The Story of American Freedom

Other Books by Eric Foner

Free Soil, Free Labor, Free Men:
The Ideology of the Republican Party Before the Civil War

America's Black Past: A Reader in Afro-American History

Nat Turner

Tom Paine and Revolutionary America

Politics and Ideology in the Age of the Civil War

Nothing But Freedom: Emancipation and Its Legacy

Reconstruction: America's Unfinished Revolution 1863–1877

A Short History of Reconstruction

A House Divided: America in the Age of Lincoln
(with Olivia Mahoney)

The New American History

The Reader's Companion to American History
(with John A. Garraty)

Freedom's Lawmakers: A Directory of Black Reconstruction Officeholders

Thomas Paine

America's Reconstruction: People and Politics After the Civil War
(with Olivia Mahoney)

The
Story of
American
Freedom

ERIC FONER

W · W · Norton & Company

New York   London

Copyright © 1998 by Eric Foner

"Words Like Freedom" from *Collected Poems* by Langston Hughes. Copyright © 1994 by the
Estate of Langston Hughes. Reprinted by permission of Alfred A. Knopf, Inc.

For information about permission to reproduce selections from this book, write to
Permissions, W. W. Norton & Company, Inc., 500 Fifth Avenue, New York, NY 10110.

The text of this book is composed in Centaur,
with the display set in Lucian Bold
Composition and Manufacturing by the Haddon Craftsmen, Inc.
Book design by Margaret Wagner

Library of Congress Cataloging-in-Publication Data
Foner, Eric.
The story of American freedom / Eric Foner.
p.   cm.
Includes bibliographical references and index.
ISBN 0-393-04665-6
1. United States—History. 2. Civil rights—United States—History. 3. Human rights—
United States—History. 4. Democracy—United States—History. 5. Liberty—History.
I. Title.
E179.F69   1998
323.44'0973—dc21   98-3290
                                                                                  CIP

W. W. Norton & Company, Inc., 500 Fifth Avenue, New York, N.Y. 10110
http://www.wwnorton.com

W. W. Norton & Company Ltd., 10 Coptic Street, London WC1A 1PU

1 2 3 4 5 6 7 8 9 0

For Daria

Contents

Words Like Freedom

There are words like *Freedom*
Sweet and wonderful to say.
On my heartstrings freedom sings
All day everyday.

There are words like *Liberty*
That almost make me cry.
If you had known what I know
You would know why.
                    —*Langston Hughes*

Civil rights demonstrators in Orangeburg,
South Carolina, 1960. (Cecil J. Williams)

Introduction

NO *IDEA* is more fundamental to Americans' sense of themselves as individuals and as a nation than freedom. The central term in our political vocabulary, "freedom"—or "liberty," with which it is almost always used interchangeably—is deeply embedded in the documentary record of our history and the language of everyday life. The Declaration of Independence lists liberty among mankind's inalienable rights; the Constitution announces as its purpose to secure liberty's blessings. The United States fought the Civil War to bring about a new birth of freedom, World War II for the Four Freedoms, and the Cold War to defend the Free World. Americans' love of liberty has been represented by poles, caps, and statues, and acted out by burning stamps and draft cards, running away from slavery, and demonstrating for the right to vote. If asked to explain or justify their actions, public or private, Americans are likely to respond, "It's a free country." "Every man in the street, white, black, red or yellow," wrote the educator and statesman Ralph Bunche in 1940, "knows that this is 'the land of the free' . . . 'the cradle of liberty.' "[1]

Foreign visitors have frequently been struck not only by Americans' commitment to freedom but by their conviction, to quote the British writer James Bryce, that they are the "only people" truly to enjoy it. The idea does seem to occupy a more prominent place in our conceptual universe than in other countries. Questions such as the justice of the economic order or the relations between racial and ethnic groups, understood in many other places as problems of equality or community, tend to be discussed here in the language of freedom. Today, when asked to choose between freedom and equality, three-quarters of Americans give priority to freedom, a far higher percentage than in Western Europe or Japan. "Being American is to be free," declared a participant in a recent survey of public opinion.[2]

Despite their devotion to freedom, Americans have not produced many abstract discussions of the concept. There is no equivalent in our literature to John Stuart Mill's *On Liberty* or the essay, "Two Concepts of Liberty," by Isaiah Berlin. American accounts of freedom tend to be historical rather than theoretical. Freedom has provided the most popular "master narrative" for accounts of our past, from textbooks with titles like *Land of the Free* to multivolume accounts of the unfolding of the idea of freedom on the North American continent. Such works, while valuable in situating the idea of freedom in historical experience, tend to give it a fixed definition and then trace how this has been worked out over time. Generally, they ground American freedom in ideas that have not changed essentially since the ancient world, or in forms of constitutional government and civil and political liberty inherited from England and institutionalized by the founding fathers. In effect, they drop a plumb line into the past, seeking the origins of one or another current definition of freedom while excluding numerous meanings that do not seem to meet the predetermined criteria. Such an approach too often fails to recognize how dissenting voices, rejected positions, and disparaged theories have also played a role in shaping the meaning of freedom. "Our story," declared the cultural critic Allan Bloom, "is the majestic and triumphant march of two principles: freedom and equality." But depicting the history of freedom as a narrative of linear progress fails to note that, as the abolitionist Thomas Wentworth Higginson put it after the Civil War, "revolutions may go backward." While freedom can be achieved, it may also be taken away.[3]

In this book, the history of what the historian Carl Becker called this "magic but elusive word" is a tale of debates, disagreements, and struggles rather than a set of timeless categories or an evolutionary narrative toward a preordained goal. The very universality of the language of freedom camouflages a host of divergent connotations and applications. It is pointless to attempt to identify a single "real" meaning against which others are to be judged. Rather than seeing freedom as a fixed category or predetermined concept, I view it as an "essentially contested concept," one that by its very nature is the subject of disagreement. Use of such a concept automatically presupposes an ongoing dialogue with other, competing meanings.[4]

"The idea of liberty," writes the French historian Marc Bloch, "is one which each epoch reshapes to its own liking."[5] Rather than discussing freedom in the abstract, I attempt to locate it in particular historical circumstances, showing how at different periods of American history different ideas of freedom have been conceived and implemented, and how the clash between dominant and dissenting views has constantly reshaped the idea's meaning. Freedom has always been a terrain of conflict, subject to multiple and competing interpretations, its meaning constantly created and recreated. Definitions of freedom relegated to the margins in one era have become dominant in the next, and long-abandoned understandings have been resurrected when circumstances changed. The meaning of freedom has been constructed not only in congressional debates and political treatises but on plantations and picket lines, in parlors and bedrooms. The story of American freedom has a rich and varied cast of characters, from Thomas Jefferson to Margaret Sanger, Franklin D. Roosevelt to former slaves seeking to breathe substantive meaning into emancipation during the Civil War.

"New circumstances," Jefferson observed in 1813, ". . . call for new words, new phrases, and for the transfer of old words to new objects." The history of freedom offers a unique vantage point from which to probe the depths of American culture, and to view the interconnection between changing patterns of thought and social experience in American history. Because of the word's very ubiquity, the study of freedom is more than a semantic exercise. "History," wrote the social critic Henry Demarest Lloyd a century ago, "is condensed in the catchwords of the people."[6] Freedom is so central to our political language that it is impossible to understand American history without knowledge of the multifaceted debates over its meaning. This history of the idea of freedom does not claim to offer a comprehensive narrative of the American past. It does contend, however, that viewing that history with freedom as the organizing theme enables us to highlight unfamiliar elements, and to see familiar events and periods in new ways. The history of freedom sheds light on the ideas and purposes of social and political movements. It shows how crises like the American Revolution, the Civil War, and the Cold War, when the language of freedom suffused politics and society, have permanently transformed the political culture. What is important is not so much the evolution of a single definition as the multiple purposes to which the idea of freedom has been put, and the broader belief systems these usages illuminate.

Since freedom embodies not a single idea but a complex of values, the struggle to define its meaning is simultaneously an intellectual, social, economic, and political contest. A morally charged idea, freedom has been used to convey and claim legitimacy for all kinds of grievances and hopes, fears about the present and visions of the future. Freedom is the oldest of clichés and the most modern of aspirations. At various times in our history it has served as a "protest ideal" and as a justification of the status quo. Freedom helps bind our culture together and exposes the contradictions between what America claims to be and what it actually is. As groups from the abolitionists to modern-day conservatives have realized, to "capture" a word like freedom is to acquire a formidable position of strength in political conflicts. "People have so manipulated the concept of freedom," the philosopher Theodor Adorno complained at the dawn of the Cold War, "that it finally boils down to the right of the stronger and richer to take from the weaker and poorer whatever they have left." Yet, not long after these words were written, the greatest mass movement of this century reinvigorated the language of freedom with its freedom rides, freedom schools, and the insistent cry, "Freedom Now."[7]

As with other central elements of our political language—independence, equality, and citizenship, for example—freedom has been defined and redefined with reference to its putative opposite. The meaning of "independence" requires a concept of dependency, "white" depends on the definition of black, and the meaning of "freedom" on the definition of unfreedom. Such binary oppositions have ordered Americans' understanding of the world, simultaneously illuminating some parts of that reality and glossing over others, while obscuring the extent to which ideas conceived as mutually exclusive are in fact ideologically interconnected.[8] Slavery helped to define American understandings of freedom in the colonial era and the nineteenth century. Indeed, much of the first part of this book explores how the existence of slavery helped to shape a racially exclusive definition of freedom, while at the same time offering those who believed themselves denied full liberty—laborers complaining of "wage slavery," women protesting the "slavery of sex"—a language with which to express their own grievances. More recently, communism helped to define American freedom when the United States declared itself the leader of the Free World.

No study of a subject as complex and multifaceted as freedom can claim to be definitive. A book of this sort inevitably reflects the personal interests and choices of the author; another historian would undoubtedly produce a very different volume. My approach to the history of freedom centers on three interrelated themes: the meanings of freedom; the social conditions that make freedom possible; and the boundaries of freedom—the definition, that is, of who is entitled to enjoy it.

In studying the first theme—how Americans have understood the idea of freedom—my concern is less with abstract definitions than with the debates and struggles through which freedom acquires concrete meanings, and how understandings of freedom are shaped by, and in turn help to shape, social movements and political and economic events. No overarching definition or single set of categories can capture the elusive meaning of freedom. Nonetheless, if freedom is a contested concept, it is not merely an empty vessel. American understandings of freedom have changed many times, but the debate itself has tended to focus on certain dimensions of the idea. That history has determined which elements of freedom I have chosen to focus on throughout the book.

One critical dimension is political freedom, or the right to participate in public affairs. The narrative begins with the American Revolution, when the prevailing understanding of freedom centered on a community's right to political self-determination. In the nineteenth century, political democracy (defined until after the Civil War as white male suffrage) became central to the meaning of freedom, and it was in the language of freedom that excluded groups claimed the right to vote. Even today, when more privatized meanings prevail, the idea of freedom as active engagement in public life has not entirely disappeared from our political culture. The question of political freedom is intimately connected to an issue that recurs throughout our history—the relationship between freedom and political institutions. Freedom is both an idea and a practice, a complex of values and an experience implemented in law and public policy. Governmental power has been seen by some Americans as a danger to liberty, and by others as a means toward what John Dewey called "effective freedom"—the ability to shape the institutions that determine the lineaments of freedom.[9]

Americans' love-hate relationship with government is reflected in another crucial strand of the history of freedom: the evolution of civil liberties, or rights that individuals can assert against authority. Today, the liberties enshrined in the Bill of Rights are central to Americans' conception of freedom. This has not always been the case; indeed, at many moments in our history, from the suppression of abolitionist meetings in the 1830s to the Red Scare after World War I and the depredations of McCarthyism during the Cold War, individual rights have been seriously curtailed—often in the name of freedom. The growth of civil liberties in this country is not a story of linear progress or simply a series of Supreme Court decisions, but a highly uneven and bitterly contested part of the story of American freedom.

Yet another understanding that has enjoyed a persistent presence in American life is a moral or "Christian" ideal of freedom. From the Puritan settlers to many modern conservatives, freedom has meant above all the capacity to act according to an ethical standard. This definition stands in uneasy tension with another recurring dimension—personal freedom, or the ability to make crucial individual choices free from outside coercion. In the revolutionary era, freedom as personal choice referred mainly to the realms of democratic politics and religious affiliation. In the nineteenth century, personal freedom came to mean each person's opportunity to develop to the fullest his or her innate talents, In the twentieth, the "ability to choose" has become perhaps the dominant understanding of freedom, a development abetted by the explosive growth of the consumer marketplace. In the name of personal liberation, the 1960s, a crucial chapter in the history of American freedom, extended freedom of choice into virtually every realm, from attire and "lifestyle" to relations between the sexes.

A final dimension is economic freedom: what kinds of economic relations constitute freedom for individuals in their working lives. The meaning of economic freedom has changed dramatically over the course of American history. For more than a century after independence, this idea centered on economic autonomy, enshrined in the glorification of the independent small producer at the time of the Revolution and the antebellum celebration of "free labor." As the industrial economy matured and the goal of proprietorship faded for most Americans, alternative definitions of economic freedom came to the fore: "liberty of contract" in the Gilded Age; "industrial freedom" (a say in corporate decision-making) in the Progressive era; economic security during the New Deal; and, more recently, the ability to partake of mass consumption within a market economy.

Useful as a method of imposing order on the myriad ways the idea has been understood and deployed, these dimensions of freedom must not be seen as either unchanging or mutually exclusive. No fixed set of categories can fully capture how freedom is actually experienced and interpreted by individuals embedded in history, or how each definition of freedom influences the others. A protean concept, freedom overspills the scholar's carefully constructed boundaries. Many people have held seemingly contradictory definitions of freedom at the same time—"negative" and "positive" liberty, for example (a distinction popularized by Isaiah Berlin), or freedom as a set of individual rights and freedom as group or national empowerment. Freedom has been applied to individuals, communities, families, persons within the family, and to the nation itself, and has been pursued through individual action and collective struggles. What is constant is the debate itself; yet the very preoccupation with freedom provides a point of unity in understanding the American past.

Discussions of freedom inevitably raise the question of what circumstances must exist to allow freedom to flourish. This issue—the social conditions of freedom—constitutes the book's second major theme. Even those who adopt a purely "negative" definition of freedom as the absence of external coercion rather than, for example, economic autonomy or political empowerment, must identify what constitutes illegitimate coercion. At one time or another, Americans have identified as obstacles to the enjoyment of individual freedom governmental authority, social pressures for conformity, bureaucratic institutions, "private" arrangements like the traditional family, and concentrated economic power. Efforts to delineate the conditions of freedom extend from the era of the Revolution, when ownership of productive property was widely seen as essential to individual autonomy, to the twentieth, when feminists sought to recast gender relations in order to afford women the same freedom as men, and Americans divided over whether poverty and lack of economic security should be seen as deprivations of freedom that the government has an obligation to alleviate. Such debates underscore the fact that discussions of freedom are inescapably political, since under almost any definition they lead directly to questions concerning how public institutions and economic and social relations affect the nature and extent of the options available to individuals. Through consideration of the social conditions of freedom, therefore, the word enters what the historian J. R. Pole has called "the language of justice."[10]

If freedom has been a battleground throughout our history, so too has been the book's third theme—the definition of those entitled to enjoy its blessings. It is hardly original to point out that the United States, founded on the premise that liberty is an entitlement of all humanity, blatantly deprived many of its own people of freedom. Less immediately apparent is how the study of freedom calls into question the universalities of what Gunnar Myrdal called "the American Creed"—a belief in the essential dignity of all human beings and their inalienable right to democracy, liberty, and equal opportunity. Many recent writers view this creed as a common theme of our history, a way of transcending the fragmentation that allegedly affects both the study of history and society itself. The study of freedom does, indeed, offer a way of responding to the criticism that the writing of history has become so fragmented and trivialized that it is no longer possible to view American society whole. Our history is more than the sum total of the experiences of the sometimes fractious groups that make up our population. Yet the history of freedom also suggests that the search for a unifying account of the American past needs to be conducted in new ways. It highlights how the universalities of our common culture have been constructed on the basis of difference and on the exclusion of considerable numbers of Americans from their benefits. "Liberty," said Louis D. Brandeis in 1915, "has knit us together as Americans."[11] But the boundaries of freedom have been as contested as the word's definition itself.

A nation, in the political scientist Benedict Anderson's celebrated definition, is more than a political entity. It is also a state of mind, "an imagined political community," with borders that are as much intellectual as geographic.[12] The greater the substantive meaning of freedom, the more important the lines of inclusion and exclusion that define American nationality. Since freedom, among other things, is a set of practical rights and entitlements that go along with being an American, its boundaries take on extreme significance. Throughout the book, therefore, I have devoted attention to the debate over a question that has never been fully resolved: who is an American (and therefore entitled to enjoy American freedom)?

If the universalistic American Creed has been a persistent feature of our history, so too have been efforts to delimit freedom along one or another axis of social existence.[13] Of the lines circumscribing the enjoyment of freedom, none have been more persistent than those drawn on the basis of race, gender, and class. I invoke these categories, whose meanings themselves have changed over time, not as a fashionable mantra but because these are among the most crucial fault lines along which limitations on freedom have so often been demarcated. Non-whites, women, and laborers experienced firsthand the paradox that one person's freedom has frequently been linked to another's servitude. The master's freedom rested on the reality of slavery, the vaunted autonomy of men on the subordinate position of women. By the same token, it has been through battles at the boundaries—the efforts of racial minorities, women, and workers to secure freedom as they understood it—that the meaning (and hence the experience) of freedom has been both deepened and transformed, and the concept extended to realms for which it was not originally intended.

The story of American freedom is not simply a saga of a fixed set of rights to which one group after another has gained access. Time and again in our history, the definition of those rights has been transformed by the demands of excluded groups for inclusion. The authors of the notion of freedom as a universal birthright, a truly human ideal, were not so much the founding fathers, who created a nation dedicated to liberty but resting in large measure on slavery, but abolitionists who sought to extend the blessings of liberty to encompass blacks, slave and free; women who seized upon the rhetoric of democratic freedom to demand the right to vote; and immigrant groups who insisted that nativity and culture ought not to form boundaries of exclusion. The struggles of such groups for freedom elevated equality to a central place in the language of liberty, challenging the views of other Americans who held that equality is the antithesis of freedom. The principles of birthright citizenship and equal protection of the law without regard to race, which became central elements of American freedom, were products of the antislavery struggle and the Civil War. The women's movement challenged the prevailing separation of public and private spheres, thereby pioneering the application of the idea of freedom to the most intimate relations of life. Judicial recognition of Americans' civil liberties originated in part in court decisions overturning World War I laws—directed against the new immigrants—that required that instruction in public and private schools be conducted in English.

The title of this book, as is perhaps obvious, is meant to be ambiguous or ironic (one might even call it postmodern). A story is both a history of actual events and an invention. Over the course of our history, American freedom has been both a reality and a mythic ideal—a living truth for millions of Americans; a cruel mockery for others. For some, freedom has been a birthright taken for granted. For others, it is "not a gift but an achievement," in the words of the philosopher Samuel DuBois Cook, a close friend of Martin Luther King, Jr. "Historically and morally speaking," Cook added, freedom "is the fruit of struggles, tragic failures, tears, sacrifices, and sorrow."[14]

Freedom, and struggles to define its meaning, have long been central to my own work as a historian. My first published article concerned the Free Soil Party and three of my previous books have had the words "Free" or "Freedom" in their titles. My graduate training at Columbia University, under the direction of Richard Hofstadter, instilled an enduring concern with the complex relationships between ideas and experience, and between social movements and political and economic institutions. The scholarship of the past thirty years has made historians far more aware than Hofstadter and his generation of the value, indeed the necessity, of bringing the varied perspectives of different Americans to bear on any account of the nation's past. But the ambition that inspires this study—to produce a coherent narrative that illuminates the evolution of American political culture and its distinctive language of politics— is much the same as theirs.

Today, chroniclers of the past are frequently called upon to contribute to a sense of common national identity by devising a unifying account based on the ideal of freedom. Historians, however, in the words of one of the preeminent practitioners of the craft, Eric Hobsbawm, are the "professional remembrancers of what their fellow citizens wish to forget."[15] Americans sometimes "forget" that things which we consider fixed and timeless are in fact constantly changing and contested. The story of freedom is not a mythic saga with a predetermined beginning and conclusion, but an open-ended history of accomplishment and failure, a record of a people forever contending about the crucial ideas of their political culture. In this extended conversation over time, the meaning of freedom is as multifaceted, contentious, and ever-changing as America itself.

The Story of American Freedom

In March 1776, James Pike, a soldier in the Massachusetts militia, carved this scene on his powder horn to commemorate the battles of Lexington and Concord eleven months earlier. Pike identified British troops as "aggressors." At the center stands the liberty tree. (Chicago Historical Society)

1

The Birth of
American Freedom

AMERICAN FREEDOM was born in revolution. During the struggle for independence inherited ideas of liberty were transformed, new ones emerged, and the definition of those entitled to enjoy what the Constitution called "the blessings of liberty" was challenged and extended. The Revolution bequeathed to future generations an enduring yet contradictory legacy. Its vision of the new nation as an asylum for freedom in a world overrun by oppression resonates in the political culture to this day. Yet the United States, a nation conceived in liberty, harbored a rapidly growing slave population, belying the founders' confident affirmation of freedom as a universal human birthright.

The Freeborn Englishman

"Liberty," of course, did not suddenly enter the American vocabulary in 1776; indeed, few words were as ubiquitous in the trans-Atlantic political discourse of the eighteenth century. Colonial America was heir to many understandings of liberty, some as old as the city-states of ancient Greece, others as new as the Enlightenment. Some laid the foundations for modern conceptions of freedom; others are quite unfamiliar today.

One common definition in British North America defined freedom less as a political or social status than as a spiritual condition. In the ancient world, lack of self-control was understood as a form of slavery, the antithesis of the free life. "Show me a man who isn't a slave," wrote Seneca. "One is a slave to sex, another to money, another to ambition." This understanding of freedom as submission to a moral code was central to the Christian cosmology that suffused the world view of the early colonists. Wherever it flourished, Christianity enshrined the idea of liberation, but as a spiritual condition rather than a worldly one. Since the Fall, man had been prone to succumb to his lusts and passions. Freedom meant abandoning this life of sin to embrace the teachings of Christ. "Where the Spirit of the Lord is," declares the New Testament, "there is liberty." In this definition, servitude and freedom were mutually reinforcing, not contradictory states, since those who accepted the teachings of Christ simultaneously became "free from sin" and "servants to God."[1]

The Puritan settlers of colonial Massachusetts, who believed their colony the embodiment of true Christianity, planted this spiritual definition of freedom on American soil. In a 1645 speech to the Massachusetts legislature that epitomized Puritan conceptions of freedom, John Winthrop, the colony's governor, distinguished sharply between "natural liberty," which suggested "a liberty to evil," and "moral liberty . . . a liberty to do only what is good." This definition of freedom as flowing from self-denial and moral choice was quite compatible with severe restraints on freedom of speech, religion, movement, and personal behavior. Individual desires must give way to the needs of the community, and "Christian liberty" meant submission not only to the will of God but to secular authority as well, to a well-understood set of interconnected responsibilities and duties, a submission no less complete for being voluntary. The most common civil offense in the courts of colonial New England was "contempt of authority." The unrestrained individual enjoying natural rights, whom later generations would imagine as the embodiment of freedom, struck these Puritan settlers as the incarnation of anarchy, the antithesis of liberty. "When each man hath liberty to follow his own imagination," declared the Puritan minister Thomas Hooker, disaster inevitably resulted, for "all prejudice the public good."[2]

Communal authority was always weaker in the more secular colonies to the south of the Puritan commonwealth. Even in New England, as jeremiads of the early eighteenth century vigorously lamented, willingness to accept community regimentation in the name of liberty soon waned. By the 1750s, the idea of New England's special place in God's plan for humanity had been subsumed in the more general celebration of the entire Anglo-American Protestant world as a bulwark against tyranny and popery. Yet the Christian understanding of liberty as spiritual salvation survived to the Revolution and, indeed, our own time. The religious revivals of the late colonial era, known to historians as the Great Awakening, reinforced this understanding of freedom. On the eve of independence, ministers like Jonathan Boucher were insisting that "true liberty" meant "a liberty to do every thing that is right, and being restrained from doing any thing that is wrong," not "a right to do every thing that we please."[3]

This equation of liberty with moral action flourished as well in a secularized form in the Atlantic world of the eighteenth century. If religious liberty meant obedience to God, "civil liberty" rested on obedience to law. As far back as the ancient world, Aristotle had cautioned men not to "think it slavery to live according to the rule of the constitution." The law was liberty's "salvation," not its adversary. Modern philosophers of liberty also distinguished sharply between "unrestrained freedom" and "a life lived under the rule of law." Liberty, wrote John Locke, meant not leaving every person free to do as he desired, but "having a standing rule to live by, common to every one of that society, and made by the legislative power." As Locke's formulation suggests, liberty in its civil form depended on obedience to the law, so long as statutes were promulgated by elected representatives and did not operate in an arbitrary manner. Here lay the essence of the idea of British liberty, a central element of social and political thought on both sides of the Atlantic. Until the 1770s, most colonists believed themselves part of the freest political system mankind had ever known.[4]

By the eighteenth century, the "invented tradition" of the freeborn Englishman had become a central feature of Anglo-American political culture and a major building block in the sense of nationhood then being consolidated in Britain. By self-definition, the British nation was a community of free individuals and its past a "history of liberty." Belief in freedom as the common heritage of all Britons and the British empire as the world's sole repository of liberty had helped to legitimize the colonization of North America in the first place. Subsequently, it served to cast imperial wars against Catholic France and Spain as struggles between liberty and tyranny, a definition widely disseminated in the colonies as well as the mother country. British freedom celebrated the rule of law, the right to live under legislation to which one's community had consented, restraints on the arbitrary exercise of political authority, and rights like trial by jury enshrined in the common law. It was closely identified with the Protestant religion and was invoked most stridently to contrast Britons with the "servile" subjects of Catholic countries.[5]

Of course, the idea of freedom as the natural condition of mankind was hardly unknown in a nation that had produced the writings of John Milton and John Locke. But British freedom was anything but universal. Nationalist, often xenophobic, it viewed nearly every other nation on earth as "enslaved"—to popery, tyranny, or barbarism. "Freedom . . . in no other land will thrive," wrote the poet John Dryden; "Freedom an English subject's sole prerogative." Britons saw no contradiction between proclaiming themselves citizens of a land of freedom precisely when British ships were transporting millions of Africans to bondage in the New World. "Britons never, never, never will be slaves," ran the popular song, "Rule, Britannia." It did not say that Britons could not *own* slaves, since for most of the eighteenth century, almost no one seemed to consider Africans entitled to the rights of Englishmen.[6]

Nor was British liberty incompatible with wide gradations in personal freedom at home—a hierarchical, aristocratic society with a restricted "political nation" (those entitled to vote and hold office). The common law's protections applied to everyone, but property qualifications and other restrictions limited the eighteenth-century electorate to less than 5 percent of the adult male population. (The "right of magistracy," wrote Joseph Priestley in his *Essay on the First Principles of Government* [1768], was not essential to British freedom. Men "may enjoy civil liberty, but not political liberty.") Nor did British law view laborers as wholly free. Vagrancy statutes punished those without visible means of support, "master and servant" laws required strict obedience of employees, and breaches of labor contracts carried criminal penalties. The very navy whose domination of the high seas secured the nation's freedom from foreign domination was manned by sailors seized by press gangs from the streets of London and Liverpool. In this sense, British freedom was the lineal descendant of an understanding of liberty derived from the Middle Ages, when "liberties" meant formal privileges such as self-government or exemption from taxation granted to particular groups by contract, charter, or royal decree. Only those who enjoyed the "freedom of the city," for example, could engage in certain economic activities. This medieval understanding of liberty assumed a hierarchical world in which individual rights in a modern sense barely existed, and political and economic entitlements were enjoyed by some social classes and denied to others. Echoes of this old, restricted idea of liberty survived in early America—for example, in New York City's rule limiting the right to work in certain trades to those who held the legal status of "freeman."[7]

Whatever its limitations and exclusions, it would be impossible, as the historian Gordon Wood writes, "to overemphasize the degree to which eighteenth-century Englishmen reveled in their worldwide reputation for freedom," an observation as applicable to the American colonies as to the mother country. One could, if one desired, subdivide British liberty into its component parts, as many writers of the era were prone to do. Political liberty meant the right to participate in public affairs; civil liberty protection of one's person and property against encroachment by government; personal liberty freedom of conscience and movement; religious liberty the right of Protestants to worship as they chose. But the whole exceeded the sum of these parts. British liberty was simultaneously a collection of specific rights, a national characteristic, and a state of mind. So ubiquitous and protean was the concept that what would later seem inconsistent elements managed happily to coexist.[8]

British freedom, for example, incorporated contradictory attitudes about political power. On the one hand, the idea's historical development was inseparable from the rise of the nation-state, and reached its apotheosis precisely when Britain emerged as the world's leading imperial power. At the same time, restraints on the exercise of political authority were central to British freedom. Power and liberty were widely believed to be natural antagonists, and in their balanced constitution and the principle that no man, even the king, is above the law, Britons claimed to have devised the best means of preventing political absolutism. These ideas sank deep roots not only within the political nation but far more broadly in British society. Laborers, sailors, and artisans spoke the language of common law rights and British freedom as insistently as pamphleteers and Parliamentarians. By the eighteenth century, the category of free person had become not simply a legal status, as in medieval times, but a powerful element of popular ideology. On both sides of the Atlantic, liberty emerged as "the battle cry of the rebellious." Frequent crowd actions protesting infringements on traditional rights gave concrete expression to the definition of liberty as resistance to tyranny. "We are *Free-men*—British subjects—Not Born Slaves," was a rallying cry of the Regulators, who protested the underrepresentation of western settlements in the South Carolina legislature during the 1760s.[9]

This tension between freedom as the power to participate in public affairs and freedom as a collection of individual rights requiring protection against governmental interference helps define the difference between two political languages that flourished in the Anglo-American world. One, termed by scholars "republicanism" (although few in eighteenth-century England used the word, which conjured up memories of the time when Charles I was beheaded), celebrated active participation in public life as the essence of liberty. Tracing its lineage back to Renaissance Florence and beyond that to the ancient world, republicanism held that as a social being, man reached his highest fulfillment in setting aside self-interest to pursue the common good. Republican freedom could be expansive and democratic, as when it spoke of the common rights of the entire community. It also had an exclusive, class-based dimension, in its assumption that only property-owning citizens possessed the quality known as "virtue"—understood in the eighteenth century not simply as a personal, moral quality but as a willingness to subordinate private passions and desires to the public good. "Only a virtuous people are capable of freedom," wrote Benjamin Franklin.[10]

If republican liberty was a civic and social quality, which could only be enjoyed by citizens of a "free state" (one ruled in accordance with the consent of the governed), the freedom celebrated by eighteenth-century liberalism was essentially individual and private. According to John Locke, the founding father of modern liberalism, government is established to offer security to the "life, liberties, and estates" that are the natural rights of all mankind, and essentially should be limited to this task. Liberty, for Locke and his eighteenth-century disciples, meant not civic involvement but personal autonomy—"not to be subject to the inconstant, uncertain, unknown Arbitrary Will of another Man." Protecting freedom required shielding a realm of private life and personal concerns—including family relations, religious preferences, and economic activity—from interference by the state. The public good was less an ideal to be consciously pursued by government than the outcome of free individuals' pursuit of their myriad private ambitions.[11]

Liberalism, as the historian Pierre Manent puts it, severed the "citizen" from the "man," the political realm of life from the social. Critics condemned it as an excuse for selfishness and lack of civic-mindedness. "The freedom . . . that I love," declared Edmund Burke, "is not solitary, unconnected, individual, selfish Liberty. As if every Man was to regulate the whole of his conduct by his own will. The Liberty I mean is *social* liberty." Yet it is easy to understand liberalism's appeal in the hierarchical Atlantic world of the eighteenth century. It called into question all the legal privileges and governmental arrangements that impeded individual advancement, from the economic prerogatives of chartered corporations to legalized religious intolerance. And in its starting point, that mankind possessed natural rights no government could violate, liberalism opened the door to the disenfranchised, women, and even slaves, to challenge limitations on their own freedom.[12]

Eventually, liberalism and republicanism would come to be seen as alternative and contradictory understandings of freedom. In the eighteenth century, however, these languages overlapped and often reinforced one another. Many leaders of the Revolution seem to the modern eye simultaneously republican (in their concern for the public good and citizens' obligations to the polity) and liberal (in their preoccupation with individual rights). Both political ideologies could inspire a commitment to constitutional government, freedom of speech and religion, and restraints on arbitrary power. Both emphasized the security of property as a foundation of freedom. The pervasive influence of Protestant morality, moreover, tempered what later would come to be seen as liberalism's amoralism.

Certainly, in the colonial era, "liberty" stood as a meeting point between liberal and republican understandings of government and society. There seemed no necessary contradiction between the personal freedom central to liberalism and the public liberty of the republican tradition. Moreover, whether liberal, republican, or some combination of the two, most eighteenth-century commentators assumed that only certain kinds of persons were fully capable of enjoying the benefits and exercising the rights of freedom. On both sides of the Atlantic, it was an axiom of political thought that dependents lacked a will of their own and thus were incapable of participating in public affairs. Liberty, wrote the influential political theorist Richard Price, rested on "one general idea . . . the idea of *self-direction* or *self-government.*" Those who did not control their own lives ought not to have a voice in governing the state. Political freedom required economic independence.[13]

Property, therefore, was "interwoven" with eighteenth-century understandings of freedom, as the New York publisher John Peter Zenger put it in 1735. The independence entailed by property was an indispensable basis of liberty. Dr. Samuel Johnson's dictionary defined "independence" as "freedom," and Thomas Jefferson insisted that dependence "begets subservience and venality, suffocates the germ of virtue, and prepares fit tools for the designs of ambition." Hence the ubiquity of property qualifications for voting in Britain and the colonies. The "true reason" for such requirements, Sir William Blackstone explained in his *Commentaries on the Laws of England* (1765–69), was that men without property would inevitably fall "under the immediate domination of others." Lacking a will of their own, their votes would threaten the "general liberty." Not only personal dependence, as in the case of a domestic servant, but working for wages was widely viewed as disreputable. In seventeenth- and eighteenth-century England, wage labor was associated with servility and loss of liberty; only those who controlled their own labor could be regarded as fully free. British popular ballads and folk tales romanticized vagabonds, gypsies, highwaymen, even beggars as more free than those who worked for wages. Many years would pass before the idea that wage labor was compatible with genuine freedom gained broad public acceptance.[14]

Those who drew up plans to colonize British North America expected to reproduce the hierarchical social structure of the mother country. But from the earliest days of settlement, migrants from Britain and the Continent held the promise of the New World to be liberation from the economic inequalities and widespread economic dependence of the Old. John Smith had barely landed at Jamestown in 1607 when he observed that in America, "every man may be master and owner of his owne labour and land." During the whole of the colonial era, most free immigrants expected to achieve economic autonomy, an anticipation encouraged by promotional literature that lured settlers by publicizing the notion of the New World as a place of exceptional opportunity for the acquisition of property. The visions of liberty that emigrants brought to colonial America always included the promise of economic independence and the ability to pass a freehold on to one's children.[15]

Defining freedom in terms of economic independence drew a sharp line between those classes capable of fully enjoying its benefits and those who were not. In the eighteenth century, economic autonomy was far beyond the reach of most Britons. Even in colonial America, most of the population was not, by this standard, truly free. Lacking a hereditary aristocracy like that of England, colonists prided themselves on having "no rank above that of freeman." But there were many ranks below. The half million slaves who labored in the mainland colonies on the eve of independence obviously stood outside the circle of free persons. For free women, whose civic identity was subsumed within that of their fathers and husbands, and who had no legal claim to their own labor, opportunities for economic autonomy barely existed. Women, moreover, were deemed by men deficient in rationality, courage, and the broad capacity for self-determination—the qualities necessary in the public-spirited citizen. Indeed, the ideal of independence was partly defined by gender; whether in the economy or polity, autonomy was a masculine trait, dependence the normal lot of women.[16]

Even among the white male population, it is sometimes forgotten, many varieties of partial freedom coexisted in colonial America, including indentured servants, apprentices, domestic laborers, transported convicts, and sailors impressed into service in the Royal Navy. Freedom in colonial America existed along a continuum from the slave, stripped of all rights, to the independent property owner, and during a lifetime an individual might well occupy more than one place on this spectrum. Indentured servants, who voluntarily surrendered their freedom for a specified time, comprised a major part of the non-slave labor force throughout the colonial era. As late as the early 1770s, nearly half the immigrants who arrived in America from England and Scotland had entered into contracts for a fixed period of labor in exchange for passage. Indentured servants often worked in the fields alongside slaves. Like slaves, servants could be bought and sold, were subject to corporal punishment, and their obligation to fulfill their duties ("specific performance," in legal terminology) was enforced by the courts. "Many Negroes are better used," complained one female indentured servant in 1756; she went on to describe being forced to work "day and night . . . then tied up and whipped." But, of course, unlike slaves, servants could look forward to freedom from their servitude. Assuming they survived their period of labor (and many in the early years did not), servants would be released from dependency and receive "freedom dues." Servants, a Pennsylvania judge remarked in 1793, occupied "a middle rank between slaves and freemen."[17]

The prevalence of so many less than free workers underpinned the widespread reality of economic independence, and therefore freedom, for propertied male heads of households. This was most obvious in the case of slaveholding planters, who already equated freedom with mastership, but also true of the countless artisans in northern cities who owned a slave or two and employed indentured servants and apprentices. (In New York City and Philadelphia, artisans and tradesmen, who prided themselves on their own independence, dominated the ranks of slaveholders.) And the vaunted independence of the yeoman farmer depended in considerable measure on the labor of dependent women. The popular adage, "Women's work is never done," was literally true; the cooking, cleaning, sewing, and assistance in agricultural chores by farmers' wives and daughters often spelled the difference between self-sufficiency and economic dependence. In the household-based economy of colonial America, autonomy rested on command over others. "Freedom and dependence," wrote the Pennsylvania jurist James Wilson in 1774, were "opposite and irreconcilable terms." Wilson failed to note that since the free man was, by definition, master of a household, freedom and dependence were also inextricably connected.[18]

The eighteenth century witnessed an increase in social stratification in colonial America and the rise of a wealthy gentry exercising more and more dominance over civil, religious, and economic institutions, and demanding deference from their social inferiors. Nonetheless, by the time of the Revolution, the majority of the non-slave male population were farmers who owned their own land. With the household still the center of economic production, the propertyless were a far smaller proportion of the population than in Britain and wage labor far less prevalent. Among the free population, property was more widely distributed than anywhere in Europe. In colonial America, writes one historian, lived "thousands of the freest individuals the Western world had ever known."[19]

Thus, an abhorrence of personal dependence and the equation of freedom with autonomy sank deep roots in British North America not simply as part of an ideological inheritance, but because these beliefs accorded with social reality—a wide distribution of productive property that made a modicum of economic independence part of the lived experience of large numbers of colonists. What the French essayist Hector St. John Crèvecoeur identified in 1782 as the hallmark of American society—its "pleasing uniformity of decent competence"—would form the material basis for the later definition of the United States as a "producer's republic," as well as its corollary, that widespread ownership of property was the social precondition of freedom.[20]

Democratizing Freedom

With its wide distribution of property (and therefore a broadly participatory political life), weak aristocratic power, and an established church far less powerful than in Britain, colonial America was a society with deep democratic potential. But it took the struggle for independence to transform this society not only into a republican polity without a king but into a nation that enshrined equality and opportunity as its raisons d'être and proudly proclaimed itself an asylum for liberty for all mankind. The Revolution unleashed public debates and political and social struggles that democratized the concept of freedom.

The American Revolution was fought in the name of liberty. On the road to independence, no word was more frequently invoked, although it rarely received precise definition. There were liberty trees, liberty poles, Sons and Daughters of Liberty, and an endless parade of pamphlets with titles like *A Chariot of Liberty* and *Oration on the Beauties of Liberty* (the latter, a sermon delivered in Boston by Joseph Allen in 1772, became the most popular public address of the years before independence). Throughout the colonies, British measures like the Stamp Act of 1765 were greeted by mock funerals of liberty, carefully choreographed spectacles in which a coffin was carried to a burial ground only to have the occupant miraculously revived at the last moment (whereupon the assembled multitude repaired to a tavern to celebrate). Liberty was more than an idea for those resisting British authority; it was a passion. Sober men spoke longingly of the "sweets of liberty." All sorts of hopes and expectations came to be embodied in the idea of freedom. Commented a British emigrant who arrived in Maryland early in 1775: "They are all liberty mad."[21]

Americans during the age of revolution did not start out to transform the rights of Englishmen into the rights of man. The very first colonial charter—Virginia's, in 1606—had granted settlers the same "Liberties, Franchises, and Immunities" as if they resided "in our Realm of *England.*" And a century and a half later, American colonists shared in the intensification of British nationalism, reaffirming their loyalty to king and constitution. Resistance to British revenue measures of the 1760s began by invoking Americans' "rights as British subjects" within the framework established by the British constitution, "the best that ever existed among men." At the outset, opposition to imperial policies invoked time-honored British principles (no taxation without representation, trial by jury) and employed modes of resistance long familiar in the mother country, from petitions and pamphlets to crowd activity. British measures of the 1760s like the Stamp Act, Quartering Act, and Townshend Duties were sometimes assailed in terms of natural rights, but far more frequently in the name of the "rights and privileges of freeborn Englishmen," especially freedom from arbitrary government, security of property, and the right to live in a political community to whose laws a people, through their representatives, had given consent. As late as 1774, appeals to natural law were often combined with a hodgepodge of other claims to liberty, as in the "ancient, constitutional, and chartered Rights" invoked by Virginians. In the same year, the first Continental Congress defended its actions by appealing to the "principles of the English constitution" and the "liberties . . . of free and natural-born subjects, within the realm of England."[22]

As the conflict deepened, however, colonial leaders came to interpret metropolitan policies as part and parcel of an immense conspiracy to destroy the liberty of America, and their own resistance not merely as a struggle over specific legislation but as an episode in a global conflict between freedom and despotism. The Intolerable Acts of 1774, which suspended the Massachusetts legislature and closed the port of Boston, represented the final stage in this British design "for enslaving the colonies." Now, the right to resist arbitrary authority and the identification of liberty with the cause of God, so deeply ingrained by the imperial struggles of the eighteenth century, were invoked against Britain itself.[23]

The coming of independence rendered the rights of freeborn Englishmen irrelevant in America. As late as March 1775, Edmund Burke assured the British Parliament that the colonists were devoted not to "abstract liberty" but to "liberty according to English ideas, and on English principles." But the deepening crisis inevitably pushed Americans to ground their claims in the more abstract language of natural rights and universal liberty. In a merging of the evangelical belief in the New World as the future seat of "perfect freedom" with the secular vision of the Old as sunk in debauchery and arbitrary rule, the idea of British liberty was transformed into a set of universal rights, with America

On both sides of the Atlantic, the liberty cap symbolized the right of self-government and, more broadly, individual freedom. In a 1770 engraving from the *Boston Gazette* by Paul Revere (top), Britannia sits with the cap and national shield, reflecting the identification of liberty with the tradition of the "free-born Englishman." Five years later, on the cover of the *Pennsylvania Magazine*, liberty has been Americanized. The shield displays the colony's coat of arms and the female figure is surrounded by weaponry (including a cartridge box marked "liberty" hanging from the tree) of the patriotic struggle. (Chicago Historical Society; American Antiquarian Society)

a sanctuary of freedom for humanity. Ironically, it took an emigrant from the lower classes of England, who only arrived in America in 1774, fully to grasp this breathtaking vision of the meaning of independence. As Thomas Paine proclaimed in January 1776 in the most widely read pamphlet of the era, *Common Sense:*

> O! ye that love mankind . . . stand forth! Every spot of the old world is over-run with oppression. Freedom hath been hunted round the globe. Asia and Africa have long expelled her. Europe regards her as a stranger, and England hath given her warning to depart. O! receive the fugitive, and prepare in time an asylum for mankind.[24]

Written, as Paine later observed, to help men "to be free," *Common Sense* announced a prophecy from which would spring the nineteenth-century idea of the United States as an "empire of liberty." Unburdened by the institutions—monarchy, aristocracy, hereditary privilege—that oppressed the peoples of the Old World, America, and America alone, was the place where the principle of universal freedom could take root. Six months later, the Declaration of Independence would legitimate American rebellion not merely by invoking British efforts to establish "absolute tyranny" over the colonies but by referring to the natural, unalienable rights of mankind, among which liberty was second only to life itself. In the Declaration, "the Laws of Nature and Nature's God," not the British constitution or the heritage of the freeborn Englishman, justified independence. The idea of liberty as a natural right became a revolutionary rallying cry, a standard by which to judge existing institutions and a justification for their overthrow. No longer a set of specific rights, no longer a privilege to be enjoyed by a corporate body or people in specific social circumstances, liberty had become a universal, open-ended entitlement. And the contradiction between the ideal of universal liberty and the reality of a society beset with inequalities would bedevil American public life during the Revolution and long thereafter.[25]

Thus, if the roots of American freedom lay in the traditions of Christian liberty and of the freeborn Englishman, its emergence as a new and distinct ideology grew out of the struggle for independence and the creation of a nation-state that defined itself, in James Madison's words, as the "workshop of liberty to the Civilized World." In this "republic of the mind," to borrow a phrase from Rousseau, a newly invented national history and a putative national destiny both revolved around the idea of freedom. "Our forefathers," Jefferson wrote in 1775, "left their native land to seek on these shores a residence for civil and religious freedom," an inspiring if somewhat limited account of the numerous motives that had brought colonists to America. As for the future, Paine's stirring remark in *Common Sense*, "we have it in our power to begin the world over again," epitomized a sense that the American Revolution was an event of transcendent historical importance, an idea reiterated in countless sermons, political tracts, and newspaper articles of the time. From the beginning, devotion to freedom formed the essence of American nationalism.[26]

A stunning repudiation of imperial authority, the Revolution also unleashed challenges to inherited structures of power at home. The real revolution, Paine would write, was intellectual: "We see with other eyes; we hear with other ears; and think with other thoughts, than those we formerly used." In rejecting the crown, as well as the principle of hereditary aristocracy, many Americans also rejected the very idea of human inequality and the society of privilege, patronage, and fixed status that these venerable traditions embodied. Jefferson's seemingly matter-of-fact assertion in the Declaration—"all men are created equal"—announced a truly radical principle, whose full implications no one could anticipate. In British North America, a well-ordered society was thought to depend on obedience to authority—the power of rulers over their subjects, husbands over wives, parents over children, masters over servants and apprentices, slaveholders over slaves. Inequality had been fundamental to the colonial social order; the Revolution in many ways made it illegitimate. Henceforth, American freedom would be inextricably linked with the idea of equality (at least for those within the circle of free citizens): equality before the law, equality in political rights, equality of economic opportunity, and, for some, equality of condition. "Whenever I use the words *freedom* or *rights*," Paine explained, "I desire to be understood to mean a perfect equality of them. . . . The floor of Freedom is as level as water."[27]

In the egalitarian atmosphere of revolutionary America, long-accepted relations of dependency and forms of unfreedom suddenly appeared illegitimate. Abigail Adams's plea to her husband to "remember the ladies," her reminder that women, no less than men, ought not to be "bound by any laws in which we have no voice or representation," is widely remembered today. Less familiar is John Adams's response, which illuminated the crumbling of all sorts of inherited ideas of deference:

> We have been told that our struggle has loosened the bonds of government everywhere; that children and apprentices were disobedient; that schools and colleges were grown turbulent; that Indians slighted their guardians, and negroes grew insolent to their masters.

To John Adams, this egalitarian upheaval, including his wife's claim to political freedom, was an affront to the natural order of things.[28]

In the end, the Revolution did not undo the obedience to which male heads of household were entitled from their wives, children, employees, and slaves. For free men, however, the democratization of freedom was dramatic, and nowhere more so than in challenges to the traditional limitation of political participation to those who owned property. "We are all, from the cobbler up to the senator, become politicians," declared a Boston letterwriter in 1774. Throughout the colonies, election campaigns became freewheeling debates on the fundamentals of government, in which annual elections, universal manhood suffrage, religious toleration, even the abolition of slavery, were debated not only by the educated elite but by artisans, small farmers, and laborers, now emerging as a self-conscious element in politics. The militia, composed largely of members of the "lower orders," including servants and apprentices, became a "school of political democracy." Its members demanded the right to elect all their officers and insisted on the enfranchisement of all soldiers, whether or not they met age and property qualifications. They thereby established a long-lasting tradition whereby service in the army enabled excluded groups to stake a claim to full citizenship.

Those who during the Revolution demanded annual elections and an expansion of the right to vote envisioned not simply severing the link between property and suffrage but a redefinition of "property" itself. By the end of the revolutionary era, the concept of property had expanded to include rights and liberties as well as physical possessions. "A man," Madison declared at the Constitutional Convention of 1787, "has property in his opinions and the free communication of them, he has property in . . . the safety and liberty of his person." A few years later, he would speak of government's obligation to protect both the right to hold property and a citizen's "property" in his rights. Rather than property serving as a requirement to qualify for freedom, in other words, freedom could be imagined as a form of property.[29]

The idea that property included ownership of one's self helped to democratize the political nation. If all persons had a property in their rights, then there was no logical reason why all should not participate in government. Before independence, the right to vote had been subject to complex restrictions, which varied from colony to colony. Everywhere, property qualifications, while less exclusionary than in England because of the wide distribution of ownership, barred those deemed incapable of independent judgment—journeymen, servants, apprentices, and the poor. Women were generally excluded from voting (although occasionally propertied females, usually widows, did cast ballots), and many colonies also imposed religious qualifications of one kind or another. The struggle for independence galvanized participation by hundreds of thousands of those outside the political nation. "Every poor man," claimed a Maryland writer, "has a life, a personal liberty, and a right to his earnings." Hence, voting was a universal entitlement, not a privilege: the "inherent right of free suffrage" was "the grandest right of a freeman." "The suffrage," declared a 1776 petition of disenfranchised North Carolinians, was "a right essential to and inseparable from freedom."[30]

Conservative patriots struggled valiantly to reassert the rationale for the old restrictions. Property, and property alone, John Adams insisted, meant independence; those without it had no "judgment of their own. They talk and vote as they are directed by some man of property." The removal of property qualifications, Adams feared, would "confound and destroy all distinctions, and prostrate all ranks to one common level." This was precisely the aim, however, of the era's radical democrats. Yet, while moving much of the way toward the idea of voting as an entitlement rather than a privilege, they generally stopped short of universal suffrage, even for free men. The most democratic new state constitutions, such as Pennsylvania's, eliminated property qualifications, but substituted a taxpaying requirement, enfranchising nearly all of the state's free male population but leaving a small number, mainly paupers and domestic servants, still barred from voting. Even Paine, who considered the right to political participation "to be inseparable from the man as man," believed it could be forfeited for a time by those who chose to work as servants in homes and therefore voluntarily surrendered their autonomy. Paine still assumed that "freedom is destroyed by dependence." Nonetheless, since paying taxes did not make a man economically independent, the taxpaying requirement for voting represented a dramatic departure from colonial practice. It elevated "personal liberty," in the words of one Maryland essayist, to a position more important than property ownership in defining the boundaries of the political nation.[31]

Overall, the Revolution witnessed a great expansion of the right to vote, through the substitution of taxpaying for property requirements in some states, the substantial reduction of the freehold qualification in others, and the widespread enfranchisement of soldiers. The debate over the suffrage would, of course, continue for many decades. For white men, the process of democratization did not run its course until the Age of Jackson; for women and nonwhites, it would take much longer. But even during the Revolution, the process had a profound effect on prevailing definitions of freedom. In the popular language of politics, if not in law, freedom and the suffrage had become interchangeable. "How can a Man be said to [be] free and independent," asked residents of Lenox, Massachusetts, in 1778, "when he has not a voice allowed him" in elections? Henceforth, political freedom—the right to self-government—would mean not only, as in the past, a people's right to be ruled by their chosen representatives, but an individual's right to political participation.[32]

In economic as well as political affairs, the Revolution redrew the boundary between the free and the unfree. In colonial America, slavery was one less-than-free system of labor among many. In the generation after independence, with the rapid decline of indentured servitude and apprenticeship, and the transformation of paid domestic service into an occupation for blacks and white females, the halfway houses between slavery and freedom disappeared (at least for white men). The demise of these forms of labor, well before they ceased to be widespread in Britain, had many causes, including the growing availability of wage workers and the actions of considerable numbers of servants and apprentices who took advantage of the turmoil of the Revolution to abscond from their masters. But the democratization of freedom played an important part. There could be no such thing as "partial liberty," and servitude increasingly came to be seen as incompatible with republican citizenship. In 1784, a group of "respectable" New Yorkers released a newly arrived shipload of indentured servants on the grounds that their status was "contrary to . . . the idea of liberty this country has so happily established."

By 1800, indentured servitude had all but disappeared from the United States, and apprenticeship was on the wane, developments that sharpened the dichotomy between freedom and slavery and between a northern economy relying on what would come to be called "free labor" and a South ever more heavily bound to the labor of slaves. In the process, the very meaning of the words "master" and "servant" were transformed. In the North, where they were deemed an affront to personal liberty, they fell into disuse. Wage laborers now referred to their employer as the "boss" rather than the "master," and domestic servants were now called "help." In the South, "master" meant slaveowner and "servant" became a euphemism for slave.[33]

Buffeted by unexpected events, Americans of the revolutionary era probed not only the definition of freedom but the means for its preservation. Preoccupied with the social conditions of freedom, they worried about whether a republic could survive with a sizable dependent class of citizens. Virginia's influential Declaration of Rights of June 1776, written by the planter and political leader George Mason, spoke of citizens as "equally free and independent," suggesting a connection between the qualities of freedom, independence, and equality. "A general and tolerably equal distribution of landed property," proclaimed Noah Webster, "is the whole basis of national freedom." "Equality," he added, was "the very soul of a republic," outstripping in importance liberty of the press, trial by jury, and other "palladia of freedom." Even a conservative like John Adams, who distrusted the era's democratic pretensions, still believed that "equal liberty" required enabling "every member of society" to acquire land, "so that the multitude may be possessed of small estates." The goal was less real equality of condition than widespread household independence, and the elimination of social conditions such as extensive poverty deemed to make autonomy impossible.[34]

When Jefferson substituted "the pursuit of happiness" for "property" in the familiar Lockean triad that opened the Declaration of Independence, he tied the new nation's star to an open-ended, democratic process whereby individuals develop their own potential and seek to realize their own life goals. Individual self-fulfillment, unimpeded by government, would become a central element of American freedom. If taken seriously as a goal, equality of opportunity can have results nearly as disruptive of traditional institutions and hierarchies as demands for equality of condition. Certainly, many leaders of the Revolution assumed that in the new republic, equality of opportunity would lead to a rough equality of condition. With hereditary privileges and mercantilist monopolies dismantled, with access to wealth thrown open to all men of talent, "perfect liberty" of trade and freedom for laborers to seek desirable employment would allow all industrious citizens to acquire property. Especially in the exceptional circumstances of the New World, with its vast areas of available land and large population of independent farmers and artisans, there seemed no contradiction between a laissez-faire economy and widespread economic autonomy. In the absence of government favoritism, the natural workings of society would produce justice, liberty, and equality. Jefferson argued that, given the rapid growth of international demand for American grain, freedom of commerce would benefit ordinary Americans, creating the material conditions for an industrious, property-owning citizenry. A limited government would allow citizens both to achieve economic independence and to become virtuous, thus reconciling order and freedom, equality and liberty.[35]

The reinforced equation of autonomy and liberty inevitably raised the question of the social preconditions of freedom. If economic dependence created political subservience, should not the citizens of a republic be guaranteed access to productive property? The linkage of property ownership and liberty, previously employed to draw the political nation's boundary so as to exclude those without property, could be transformed into a political entitlement by those seeking land. From conflict over access to western lands not only with

Britain but with creditors, landlords, and Indians, for example, settlers on the frontier forged their own distinctive language of freedom. When a group of Ohioans petitioned Congress in 1785 assailing landlords and speculators who engrossed available acreage, their motto was "Grant us Liberty." Settlers' claims for preferential access to land rested on the idea that possession of property, as a North Carolina congressman put it, was "a situation incident to freedom and desired by all."

Others sought different ways for the government to ensure economic autonomy—and therefore freedom—to those who did not possess it. At the Revolution's radical edge, the cry of equality led to demands for government to ensure that all Americans enjoyed equally "the blessings and benefits" arising from national independence. The democratization of state government after independence unleashed a flood of enactments aimed at bolstering economic autonomy: debtor relief, more equitable taxation, and direct grants of land to those who did not possess it. In the name of liberty, demands were even raised for limits on the amount of property any individual could accumulate. Whatever the wisdom of individual measures (and taken together, they so alarmed proponents of prudent fiscal and economic policy that they inspired the movement for a stronger national government that culminated in the writing of the U.S. Constitution), the debate itself suggested that the Revolution had thrust to the forefront of politics the question of the economic conditions of freedom.[36]

Like many other Americans of his generation, Thomas Jefferson believed that to lack economic resources was to lack freedom. Jefferson favored a limited state, but simultaneously believed government could help create freedom's institutional framework. Among his proudest achievements were the Virginia laws abolishing entail (the limitation of inheritance to a specified line of heirs to keep an estate within a family) and primogeniture (a law providing for the passing of a family's land entirely to the eldest son), so as to prevent the rise of a "future aristocracy" and lay the foundation for "a government truly republican." To the same end, Jefferson proposed to award fifty acres of land to "every person of full age" who did not already possess it, another way government could enhance the liberty of its subjects.[37]

Jefferson's lifelong friend and colleague, James Madison, agreed that the small, independent farmer constituted "the best basis of public liberty." Legislation in a republic, Madison wrote, should aim to "reduce extreme wealth toward a state of mediocrity, and to raise extreme indigence toward a state of comfort." But lacking Jefferson's congenital optimism, Madison was obsessed by fear that conditions of relative economic equality would prove temporary.

Economic development, he warned the Constitutional Convention, would inevitably produce a society with a non-propertied majority and class conflict between rich and poor. How could government resting on the popular will survive when a democratic majority, resenting its propertyless status, might seek to despoil the rich? For Madison, the answer was to structure government so as to prevent any single economic interest from achieving power. With its elaborate system of checks and balances and divided sovereignty, the Constitution was designed, in part, to enable republican government to survive the rise of economic inequality (and to render unequal concentrations of property immune from governmental interference). But Madison and Jefferson also believed that the new nation's unique circumstances could long delay the rise of economic inequalities on the scale of Great Britain and Europe. Westward expansion, an option obviously not available to the Old World, would underpin the "regime of liberty" in the New. Here, indeed, was a powerful and enduring American dream—a society of free individuals made equal by the bounty of nature.[38]

Was energetic government a threat to liberty, or, in the hands of a virtuous citizenry, the embodiment of political freedom? For Paine, government was a necessary evil, a "badge of lost innocence." To Samuel Adams, writing in 1785, political authority could hardly be seen as a danger to freedom, since "our government at present has liberty for its object."[39] Yet the egalitarian upsurge unleashed by the Revolution produced fears among influential leaders in many states that the experiment in independence would founder unless ways were found to insulate government from popular passions. In creating a structure of government that aimed, among other things, at securing "the blessings of liberty," the writers of the Constitution institutionalized new understandings of political freedom and civil liberty that would profoundly affect the future course of American history.

During the struggle for independence, a Massachusetts writer commented while the Constitution was being debated, "the public rage was on the side of liberty." Among the framers, however, liberty had lost some of its luster. In 1775, John Adams had insisted that "a democratic despotism is a contradiction in terms." But nationalists like Madison became convinced during the 1780s that popular self-government, the essence of political freedom, threatened the security of property and must be restrained so that freedom might flourish. "Liberty," Madison would write in *The Federalist*, "may be endangered by the abuses of liberty as well as the abuses of power." Or to put it another way, private liberty could be endangered by public liberty, personal liberty by political liberty—that is, by power in the hands of the people. Madison had in mind the boisterous state-level democracy of the 1780s and collective attacks on pub-

AMERICA TRIUMPHANT and BRITANNIA in DISTRESS

An elaborate allegory representing American independence as a triumph of liberty, from an almanac published in Boston in 1781. An accompanying key explains the symbolism: "1. America sitting on that quarter of the globe with the flag of the United States displayed over her head, holding in one hand the olive branch, inviting the ships of all nations to partake of her commerce, and in the other hand supporting the cap of liberty. 2. Fame proclaiming the joyful news to all the world. 3. Britannia weeping at the loss of the trade of America, attended with an evil genius [the devil]. 4. The British flag struck, on her strong fortress. 5. French, Spanish, Dutch shipping in the harbors of America. 6. A view of New York, wherein is exhibited the Traitor [Benedict] Arnold, taken with remorse for selling his country, and Judas-like hanging himself." (American Antiquarian Society)

lic order like Shays' Rebellion of 1786–87, when debt-ridden farmers, many of them former soldiers in the War for Independence, closed the courts in western Massachusetts to prevent the loss of their property to creditors. That they employed liberty trees and liberty poles, the emblems of the struggle for independence, as symbols of their own cause did nothing to endear them to defenders of law and order.[40]

Ultimately, the framers of the Constitution sought to reconcile republican government and social stability by diffusing political power, barring states from abridging the rights of property, and balancing the self-interested ambitions of competing social groups against one another. Madison did not abandon the idea that "virtue in the people" was the essential underpinning of freedom. But in a world in which self-interest appeared to overwhelm civic virtue, the preservation of liberty would have to rely on the machinery of government itself, not the character of the people—a major step in the shift from republican to liberal premises among the political elite. Nonetheless, the republican idea that political decisions and economic relationships ought to reflect concern for the common good rather than private gain long survived the revolutionary era.

Madison, Alexander Hamilton, and the other architects of the Constitution were nation-builders. Hamilton was perhaps the most vigorous proponent of an "energetic" government that would enable the new nation to become a powerful commercial and diplomatic presence in world affairs. Power and liberty, he insisted, were complementary, not antithetical, for freedom required "a proper degree of authority, to make and execute the laws with vigor." Although he did not envision the federal government as quite so assertive a power as Hamilton did, Madison too sought to enhance national authority. The danger to liberty, Madison believed, lay in unchecked majority power at the state level. While the convention rejected Madison's proposal to empower Congress to override state laws, the Constitution created a central government far more powerful than the weak authority established by the Articles of Confederation, the preceding frame of government.[41]

Thus the framers of the Constitution viewed freedom both as the foundation of governmental authority and as a threat to proper governance that must be kept in check. In this sense, it represented a retreat from the ebullient democratic upsurge that had accompanied the struggle for independence. "The same enthusiasm, *now* pervades all classes in favor of *government*," observed Benjamin Rush, a leader of the independence struggle in Pennsylvania, "that actuated us in favor of *liberty* in the years 1774 and 1775." Whether "all classes" truly concurred may be doubted, for the ratification process unleashed a nationwide debate over the best means of preserving political freedom. Anti-Federalists, as opponents of ratification were called, insisted that the Constitution shifted the balance between liberty and authority too far in the direction of the latter. Freedom, they believed, was more secure in the hands of smaller communities pursuing the common good than a distant federal power protecting private interests. The "consolidated government" envisioned by the Constitution, complained Patrick Henry, might produce "a great and mighty empire," but at the cost of freedom. "What is Liberty?" asked James Lincoln of South Carolina. "The power of governing yourselves. If you adopt this Constitution, have you this power? No."[42]

In the end, of course, ratification was achieved, partly in exchange for adding the Bill of Rights. The original document, Anti-Federalists charged, left un-continued to reinforce one another, in requirements barring non-Christians from office and in the continued prosecution of blasphemy and breaches of the sabbath. Nevertheless, the Constitution, which contains no reference to God, is a purely secular document. In prohibiting religious tests for federal office-holders and, in the First Amendment, barring the federal government from legislating on the subject of religion, it departed dramatically from both British and colonial practice. Under the Constitution, it was and remains possible, as one critic at the time complained, for "a papist, a Mohomatan, a deist, yea an atheist," to become president of the United States.[47]

Like freedom of speech and the press, religious freedom reflected the conviction that, as Madison put it, conscience was the most "sacred" of all rights, and that no political authority should influence or punish its free exercise. Even more than other freedoms, religious liberty became the paradigm for the revolutionary generation's definition of "rights" as private matters that must be protected from governmental interference. Religious freedom offered a new rationale for the idea of the United States as a beacon of liberty. In successfully opposing a Virginia tax for the general support of Christian churches, Madison insisted that one reason for the complete separation of church and state was to reinforce the meaning of independence as "offering asylum to the persecuted and oppressed of every nation and religion." And religious liberty provided a model for the Madisonian system of preserving freedom. In a free society, Madison wrote, "the security for civil rights must be the same as for religious rights. It consists in the one case in the multiplicity of interests and, in the other, in the multiplicity of sects." A free market in religion would prevent any one group from using political power to impose its views on the others. In an overwhelmingly Christian (though not necessarily churchgoing) nation, the separation of church and state drew a sharp line between public authority and a realm defined as "private," reinforcing the idea that rights exist as restraints on the power of government.[48]

Thus, the Revolution democratized not only American Christianity but also the idea of religious liberty itself. Ironically, even as the separation of church and state created the social and political space that allowed a myriad of religious institutions to flourish, the culture of individual rights of which that separation was a part threatened to undermine the authority of churches. One telling example lay in the experience of the Moravian Brethren, who had emigrated from Germany to North Carolina on the eve of independence. According to the Moravian elders, younger members of the community, like so many other Americans of the revolutionary generation, insisted on asserting "their alleged freedom and human rights." To the elders, "the American freedom" was little more than "an opportunity for temptation," a threat to the spirit of self-sacrifice and communal loyalty essential to Christian liberty. But despite such fears, disestablishment did not end the influence of religion on American society; quite the reverse. Thanks to religious freedom, the post-revolutionary era witnessed an amazing proliferation of religious denominations. Today, even as debates continue over the proper relationship between spiritual and political concerns, more than one thousand three hundred religions are practiced in the United States.[49]

"Yield to the mighty current of American freedom." So a member of the South Carolina legislature implored his colleagues in 1777.[50] And the current of freedom swept away not only British authority but also the principle of hereditary rule, the established churches, long-standing habits of deference and hierarchy, and old limits on the political nation. Yet in one crucial area, the tide of freedom encountered an obstacle that did not yield to its powerful flow. For freedom's antithesis—slavery—emerged from the Revolution more firmly entrenched than ever in American life.

2

To Call It Freedom

Slavery and the Republic

$A_{PART\ FROM}$ "liberty," the word most frequently invoked in the legal and political literature of the eighteenth century was its opposite, "slavery." The institution of slavery is as old as civilization and its metaphorical meanings go back to ancient times. Virtually every form of oppression has at one time or another been described as a form of slavery. In the eighteenth century, freedom and slavery were frequently juxtaposed as "the two extremes of happiness and misery in society." The condition of the slave was widely considered odious. "When an Englishman would paint the greatest curse that can befall him," commented Boston merchant Nathan Appleton, "it is to be no better off than an African slave." Yet in the era's political discourse, slavery was primarily a political category, shorthand for the denial of one's personal and political rights by arbitrary government. Those who lacked a voice in public affairs, declared a 1769 petition demanding an expansion of the British franchise, were "enslaved." In the years preceding independence, slavery assumed a central place in the language of colonial resistance. Many Americans came to describe their relationship to the mother country as a form of enslavement.[1]

Occasionally, colonial writers of the 1760s made a direct connection between slavery as a reality and slavery as a metaphor. Few were as forthright as James Otis of Massachusetts, whose pamphlets did much to popularize the idea that Parliament lacked the authority to tax the

Liberty Displaying the Arts and Sciences (1792). This painting by Samuel Jennings, commissioned by the Library Company of Philadelphia, is one of the few visual images of the early republic explicitly to link slavery with tyranny and liberty with abolition. The female figure of Liberty offers books to newly freed slaves; beneath her left foot is a broken chain. (Winterthur Museum)

colonies and regulate their commerce. Freedom, Otis insisted, must be universal: "What man is or ever was born free if every man is not?" Blacks, for Otis, were not allegorical figures whose status illustrated the dire fate awaiting free Americans, but flesh and blood British subjects "entitled to all the civil rights of such."[2]

Otis, however, was hardly typical. When most patriot leaders spoke of slavery, they meant the denial of the right of self-government or dependence on the will of another, not being reduced to a species of property. "Those who are taxed without their own consent," said John Dickinson of Pennsylvania, "are slaves." Thomas Paine identified hereditary rule as "a species of slavery." "Representative government," he asserted, "is freedom." Until the 1760s, colonists had shared in the celebration of Britain as a land of freedom. But as part and parcel of the patriotic struggle, their image of the mother country was transformed. By the eve of independence, the contrast between Britain, "a kingdom of slaves," and America, a "country of free men," had become a standard part of the idiom of resistance. "Liberty or slavery is now the question," declared the Philadelphia radical James Cannon in April 1776. Such language was employed without irony even in areas where a majority of the population in fact consisted of slaves. South Carolina, one writer declared in 1774, was a "sacred land" of freedom, where it was impossible to believe that "slavery shall soon be permitted to erect her throne."[3]

While rarely mentioned explicitly, the proximity of hundreds of thousands of real slaves was intimately related to the meaning of freedom for the men who made the American Revolution. In his famous speech to the British Parliament warning against attempts to coerce the colonies, Edmund Burke suggested that in the South, at least, it was familiarity with actual slavery that made colonial leaders so sensitive to the threat of metaphorical slavery. Where freedom was a privilege, not a common right, he observed, "those who are free are by far the most proud and jealous of their freedom." Much the same point was made by David Ramsay, a South Carolinian whose *History of the American Revolution*, published in 1789, helped to popularize an understanding of the American past as a progress of freedom. In the southern colonies, wrote Ramsay, slavery "nurtured a spirit of liberty among the free inhabitants," since nothing could excite slaveholders' opposition to British rule more effectively than fear of being "degraded" to a position analogous to that of their slaves.[4]

Americans were not the only people to worship liberty while profiting from slavery. In the ancient world, "one element of freedom was the freedom to enslave others." Christian liberty, a spiritual state, did not preclude slaveholding, a worldly condition recognized in the Bible. During the eighteenth century,

Britain, France, and Holland, countries where ideas of freedom flourished, were all deeply involved in the Atlantic slave trade; indeed, the freedom of the seas so cherished by Britons included the right to carry slaves to any port their merchants desired. British observers, while hardly above criticism on the same grounds, were fond of pointing out the colonists' apparent hypocrisy. "How is it," asked Dr. Samuel Johnson, "that we hear the loudest yelps for liberty from the drivers of negroes?" The Declaration of Independence inspired Thomas Hutchinson, the former royal governor of Massachusetts, to wonder how, "if these rights are so absolutely inalienable," Americans justified depriving "Africans of their rights to liberty, and the pursuit of happiness." British friends of American independence like Richard Price feared that slavery fatally compromised the Revolution's promise. If "the people who have been struggling so earnestly to save *themselves* from slavery are very ready to enslave *others,*" he wrote to Jefferson in 1785, American independence would mean little more than a new chapter in the timeless story of "aristocratic tyranny and human debasement," and the "friends of liberty and virtue in Europe" would be "mortified."[5]

Indeed, the contradiction between freedom and slavery is so self-evident that it is difficult today to appreciate the power of the obstacles to abolition. At the time of the Revolution, slavery was already an old institution in America; it existed in every state and formed the basis of the economy and social structure from Maryland southward. It was slavery that made the staple-producing colonies the richest region in British America. Already, as a French visitor observed, "command of a few negroes" was essential to the self-definition, the social standing, of southern planters. Thomas Jefferson, as is well known, owned over one hundred slaves at the time he wrote the immortal lines affirming the inalienable right to liberty, and everything he cherished in his own manner of life, from lavish entertainments to the leisure that made possible the pursuit of arts and sciences, ultimately rested on slave labor.[6]

Slavery for blacks did not necessarily contradict white Americans' understanding of freedom. It could in fact be argued that slavery made republican freedom possible, for by eliminating the great bulk of the dependent poor from the political nation, it left the public arena to men of propertied independence. For many Americans, owning slaves offered a route to the economic autonomy widely deemed indispensable to genuine freedom (a point driven home by a 1780 Virginia law that rewarded veterans of the War for Independence with three hundred acres of land—and a slave). The republican vision of a society of independent men actively pursuing the public good could easily be reconciled with slavery for those outside the circle of citizenship. In a republic, Adam Smith pointed out, it would be all the more difficult to abolish slavery since "the persons who make all the laws in that country are persons who have slaves themselves"—thus, the "freedom of the free" helped to produce "the great oppression of the slaves." So, too, the liberal definition of freedom as essentially private and of the political community as a group of individuals seeking protection for their natural rights could readily be invoked to defend bondage. Nothing was more essential to liberal freedom than the right of self-government and protection of property against interference by the state. These principles suggested that it would be an infringement of liberty to relieve a man of his property (including slave property) without his consent. The right to property, Virginian Arthur Lee insisted, was "the guardian of every other right, and to deprive a people of this, is in fact to deprive them of their liberty." If government by the consent of the governed was the essence of political freedom, then to require owners to give up their slave property would reduce *them* to slavery.[7]

Nonetheless, by imparting so absolute a value to liberty, sweeping away forms of partial freedom so prevalent in the colonial era, and positing freedom as a universal entitlement rather than a set of rights specific to a particular place or people, the Revolution inevitably raised questions about the status of chattel slavery in America. Before independence, the nation's first chief justice, John Jay, later remarked, "very few . . . doubted the propriety and rectitude" of slavery, even though enlightened opinion in the Atlantic world (exemplified, for example, in the writings of Montesquieu, David Hume, and Adam Smith) had come to view slavery as morally wrong and economically inefficient, the relic of a barbarous past. During the revolutionary era, slavery for the first time became a focus of public debate in America. It was not a British critic but the Pennsylvania patriot Benjamin Rush who in 1773 called upon "advocates for American liberty" to "espouse the cause of . . . general liberty," and warned that slavery was one of those "national crimes" that one day would bring "national punishment." In the following year, Massachusetts clergyman John Allen lamented that Americans were making a "mockery" of their professed love of liberty "by trampling on the sacred natural rights and privileges of the *Africans*." Not all these comments emanated from the North, where slavery was far less powerfully entrenched than in the plantation regions of Maryland, Virginia, the Carolinas, and Georgia. Jefferson, at least in private, strongly condemned chattel slavery as a system "one hour of which is fraught with more misery, than ages of that which [the colonists] rose in rebellion to oppose."[8]

The Revolution inspired widespread hopes that slavery could be removed from American life. Most dramatically, slaves themselves appreciated that by defining freedom as a universal right, the revolutionists had devised a rhetoric that could be deployed against chattel bondage. The language of liberty echoed in slave communities, North and South. Living amid freedom but denied its substance, slaves appropriated the patriotic ideology for their own purposes. The first concrete steps toward emancipation were "freedom petitions"—arguments for manumission presented to New England's courts and legislatures in the early 1770s by enslaved African-Americans. Once the War for Independence began, the British offered freedom to slaves who joined the royal cause. Nearly one hundred thousand, including one-quarter of all the slaves in South Carolina, deserted their owners (although not a few were subsequently reenslaved in the West Indies). George Washington himself saw seventeen of his slaves flee to British lines. Thousands more escaped bondage by enlisting in the Revolutionary Army.

Blacks recognized both hypocrisy and opportunity in the ideology of freedom. The most insistent advocates of freedom as a universal entitlement were African-Americans, who demanded that the leaders of the struggle for independence live up to their professed creed, thus extending the concept of liberty into unintended realms. As early as 1766, white Charlestonians had been shocked when their opposition to the Stamp Act under the slogan, "Liberty and stamp'd paper," inspired a group of blacks to parade about the city crying "Liberty." Nine years later, the Provincial Congress of South Carolina felt compelled to investigate the "high notions of liberty" the struggle against Britain had inspired among the slaves.[9]

In 1776, the year of American independence, Lemuel Haynes, a black member of the Massachusetts militia and later a celebrated minister, urged that Americans "extend" their conception of freedom. If liberty were truly "an innate principle" for all mankind, Haynes insisted, "even an African [had] as equally good a right to his liberty in common with Englishmen." Throughout the revolutionary period, petitions, pamphlets, and sermons by blacks expressed "astonishment" that white patriots failed to realize that "every principle from which America has acted" demanded emancipation. Blacks sought to alter the language of politics, insisting that the nation understand slavery as a concrete, brutal reality, not an abstract condition or metaphor. Petitioning for their freedom in 1773, a group of New England slaves exclaimed: "We have no property! We have no wives! No children! We have no city! No country!" For blacks, slavery meant the denial of all the essential attributes of freedom, not merely the loss of personal autonomy or lack of political self-determination.[10]

Most slaves of the revolutionary era were only one or two generations removed from Africa. They did not need the ideology of the Revolution to persuade them that freedom was a birthright; the experience of their parents and grandparents suggested as much. In contrast to Edmund Burke and David Ramsay, blacks insisted that the slave, not the master, genuinely craved liberty. "My love of freedom," wrote the black poet Phillis Wheatley in 1783, arose from the "cruel fate" of being "snatch'd from Afric's" shore. Yet, if traditional African societies knew the desire not to be a slave, the modern idea of freedom was born in the West. In the world from which the slaves had been forcibly removed, where individuals existed within a wide network of communal and kin relationships and social identity depended on being anchored in a web of power and authority, personal freedom was an oxymoron. By invoking the Revolution's ideology of liberty to demand their own rights and defining freedom as a universal entitlement, blacks demonstrated how American they had become, even as they sought to redefine what American freedom in fact represented.[11]

For a brief moment, the "contagion of liberty" appeared to threaten the continued existence of slavery. During the 1780s, a considerable number of southern slaveholders, especially in Virginia and Maryland, voluntarily emancipated their slaves. Father south, however, the abolition process never got underway. In the North, every state from New Hampshire to Pennsylvania took steps toward emancipation, the first time in recorded history that legislative power had been invoked to eradicate slavery. But even here, where slavery was peripheral to the economy, the slowness of abolition reflected how powerfully the sanctity of property rights impeded emancipation. Generally, abolition laws provided for the liberty of any child henceforth born to a slave mother, but only after he or she had served the mother's master until adulthood as compensation for the owner's future loss of property rights.[12]

At the Constitutional Convention of 1787, as Madison recorded, "the institution of slavery and its implications formed the line of discrimination" in many debates. The fifty-five men who gathered in Philadelphia to draft the document included numerous slaveholders, as well as some dedicated abolitionists. Madison, who, like Jefferson, was a Virginia slaveholder who despised slavery, told the convention that the "distinction of color" had become the basis for "the most oppressive dominion ever exercised by man over man." Yet later, Madison assured delegates to the Virginia ratifying convention that the Constitution offered slavery "better security than any that now exists." And so it did. For the Constitution prohibited Congress from abolishing the African slave trade for two decades; required states to return to their owners fugitives from bondage; and provided that three-fifths of the slave population be counted in determining each state's representation in the House of Representatives and its electoral votes for president. To be sure, the words "slave" and "slavery" did not appear in the original Constitution—a concession to the sensibilities of dele-

gates who feared they would "contaminate the glorious fabric of American liberty." As Luther Martin, a Maryland attorney who opposed ratification, wrote,
his fellow delegates "anxiously sought to avoid the admission of expressions
which might be odious to the ears of Americans." But, he continued, they were
"willing to admit into their system those *things* which the *expressions signified.*"[13]

Clearly, the Constitution's slavery clauses were compromises, efforts to find
a middle ground between the institution's critics and defenders. Taken together,
however, they managed to strengthen the institution of slavery and leave it
more deeply embedded in American life and politics. The slave trade clause allowed a commerce condemned by civilized society, and which had been suspended during the War for Independence, to continue until 1808. Partly to
replace slaves who had escaped to the British, and partly to provide labor for
the expansion of cotton production into the upcountry, South Carolina and
Georgia took advantage of the twenty-year hiatus before the trade's abolition
to import some ninety thousand additional Africans, about one-quarter of all
the slaves brought to British North America after 1700. The fugitive slave clause
accorded slave laws "extraterritoriality," that is, the condition of bondage adhered to a person even after he or she had escaped to a jurisdiction where slavery had been abolished. John Jay, while serving in Madrid on a diplomatic
mission, once wrote of how he missed the "free air" of America. Jay was probably unaware of the phrase's ironic implications, for in the *Somerset* case of 1772,
the lawyer for a West Indian slave brought to Britain had obtained his client's
freedom by invoking the memorable words, "the air of England is too pure for
a slave to breathe." Yet in the United States, the Constitution's fugitive slave
clause made all the states, including those that had abolished slavery, complic-
itous in maintaining the institution's stability. For slaves, there was no "free air"
in America.

The federal structure, moreover, insulated slavery in the states from outside
interference, while the three-fifths clause allowed the white South, and especially
the planter class, to exercise far greater power in national affairs than the size
of its free population warranted. Partly as a result, of the first sixteen presidential elections, between 1788 and 1848, all but four placed a southern slaveholder in the White House. Even the initial failure to include a Bill of Rights
resulted, in part, from the fact that, as South Carolina delegate Charles
Cotesworth Pinckney explained, "such bills generally begin with declaring that
all men are by nature born free," a declaration that would come "with a very
bad grace, when a large part of our property consists in men who are actually
born slaves."[14]

All in all, the Revolution had a contradictory impact on American slavery and, therefore, on American freedom. Gradual as it was, the abolition of slavery in the North drew a geographical line across the new nation, creating the portentous division between free and slave states. Abolition in the North, voluntary emancipation in the Upper South, and the escape of thousands from bondage created, for the first time in American history, a sizable free black population (not a few of whose members took new family names like Freeman or Freeland). On the eve of independence, virtually every black person in America had been a slave. Now, a free community, with its own churches, schools, and leadership class, came into existence, constituting a standing challenge to the logic of slavery, a haven for fugitives, and a springboard for further efforts at abolition.[15]

For many Americans, white as well as black, the existence of slavery would henceforth be recognized as a standing affront to the ideal of American freedom, a "disgrace to a free government," as a group of New Yorkers put it. In 1792, when Samuel Jennings of Philadelphia painted *Liberty Displaying the Arts and Sciences*, he included among the symbols of freedom a slave's broken chain, graphically illustrating how freedom had become identified not simply with political independence but with emancipation. Certainly, after the Revolution it would be difficult to employ slavery as a metaphor without triggering thoughts about actual slaves. Nonetheless, the stark fact is that the Revolution did not rid American society of slavery. Indeed, thanks to the natural increase of the slave population, soon to be supplemented by a reopened slave trade, there were considerably more slaves at the end of the revolutionary era than at the beginning. The first national census, in 1790, revealed that the half-million slave population of 1776 had grown to some 700,000.[16]

Throughout the Atlantic world, the upheavals of the age of revolution posed a threat to slavery. In 1794, the French Convention proclaimed abolition (only to see slavery restored by Napoleon a few years later). Emancipation was a goal of the leaders of independent Haiti and nearly all the Latin American liberators. Only in the United States did the creation of a new nation-state strengthen the institution. The British poet Oliver Goldsmith might well have been speaking of the revolutionary generation when he commented on mankind's propensity "to call it freedom, when themselves are free."[17]

We the People

If the Revolution created a new nation, it also invented a new public entity: the American people. From a colonial population divided by ethnicity, religion, class, and status, and united largely by virtue of their allegiance to Britain, the Revolution created a new collective body whose members were to enjoy rights and freedom as citizens in a new political community.[18] The capacious nature of American freedom made it all the more imperative to identify "the people" entitled to enjoy it. "We the people," the words that open the Constitution, describe those who, among other things, are to possess "the blessings of liberty" as a birthright and bequeath them to "posterity." Although one might assume that "the people" of the United States included all those living within the nation's borders, the subsequent text made clear that this was not the case. The Constitution identified three populations inhabiting within the United States: Indians, treated as members of their own tribal sovereignties and not, therefore, part of the American body politic; "other persons"—that is, slaves; and "the people." Only the third enjoyed the blessings of liberty.

The debate unleashed by the Revolution about who was entitled to American freedom continues to this day. Americans' persistent disagreements about the bases of our "imagined community" reflect a larger contradiction in the Western tradition itself. For if the West, as we are frequently reminded, created the idea of liberty as a universal human right, it also invented the concept of race and ascribed to it all sorts of predictive powers about human behavior. Nationalism, in America at least, is the child of both these beliefs. Traditionally, scholars have distinguished between civic nationalism—which envisions the nation as a community based on shared political institutions and values, with membership open to all who reside within its territory—and ethnic nationalism, which defines the nation as a community of descent based on a shared ethnic and linguistic heritage. At first glance, the United States appears to conform to the civic model. Lacking a clear ethnic identity or long-established national boundaries, it was the political creed of the Revolution that held Americans together. To be an American, all one had to do was commit oneself to an ideology of liberty, equality, and democracy.[19]

From the outset, however, American nationality combined both civic and ethnic definitions. Americans, one scholar has written, are given to hiding their "particularism in the universals of 'freedom' and 'liberty.' " For most of our history, American citizenship has been defined by blood as well as by political allegiance. Both definitions can be traced to the earliest days of the republic, when a nation was created committed to liberty, yet resting, to a considerable extent, on slavery. Slavery helped to shape the identity, the sense of self, of all Americans. Constituting the most impenetrable boundary of citizenship, slavery rendered blacks all but invisible to those imagining the American community.[20]

Already, Americans were speaking of their country as a place where "individuals of all nations" were transformed into a new people, "melted into a new race of men." But the popular idea that the shared experience of fleeing tyranny in the Old World for freedom in the New made Americans one people automatically excluded Africans. When the era's master mythmaker, Hector St. John Crèvecoeur, posed the famous question: "What then is the American, this new man?", he answered: "a mixture of English, Scotch, Irish, French, Dutch, Germans, and Swedes. . . . He is either a European, or the descendant of a European." This at a time when fully one-fifth of the population (the highest proportion in our history) consisted of Africans and their descendants. Slaves, as Edmund Randolph, the nation's first attorney general, wrote, were not "constituent members of our society," and the language of liberty and citizenship did not apply to them.[21]

Did blacks form part of the "imagined community" of the new republic? Nowhere does the original Constitution define who in fact are citizens of the United States, or what privileges and immunities they enjoy. The individual states were to determine the boundaries of citizenship and citizens' rights. The North's Emancipation Acts assumed that former slaves would remain in the country, not be colonized abroad, and during the era of the Revolution, free blacks enjoyed at least some of the legal rights accorded to whites. Most of the new state constitutions, including those in the Upper South, allowed newly emancipated black men to vote if they could meet property qualifications.

The Constitution, however, empowered Congress to create a uniform system of naturalization, and the Naturalization Act of 1790 offered the first legislative definition of American nationality. With no debate, Congress restricted the process of becoming a citizen to "free white persons." Thus, at the very outset, a nation that defined itself as an asylum for liberty excluded the vast majority of the world's population from partaking in the blessings of American freedom (a fact that belies the common description of the initial policy as "open" immigration). This limitation lasted a long time. For eighty years, only white immigrants could become naturalized citizens. Blacks were added in 1870, but not until the 1940s did persons of Asian origin become eligible. Only in the last quarter of the nineteenth century were groups of whites barred from entering the country and becoming citizens. Beginning with prostitutes, convicted felons, lunatics, polygamists, and persons likely to become a "public charge," the list of excluded classes would be expanded in the twentieth century to include, among others, anarchists, Communists, homosexuals, and the illiterate. But for the first century of the republic, while all non-whites were barred, virtually the only white persons in the entire world ineligible to claim American citizenship were those unwilling to renounce hereditary titles of nobility, as required in an act of 1795.[22]

The two groups excluded from naturalization—European aristocrats and non-whites—had more in common than might appear at first glance. Both were viewed as deficient in the qualities that made freedom possible: the capacity for self-control, rational forethought, and devotion to the larger community. These were the characteristics that Jefferson, in his famous comparison of the races in *Notes on the State of Virginia* (1785), claimed blacks lacked, partly due to natural incapacity and partly because the bitter experience of slavery had (quite understandably, he felt) rendered them disloyal to the nation. (Jefferson also thought that slavery had a disastrous impact on the morals of whites, since the "perpetual exercise" of despotic rule over other human beings rendered self-control impossible; he did not conclude from this, however, that slaveholders should be barred from citizenship.) Jefferson was obsessed with the connection between heredity and environment, race and intelligence. His environmentalism, combined with his belief that all men possessed an inner moral sense, inclined him not only to democratic values but to the hope that no group was fixed permanently in a status of inferiority. His racism led him to the "suspicion" that nature had rendered blacks permanently deficient in the qualities that made freedom possible.

In holding these two apparently contradictory beliefs—environmentalism and racism—in uneasy tension, Jefferson reflected the divided mind of his generation. He believed black Americans should eventually enjoy the natural rights enumerated in the Declaration of Independence, but in Africa or the Caribbean, not the United States. Madison, too, always coupled the idea of emancipation with colonization. America should have a homogenous citizenry whose common experiences, values, and innate capacities made it possible to realize the idea of the public good, and whose essential sameness underpinned the ideal of equality.[23]

By narrowing the gradations of freedom among the white population, the Revolution widened the divide between free Americans and those who remained in slavery. Race, which had long constituted one of many kinds of legal and social inequality among colonial Americans, now emerged as a convenient justification for the existence of slavery in a land ideologically committed to freedom as a natural right. Man's liberty, John Locke had written, flowed from "his having reason." To deny liberty to those who were not rational beings was not a contradiction. By the nineteenth century, the idea of innate black inferi-

ority, advanced by Jefferson as a suspicion, would mature into a full-fledged ideology, central to many definitions of American nationality itself.[24]

Gender, too, formed a boundary limiting those entitled to the full blessings
of American freedom. Free women were certainly members of the nation; they
could be naturalized if emigrating from abroad, and were counted fully in determining representation in Congress. Until after the Civil War, the word
"male" did not appear in the Constitution, and there was nothing explicitly limiting the rights outlined in that document by sex. The pronoun "he" describing officeholders, however, expressed an assumption so pervasive that it scarcely
needed explicit defense: politics was a realm for men. Political freedom for
men meant the right to self-government, the power to consent to the individuals and political arrangements that ruled over them. For women, however, the
marriage contract superseded the social contract, and their relationship to the
larger society was mediated through their relationships with men. For many
women, the Revolution did produce an improvement in status. According to the
ideology of "republican motherhood" that emerged as a result of independence, women played an indispensable political role by training future citizens. The "foundation of national morality," wrote John Adams, "must be
laid in private families." Even though republican motherhood ruled out direct
female involvement in politics, it encouraged the expansion of educational opportunities for women, to enable them to inculcate political wisdom in their
children.[25]

In both law and social reality, however, women lacked the essential qualification of political participation—the opportunity for autonomy based on
ownership of property or control of one's own person. Since the common law
subsumed women within the legal status of their husbands, women could not
be said to have property in themselves in the same sense as men. Their very subordinate status within the family heightened the contrast between masculine autonomy and female dependence. Indeed, among the deprivations of slavery
cited by a group of male black petitioners in 1774 was that it prevented their
wives from "submitting themselves to husbands in all things," as the natural
order of the universe required. For women, as well as for blacks, the denial of
full freedom rested on the assumption of natural incapacity, since women were
widely thought (by men) to be naturally submissive and irrational, creatures of
sentiment unfit for citizenship. The subordination of free women, however, did
not become a source of public debate until long after American independence;
Mary Wollstonecraft's *Vindication of the Rights of Woman*, a stirring call for civil and
political equality published in Britain in 1792, inspired a few similar efforts in

the young republic, and even a short-lived women's rights magazine in New York City. But the time had not yet arrived for a broad assault on gender inequality. Although New Jersey's constitution of 1776, which granted suffrage to all "inhabitants" who met a property qualification, inadvertently enfranchised some women until 1807, the republican citizen was, by definition, male.[26]

Despite these limitations, most Americans would probably have agreed with the members of the first Congress, who, in congratulating George Washington on his inauguration, spoke of their countrymen as "the freest people on the face of the earth." To Washington's dismay, however, freedom did not produce public harmony, for his accession to office was soon followed by the outbreak of fierce political conflict. Yet the very passion of the partisan debates of the 1790s revealed how deeply the idea of freedom had taken root in American political culture. Parties and social movements laid claim to the language of liberty, each accusing their opponents of engaging in a conspiracy to undermine freedom. Federalists, who were generally elitist in their view of politics and society, feared, as Washington put it, that the "spirit of liberty" unleashed by the Revolution was degenerating into "licentiousness." This conviction was reinforced by the Whiskey Rebellion of 1794, when backcountry Pennsylvania farmers invoked the symbols of 1776, such as liberty poles, as they sought to block enforcement of a new excise tax. When the Federalist leader Rufus King wrote an essay on the "words . . . with wrong meaning" that had "done great harm" to American society, his first example was "Liberty." Freedom, Federalists insisted, did not mean the right to set one's self up in opposition to government, but rested on deference to authority.[27]

Jeffersonian Republicans were more prone to accept what a New Hampshire editor called the "boisterous sea of liberty" as preferable to the "calm of despotism." Their outlook was far more egalitarian and critical of social and economic hierarchies, more accepting of democratic participation as essential to freedom. Each side accused the other of undermining the liberty bequeathed to Americans by the Revolution. Jeffersonians feared that the program of national economic development pursued by Secretary of the Treasury Alexander Hamilton, involving close commercial ties with Great Britain, a national debt, and a national bank to stabilize and regulate the currency, were harbingers of the same political corruption that had undermined liberty in Britain in the decades before the American Revolution. To Jeffersonian Republicans, the greatest threat to American freedom lay in the alliance of a powerful central government and an emerging class of commercial capitalists, such as Hamilton appeared to envision.[28]

The debates of the 1790s produced not only one of the most intense periods of partisan warfare in American history but an enduring expansion of the democratic content of American freedom. The decade witnessed the rapid expansion of the American press and a vigorous debate over public policies, with hundreds of "obscure men" writing pamphlets and newspaper essays and forming political organizations. The emergence of the Democratic-Republican societies, organized by critics of the Washington administration, suggested that political liberty meant not simply voting at elections but constant involvement in public affairs. Denounced by the president as "self-created" and divisive, these societies were forced to justify their existence. In so doing they articulated a defense of what scholars would later call the "public sphere"—a realm independent of government where debate on political issues can take place and citizens organize themselves to affect public policy. To the societies, "free inquiry" and "free communication"—the right of "any portion of the people," regardless of station in life, to express political opinions—were among "the inalienable rights of free men." The political crisis came to a head in 1798, when, beset by foes at home and abroad, the administration of John Adams enacted the Alien and Sedition Acts. The first allowed the deportation of aliens deemed dangerous by federal authorities, a repudiation, Republicans claimed, of the idea of the United States as an asylum of liberty. The second authorized the prosecution of virtually any public assembly or publication critical of the government.[29]

The Alien and Sedition Acts and the subsequent jailing of a number of Republican editors thrust freedom of speech and of the press to the center of discussions of American liberty. In denouncing these measures, Jefferson and Madison repudiated the common law tradition that the national government enjoyed the power to punish "seditious" speech (although Jefferson was careful to insist that the states "fully possessed" this power). Other Republicans went further, challenging the entire idea of legal restraints on the free expression of ideas. State-level prosecutions of newspapers for seditious libel did not end when the Sedition Act expired in 1801. But the "crisis of freedom" of the late 1790s strongly reinforced the idea that "freedom of discussion" was an indispensable attribute of American liberty. The broad revulsion against the Alien and Sedition Acts contributed greatly to Jefferson's election as president in 1800. As the campaign slogan, "Jefferson and Liberty," indicated, Republicans saw their victory not simply as a partisan success but as the triumph of American freedom, securing for posterity the fruits of the Revolution.[30]

Yet the events of the 1790s, culminating in Jefferson's victory, also underscored how powerfully slavery defined and distorted American freedom. The same Jeffersonians who hailed the French Revolution as a step in the universal progress of liberty reacted in horror against the slave revolution that began in 1791 in Saint-Domingue, the jewel of the French overseas empire, situated not far from the southern coast of the United States. The slave uprising affirmed the universality of the revolutionary era's credo of liberty. But the reaction to it revealed how easily slavery could be subsumed into the revolutionary cause. The rebellious slaves were viewed not as men and women seeking their liberty in the tradition of 1776, but as a danger to American institutions. Their resort to violence was widely taken to illustrate that blacks were unfit for republican freedom. Ironically, it was the Adams administration, which hoped that American merchants could replace their French counterparts in the island's lucrative sugar trade, that encouraged the independence of black Haiti, whereas Jefferson as president sought to quarantine and destroy the hemisphere's second independent republic. But then, the triumph of "Jefferson and Liberty" would not have been possible without slavery. Had three-fifths of the South's slaves not been counted in apportioning electoral votes, John Adams would have won reelection in 1800.[31]

Jefferson referred to his election as the "Revolution of 1800." Yet that momentous year witnessed not only a metaphorical revolution but an attempted real one, a plot by slaves in Virginia itself to gain their freedom. Organized by a Richmond blacksmith, Gabriel, and his brother Martin, a slave preacher, the conspirators evidently planned to march on the city from surrounding plantations and kill most of the white residents. On the night they were to gather, a storm washed out the roads to Richmond. The plot was soon uncovered and the leaders arrested. Like other Virginians, participants in Gabriel's conspiracy spoke the language of liberty forged in the American Revolution. The rebels even planned to carry a banner emblazoned with a slogan borrowed from Patrick Henry: "Death or Liberty." "We have as much right," one conspirator declared, "to fight for our liberty as any men." Another likened himself to George Washington, who had also rebelled against established authority to "obtain the liberty of [his] countrymen" (an analogy that carried the disturbing implication that American officials had now replaced the British as enemies of freedom).[32]

If the Gabriel conspiracy demonstrated anything, George Tucker, a member of one of Virginia's most prominent families, commented, it was that slaves possessed "the love of freedom" as fully as other men. Tucker believed Virginians should emancipate their slaves and colonize them outside the state. The legislature, however, moved in the opposite direction: it tightened controls over the black population and severely restricted opportunities for voluntary manumission. Any slave emancipated after 1806 was required to leave Virginia.

Did not closing the door to freedom violate the ideals of the Revolution? "Tell us not of principles," a Richmond newspaper declared. "Those principles have been annihilated by the existence of slavery among us."[33]

In March 1776, on the eve of independence, Boston lawyer Peter Thatcher identified the central dilemma confronting the new nation: would the "rising empire of America," he asked, "be an empire of slaves or of freemen?"[34] By the time the revolutionary era drew to a close, history had provided the answer: it would be both.

In 1792, Congress formalized the choice of the female personification of Liberty as a symbol of American nationhood by directing that coins bear "an impression emblematic of liberty, with an inscription of the word Liberty." (Chicago Historical Society)

3

An Empire of
Liberty

In 1824, the marquis de Lafayette visited the United States. Nearly fifty years earlier, as a youth of twenty, the French nobleman had fought at Washington's side in the War for Independence. Now, his thirteen-month tour became a triumphant Jubilee of Liberty. Americans had good reason to celebrate Lafayette's visit and their own freedom. Since the Revolution, the nation's population and territorial expanse had more than doubled and its political institutions had thrived, vindicating the promise of government by popular consent. Yet if Lafayette's tour underscored what Walt Whitman would later call his countrymen's "deathless attachment to freedom," it also drew attention to the central contradiction of liberty in America half a century after the winning of independence. For in all the speeches addressed to Lafayette at receptions, banquets, and parades, one subject was studiously avoided—the existence of slavery. In several southern cities, public notices warned all "persons of color" to stay away from the ceremonies honoring the distinguished guest. When, at Gallipolis, Ohio, Lafayette took it upon himself to point out "the disadvantages of slavery," his remarks evoked little interest.[1]

Americans in the era between the Revolution and the Civil War were prone to describe freedom as the defining quality of their new nation, the unique genius of its institutions. When the nation's first coins were issued, republican fears of a monarchial presidency led Congress to direct that they bear not the image of the head of state but "an impression emblematic of liberty, with an inscription of the word Liberty." Images of the goddess of liberty, a familiar figure in eighteenth-century British iconography, became even more ubiquitous in the United States, appearing in paintings and sculpture, and on folk art from weathervanes to quilts and tavern signs. "Liberty," declared the popular orator Edward Everett, "is the lesson, which we are appointed to teach" the world. In 1835, in *Democracy in America*, the French aristocrat and political philosopher Alexis de Tocqueville wrote of the "holy cult of freedom" he had encountered on a tour of the United States. "Do not ask me," he later observed, "to analyze this sublime sentiment; it must be felt. It enters of itself, into the great hearts of those God has prepared to receive it; it fills them; it enraptures them."

Immigrants shared in this equation of America's destiny with freedom. "I feel free and independent among a free people . . . ," one emigrant from Norway wrote home, "and I am very proud of belonging to a mighty nation, whose institutions must in time come to dominate the entire civilized world." This language of self-congratulation knew no geographical borders; it could be found in newspaper editorials, public addresses, and sermons North and South, and became standard fare in political papers. Never, declared Andrew Jackson in his farewell address in 1837, had any population "enjoyed so much freedom and happiness as the people of these United States."[2]

Three historical processes unleashed by the Revolution—territorial expansion, political democratization, and the rapid spread of market relations—powerfully affected the idea of American freedom in the antebellum decades. They reinforced its identification with the westward movement, political participation, and the promise of economic opportunity. But freedom was also profoundly shaped by the continuing growth of slavery. Slavery affected the lives of all Americans, white as well as black. It helped to determine where they lived and how they worked, and under what conditions they could exercise their freedom of speech, press, and assembly. Eventually, the nation's politics would come to center on the future of the West, and whether slavery or freedom would take root there. Fostering the illusion of equality among whites, slavery obscured the many forms of coercion experienced by free men and women. Yet slavery also provided a standard against which to judge free society. In such metaphors as "wage slavery" and "the slavery of sex," it came to be employed as a language of protest by social movements of those who feared they were being denied the promise of American freedom.[3]

An 1804 embroidery by sixteen-year-old Mary Gray, based on *Liberty as Goddess of Youth Feeding the American Eagle*, a widely distributed engraving by Edward Savage, reflects the popularity of images linking liberty and nationhood. Atop the American flag sits the cap of liberty. At the goddess's feet lie symbols of Old World monarchy and aristocracy—the key to the Bastille, the British crown, and the Order of the Garter. (Worcester Art Museum)

Democracy in America

The most dramatic development in the life of the young republic was the rise of the West. The term "manifest destiny," suggesting that the United States had a divinely appointed mission to overspread the entire North American continent, was first employed by a New York journalist, John L. O'Sullivan, in 1845. But the core idea was familiar much earlier. The United States had been selected by God for the greatest experiment in human history, the achievement of liberty, and its expansion was part and parcel of this providential destiny. Unlike other nations, America, with its federal structure, separation of powers, increasingly democratic political system, and practice of admitting new territories into the Union as equal states, could enjoy both empire and self-government. Indeed, a sense of spatial openness, of the constant opportunity to pick up and move when the pursuit of happiness seemed to demand it, became in these years a central component of American freedom. In national myth and ideology the West would long remain, as Wallace Stegner would later put it, "the last home of the freeborn American."[4]

The rise of the West was not simply a mythic adventure but an inescapable fact of American life. Between 1791 and 1850, no fewer than eighteen new states entered the Union. Liberty in the United States, wrote the French historian Michel Chevalier, who visited the country in the 1830s, was a "practical idea" as much as a "mystical one"—it meant "a liberty of action and motion which the American uses to expand over the vast territory that Providence has given him and to subdue it to his uses." National boundaries made little difference to expansion; in Florida, Louisiana, Texas, and other areas, American settlers rushed in to claim land under the jurisdiction of Spain, France, Mexico, and Indian tribes, confident that American sovereignty would soon follow in their wake. The land hunger of those who saw the "empty" continent as a guarantee of future economic opportunity supported the "practical" side of manifest destiny. Indeed, by allowing for the continuing reinvigoration of a social order based on independent small producers, the settlement and economic exploitation of the West promised to prevent the United States from following down the path of Europe and becoming a stratified society with a large class of dependent poor. The West, therefore, was essential to maintaining the social conditions of freedom. When Jefferson purchased the vast Louisiana Territory from France in 1803, doubling the size of what he called "the Empire of Liberty," he believed that he had pushed far into the future the dreaded day when an overpopulated, class-divided America would cease to be home to freedom.[5]

John Gast's painting *American Progress* (1872) reflects the ebullient spirit of Manifest Destiny. A female figure descended from earlier representations of Liberty wears the Star of Empire and leads the march of pioneers, enlightenment, and technological progress westward, while Indians and the buffalo retreat before her. (Library of Congress)

The idea that theirs was an empire of liberty enabled Americans to ignore some unpleasant truths about westward expansion. For one thing, the continent was not, in fact, empty. For centuries, the West had been a meeting ground of peoples, whose relationships were shaped by conquest as much as free choice. It was also, therefore, the site of clashing definitions of liberty. "The life my people want is a life of freedom," the great leader of the Lakota Sioux, Sitting Bull, would later proclaim. The Native American idea of freedom, however, which centered on preserving their cultural and political autonomy and retaining control of ancestral lands, was incompatible with that of western settlers, for whom freedom entailed the right to expand across the continent and establish farms, ranches, and mines on land that Indians considered their own. Indian removal—accomplished by fraud, intimidation, and violence—was indispensable to the triumph of manifest destiny and the American mission of spreading freedom.[6]

Territorial expansion was intimately connected with a second central element of American freedom: political democracy. The challenge to property qualifications for voting, begun during the American Revolution, reached its culmination in the early nineteenth century as western states entered the Union with laws allowing all adult white males to vote. The older states quickly followed suit. In the state constitutional conventions of the 1820s and 1830s, delegates considered anew the relationship between democracy and property. At the Virginia Constitutional Convention of 1829, James Madison reiterated his warning that economic change would eventually produce a propertyless majority likely to imperil "the rights of property" and "the claims of justice." Four decades earlier, at the Constitutional Convention, Madison had tentatively endorsed property qualifications for voting to curb popular excesses, Now, reflecting the democratic spirit of the age, he concluded that such restrictions violated "the vital principle of free government," rule by consent.[7]

Although the speed of the process varied from state to state, by 1860 every one had eliminated property qualifications for voting. The result was to sever the traditional link between propertied independence and membership in the political community. The autonomy necessary in the citizen now rested not on ownership of property, but ownership of one's self. Advocates of democratic change pointed out that property was "not even named" among the inalienable rights enumerated in the Declaration of Independence and challenged the idea that wealth was a guarantee of either wisdom or virtue. There were "thousands of men without property," wrote Francis Lieber, the founding father of American political science, "who have quite as great a stake in the public welfare as those who may possess a house or enjoy a certain amount of revenue."[8]

By the 1830s, a flourishing democratic system had been consolidated. American democracy was boisterous, highly partisan, and sometimes violent. It engaged the energies of massive numbers of citizens (by the 1840s, voter turnout exceeded 80 percent of those eligible). The strength of democratic politics lay in self-governing local communities, not Washington. Indeed, to emphasize the wide diffusion of political power, Tocqueville began his examination of American political culture with a chapter on the necessity of "examining the condition of the states" before turning to "the Union at large."[9] In a country that lacked more traditional bases of nationality—a powerful and menacing neighbor, historic ethnic, religious, and cultural unity—America's democratic political institutions came to define the nation as a whole.

As Tocqueville recognized, democracy meant far more than the right to vote. A social innovation of profound significance, it reinforced a sense of equality among those who belonged to the political nation and deepened the divide separating them from those who did not. "Civil liberty," wrote Lieber, was "a state of union with equals." Participation in elections and the pageantry surrounding them—parades, bonfires, mass meetings, party conventions—helped to define "the people" of the United States who enjoyed an entitlement to equality. Increasingly, the right to vote became the emblem of American citizenship—if not in law (since suffrage was still, strictly speaking, a privilege rather than a right, subject to regulation by the individual states), then in common usage and understanding. Noah Webster's *Dictionary of the English Language* noted that the term "citizen" had, in America although not in Europe, become synonymous with the right to vote. Political democracy was thus an essential attribute of American freedom. The vote, said one advocate of democratic reform, was "the first mark of liberty, the only true badge of the freeman."[10]

In a democratic society, political freedom was simultaneously an individual right and a collective attribute of self-governing communities, a restraint on unaccountable authority and a form of citizen empowerment. It would be quite wrong to view antebellum Americans as hostile to all action by the state. "Freedom in this country," declared a Tennessee court in 1827, was not "confined in its operations to privacy," but was a public quality that flourished at "the court house and the election ground." No society that harbored a slave population numbering in the millions could be unfamiliar with vigorous action by government. Territorial expansion and economic growth depended on the energetic exercise of public authority—from the Louisiana Purchase and the dispossession of Indians and Mexicans to direct interventions in the economy like New York State's construction of the Erie Canal and the granting of incorporation privileges to stimulate investment and entrepreneurship.[11]

"A weak government," wrote Lieber, was "a negation of liberty," reflecting a view not without adherents in antebellum America. At the national level, Whigs like John Quincy Adams and Henry Clay insisted that government could enhance the realm of freedom. Freedom, wrote Adams, meant more than the absence of restraint: "individual liberty is individual power," the capacity to act to achieve one's ends. Freedom required a prosperous America, which government could help to achieve by creating the conditions for balanced and regulated economic development, thereby promoting a prosperity in which all classes would share. Whigs, moreover, rejected the liberal premise that private life must be insulated from public action. To function as free—that is, as self-directed and self-disciplined—moral agents, individuals required certain character traits that government could help instill. Via public education, temperance legislation, and the like, democratic governments could inculcate the "principles of morality." And, indeed, popularly elected local authorities in Jacksonian America enacted a plethora of laws, ordinances, and regulations that governed how goods were bought and sold, controlled the spread of infectious diseases, and shaped public morals in such areas as prostitution and the consumption of alcohol. Pennsylvania was as renowned in the nineteenth century for its stringent laws against blasphemy, profanity, and desecrating the sabbath as it had been in the colonial era for its commitment to religious liberty.[12]

Nonetheless, even as democratic politics expanded, the power of government waned. Ralph Waldo Emerson called antebellum Americans "fanatics in freedom," whose obsession expressed itself in hatred of "tolls, taxes, turnpikes, banks, hierarchies, governors, yea, almost laws." The old conviction that history involved an endless struggle between liberty and political power persisted into the first half of the nineteenth century, even though in many respects a national state barely existed. By the Age of Jackson, the Democratic Party regularly condemned the faraway federal government as the greatest "danger to liberty" in America. It was no coincidence that the slave South, for whom state rights served as the "peculiar institution's" first line of defense, was a Democratic stronghold. But Democrats' positioning of freedom in opposition to government represented far more than a shield for slavery. Building upon laissez-faire economics and its distinction between government and society, Democrats identified government-granted privilege as the root cause of social injustice. If the state removed itself from the economy, eliminating tariffs, special charters for banks and corporations, and other forms of privilege, ordinary Americans could test their abilities in the fair competition of the self-regulating market, rather than being trapped in a system of lifetime privilege as in Europe.

Weak government, in the Democratic view, was essential to both private and public freedom—"the freedom of the individual in the social union, [and] the freedom of the State in the Federative Union." Individual morality, moreover, was a private matter, not a public concern. Democrats opposed temperance legislation and other attempts to impose a moral vision on society as a whole, a stance especially welcomed by the Irish Catholic immigrants who flocked to the party beginning in the 1830s. Opposition to temperance legislation was couched in terms of personal freedom. A "Liberty Loving Citizen" of Worcester, Massachusetts, wondered what gave one group of citizens the right to dictate to others how to conduct their personal lives. "The limitation of power, in every branch of our government," wrote a Democratic newspaper in 1842, "is the only safeguard of liberty."[13]

The tension between these "positive" and "negative" definitions of government and its relationship to freedom has been a persistent feature of the nation's politics, surviving to the present day. But by the mid-nineteenth-century, the Whigs' "American System" of government-coordinated economic development was a thing of the past and the Democratic belief in limited government was definitely in the ascendancy. "In this country," declared the New York *Journal of Commerce* in 1848, contrasting American definitions of freedom with those of French socialists, "liberty is understood to be the *absence* of government from private affairs." The test of public policies was no longer whether they enhanced the common good, but the extent to which they allowed scope for "free agency," that is, for individuals to pursue their interests and cultivate their unique talents without outside interference.[14]

Like the democratization of politics, which defined political freedom as a function of self-ownership rather than control of property, changes in economic and religious life strongly encouraged the spread of a liberal understanding of freedom as the absence of external constraints upon autonomous, self-directed individuals. In the first half of the nineteenth century, an economic transformation known to historians as the "market revolution" swept over the United States. Technological innovations in transportation and communication—the steamboat, canal, railroad, telegraph—linked farmers to national and international markets and, at least in the North, made them major consumers of manufactured goods. Banks and corporate endeavors of all kinds became central to economic enterprise. In industries such as textiles and shoe production, the first factories made their appearance; in others, merchants gathered formerly independent artisans into workshops, subjecting them to unprecedented forms of labor discipline. These changes produced what a Connecticut minister, Horace Bushnell, in 1851 called a "complete revolution of domestic life and manners."[15]

The decline of the household as the center of economic production, combined with westward movement and urban development, created a large mobile population no longer tied to local communities and seeking, as enterprising men, to seize the opportunities offered by economic change. Increasingly, the right to compete for advancement in the marketplace became a touchstone of American freedom. "The whole question of freedom or slavery for man," argued Henry C. Carey, among the era's most prominent economists, was bound up with market relations. When individuals competed to purchase a commodity, "its owner becomes a free man." As the market revolution progressed, official iconography linked the goddess of liberty ever more closely to emblems of material progress. New Jersey, whose official seal, adopted in 1776, had paired the goddess of liberty with Ceres, the Roman goddess of agriculture, holding a cornucopia, in 1821 made the link explicit by adding the motto: "Liberty and Prosperity." In the state seal of Arkansas, admitted to the Union in 1836, liberty was accompanied by an image of a steamboat and two overflowing horns of plenty.[16]

The revivals that swept the country during the Second Great Awakening of the 1820s and 1830s added a religious underpinning to the celebration of per-

The official seals of New Jersey (1776, with the motto, "Liberty and Prosperity" added in 1821) and Arkansas (1836) reflect the widespread identification of freedom with technological progress and material prosperity. (J. Franklin Reigart, *The United States Album* [Lancaster, 1844])

sonal self-improvement and self-determination. Rejecting the idea that man is a depraved creature with a preordained fate, revivalists propagated the explosive doctrines of a benevolent God and human free will. Although some Calvinists objected, free will in these years became "virtually an American dogma." Since each human being was a moral free agent, sinners could choose spiritual freedom, defined, in the words of the evangelical minister Jonathan Blanchard, as "Christ ruling in and over rational creatures who are obeying him freely and from choice." The revivals' opening of religion to mass participation and their message that ordinary Americans, not simply a small body of the "elect," could shape their spiritual destinies resonated with the democratization of politics and the spread of market values. Evangelical preachers were hardly conscious cheerleaders for a market society; indeed, the sins they regularly railed against included greed, selfishness, and indifference to the welfare of others. Yet in exalting the "individualization of conscience" and stressing the importance of industry, sobriety, and self-discipline as the epitome of freely chosen moral behavior, they promoted the very qualities necessary for success in a market culture.[17]

The idea of Christian freedom as essentially an inner condition unrelated to worldly status, of course, had a long history. In antebellum America, it took on a secular as well as a religious form. Looking back from 1880, Ralph Waldo Emerson remembered the antebellum era as a time when "social existence" gave way to "the enlargement and independency of the individual . . . driven to find all his resources, hopes, rewards, society, and deity within himself." For Emerson, the spirit of self-reliance and self-improvement was an antidote to the pressure for conformity that Tocqueville had recognized as one of the most salient characteristics of a democracy. The opportunity for personal growth offered a new definition of Jefferson's pursuit of happiness, one well suited to a world in which democracy, territorial expansion, and the market revolution were shattering traditional spatial and social boundaries and making moving from place to place and status to status ubiquitous features of American life. Freedom suggested an unending process of self-realization by which individuals could remake themselves and their own lives.[18]

Ironies abounded in the era's "individualism" (a term that first entered the vocabulary in the 1820s and 1830s). For if democracy and the market revolution promoted political and commercial intercourse, the idea of the "sovereign individual" proclaimed that Americans should be beholden to no one but themselves. And if personal self-development—for men at least—required pursuing economic gain in the turbulent world of the marketplace, the home, now emptied of productive functions, was exalted as the site where the self could reach its fullest expression via love, friendship, and mutual obligation—distinctly non-market values. The boundary of the sovereign self—which came to be called "privacy"—was increasingly understood as a realm with which neither other individuals nor government had a right to interfere. Freedom, in this definition, lay within.[19]

Labor, Free and Slave

In a world in which personal freedom increasingly meant the opportunity to compete for economic gain and individual self-improvement, slavery remained a master metaphor for describing impediments to advancement. To temperance advocates, drink, which deprived an individual of the capacity for moral choice and self-realization, was a form of enslavement; indeed, some described the "chains of intoxication" as "heavier than those which the sons of Africa have ever worn." Those favoring liberalization of bankruptcy laws frequently invoked the phrase "debt slavery" to evoke how temporary economic failure impeded future advancement in the marketplace. For those steeped in the tradition that identified freedom with the Reformation, Catholicism was a form of slavery at odds with American conceptions of liberty, since Catholics were allegedly obligated to follow church authority rather than displaying the manly independence of Protestants. And the discontent of those Americans who believed the material conditions of freedom were slipping from their grasp even as the rhetoric of freedom flourished crystallized in the idea of "wage slavery."[20]

It was a paradox of antebellum American life that as ownership of property disappeared as a prerequisite of political freedom, and the idea of autonomy took on an inner rather than a social meaning, independence survived as a popular measure of economic freedom. The market revolution had a contradictory impact on the inherited definition of economic autonomy as a condition of freedom. On small farms, North and South, the ideal of the independent small producer retained its vitality, even though farmers found themselves more and more enmeshed in market relations. Of course, no household could be truly independent in the age of the market revolution. Property-owning farmers, however, retained considerable choice as to the extent of market participation, and a degree of shelter from the vicissitudes of commerce. So long as yeoman families controlled productive property and had the realistic expectation of passing it on to their children, an expectation greatly enhanced by the opening for settlement of vast areas of land in the West, it remained plausible to think of America as a "paradise" for small producers.[21]

Far different were the consequences of capitalism's development in the nation's commercial and manufacturing cities. Market capitalism opened numerous new jobs to skilled workers, and in many crafts, owning a shop remained well within reach. Yet the increased scale of manufacturing undermined traditional skills and diminished opportunities for journeymen to rise to the status of independent master. Increasingly, wage labor, rather than ownership of productive property, became the economic basis of family survival. After 1830, the rapid increase of immigration swelled the bottom ranks of the labor force. At midcentury, over two-thirds of the workforce in Boston and New York City consisted of wage workers, and for the nation as a whole, the number of wage earners for the first time exceeded the number of slaves. Ten years later, according to one estimate, wage laborers outnumbered self-employed members of the labor force. The legal order increasingly served to support the system of wage labor. Judges defined any decision to labor for another as a voluntary contractual agreement that allowed employers full authority over the workplace. At the same time, they invoked the definition of laborers as autonomous individuals to impede them, through an anti-union interpretation of conspiracy laws, from organizing collectively to seek higher pay.[22]

The rise of wage labor and its institutionalization in the law posed a profound challenge for the ethos that defined economic dependence as incompatible with freedom. The market revolution, the historian Thomas Haskell has argued, encouraged a humanitarian sensibility by promoting a sense of individual control over one's own future and responsibility for the fate of others. But many Americans experienced the expansion of capitalism not as an enhancement of the power to shape their world, but as a loss of control over their own lives. Invigorated by the popular conviction, which dated back at least as far as John Locke, that labor was the source of all wealth and the worker entitled to the fruits of his toil, the ideal of the autonomous small producer reemerged in Jacksonian America as a full-fledged critique of early capitalism and its transformation of free labor into a commodity.[23]

There was, of course, nothing new, or uniquely American, in the rhetorical mobilization of chattel slavery to criticize the freedom of labor relations under capitalism. In Britain, description of wage laborers as subject to coercion akin to slavery dated back to the eighteenth century, and even as the Jacksonian labor movement adopted this rhetoric in the 1830s and 1840s, the Chartist press was employing much the same language to describe the conditions of the English working class. But in the United States, where slavery was an immediate reality, not a distant symbol, and the small producer still a powerful element in the social order, the idea that the wage earner, because of economic dependence, was less than free took on a special power. The idea of wage slavery served to deconstruct, as it were, the sharp contrast between slavery and freedom, to expose the forms of coercion and hidden inequalities inherent in ostensibly free economic institutions, to challenge the marketplace idea of contract as an adequate definition of freedom. Freedom, Noah Webster's *American Dictionary* declared in 1828, was "a state of exemption from the power or control of another." The Jacksonian labor movement asked how many wage earners truly enjoyed such "exemption." Wage labor, insisted Philadelphia labor spokesman Langdon Byllesby, was the "very essence of slavery."[24]

The metaphor of wage slavery (or, in New England, its first cousin, "factory slavery") drew on immediate grievances such as low wages, irregular employment, the elaborate and arbitrary work rules of the early factories, and the use of conspiracy indictments to impede union organization. "The name of freedom is but a shadow," declared a group of Philadelphia shoemakers in 1806 after their leaders were found guilty of conspiracy for seeking to combine to raise wages; thirty years later, a similar conviction of twenty journeymen tailors in New York inspired a public procession marking the "burial of liberty." The elaborate system of rules and regulations in the era's factories and workshops also evoked complaints of a loss of freedom. One operative in the Amoskeag mills in Manchester, New Hampshire, likened the factory bell to a "slave driver's whip."[25]

But at its core, the idea of wage slavery rested on a critique of economic dependence as incompatible with freedom. In 1840, in his essay "The Laboring Classes," the era's most influential statement of the argument, the New England social philosopher Orestes A. Brownson, described wages as "a cunning device of the devil for the benefit of tender consciences who would retain all the advantages of the slave system without the expense, trouble, and odium of being slaveholders." His essay, Brownson later recalled, elicited "one universal scream of horror" from respectable opinion. But the idea that permanent wage labor bore some resemblance to slavery was not confined to labor radicals and allied intellectuals. In Herman Melville's strange tale "The Tartarus of Maids," workers in a New England paper mill stand by their machines "mutely and cringingly as the slave." Within the Jacksonian Democratic Party, from the colorful Mike Walsh (who told New York workingmen, "you are slaves, and none are better aware of the fact than the heathenish dogs who call you freemen") to less demagogic political figures, it remained axiomatic that the ideal citizen was a farmer or independent mechanic, and that the factory system and merchant-dominated craft workshop were introducing a system of despotism incompatible with American freedom.[26]

"The Shoemakers' Strike in Lynn, Mass.—Procession, in the Midst of a Snow-Storm, of Eight Hundred Women Operatives," from *Frank Leslie's Illustrated Newspaper,* 17 March 1860. Comparisons between the condition of slaves and that of Northern "wage slaves," were a standard part of the nineteenth-century labor movement's rhetoric. (Library of Congress)

Today, when the level of wages, not the fact of working for wages, excites labor protest, the phrase "wage slavery" and its corollary that wage laborers lack true freedom seem hopelessly arcane. In the nineteenth century, both defined a vision of liberty that encompassed economic autonomy. "We are free," wrote Peter Rödel, an immigrant German shoemaker, "but not free enough. . . . We want the liberty of living." Rooted in the traditions of the small producer and popular understandings of the promise of the American Revolution, the identification of freedom with economic autonomy suggested a different conception of society from one determined by market values. It directly challenged the idea of Emerson and other reformers that "self-trust, self-reliance, self-control, self-culture" could be counted on to bring about personal freedom and social change. Workers' problems, Brownson insisted, were institutional, not individual; they had their root in "the constitution of society," and would not be addressed by those unwilling to "disturb existing social arrangements." This sensibility would inspire nineteenth-century protest movements from the Jacksonian era to the Populists of the 1890s.[27]

It proved far easier to persuade wage earners that they enjoyed only the "skeleton of liberty," in the words of the Philadelphia labor leader Stephen Simpson, than to devise ways of reversing the trend toward economic dependency. One approach was offered by the era's communitarians, followers of Robert Owen, Albert Fourier, and other utopian socialists, who insisted that genuine freedom required the abolition of private property, thereby eliminating the distinction between employer and employee. To outsiders, the dozens of communal experiments established in antebellum America, many of which practiced great austerity while adhering to exacting rules laid down by a charismatic religious or secular leader, seemed a form of "voluntary slavery." To their devotees, joining a community like New Harmony, Brook Farm, or Oneida offered the way to personal freedom through rejection of the market economy, the "grave of liberty."[28]

Since most Americans viewed property as the basis of liberty, not a threat to it, the appeal of communitarianism was limited. Labor's aim was to make private property more accessible rather than abolishing it. One proposal came from Thomas Skidmore, a machinist, teacher, and early leader of New York City's Workingmen's Party. Skidmore regarded the entitlement to property as so fundamental that he criticized Jefferson for eliminating it from the Declaration's triad of inalienable rights. But to form the basis for genuine freedom, he insisted, property must be equally distributed. Skidmore proposed that the government provide each person reaching adulthood (and he did not exclude women or blacks) with a "comfortable subsistence."

In the aftermath of the economic depression of 1837–42, the most severe in American history to that date, a different mode of securing economic autonomy for workingmen rose in popularity: the movement for free land. Of course, American ideas about freedom had long been tied up with the promise of the West. For years, the Democratic Party had advocated a policy of easy access to government land, "to afford every American citizen of enterprise," as Andrew Jackson put it, "the opportunity of securing an independent freehold." But in the 1840s, it was George Henry Evans, a journalist and veteran of the Jacksonian labor movement, and the iconoclastic Horace Greeley, a sometime Whig, communitarian socialist, and antislavery reformer, who popularized the idea of free homesteads in the West. "Freedom of the soil," Evans insisted, offered "emancipation" to the wage slave, the only alternative to permanent dependence.[29]

Northern laborers and reformers were not alone in criticizing marketplace notions of freedom. The South shared as fully in the process of westward expansion as the free states, but here the process further entrenched plantation slavery as the central institution of southern life, rather than promoting economic modernization. The rapid expansion of slavery and the consolidation of a distinctive southern ruling class led inexorably to the rise of a proslavery ideology that employed the contrast between freedom and slavery as a weapon against the self-proclaimed "free society" of the North. The free laborer, insisted defenders of slavery like John C. Calhoun and George Fitzhugh, was little more than "the slave of the *community*," a situation far more oppressive than to be owned by a paternalistic master and shielded from the exploitation of the competitive marketplace. Indeed, proslavery writers claimed, the very idea of free labor was a brutal fiction, which allowed the propertied classes to escape a sense of responsibility for the well-being of social inferiors. Slavery for blacks was the surest guarantee of "perfect equality" among whites, liberating them from the "low, menial" jobs like factory labor and domestic service performed by wage laborers in the North, and allowing for a considerable degree of economic and social autonomy on the part of non-slaveholders. Because of slavery, claimed one congressman, white southerners were as "independent as the bird which cleaves the air."[30]

As in the North, the egalitarian ethos sank deep roots in the white South. Southern state constitutions, like those of the North, enshrined the idea of equal rights for free men, and the South participated fully in the movement toward political democracy. Indeed, South Carolina in 1810 became the first of the original thirteen states to adopt white manhood suffrage (although it retained property requirements for many offices). White southerners in antebellum

America claimed to be the genuine heirs of the Revolution, motivated by "the same spirit of freedom and independence" as the founding generation. Contrasts between liberty and slavery suffused their political language, as did complaints that northerners proposed to reduce them to slaves. One group of white Mississippians charged that if their right to spread slavery westward were restricted, southerners would become "the enslaved children of the North." Southern spokesmen returned to the older definition of freedom as a privilege, a "reward to be earned, not a blessing to be gratuitously lavished on all alike." The white man was "made for liberty," while blacks, said Governor George McDuffie of South Carolina, were "utterly unqualified . . . for rational freedom."[31]

As the sectional controversy intensified after 1830, a number of southern ideologues came to defend slavery less as the basis of equality for whites than as the foundation of an organic, hierarchical society. Freedom meant more than being uncoerced or the ability to reinvent one's self in a competitive society: it rested on sovereignty over subordinates, not simply within the family, where northerners agreed relations of dependency were indispensable, but in society at large, where all sorts of weak and inferior groups "require masters of some kind." Disavowing Jefferson's rhetoric of universal natural rights, James Henry Hammond, a leading planter of South Carolina, called the idea of human equality "ridiculously absurd." Many southern clergymen, in the course of offering a religious defense of slavery, also argued that inequality and hence the submission of inferior to superior was a "fundamental law" of human existence. A hierarchy of "ranks and orders in human society," insisted John B. Alger, a Presbyterian minister in South Carolina, was part of the "divine arrangement" of the world. George Fitzhugh took the argument to its most radical conclusion, repudiating not only Jeffersonian ideals but the notion of America's special mission in the world. To Fitzhugh, southern secession was a far more significant act than the "commonplace affair" of 1776, since it rebelled not merely against a particular government but against Locke, Smith, Jefferson, and Paine, authors of the erroneous modern idea of freedom based on "human equality" and "natural liberty." Far from being the natural condition of mankind, Fitzhugh wrote, "universal liberty" was an aberration, an experiment carried on "for a little while" in "a corner of Europe" and the northern United States, with disastrous results. Taking the world and its history as a whole, slavery, "without regard to race and color," was "the general . . . normal, natural" basis of "civilized society."[32]

"Nobody," Edmund Burke once remarked, "will be argued into slavery." And it seems safe to assume that few non-slaveholding white southerners believed they required "masters," or that enslavement would offer them greater freedom than they already enjoyed. Racial and class assumptions mingled in proslavery definitions of freedom. Fitzhugh himself sometimes argued that all labor would be better off as slaves, and on other occasions spoke of slavery only for blacks, perpetual "children" for whom liberty would be "a curse." Yet, whatever the philosophical basis, the majority of white southerners came to believe, in the words of the *Richmond Enquirer*, that "freedom is not possible without slavery."[33]

Whether emanating from protesting northern laborers or southern defenders of slavery, the analogy between free worker and slave posed a fundamental challenge to the emerging market definition of economic freedom. In a society of rapidly expanding capitalism, this critique of northern wage labor inevitably called forth a defense of "free labor" as the foundation of individual liberty and social progress, a defense celebrating the benefits of the marketplace and the laborer's juridical freedom. Many currents flowed together in forming the free labor ideology, which by the eve of the Civil War would help to define popular understandings of the difference between free and slave societies. One source lay in the effort of antebellum economists to reconcile belief in economic progress with the rise of a large number of wage earners. To do so, they turned to Adam Smith and other exponents of eighteenth-century liberalism, who had insisted that slavery was a far more costly and inefficient means of obtaining labor than the payment of wages, since it prevented the worker's self-interest from being harnessed to the public good. The ever-expanding wants stimulated by participation in the marketplace offered the most effective incentive to productive labor.[34]

In the 1850s, the newly created Republican Party would hammer home Smith's antislavery message: freedom meant prosperity, and slavery retarded economic growth. A generation earlier, however, it was not Smith's hostility to slavery that appealed to defenders of northern labor relations as much as his contention that the transformation of labor into a commodity did not contradict the autonomy of free labor. But Smith's American disciples added a new wrinkle to the argument, one in keeping with the vitality of small producer ideals in America. Smith had seen intractable class divisions as an inevitable consequence of economic development. American economists sought to reconcile wage labor with the idea of the New World as a classless utopia by insisting that in the United States industrious and frugal laborers could save money, purchase their own homes, and eventually acquire a farm or shop, thereby escaping the status of wage labor and assimilating into the republic of property holders. Craft employers and manufacturers embraced this defense of entrepreneurship in the name of equal opportunity, as did leaders of the Whig Party. The Democrats' rhetoric of class conflict, Whigs insisted, was a European import irrelevant to a society of "self-made men" where the vast majority of the population either owned productive property or had a reasonable expectation of acquiring it. In America, wage labor was a temporary status, and "laborers for hire do not exist as a class." Indeed, wrote the Whig economist Calvin Colton, in the United States, "high wages" were "identical with freedom."[35]

As an intersectional party, the Whigs were understandably reluctant to contrast free labor with slavery. That task, so essential to the development of a mature ideology of free labor, emerged from a different quarter in Jacksonian America—the antislavery crusade. By and large, the defense of free labor was a minor strand in abolitionist thought, which always regarded morality, not economics, as paramount. Nonetheless, abolitionists understandably resented equations of northern labor with southern bondage. Northern workers, said the abolitionist orator Wendell Phillips, would find the idea of wage slavery "utterly incomprehensible." As far as laborers were concerned, Phillips wrote, the "idea of Massachusetts liberty" meant an unfettered wage relationship and the right to quit a job at will. After the Civil War, Phillips would come to a different conclusion about northern labor relations, even accepting the Labor Reform Party's nomination for governor of Massachusetts. But in the antebellum era, by insisting upon the uniqueness of the evil of slavery, he and other abolitionists reinforced the sharp dichotomy between slavery's illegitimate coercions and the condition of labor in the North. They also popularized the related concept that freedom was a matter of property in one's self and the right to dispose of the fruits of one's labor as one saw fit, not the ownership of productive property. "Does he not own himself?" one abolitionist asked, in explaining why the northern laborer could not be considered a slave.[36]

To black abolitionists, the wage slavery analogy seemed particularly spurious. When Frederick Douglass, soon after escaping from slavery, took his first paying job in New Bedford, Massachusetts, his wage was an emblem of freedom: "I was now my own master." To Douglass, the wage represented not a mark of oppression but a symbol of a fair exchange, reflecting the fact that for the first time in his life he enjoyed the fruits of his labor. By sharpening the ideological contrast between free and slave labor, the abolitionist movement helped to legitimize the wage relationship even as it was coming under bitter attack. Wage slavery, wrote William Lloyd Garrison, was an "abuse of language." "We cannot see that it is wrong to give or receive wages."[37]

Despite the popularity of the rhetoric of wage slavery, the emerging ideology of free labor had considerable appeal among northern workers. Indeed, another root of the free labor ideology lay in the divided mind of labor itself, which celebrated the independence and equal rights of workingmen while also insisting that they were reduced to wage slavery when forced to market their labor. The very struggles to incorporate propertyless men into political democracy had reinforced the definition of self-ownership as the foundation of freedom. Political enfranchisement subtly contradicted the rhetorical image of the worker as a wage slave.[38]

The decades after the Revolution witnessed what Gordon Wood has called a "transvaluation of labor." In a tradition passed down from the ancient world to the eighteenth century, freedom *from* labor had been deemed far superior to freedom *of* labor, since the progress of civilization rested on the leisure of the educated, propertied classes. Although the roots of an alternative point of view can be traced back to the Protestant Reformation, it was not until the nineteenth century that idleness, not manual labor, came to be viewed as disreputable in the United States (except in the South) and "non-producer" emerged as a popular term of abuse. The glorification of labor of all kinds as dignified and not degraded—a standard element of political rhetoric by the 1830s—had its appeal to working people. Earning an honest living could appear as part of the definition of independence and freedom, setting northern laborers off from both southern slaves and aristocratic non-producers.[39]

Indeed, at a time of rapid economic fluctuations, a good wage might offer more genuine independence than the uncertain prospects of operating one's own business (in some industries, eight out of ten new enterprises failed during the 1850s). The contrast between the slave bound to an owner and the free worker able to leave his job was more than mere rhetoric: it defined a central reality of social life. "No one who enters the factory," said a worker in Waltham, Massachusetts, "thinks of remaining there his whole life-time." Turnover rates were extremely high, and for many laborers physical mobility, the "freedom to move," served as a means of obtaining leverage in the labor market, an essential strategy for survival and possible advancement in a market society. "In America," a German immigrant miner wrote home from California, "there aren't any masters, here everyone is a free agent, if you don't like one place you can go to another for we're all equal here."[40]

Nowhere was the broad appeal of the free labor ideology more apparent, or its internal tensions more evident, than in the speeches and writings of Abraham Lincoln. Even though he lived in a society firmly in the grasp of the market revolution (and served as attorney for the Illinois Central Railroad, one of the nation's largest corporations), Lincoln's America was the world of the small producer. His life and that of thousands of his contemporaries in Illinois, a state where in 1860, property-owning farmers, artisans, and small shopkeepers far outnumbered wage earners, embodied the opportunities northern society offered to laboring men. Lincoln was fascinated and disturbed by the writings of proslavery ideologues like George Fitzhugh. The southern critique of wage slavery catalyzed in Lincoln a defense of free society. Most northerners, he insisted, were "neither *hirers* nor *hired*," but worked "for themselves, on their farms, in their houses, and in their shops, taking the whole product to themselves, and asking no favors of capital on the one hand, nor hirelings or slaves on the other." Wage earners were generally young "beginners," hired "by their own consent"; contrary to southern charges, they were not "fatally fixed in that condition for life." Yet even Lincoln's eloquent exposition could not escape free labor's inherent ambiguities. Was wage labor a normal, acceptable part of the northern social order or a temporary status, associated with the lack of genuine freedom?[41]

Despite these ambiguities, by the eve of the Civil War, "free labor" had become a central component of northern definitions of freedom. Its meaning depended on juxtaposition with its ideological opposite, "slave labor." Under the rubric of free labor, northerners of diverse backgrounds and interests could rally in defense of the superiority of their own society, even as critical voices questioned whether the contrast with slavery did not disguise the forms of compulsion to which free laborers were themselves subjected. Whatever their differences in economic status, however, all northerners had in common the fact that they neither were nor owned slaves. By the mid-1850s, the Republicans, a party that exalted the virtues of free labor, had become the political majority in the North. To southern claims that slavery was the foundation of liberty, Republicans responded with the rallying cry, "Freedom national." Slavery was an aberration that time would do away with. The "universal principle" of the American republic was freedom.[42]

4

The Boundaries
of Freedom in the
Young Republic

The Imagined Community

BY THE 1830S, the time of Andrew Jackson's presidency, the axiom
that "the people" ruled had become a cliché of American political discourse. But the very vigor of American democracy, and the centrality
of democracy to the definition of both freedom and nationality itself,
made it all the more imperative to define the political nation. As older
exclusions fell away—notably, property and religious qualifications
for voting—others were retained and new ones added. The vigorous
public life of antebellum America was simultaneously expansive and
exclusive, and its limits were as essential to its nature as its broad
scope. Democracy in America was capable of absorbing poor white
men at home and waves of immigrants from abroad, yet erected impenetrable barriers to the participation of women and non-white men.
These groups were also excluded from full participation in the market revolution.[1]

If the rhetoric of freedom obscured the new republic's considerable
economic dependence on slave labor, slavery's presence gave new and
contradictory meanings to such core ideas of nineteenth-century
Americans as nationality, class, and freedom. Slavery gave American
freedom a powerful exclusionary dimension and reinforced a racialized
outlook on the world. Its presence sustained the reality of rapid eco-

Abolitionists adopted the Old State House bell in
Philadelphia as an emblem of their cause, renaming it
the Liberty Bell. It would eventually become one of the
nation's most venerated symbols of freedom.
(Massachusetts Anti-Slavery Fair, *The Liberty Bell*
[Boston, 1839])

nomic growth and expanding economic opportunity for many white Americans, while severely limiting the rights enjoyed by free blacks. Yet simultaneously, the contrast between liberty and slavery provided a rhetoric through which those outside the boundaries of American freedom could challenge their exclusion and, in so doing, transform the meaning of freedom itself.

How could belief in freedom as a universal human right be reconciled with the exclusion of blacks from liberty in the South and the rights of free men in the North, and of women from political participation and the opportunities of free labor? As democracy triumphed, the intellectual grounds for exclusion shifted from economic dependency to natural incapacity. A boundary drawn by nature itself was not really exclusion at all. Of course, as John Stuart Mill once asked, "was there ever any domination which did not appear natural to those who possessed it?" Yet even Mill's argument for universal freedom, in his great work *On Liberty* (1859), applied "only to human beings in the maturity of their faculties." The immature included not only children but entire "races" of less than "civilized" peoples, deficient in the qualities necessary in the democratic citizen. In the United States, too, gender and racial differences were widely understood as being part of a single, natural hierarchy of innate endowments. "How did woman first become subject to man, as she now is all over the world?" asked the *New York Herald* in 1852. "By her nature, her sex, just as the negro is and always will be, to the end of time, inferior to the white race, and, therefore, doomed to subjection." Paradoxically, therefore, while freedom for white men involved an open-ended process of personal transformation, developing to the fullest the potential inherent within each human being, discussion of citizenship, race, and gender rested on the essentialist premise that the character and abilities of non-whites and women were fixed by nature.[2]

Thus, the common description of American democracy as based on "universal white manhood suffrage" did not seem self-contradictory to those who enjoyed American freedom. Everywhere, with the quixotic exception of New Jersey between 1776 and 1807, women, whether married or single, propertied or dependent, were denied the suffrage. The Creator, said a delegate to Virginia's 1829 constitutional convention, had rendered woman "weak and timid, in comparison with man, and had thus placed her under his *control*, as well as under his protection." Since the right of suffrage "necessarily implied *free-agency* and *intelligence*," nature itself had decreed women's "incapacity to exercise political power."[3]

Subtly, the early republic's ideology of "republican motherhood," which offered women a kind of public role as the mothers of future citizens, evolved into the mid-nineteenth-century "cult of domesticity." If this allowed women greater power within the family by affirming their role as its moral leaders, it minimized even their indirect participation in public affairs. For both sexes, freedom meant fulfilling their respective inborn qualities. Men were rational, aggressive, and domineering; women nurturing, selfless, ruled by the emotions, and thus less fitted for public life. If submission to the will of another increasingly seemed inadmissible for free men, it remained a condition natural to women and expected of them. The sphere of politics and the competitive marketplace were male preserves, while the home, ostensibly shielded from public life and of declining economic importance, stood as women's domain. Men moved freely from one "sphere" to the other; women were cloistered in the private realm of the family.[4]

Separate spheres was an ideology, from which reality often diverged. By the 1830s, through participation in temperance, abolition, and other reform movements, thousands of women had established a public presence. Nonetheless, the political world of the nineteenth century, so crucial an arena for the exercise of American freedom, was in part constructed in contrast to the feminine sphere of the home. Back in 1776, Jefferson had advocated "extending the right of suffrage (or in other words the rights of a citizen)" to all Americans with a permanent stake in society. Evidence of such a stake, he went on, included "having a family." If the consolidation of democracy meant that political identity no longer required ownership of property, "having a family" remained central to the political order. The free man was still defined, in part, as the master of a household. The institution of marriage continued to shape the civic status of both men and women, empowering the former, disempowering the latter, and affecting even those who chose to remain single. The idea that women were represented by men in the political world survived long after the analogous notion that workers could be represented by their employers had been laid to rest.

The ideology of separate spheres had profound implications for the idea of American freedom, for it severely limited the reach of the nation's egalitarian and democratic ideals. Freedom in the public realm in no way implied freedom in the private. The "most rabid Radical," Ralph Waldo Emerson remarked in his journal in 1841, was likely to be conservative "in relation to the theory of Marriage." Beyond the right to "decent treatment" by her husband and to whatever property the law allowed her to control, women, declared the New York Herald, had "no rights . . . with which the public have any concern."[5]

Domesticity also excluded women from the opportunities of free labor. In a market economy where labor increasingly meant work that produced monetary value, it became more and more difficult to think of free labor as encompassing anyone but men. Women could not compete freely for employment, since only a few low-paying jobs were available to them. Nor could they be considered freely contracting wage workers. According to common law, married women could not sign independent contracts or sue in their own name, and not until after the Civil War did the states accord them control over the wages they earned. Even then, the husband retained a proprietary claim to his wife's domestic work.[6]

Prevailing ideas concerning gender, which defined women as existing outside the labor market, bore little relation to the experience of those women who worked for wages at least some time in their lives. Even for the middle class, the cult of domesticity concealed the fact that the home was, in fact, a place of work. Lydia Maria Child, whose popular book *The Frugal Housewife*, published in 1829, sought to prepare women for the real world of the market revolution (one chapter was entitled "How to Endure Poverty"), supported her family by her writing, but her diary reveals that in a single year she also sewed thirty-six pieces of clothing and prepared over seven hundred meals. Through servants— the largest employment category for women in the nineteenth century and a ubiquitous emblem of middle-class status—wage labor itself entered the home, even though relations with servants were generally understood as questions of morality and discipline rather than a labor problem.[7]

Among urban artisans and wage laborers, women's work often spelled the difference between independence and dependence, even outright survival. Their homes, too, sheltered paid work by women—especially the sweated labor of outworkers toiling at subsistence wages. By 1850, Boston's seamstresses outnumbered the entire male labor force. On small farms, North and South, women's work—including labor in the fields, childrearing, cleaning, cooking, laundering, producing clothing and other items for use at home or for sale— was constant. Early industrialization enhanced the importance of women's work in the North, as the spread of the putting-out system in such industries as shoemaking, hatmaking, and clothing manufacture allowed women working at home to contribute to family income even as they retained responsibility for domestic chores. At the same time, the early factories offered new employment opportunities for the teenaged daughters of farm families. In either case, the vaunted independence of the small producer depended in considerable measure on the labor of women, whether unremunerated within the household or paid wages at home or outside. Thus, free labor embodied a contradiction obscured by the rhetorical contrast between "free" and "slave" societies: independence for some rested on dependent labor for others.[8]

Identifying the workplace as the world outside the home had the effect of rendering women's actual labor virtually invisible. Housewives, domestic servants, and the army of female outworkers were rarely mentioned in discussions of free labor, except as an indication of how the spread of capitalism was degrading men. The idea that the male head of household should command a "family wage" enabling him to support his wife and children became a popular definition of social justice. It sank deep roots among middle-class Americans, for whom the ability to maintain a home in which women devoted themselves to the family became a defining characteristic of bourgeois status, and among working-class men as well. Capitalism, said the *Workingman's Advocate*, tore women from their role as "happy and independent mistresses" of the domestic sphere and forced them into the labor market, thereby undermining the natural order of the household and the authority of its male head. The fight for a family wage mobilized successive generations of labor organizations. Indeed, the contrast between a "family wage" or a "man's wage" (increasingly a badge of honor) and a "woman's wage" (a term of opprobrium) helped to legitimate the idea that wage labor, if equitably rewarded, was an appropriate status for American men.[9]

If the exclusion of women from political and economic freedom continued a practice of long standing, the increasing identification of democracy and race marked something of a departure. Even as Americans' rhetoric grew ever more egalitarian, the somewhat tentative thinking of the revolutionary era flowered into a fully developed racist ideology, complete with "scientific" underpinnings. "Race" gained broad acceptance as the explanation for the boundaries of nationality. Blacks, as a delegate to Oregon's constitutional convention of 1857 put it, were "born to servility," an idea widely disseminated in newspapers, lithographs, and popular theatrical performances such as minstrel shows. In the revolutionary era, only Virginia, South Carolina, and Georgia explicitly confined the vote to whites, although elsewhere, custom often made it difficult for free blacks to exercise the franchise. As late as 1800, no northern state limited the suffrage on the basis of race. But every state that entered the Union after that year, with the single exception of Maine, restricted the right to vote to white males. And in states such as New York and Pennsylvania, the right of free blacks to vote was either narrowed or eliminated entirely. In 1821, the same New York Constitutional Convention that removed property qualifications for white voters raised the requirement for blacks to $250, a sum beyond the reach of nearly all the state's black residents. Sixteen years later, Pennsylvania, home of an articulate, economically successful black community in Philadelphia, eliminated black voting altogether. By 1860, blacks could vote on the same basis as whites only in five New England states.[10]

Despite racial inequalities, many whites of the revolutionary generation had thought of African-Americans as "black Yankees," entitled to at least some of the rights of citizens and potential members of the body politic. But in the nineteenth century, as southern states tightened their laws to make manumission almost impossible and blacks in the North were subjected to political disenfranchisement, social segregation, and severe economic discrimination, the racial boundaries of the political nation became more and more impermeable. By 1837, a delegate to the Pennsylvania Constitutional Convention could describe the United States as "a political community of white persons." Blacks were aliens, not Americans, "intruders among us," declared a political leader in Minnesota. As the slavery controversy intensified, the rhetoric of racial exclusion suffused the political language, adopted, by the eve of the Civil War, even by the Supreme Court. In ancient Rome, manumission had entailed citizenship as well as freedom. In America, according to Chief Justice Roger B. Taney in the *Dred Scott* decision of 1857, blacks could not be citizens; they "had no rights which the white man was bound to respect." The American people, Taney argued, constituted a "political family" restricted to whites. It was a family of which blacks, descended from different ancestors and lacking a history of freedom, could never be a part. In effect, race had replaced class as the boundary separating which American men were entitled to enjoy political freedom and which were not.[11]

Nor did the glorification of free labor as the most salient characteristic of northern society include the region's African-Americans. At its base, the idea of free labor rested on universalistic assumptions. Human nature itself, which responded more favorably to incentive than coercion, explained why free labor outstripped slave in economic progress. Like political democracy, however, free labor was defined, in part, by lines of exclusion understood as arising from the natural order of things. Lincoln himself hinted at these boundaries when he remarked that only those with a "dependent nature" did not take advantage of the opportunity to escape the status of wage earner for propertied independence.[12]

Who were those "dependent" by nature and hence outside the bounds of free labor? As in the case of political democracy, the answer was provided by the historical experience of American society. By 1860, nearly 4 million African-Americans toiled as slaves; in addition, neither free blacks nor members of other racial minorities could easily be assimilated into the rigid compartmentalization of labor systems as either "free" or "slave." Among them, apprenticeship and indentured servitude—the halfway houses of semifree labor, which had disappeared for whites by the early nineteenth century—long endured.[13]

The West's promise of economic autonomy did not apply universally. Imagined (and often experienced) by whites as a land of economic independence, the West simultaneously harbored indentured Indian labor, Mexican-American peonage, and work under long-term contracts for Chinese immigrants. These labor systems persisted well past midcentury; indeed, they were reinvigorated by the expansion of highly market-oriented, labor-intensive enterprises in mining, manufacturing, and commercial agriculture. In 1850, California placed as many as ten thousand Indians in "apprenticeships" on ranches owned by Mexicans and white migrants to the state. Most strikingly, territorial expansion carried with it the expansion of slavery. Jefferson had believed European demand for American grain would underpin the nation's economic growth and the autonomy of the small farmer. But demand for mass-produced textiles proved even more resilient than the market for American food. It was cotton, a crop produced on slave plantations, not grain grown by sturdy yeomen, that became the linchpin of the southern economy as it expanded westward, and the leading export of the entire empire of liberty.[14]

If any group in American society could be identified as wage slaves, it was the free blacks of the antebellum North. They were the last to experience indentured servitude, for emancipation generally required children of slave mothers to work for their owners for a period of time before being freed (twenty-eight years in Pennsylvania, far longer than had been customary for white indentured servants). Until the onset of large-scale immigration after 1830, African-Americans formed a significant portion of the region's wage-earning proletariat. While the free labor ideology celebrated social advancement, blacks' actual experience was downward mobility. At the time of abolition, because of widespread slave ownership among eighteenth-century artisans, a considerable number of northern blacks were skilled craftworkers. Though many white artisans were critics of southern slavery, however, few viewed the free black as anything but a low-wage competitor and most sought to bar them from skilled employment. "They are leaders in the cause of equal rights for themselves," a black editor commented of New York City's radical artisans in the 1830s. Hostility from white craftsmen, however, was only one among many obstacles that kept blacks confined to the lowest ranks of the labor market. White employers refused to hire them in anything but menial positions, and white customers did not wish to be served by them. The result was a rapid decline in economic status, until by midcentury the vast majority of northern blacks labored for wages in unskilled jobs and as domestic servants. Nor could free blacks take advantage of the opening of the West to improve their economic status, a central component of American freedom. Federal law barred them from access to the public domain and four states—Indiana, Illinois, Iowa, and Oregon—prohibited them from entering their territory altogether. The goal of economic independence held as much appeal to free blacks as white Americans. But it was almost unimaginably remote; the vast majority could only look forward to a lifetime of economic subservience.[15]

In a country whose economic growth and territorial expansion required appropriating the land of one non-white group (Native Americans), exploiting the labor of another (slaves), and annexing much of a nation defined as non-white (Mexico), it was inevitable that nationhood and freedom would acquire powerful racial dimensions. During the 1840s, as the nation acquired vast new lands from Mexico and the ideology of manifest destiny reached its greatest influence, territorial expansion came to be seen as proof of the innate superiority of the "Anglo-Saxon race" (a mythical construct defined largely by its opposites: blacks, Indians, Hispanics, Catholics). *"Race,"* declared the *Democratic Review* on the eve of the Mexican War, was the "key" to the "history of nations" and the rise and fall of empires. "Race" in the mid-nineteenth century was an amorphous notion involving color, culture, national origin, and religion. But the idea that American freedom was linked to the innate liberty-loving qualities of Anglo-Saxon Protestants was widely popularized in the press and popular magazines, political treatises, and the writings of the era's philosophers and historians. There had always been a small Catholic population in the colonies and young republic, but only in the 1840s with the Irish Potato Famine and the Mexican War did large numbers of Catholics suddenly became part of the population. The result was to reinvigorate long-standing Protestant hostility to "Popery" and further reinforce the identification of liberty with the nation's putative Anglo-Saxon heritage. In lectures such as Ralph Waldo Emerson's "Genius of the Anglo-Saxon Race," public orators amalgamated Anglo-Saxon superiority, a racial definition of nationality, and manifest destiny into a single account of the nation's mission.[16]

Providing an intellectual grounding for the new republic, gentleman-scholars like Walter H. Prescott, Francis Parkman, and George Bancroft constructed a patriotic historical narrative that had no place for Indian tribes, African-Americans, or the Spanish- and French-derived cultures of the trans-Mississippi West. In their grand narrative of American freedom, the seeds of liberty, planted in Puritan New England, had reached their inevitable flowering in the American Revolution and westward expansion. The annexation of Texas in 1845 and conquest of much of Mexico shortly thereafter became triumphs of civilization, progress, and liberty over the tyranny of the Catholic Church and the innate incapacity of "mongrel races." Since territorial expansion meant "extending the area of freedom," those who stood in the way—European powers, Native Americans, Mexicans—were by definition obstacles to the progress of liberty. (The equating of the country's national interests with the liberation of mankind and of its antagonists with hostility to freedom has infused the rhetoric of American statecraft to the present day, often to the bemusement or annoyance of other nations.)[17]

Throughout the nineteenth century, westward expansion inevitably raised the question of whether the inhabitants of newly acquired territories could be absorbed into the American people and were capable of enjoying the blessings of American freedom. For the most part, inhabitants of European descent— French, Spanish, Russians—were welcome to become American citizens. Jefferson and many of his generation had hoped that by abandoning their traditional ways and learning the benefits of settled agriculture and Christianity, Indians could also be assimilated into the American population. Though this idea never completely died out, the experience of the Cherokee nation, who had become everything republican citizens should be (they adopted a written constitution, become farmers, owned slaves, and, in good American fashion, went to court when their rights were violated), suggested that exclusion was to be the Indians' fate. Despite heroic resistance, the Cherokees and other "civilized tribes" were removed from the Southeast during the 1830s. The effort of the state of Georgia to extend its jurisdiction over the Cherokees and seize much of their land led Chief Justice John Marshall to try to define the unique status of American Indians. The best he could do was to describe them as "wards" of the federal government, worthy of paternal regard and protection. Legally, however, they lacked the standing as citizens that would allow the Supreme Court to enforce their natural or treaty rights. In effect, the 1831 decision in *Cherokee Nation* v. *Georgia* accepted the "contingency of liberty" in America, freedom's dependence on group membership.[18]

Ironically, the status of non-whites in the West to some extent depended on what rights a foreign power had previously acknowledged and whether it insisted that the United States continue to recognize them. The treaty that transferred Louisiana to the United States in 1803 promised that all free inhabitants would enjoy "the rights, advantages, and immunities of citizens." Although American rule led to a steady diminution in the status of Louisiana's free blacks, they continued to enjoy privileges unknown by their counterparts elsewhere in the country, such as the right to form militia units—a legacy of Spanish and French rule. The Treaty of Guadalupe Hidalgo of 1848 allowed Mexicans in territories annexed by the United States to enjoy "all the rights" of American citizens, a provision designed to protect the property of large landowners in California. The case of Mexican Americans illustrates how racial lines could sometimes be quite indeterminate, and affected by local circumstances. When California entered the Union in 1850, it excluded non-whites from voting. Unlike blacks, Indians, and Asians, Mexicans in California, many of whom claimed Spanish descent or had intermarried with Anglo-Saxons or Irish immigrants, were deemed to be white. The population of New Mexico, however, was deemed "too Mexican" (that is, too Indian) for democratic self-government, with the result that statehood was delayed in 1912, long after the necessary number of inhabitants had been reached.[19]

Even as this focus on race drew ever more tightly the lines of exclusion of America's imagined community, it helped to solidify a sense of national identity among the diverse groups of British and European origin that made up the free population. Before 1830, immigrants from abroad contributed only marginally to American population growth. But between that year and 1860, nearly 5 million people (more than the entire population of 1790) entered the United States, the vast majority from England and Ireland. Though immigrants from England were easily absorbed, those from Ireland faced considerable hostility. Nativists contended that the Irish, ostensibly unfamiliar with American conceptions of liberty and subservient to the Roman Catholic Church, posed a threat to democratic institutions. Stereotypes similar to those directed at blacks flourished regarding the Irish as well—childlike, indolent, and slaves of the passions, they were unsuited for republican freedom. Yet despite the reality of severe anti-Irish discrimination in jobs, housing, and education, it is remarkable how little came of demands that immigrants be barred from the political nation. The vast majority had the good fortune to arrive after white manhood suffrage had become the norm and thus were automatically accorded political freedom. Indeed, even as New England states explored ways to reduce immigrant voting power (the most extreme being the two-year waiting period between naturalization and voting mandated by Massachusetts in 1859), western states desperate for labor offered white immigrants the franchise well before they became citizens. In a country where the right to vote had become intrinsic to understandings of freedom, it is difficult to overstate the importance of the fact that white male immigrants could vote almost from the moment they disembarked in America, while blacks, whose ancestors had lived in the country for centuries (and Indians, who had been there even longer), could not.[20]

Battles at the Boundaries

Given the pervasiveness of the language of liberty, it is hardly surprising that those excluded from the blessings of American freedom should adopt it to their own purposes. One is tempted to view demands that non-whites and women be admitted to democratic participation, the opportunity for personal self-realization, and the rights of free labor as efforts to expand freedom's boundaries without altering its definition. But since race and sex were crucial constitutive elements in how freedom was understood and experienced, re-drawing the boundaries of freedom inevitably required rethinking its content. If the language of the abolitionist and women's rights movements was thoroughly American, they used it to try to transform the meaning of American freedom.

One did not have to belong to women's rights associations to believe that gender should not delimit economic freedom. But the very fact of women working outside the home implicitly challenged prevailing gender conventions. Working women of the Jacksonian era adopted for themselves the language of equal liberty so prominent among male unionists. "Equal rights should be extended to all," declared a group of striking female shoebinders, "to the weaker sex as well as to the stronger." Some female workers (especially those who were unmarried) challenged the idea of the male family wage, insisting that women were equally entitled to "a comfortable support" from their labor.[21]

While most American women of this generation doubtless accepted the premise that their first responsibility was to their families, not all agreed that earning a living contradicted a woman's dignity. If blacks saw wage labor as a definite improvement over slavery, many nineteenth-century women found in working for wages an escape from the paternalistic bonds and personal dependence of the household. As Harriet Hanson Robinson later recalled about her time in the Lowell textile mills, work outside the home offered women autonomy: for the first time, "they could earn money, and spend it as they pleased. . . . For the first time in this country a woman's labor had a money value." Equal opportunity to enter the labor market was a recurring demand of the early movement for women's rights, which rejected the domestic ideology's celebration of the "idle" housewife. Isolated within the home, cut off from the opportunity to earn wages, economically dependent women, argued nineteenth-century feminists from Susan B. Anthony to Charlotte Perkins Gilman, could make no significant contribution to society. Women, wrote Pauline Davis in 1853, "must go *to work*" to emancipate themselves from "bondage."[22]

Whether married or not, early feminists insisted, women deserved the autonomy and range of individual choices, the possibility of self-realization, that constituted the essence of freedom. "Under the expanded wings of liberty," proclaimed Frances Wright, who in the late 1820s became the first female to lecture in public on political subjects, women would be able to develop their talents as fully as men. Women, wrote Margaret Fuller two decades later, had the same right as men to "grow . . . to live freely and unimpeded." To the end of her long life, Elizabeth Cady Stanton maintained that woman, like man, was ultimately the "arbiter of her own destiny," and must rely on her own inner resources for self-realization and the "full development of her faculties." In her 1892 speech, "The Solitude of Self," Stanton (who had given birth to seven children) offered a rather chilling portrait of a society of sovereign individuals, each like "Robinson Crusoe . . . on a solitary island," with the roles of "mother, wife, sister, daughter" pertaining only to the "incidental relations of life." The speech claimed for women full inclusion in American individualism, and anticipated the feminism of personal fulfillment that would flourish in the twentieth century.

By the 1840s, women's rights advocates had concluded that in a democratic society, freedom was impossible without the ballot. The demand for the "sovereignty of free citizens" assumed a central place in the women's movement. The argument was simple and irrefutable: in the words of Lydia Maria Child, "either the theory of our government is *false*, or women have a right to vote." Women had never consented to their inferior legal status; second-class citizenship had been imposed upon them. As Stanton told the Seneca Falls Convention of 1848—the first public meeting to demand equal political rights for women—only the vote would make women "free as man is free."[23]

Feminism, therefore, was an extension of nineteenth-century market, individualist, and democratic principles, a demand that women, in the words of Francis D. Gage, enjoy "the rights and liberties that every 'free white male citizen' takes to himself as God-given." But it was also much more. In every realm of life, not excluding the family, declared Stanton, there could be "no happiness without freedom." Even as it sought to apply prevailing notions of freedom to women, the movement posed a fundamental challenge to some of their central tenets—that the capacity for independence and rationality were male traits, that the world was divided into autonomous public and private realms, and that the family's internal relations fell beyond the bounds of scrutiny on the basis of justice and freedom. "Women's Rights," declared a Boston meeting in 1859, did not imply eliminating the "divine" institution of the family, but did demand "freedom and equal rights for her in the family." Yet this requirement portended a fundamental redefinition of freedom itself.[24]

The dichotomy between freedom and slavery powerfully shaped early feminists' political language. Just as "wage slavery" enabled northern workers to unmask the inequalities inherent in market freedom, the concept of the "slavery of sex" empowered the women's movement to develop an all-encompassing critique of male authority and the subordination of their sex. Despite the prevalent notion that the public sphere was a male preserve, northern women served as the foot soldiers of abolitionism. Tens of thousands gathered petitions, raised funds, and in other ways promoted the cause. This activism inevitably led some to think in new ways about the constraints affecting their own lives. "In striving to strike [the slave's] irons off," wrote the abolitionist orator Abby Kelley, "we found most surely that *we* were manacled *ourselves.*" The inclusion of female slaves in the category of woman enabled feminists to redefine social difference as sexual inequality. The analogy with slavery suggested the remedy—emancipation—understood to include not only political enfranchisement but also such demands as access to all the educational and economic opportunities of men, liberalization of divorce laws, and changes in the institution of marriage. "There is no private life," George Eliot would write in *Felix Holt, the Radical* (1866), "which is not determined by a wider public life." Antebellum feminists pointed out that the law of marriage made nonsense of contentions that the family was a "private" institution independent of public authority. When Lucy Stone and Henry Blackwell married, they felt obliged to repudiate New York's laws that clothed the husband "with legal powers which . . . no man should possess."[25]

Feminist abolitionists did not invent the analogy between marriage and slavery. Mary Wollstonecraft had invoked it in the 1790s and it had been prominent in the writings and speeches of Frances Wright. But the analogy between free women and slaves gained prominence as it was swept up in the accelerating debate over chattel slavery. Even Sarah J. Hale, editor of *Godey's Lady's Book* and a strong opponent of the movement for women's rights, spoke of how the common law reduced "woman to the condition of a slave." "Woman is a slave, from the cradle to the grave," asserted Ernestine Rose. "Father, guardian, husband—master still. One conveys her, like a piece of property, over to the other." Southern ideologies used much the same argument for the very different purpose of defending slavery. Both slavery and marriage, wrote George Fitzhugh, were systems of subordination based upon natural differences in the capacity for freedom. "Marriage," he proclaimed, "is too much like slavery not to be involved in its fate."[26]

There were indeed real and disturbing parallels between chattel slavery and marriage. Marriage was "voluntary," but the common law reduced the wife to an appendage of her husband, who did not enjoy the fruits of her own labor or ownership of her own person—central elements of freedom. Jefferson believed slavery daily inculcated the spirit of domination; John Stuart Mill called the family "a school of despotism." The early socialists took the critique even

further, insisting that only if private property were abolished could relations between the sexes be transformed. At New Harmony, Robert Owen promised,
women would no longer be "enslaved" to their husbands, and "false notions"
about innate differences between the sexes would be abandoned. From Oneida's
"complex marriage" to Mormon polygamy, Shaker celibacy, and "free love" at
Modern Times, the era's communal experiments witnessed numerous efforts to
respond to tensions within the traditional family structure by creating alternative arrangements that emancipated women. (Actual conditions for women in
these communities tended to be less than utopian. In general, positions of
power were monopolized by men, and despite noble professions of equality,
cooking, child care, and other domestic labor remained female responsibilities.)[27]

"Personal freedom," an influential treatise of the 1820s declared, was the
essence of liberty: "nothing can be considered more strictly our own property
than our own persons." Women's rights advocates turned this popular understanding of freedom as self-ownership in an entirely new direction. Among the
foremost aims of the American Anti-Slavery Society was to restore to the slave
"the inalienable right to his own body." The emphasis in abolitionist literature
on the physical violation of the slave woman's body helped give the idea of self-
ownership a concrete reality, a literalness that encouraged application to free
women as well. The law of domestic relations presupposed the husband's right
of sexual access to his wife and courts were reluctant to intervene in cases of
physical chastisement so long as it was not "extreme" or "intolerable." The
idea that women should enjoy the rights to regulate their own sexual activity and
procreation and to be protected by the state against violence at the hands of
their husbands fundamentally challenged the notion that claims for justice,
freedom, and individual rights should stop at the household's door. The woman
forced to submit to her husband, wrote Henry C. Wright, an abolitionist, feminist, and advocate of what in the twentieth century would be called family
planning, did not enjoy freedom; she was "the veriest slave alive." To be sure,
few Americans, male or female, were willing to raise such issues in public. But
the dramatic fall in the birth rate (from 278 to 130 births per 1,000 white women
of childbearing age over the course of the nineteenth century) suggests that
many women were exercising "personal freedom" in their most intimate relationships.[28]

Like the metaphor of wage slavery, the description of free women as living
in "legalized slavery" simultaneously illuminated and obscured social realities.
Just as most abolitionists repudiated the wage slavery metaphor, there were
black women, such as Sarah Parker Remond, who rejected the analogy between

marriage and slavery because they understood that a stable family life had special meaning to those in bondage. Free women certainly deserved more rights, Remond declared, but slavewomen, as the "worst victims" of slavery, stood in dire need of "the protection . . . enjoyed by the white." Indeed, many abolitionists, male and female, contended that among slavery's gravest abuses was destroying male authority and making it impossible for women to fulfill their roles as mothers and wives.[29]

Many feminists understood that the intense individualism of an Elizabeth Cady Stanton or a Lucy Stone was far removed from family life as actually experienced by most women, and that their theories did not take into account the emotional dependencies that marriage and parenthood inevitably entail. Even those who grasped the important insight that the interests of men and women within a family were not necessarily the same hoped and expected to enjoy a harmonious relationship with their spouse. Many feminists were powerfully influenced by the Second Great Awakening of the 1820s and 1830s, which not only inspired the hope for individual salvation but exalted "companionate marriage" as the ideal relationship for a Christian family, and celebrated women's natural moral superiority and maternal instincts. Such women viewed abstinence as the route to sexual self-determination, not birth control or easy divorce, which, they feared, would give even greater scope to male lust. Egalitarianism and belief in the natural differences between the sexes coexisted in antebellum feminist thought, as they do even today.[30]

Lucy Stone, who believed a woman must have an "absolute right" to her "body and its uses," admitted that the movement was not yet ready for this question, since "no two of us think alike about it." Most feminists deemed the issue of women's private freedom so explosive that they rarely raised it in public before the Civil War. When a heated debate arose at the National Women's Rights Convention of 1860 on whether marriage laws should be reformed, Wendell Phillips, not normally known for timidity, proposed that the entire discussion be omitted from the published proceedings. Such questions frequently arose, however, in the private correspondence of feminist leaders. "Social Freedom," Susan B. Anthony observed to Stone, " . . . lies at the bottom of all—and until woman gets that, she must continue the slave of men in all other things." Not until the twentieth century would the demand that freedom be extended to intimate aspects of life inspire a mass movement. But the foundation was laid in antebellum America.[31]

Like the movement for women's rights, the crusade against slavery challenged fundamental elements of freedom as conceived and experienced in antebellum America. The antislavery contribution to redefining the meaning of freedom was profound and complex. Abolitionists, as has been related, rejected the equation of northern labor with southern bondage, whether emanating from the slave South or the labor movement of the free states. In affirming the uniqueness of the evil of slavery, abolitionists helped to popularize the sharp dichotomy between slavery's illegitimate coercions and the condition of labor in the North, as well as the related concept, fortified by the market revolution, that autonomy derived not from the ownership of productive property but from property in one's self and the ability to enjoy the fruits of one's labor. Only slavery, wrote the poet John Greenleaf Whittier, "lays its grasp upon the right of personal ownership—that foundation right, the removal of which uncreates the man."

Abolitionists of the Garrisonian persuasion, who eschewed voting under a proslavery constitution, extended the definition of freedom as personal self-direction to a critique of all coercive institutions, including government, the church, and, on occasion, the family. Others, particularly those who led the antislavery movement into politics in the 1840s, rejected the practice of "confounding" slavery "with other relations and institutions from which it is in reality and essentially distinct." The cause of freedom meant emancipating the slaves, not transforming northern society. It would be counterproductive to identify abolitionists as enemies of institutions "which the great body of its members cherish as objects of great regard—family authority and our republican government." Stripping away many of the metaphorical usages of slavery, these political abolitionists helped to focus the debate over freedom on actually existing chattel slavery.[32]

The long contest over slavery gave new meaning to personal liberty, political community, and the rights attached to American citizenship. Initially, the nation responded to the crusade against slavery by attempting to suppress it. In Washington, the House of Representatives in 1836 adopted the notorious gag rule, prohibiting the consideration of abolitionist petitions, and Andrew Jackson's Postmaster General, Amos Kendall, allowed local authorities in the South to remove material critical of slavery from the U.S. mails. Throughout the 1830s, northern mobs (more than a hundred by one count) broke up abolitionists' meetings and destroyed their printing presses. In 1838, Pennsylvania Hall, built at great expense by Philadelphia's antislavery movement, was burned to the ground, although only after the mob had removed a portrait of George Washington to safety. "The struggle over what gets included in the public agenda," the scholar Seyla Benhabib has written, "is itself a struggle for . . . freedom." For many years, the American public sphere excluded discussion of slavery. The fight for the right to debate slavery openly and without reprisal led abolitionists to elevate "free opinion"—freedom of speech and of the press and the right of petition—to a central place in what Garrison called the "gospel of freedom." The struggle for free speech also reinforced the contention that slavery threatened the liberties of white Americans as well as black. Free expression, abolitionists insisted, should be a national standard, not subject to limitation by those who held power within local communities. The abolitionist movement rejuvenated the Bill of Rights as a fundamental definition of American liberties and tried to devise ways—through elaborate theories of natural or "higher" law—to make it applicable to state as well as federal authorities. In defending the Bill of Rights, every provision of which slavery violated, the antislavery movement had, it claimed, become custodians of the "rights of every freeman."[33]

The antislavery movement also sought to reinvigorate the idea of freedom as a truly universal entitlement. Regardless of race, abolitionists maintained, every human being was a "free moral agent." Drawing on eighteenth-century traditions of natural rights, the Declaration of Independence, and the perfectionist creed of evangelical Protestantism, they insisted that the inherent, natural, and absolute right to personal liberty took precedence over other forms of freedom, such as the right of citizens to accumulate and hold property or self-government by local political communities. The slaveowner's power over the slave represented a throwback to hierarchy and inequality, traditions no longer acceptable in nineteenth-century America.[34]

Even as slavery spawned a racialized definition of American freedom, the struggle for abolition gave rise to its opposite, a purely civic understanding of nationhood. The origins of the idea of an American people unbounded by race lies not with the founders, who by and large made their peace with slavery, but with the abolitionists. The antislavery crusade insisted on the "Americanness" of slaves and free blacks, a position summarized in the title of Lydia Maria Child's popular treatise of 1833, *An Appeal in Favor of That Class of Americans Called Africans.* Child's text insisted that blacks were compatriots, not foreigners; they were no more Africans than whites were Englishmen. At a time when the authority to define the rights of citizens lay almost entirely with the states, abolitionists maintained that "birth-place" should determine who was an American. This idea of birthright citizenship, later enshrined in the Fourteenth Amendment, was a truly radical departure from the traditions of American life. "We do not admit," declared the *New England Magazine* in 1832, "that America is as much the country of the blacks, bound and free, as it is ours."[35]

The crusade against slavery, wrote Angelina Grimké, the daughter of a South Carolina slaveholder who became a prominent abolitionist and feminist, was the nation's preeminent "school in which *human rights* are . . . investigated." Even as they debated the Constitution's relationship to slavery (William Lloyd Garrison burned the document, calling it a covenant with the devil; Frederick Douglass came to believe it offered no national protection to slavery), abolitionists developed an alternative, rights-oriented constitutionalism, grounded in a universalistic understanding of liberty. Seeking to define the core rights to which all Americans were entitled—the meaning of freedom in concrete legal terms—abolitionists invented the concept of equality before the law regardless of race, one all but unknown in American jurisprudence before the Civil War. Abolitionists challenged both southern slavery and the racial proscription that confined free blacks to second-class status throughout the nation. Before the Civil War, the movement was thoroughly alienated from a succession of administrations that seemed firmly in the grasp of the Slave Power (as antislavery northerners came to call the planter class). Borrowing a leaf from their southern adversaries, abolitionists drew on the idea of state sovereignty to try to nullify the Fugitive Slave Law of 1850, among the most energetic exercises of federal authority in the entire antebellum era. Yet in the ideas of a national citizenship and of equal rights for all Americans, abolitionists developed a "vocabulary of freedom" that would flourish during and after the Civil War. They glimpsed the possibility that the national state might become the guarantor of freedom, rather than its enemy.[36]

Most adamant in contending that the struggle against slavery required a redefinition of both freedom and Americanness were black members of the abolitionist crusade. "He who has endured the cruel pangs of slavery," wrote Frederick Douglass in 1847, "is the man to advocate liberty," and black abolitionists developed an understanding of freedom that went well beyond the usage of most of their white contemporaries. Those who had actually experienced slavery were among the most penetrating critics of the proslavery argument ("flimsy nonsense," Douglass called it, which men would be "ashamed to remember" once slavery had been abolished). Equally absurd were the nation's pretensions as a land of liberty, which black abolitionists repudiated at every opportunity. Indeed, free blacks dramatically reversed the common association of the United States with the progress of freedom. In devising an alternative calendar of "freedom celebrations" centered on January 1, the date in 1808 on which the slave trade became illegal, and August 1, the anniversary of West Indian emancipation, rather than July 4 (from which they were forcibly barred in many localities), black communities in the North offered a stinging rebuke to white Americans' claims to live in a land of freedom. Thanks to its embrace of emancipation in the 1830s, declared a group of black abolitionists in Philadelphia, Great Britain, from which America had "wrested [her] freedom," had become a model of liberty and justice, while the United States remained a land of tyranny. Black abolitionists also challenged the identification of American freedom with the genius of the Anglo-Saxon "race." (Many ancient Anglo-Saxons, Douglass pointed out sardonically, were themselves slaves.)[37]

Though hardly free from the racial preconceptions so prevalent in their society, white abolitionists insisted that genuine freedom meant civic equality. "While the word 'white' is on the statute-book of Massachusetts," declared Edmund Quincy, an active associate of William Lloyd Garrison, "Massachusetts is a slave state." Defying overwhelming odds, abolitionists launched legal and political battles against racial discrimination in the North, occasionally achieving victories like the end of school segregation in Massachusetts in 1855. Even more persistently than their white counterparts, black abolitionists articulated the ideals of egalitarian constitutionalism and color-blind citizenship. "The real battleground between liberty and slavery," wrote Samuel Cornish, "is prejudice against color." (Cornish in 1827 had established the nation's first black newspaper in New York City, choosing the expressive title *Freedom's Journal.*) More than white abolitionists, as well, blacks identified the widespread poverty of the free black population as a consequence of slavery and insisted that freedom possessed an economic dimension. It must be part of the "great work" of the antislavery crusade, insisted Charles L. Reason, "to abolish not only chattel slavery, but that other kind of slavery, which, for generation after generation, dooms an oppressed people to a condition of dependence and pauperism."[38]

African-Americans understood that the sharp dichotomy between freedom and slavery failed to encompass the actual experience of free blacks, who in the South lived, worked, and worshipped alongside slaves and were subjected to many of the same prohibitions on physical movement, economic opportunity, and access to the courts, and, in the North, were relegated to a quasi-freedom of inequality. When followed by the noun "black" or "Negro," the word "free" took on an entirely new meaning. Whites defined their freedom, in part, via their distance from slavery. Among blacks, wrote Douglass, "the distinction between the slave and the free is not great." True liberty, the free black experience suggested, was more than a juridical status. "No people can be free," wrote the black abolitionist Martin Delany, "who themselves do not constitute an essential part of the *ruling element* of the country in which they live." Delany believed blacks could never achieve equality in the United States; he was neither the first nor the last black American to look abroad for freedom. Having experienced "the legal slavery of the South and the *social slavery* of the North," wrote one emigrant on departing for Liberia, he knew he could "never be a *free man* in this country."[39]

Emigration became a mass movement after the passage of the Fugitive Slave Act of 1850, when several thousand northern blacks fled to Canada. The law for the first time empowered the federal government to apprehend fugitives, and offered little protection against enslavement to northern blacks who had been born free. The spectacle of men and women native to the United States seeking asylum in another country in order to preserve their liberty struck a discordant note in the familiar story of American freedom. Indeed, abolitionists developed an alternative account, an antinarrative, of the nation's development as a chronicle of declension, not progress. The United States, declared Douglass, was "unworthy of the name of great or free." In perhaps his most celebrated speech, Douglass proclaimed that Fourth of July celebrations revealed to blacks the "hypocrisy" of a nation that proclaimed belief in liberty yet daily committed "practices more shocking and bloody" than any other country on earth. "This Fourth of July," said Douglass, "is *yours*, not *mine*."

Simultaneously, however, Douglass laid claim to the founders' legacy. The Revolution had bequeathed a "rich inheritance of justice, liberty, prosperity and independence," from which subsequent generations had tragically strayed. Only by abolishing slavery and freeing the "great doctrines" of the Declaration from the "narrow bounds of races or nations" could the United States recapture its original mission. Indeed, in his autobiographical narrative *My Bondage and My Freedom* (1855), Douglass created a new pantheon of historical heroes for American freedom, explicitly linking himself both with the founding fathers and with slave rebels like Gabriel, Denmark Vesey, and Nat Turner. In effect, Douglass argued that in their desire for freedom, the slaves were truer to the nation's underlying principles than the white Americans who annually celebrated the Fourth of July.[40]

Douglass was not the only abolitionist to identify himself with the revolutionary heritage. The Declaration of Independence was not as fundamental to public oratory in the early republic as it would later become. It was abolitionists who seized upon it, interpreting the Declaration as a condemnation of slavery. The Liberty Bell, later one of the nation's most venerated symbols of freedom, did not achieve that status until abolitionists adopted it as a symbol and gave it its name, as part of their effort to identify their principles with those of the founders. (Prior to the 1830s, it was simply the Old State House bell, used at various times to mark the deaths of prominent citizens, summon students at the University of Pennsylvania to their classes, and celebrate patriotic

The top portion of an engraving produced by the American Anti-Slavery Society in 1836 illustrates how abolitionists sought to identify their cause with American traditions even as they mocked the nation's claim to be a "land of the free." (Library of Congress)

holidays.) Of course, Americans of all regions and political beliefs claimed the Revolution's legacy. Mobs that disrupted abolitionist meetings invoked the spirit of '76, as did southern defenders of slavery. But as the slavery controversy intensified, the belief spread far beyond abolitionist circles that chattel slavery contradicted the nation's heritage of freedom.[41]

By the 1850s, the antithesis between "free society" and "slave society" had co-alesced into a comprehensive world view glorifying the North as the home of progress, opportunity, and freedom. No one expressed this vision more eloquently than Abraham Lincoln. Lincoln was not an advocate of immediate abolition. But in his speeches opposing the expansion of slavery, he hammered away

T OF AMERICA.

D OF GOD.

DO YE EVEN SO TO THEM, FOR THIS IS THE LAW AND THE PROPHETS."
CAME UP UNTO GOD BY REASON OF THE BONDAGE, AND GOD HEARD THEIR GROANING."
AS OF THE OPPRESSOR, LEST MY FURY GO OUT LIKE FIRE, AND BURN THAT NONE CAN QUENCH IT, BECAUSE OF THE
IR DOINGS."

IERICAN INDEPENDENCE.

CREATOR WITH CERTAIN UNALIENABLE RIGHTS; THAT AMONG THESE ARE LIFE, LIBERTY, AND THE PURSUIT OF HAPPINESS."

THE UNITED STATES.

ID IMMUNITIES OF CITIZENS OF THE SEVERAL STATES." Article 4, Section 2.
OPLE PEACEABLY TO ASSEMBLE, AND TO PETITION THE GOVERNMENT FOR A REDRESS OF GRIEVANCES."—Article 1, Amendment.
S MAY, BY CESSION OF PARTICULAR STATES AND THE ACCEPTANCE OF CONGRESS, BECOME THE SEAT OF GOVERNMENT OF THE UNITED STATES."—Article 1, Section 8.

F THE STATES.

LIBERTY." *Constitutions of Maine, Connecticut, New-York, Pennsylvania, Delaware, Ohio, Indiana, Illinois, Tennessee, Louisiana, Alabama,*
vi, and Missouri.
TY, AND THEREFORE OUGHT NEVER TO BE RESTRAINED."—*North Carolina.*
E INVIOLABLY PRESERVED."—*Maryland.*
BE RESTRAINED BUT BY DESPOTIC GOVERNMENTS."—*Virginia. Other States nearly the same.*

COLUMBIA.

7000 SLAVES.   *"THE HOME OF THE OPPRESSED."*

HINGTON CITY.   CAPITOL OF THE UNITED STATES. "HAIL COLUMBIA."

TERFERE.

at the theme that slavery was incompatible with the founders' ideals and the nation's world-historical mission. Slavery violated the essential premises of American freedom—personal liberty, political democracy, and the opportunity to
better one's condition in life. The slave, quite simply, was an individual illegit-
imately deprived of liberty and the fruits of his labor, and denied the social opportunity that should be the right of all Americans.

In the 1850s, the relationship between American slavery and American freedom became the pivot on which political debate turned. Illinois senator Stephen
A. Douglas, Lincoln's great antagonist and the decade's leading political figure,
insisted that the essence of freedom lay in local self-determination. Thus, the

right to hold slaves was essential to American liberty; a people denied that right, one of Douglas's allies declared, was itself "sold into slavery." For Lincoln, by contrast, democracy was inconceivable in the absence of freedom. "As I would not be a *slave*, so I would not be a master": this, Lincoln mused in 1858, was his "idea of democracy." Yet southerners, he observed, claimed that freedom meant "the liberty of making slaves of other people." If such a definition came to be accepted, the "love of liberty" would be extinguished, and with it the nation's "genius."[42]

Like abolitionists, Lincoln enunciated an account of American history that effectively stigmatized southern ideas as alien to the nation's traditions. "We" Americans had created a nation dedicated to universal liberty through the Declaration of Independence, and "we" were forced to compromise with slavery to "get our Constitution." Yet the founders, who had set forth "a standard maxim for free men," believed slavery would eventually die. Yoking the nation's future ever more tightly to "free soil"—land free of cost and free of slavery— Republicans like Lincoln powerfully invoked the image of America as an empire of liberty and the idea that access to land in the West guaranteed economic autonomy, and therefore freedom. By reinvigorating slavery and demanding its spread into the West, southerners and their northern allies repudiated the nation's purpose, and gave aid and comfort to the "enemies of free institutions" throughout the world.[43]

Lincoln was not a racial egalitarian; he accepted without dissent many of the proscriptions so prevalent in his society. Almost to the end of his life he opposed black suffrage, and on occasion spoke of colonizing blacks outside the country. Yet, like the abolitionists, he insisted that America's professed creed was broad enough to encompass all mankind. Lincoln rejected Stephen A. Douglas's race-based definition of liberty. "I believe this government," said Douglas, "was made . . . by white men for the benefit of white men and their posterity for ever, and I am in favor of confining citizenship to white men . . . instead of conferring it upon negroes, Indians, and other inferior races." Lincoln responded that the rights enumerated in the Declaration applied to "all men, in all lands, everywhere," not merely to Europeans and their descendants. When Lincoln insisted that the right to the fruits of one's labor was a natural right, not confined to any particular set of persons, he drove home the point by choosing as his example a black woman: "In some respects she is certainly not my equal, but in her natural right to eat the bread she earns with her own hand . . . she is my equal and the equal of all others." As for European immigrants, their membership in the American community derived neither from "blood" nor ancestral connection with the Revolution. It was the "moral sentiment" expressed in

Thomas Crawford's original design for a "Statue of Freedom" to stand atop the Capitol's dome depicted a female figure wearing a cap of liberty. At the insistence of Secretary of War Jefferson Davis of Mississippi, the cap, which originated in Roman times as a symbol of emancipated slaves, was replaced by a helmet. (Library of Congress; Architect of the Capitol)

the Declaration of Independence, the ideal of universal liberty, that made them part of a unified America.[44]

In 1855, as the sectional controversy approached its final crisis, the sculptor Thomas Crawford was asked to design a statue to adorn the Capitol's dome. He proposed a "Statue of Freedom," a female figure wearing a cap of liberty. To this, Secretary of War Jefferson Davis, one of the South's largest slaveholders, objected. A familiar symbol in colonial America and the young republic, the liberty cap had become closely associated with the French

Revolution and for this reason had been outlawed in Great Britain. Davis's objection, however, rested on other grounds. In Roman times, the cap of liberty had been bestowed on emancipated slaves and thus, Davis noted, was regarded as "the badge of the freed slave." Such a symbol would be highly inappropriate, he felt, for it would suggest that an analogy existed between the slaves' longing for freedom and the liberty of freeborn Americans. In deference to Davis's sensibilities, Crawford replaced the liberty cap with a feathered helmet.[45]

The colossal *Statue of Freedom,* cast in several pieces in Rome, was transported to the United States in 1859 and assembled at a Maryland foundry under the direction of Philip Reed, a slave craftsman. It was not installed atop the Capitol until 1863. By then, Davis was president of the Confederate States of America, Lincoln had proclaimed the emancipation of the slaves, and a "new birth of freedom" was sweeping over the empire of liberty.

5

A New Birth of Freedom

"We All Declare for Liberty"

BOTH SIDES fought the Civil War in the name of freedom. To be sure, shortly before the war began in 1861, Alexander H. Stephens, the South's vice president, identified slavery as the "cornerstone" of the Confederacy. But those who took up arms for southern independence understood the conflict as a "struggle for liberty." White southerners had inherited from the antebellum era a definition of freedom that centered on local self-government, opportunities for economic self-sufficiency, security of property—including property in slaves—and resistance to northern efforts to "enslave" their region. Confederate victory was indispensable to maintaining these traditions. "I am engaged in the glorious cause of liberty and justice," wrote an Alabama corporal, with no sense of incongruity, in 1862.[1]

"The magic word *Freedom*," in the words of one Pennsylvania recruit, also shaped how Union soldiers understood the conflict. The war's purpose, wrote Samuel McIlvaine, a sergeant from Indiana, was to preserve the American nation as "the beacon light of liberty and freedom to the human race." But as the war progressed, prewar understandings of liberty gave way to something new. Millions of northerners who had not been abolitionists before the war became convinced that securing the Union as an embodiment of liberty required the destruction of slavery. "The maintenance of our free institutions," wrote a Massachusetts private in 1863, "must of *necessity* result in the freedom

9 5

The illustration adorning a piece of patriotic sheet music exemplifies how the Civil War fused even more emphatically than in the past the symbols of liberty and nationhood. (Library of Congress)

of every human being over whom the stars and stripes wave." For Lincoln, the war's deepest meaning lay in the "new birth of freedom" occasioned by the abolition of slavery. "In giving freedom to the slave," he told Congress in December 1862 on the eve of the Emancipation Proclamation, "we assure freedom to the free—honorable alike in what we give and what we preserve."[2]

Never was freedom's protean and contested nature more evident than during the Civil War. "We all declare for liberty," Lincoln observed in 1864, "but in using the same *word* we do not all mean the same *thing*." To the North, freedom meant for "each man" to enjoy "the product of his labor"; to southern whites, it conveyed mastership—the power to do "as they please with other men, and the product of other men's labor."[3] The Union's triumph consolidated the northern understanding of freedom as the national norm. In the process, the meaning of freedom, and the identity of those entitled to enjoy its blessings, were themselves transformed.

Throughout American history, wars have been a vital force in expanding the boundaries of the nation's "imagined community." The War for Independence catalyzed abolition in the North. Women would win the right to vote after World War I, eighteen-year-olds during the war in Vietnam. With the Union's victory in 1865, the abolitionist vision of America also triumphed. Liberty became a universal principle; citizenship was proclaimed the birthright of all Americans. "It is a singular fact," Wendell Phillips wrote in 1866, "that, unlike all other nations, this nation has yet a question as to what makes or constitutes a citizen." From the Civil War emerged the principle of a national citizenship whose members enjoyed the equal protection of the laws, regardless of race.

Early in 1865, the Supreme Court, which eight years earlier had declared blacks forever excluded from the American "family," admitted an African-American lawyer, John S. Rock of Boston, to practice before it. There could no longer be "even the shadow of a doubt," wrote Francis Lieber, that blacks were citizens, entitled to protection by the federal government. Not simply the logic of liberty but the enlistment of 200,000 black men in the Union armed forces during the second half of the war placed black citizenship on the postwar agenda. The inevitable consequence of black military service, one senator observed in 1864, was that "the black man is henceforth to assume a new status among us." In the same year Lincoln, who before the war had never supported suffrage for African-Americans, urged Governor Michael Hahn of Unionist Louisiana to work for the partial enfranchisement of blacks, singling out soldiers as especially deserving. At some future time, he observed, they might again be called upon to "keep the *jewel of Liberty* in the family of freedom." Racism was hardly eradicated from national life. But by 1865, declared George

William Curtis, editor of *Harper's Weekly*, the war and emancipation had transformed a government "for white men" into one "for mankind."[4]

But more than redrawing the boundaries of citizenship, the Civil War linked the progress of freedom directly to the power of the national state. "It is war," declared the nineteenth-century German historian Heinrich von Treitschke, "which turns a people into a nation." Begun to preserve the old Union, the Civil War brought into being a new American nation-state. The mobilization of the Union's resources for modern war created what one Republican leader called "a new government," with greatly expanded powers and responsibilities. Equally important, the war forged a new national self-consciousness. "Liberty . . . true liberty," Lieber proclaimed, "requires a country." This was the moral of one of the era's most popular works of fiction, Edward Everett Hale's short story "The Man Without a Country," published in 1863. Hale's protagonist, Philip Nolan, in a fit of anger curses the land of his birth. As punishment, he is condemned to live on a ship, never to set foot on American soil or hear the name "the United States" spoken. He learns that to be deprived of national identity is to lose one's sense of self.[5]

This intense new nationalism, reinforced by the identification of the nation with freedom, automatically made criticism of the war effort—or, in Republican eyes, opposition to the policies of the Lincoln administration—seem equivalent to treason. Although there had been sporadic persecution of opponents of the Mexican War, the Civil War presented, for the first time since the Revolution, the issue of the limits of wartime dissent. "War," insisted Horatio Seymour, the Democratic governor of New York, "does not extinguish liberty." During the conflict, replied the Republican *New York Times*, "the safety of the nation is the supreme law." Lincoln was hardly an aspiring despot, but neither was preserving civil liberties, according to one of his biographers, David Donald, his "primary concern." The same could be said of Confederate officials, who allowed hundreds of Unionists to be imprisoned by military tribunals, many others to be violently driven from their homes, and a few to suffer summary execution by the army or civilian authorities. But since the North emerged victorious, it was the Lincoln administration's policies that established precedents for the future.

Although recent research has considerably reduced the estimate of arbitrary arrests by military authorities in the North, they still numbered in the thousands, ranging from opposition newspaper editors and Democratic politicians to ordinary civilians like the Chicago man briefly imprisoned for calling the president a "damned fool." With the Constitution unclear as to who possessed the authority to suspend the writ of habeas corpus (that is, to hold a prisoner without charge), Lincoln claimed the right under the presidential war powers and twice suspended the writ throughout the entire Union for those accused of "disloyal activities." To be sure, the Democratic press continued to flourish, evincing little sign of intimidation, and both Union and Confederacy held contested elections during the war. But the Civil War experience offered yet another demonstration—to be amply reinforced during World War I—of the fragility of civil liberties in the face of wartime demands for national unity.[6]

While many northern Republicans interpreted the new nationalism as a force for stability and order, equating patriotism with unconditional loyalty to whatever administration happened to hold office, emancipation demonstrated that the newly empowered national state could disrupt existing institutions and expand the realm of freedom. Among reformers, the war inspired a shift from antebellum anti-institutionalism, which saw the purification of the individual as the route to social change, to a state-centered vision in which political power could be harnessed to social betterment. Emancipation would long remain a model of social change, a touchstone for movements demanding other forms of liberation.[7]

The attack on Fort Sumter crystallized in northern minds the direct conflict between freedom and slavery that abolitionists had insisted upon for decades. Before the war, many Americans, North and South, could speak with no sense of irony of their slaveholding republic as an "empire of liberty." But the war, as Frederick Douglass recognized as early as 1862, merged "the cause of the slaves and the cause of the country." To be sure, a generation of northern schoolchildren had learned to recite Daniel Webster's impassioned words spoken on the Senate floor in 1830: "Liberty *and* Union, now and forever, one and inseparable." But Webster was condemning the doctrine of states' rights, not the South's "peculiar institution." When Douglass proclaimed that "Liberty and Union have become identical," his target was chattel slavery—now viewed as not simply a moral abomination but an affront to national power. The master's undiluted sovereignty over his slaves, insisted Charles Sumner, the antislavery senator from Massachusetts, was incompatible with the "paramount rights of the national Government." And the destruction of slavery—by presidential proclamation, legislation, and constitutional amendment—was a key act in the nation-building process. It announced the appearance of a new kind of national state, one powerful enough to eradicate the central institution of southern society and the country's largest concentration of wealth.[8]

The scale of the Union's triumph and the sheer drama of emancipation fused nationalism, morality, and the language of freedom in an entirely new combination. As during the American Revolution, religious and secular understandings of freedom were joined in a rhetoric of national destiny. "As He died to make men holy, let us die to make men free," proclaimed "The Battle Hymn of the Republic." Proponents of America's millennial mission interpreted the Civil War as a divine chastisement for this paramount national sin (a vocabulary the non-churchgoing Lincoln himself adopted in his second inaugural address). But with emancipation the war also offered an opportunity for national regeneration, as well as providing incontrovertible proof of the progressive nature and global significance of the country's historical development. Long after the war had ended, Lincoln and the emancipated slave would remain symbols of freedom and American patriotism.[9]

"What Is Freedom?"

With the Union's triumph, freedom truly defined the nation's existence. A "new nation" emerged from the war, declared Illinois congressman Isaac N. Arnold, new because it was "wholly free." Central to this vision was the antebellum principle of free labor, now further strengthened as a definition of the good society by the North's triumph. In the free labor vision of a reconstructed South, emancipated blacks, enjoying the same opportunities for advancement as northern workers and motivated by the same quest for self-improvement, would labor more productively than slaves. Meanwhile, northern capital and migrants would energize the economy. Eventually, the South would come to resemble the "free society" of the North, with public schools, small towns, and independent producers. Unified on the basis of free labor, proclaimed Carl Schurz, a refugee from the failed German revolution of 1848 who rose to become a leader of the Republican Party, America would become "a republic, greater, more populous, freer, more prosperous, and more powerful, than any state" in history.[10]

The concrete reality of emancipation posed freedom as a historical and substantive issue, rather than a philosophical or metaphorical one. It raised in the most direct possible form the question of the relationship between property rights and personal rights, between personal, political, and economic liberty. "What is freedom?" asked Congressman James A. Garfield in 1865. "Is it the bare privilege of not being chained? If this is all, then freedom is a bitter mockery, a cruel delusion." Did freedom mean simply the absence of slavery, or did it imply other rights for the emancipated slaves, and if so, which ones: civil equality, the suffrage, ownership of property? If the abolition of slavery reinforced freedom's status as the keyword of political discourse, this made control of its definition all the more important. Instead of a predetermined category or static concept, freedom became a terrain of conflict, its substance open to different, sometimes contradictory interpretations.[11]

"Freedom," declared one black minister, "lived in the black heart long before freedom was born." In the slave quarters, a fugitive who reached the North later recalled, the "constant theme" of conversations was "the desire for freedom." Slaves could hardly remain indifferent to the currents of thought unleashed by the American Revolution, or the language of democracy and liberty that circulated in the antebellum South no less than in the North. Nor were they unaware of the growing national struggle over slavery's future. Indeed, on the eve of the Civil War, President James Buchanan warned that "agitation of the slavery question" had inspired among the slaves "vague notions of freedom."[12]

Slaves' ideas, however, were anything but vague. In bondage, African-Americans had forged their own understanding of freedom, shaped by their experience as slaves and observation of the free society around them. Adopting the nation's democratic and egalitarian rhetoric as their own, slaves interpreted it in light of the compelling biblical story of Exodus, in which a chosen people suffers a long period of bondage only to be released through divine intervention. Slaves saw themselves simultaneously as individuals deprived of their rights and as a people lacking self-determination. Thus, freedom meant both escaping the myriad injustices of slavery—punishment by the lash, the separation of families, denial of access to education, the sexual exploitation of black women by their owners—and collective empowerment, a share in the rights and entitlements of American citizens.[13]

If slavery was part of God's plan, the outbreak of the Civil War heralded blacks' impending passage to the Promised Land of American freedom. Attitudes and aspirations long hidden from outside scrutiny now burst forth, as the South's 4 million slaves, uninvited, entered nineteenth-century America's "public sphere." Black preachers and political leaders (often one and the same persons) proclaimed a new Gospel of Freedom. God had answered His people's prayers and the day of Jubilee had come. Long before Lincoln made emancipation a war aim, blacks, North and South, were calling the conflict the "freedom war." Acting on this understanding, slaves by the thousands in 1861 and 1862 fled the plantations and headed for Union lines, placing the future of slavery on the political agenda and helping to propel a reluctant North down the road to emancipation.[14]

In a society that had made political participation a core element of freedom, the right to vote inevitably became central to the former slaves' desire for empowerment and autonomy. As Frederick Douglass put it soon after the South's surrender in 1865, "slavery is not abolished until the black man has the ballot." Democracy itself dictated this conclusion. In a "monarchial government," Douglass explained, no "special" disgrace applied to those denied the franchise. But "where universal suffrage is the rule," to exclude blacks was to brand them with "the stigma of inferiority." As soon as the Civil War ended, and in some parts of the South even earlier, free blacks and emancipated slaves came together in conventions, parades, and petition drives to demand the suffrage and, on occasion, to organize their own "freedom ballots." Anything less than full citizenship would betray the nation's democratic promise and the war's meaning and doom former slaves to the quasi-freedom to which free blacks had previously been subjected.

Throughout Reconstruction, blacks remained "irrepressible democrats." And long after they had been stripped of the franchise, they would recall the act of voting as a defiance of the norms of white supremacy and regard "the loss of suffrage as being the loss of freedom." Having received their freedom through an unparalleled exercise of national power, moreover, African-Americans identified fully with the new nation-state. On July 4, 1865, Charleston blacks, a young white resident of the city recorded in her diary, held a "grand celebration," while whites "shut themselves within doors." For years after the Civil War, white southerners would shun celebrations of Independence Day, while former slaves appropriated the holiday for themselves. To this day, few African-Americans share the instinctive sense among so many whites that freedom requires reining in federal authority.[15]

Also crucial to the former slaves' definition of freedom was economic autonomy. When General William T. Sherman met with a group of black ministers in Savannah in January 1865, shortly after cutting a swath through Georgia in his March to the Sea, their spokesman, Garrison Frazier, offered a succinct definition of slavery and freedom as understood by those just emerging from bondage. Slavery, said Frazier, was "receiving . . . the work of another man, and not by his consent." Freedom meant "placing us where we could reap the fruit of our own labor." Genuine economic freedom, Frazier insisted, could only be attained through ownership of land, for without land, blacks' labor would continue to be exploited by their former owners. On the land, communities would arise where former slaves could enjoy a modicum of economic independence, complete with churches, schools, and newly stabilized families. Only land, wrote Merrimon Howard, a former slave, would enable "the poor class to enjoy the sweet boon of freedom."[16]

In its individual elements and much of its language, the attempt by former slaves to breathe substantive meaning into emancipation recalled definitions of freedom widely shared among white Americans: self-ownership, family stability, religious liberty, marketplace equality, political participation, and economic autonomy. But these elements coalesced into a vision very much their own. Freedom meant something quite different to men and women who had long enjoyed its blessings than to those to whom it had always been denied. For whites, freedom, no matter how defined, was a given, a birthright to be defended. For African-Americans, it was an open-ended process, a broad, multifaceted concept, a millennial transformation of every facet of their lives and of the society and culture that had sustained slavery in the first place. Rather than a metaphor, slavery was a traumatic experience, which would long help to shape their conception of themselves and their place in American society. Although the freedpeople failed to achieve full freedom as they understood it, their expansive definition did much to shape the nation's political agenda during the turbulent era of Reconstruction that followed the Civil War.[17]

Blacks, of course, were not to chart their path from slavery to freedom alone. Southern whites, especially a planter class devastated by wartime destruction and the loss of their slave property, sought to implement a different understanding of emancipation's consequences. Early in 1865, a local white resident wrote to an Atlanta newspaper that the war had kindled the "spirit of freedom . . . in the breast of the slaves." Southern whites, the author concluded, failed to appreciate that blacks, no less than themselves, possessed the "love of freedom." Still, in the war's immediate aftermath, the South's white leadership defined black freedom in the narrowest conceivable manner. As the northern journalist Sidney Andrews discovered late in 1865, "the whites seem wholly unable to comprehend that freedom for the negro means the same thing as freedom for them. They readily enough admit that the Government has made him free, but appear to believe that they have the right to exercise the same old control." Convinced that the survival of the plantation system was essential to maintaining economic stability and racial supremacy, southern leaders sought to revive the antebellum definition of freedom as if nothing had changed. Freedom still meant hierarchy and mastery; it was a privilege, not a right, a legal status rather than an open-ended entitlement. Certainly, it implied neither economic autonomy nor civil and political equality. "A man may be free and yet not independent," Mississippi planter Samuel Agnew observed in his diary in 1865. "A man may be free and still not have the right to vote," echoed a delegate to Virginia's constitutional convention two years later. The white South's general stance was summed up by a Kentucky newspaper: the former slave was *free, but free only to labor.*"

Rejecting the idea that emancipation implied civil or political equality or opportunities to acquire property or advance economically, rights northerners deemed essential to a free society, most white southerners insisted that blacks must remain a dependent plantation workforce in a laboring situation not very different from slavery. During Presidential Reconstruction—the period from 1865 to 1867 when Lincoln's successor, Andrew Johnson, gave the white South a free hand in determining the contours of Reconstruction—southern state governments enforced this view of black freedom by enacting the notorious Black Codes, which denied blacks equality before the law and political rights, and imposed on them mandatory year-long labor contracts, coercive apprenticeship regulations, and criminal penalties for breach of contract. Through these laws, the South's white leadership sought to ensure that plantation agriculture survived emancipation.[18]

Thus, the death of slavery did not automatically mean the birth of freedom. But the Black Codes so flagrantly violated free labor principles that they invoked the wrath of the Republican North. Southern reluctance to accept the reality of emancipation resulted in a monumental struggle between President Andrew Johnson and the Republican Congress over the legacy of the Civil War. The result was the enactment of laws and constitutional amendments that redrew the boundaries of citizenship and expanded the definition of freedom for all Americans.

"Will the United States give them freedom or its shadow?" a northern educator asked from North Carolina in 1865. As the war drew to a close, the Republican-dominated Congress struggled to define precisely the repercussions of the destruction of slavery. Even Congressman William Holman, an Indiana Democrat hardly known as an advocate of emancipation, noted that "mere exemption from servitude is a miserable idea of freedom." By 1865, virtually all northerners agreed that property rights in man must be abrogated, contractual relations substituted for the discipline of the lash, and the master's patriarchal authority over the former slaves abolished. The phrase most often repeated in these debates—the "right to the fruits of his labor"—was thought to embody the essential distinction between slavery and freedom.[19]

Much of the ensuing conflict over Reconstruction revolved around the problem, as Senator Lyman Trumbull of Illinois put it, of defining "what slavery is and what liberty is." The Thirteenth Amendment, ratified in 1865, irrevocably abolished slavery; "that I think," said one Democratic senator, "ought to be sufficient for the lovers of freedom in this country." But it was not. "We must see to it," announced Senator William Stewart at the opening of Congress in December 1865, "that the man made free by the Constitution of the United States . . . is a freeman indeed." Most insistent on identifying and protecting the basic rights of the freedpeople were the Radical Republicans, longtime foes of slavery and advocates of freedom as a principle limited to "neither black nor white," in the words of Senator Henry Wilson of Massachusetts. Freedom, said another Radical, William D. Kelley of Pennsylvania, was "a right so universal . . . that we will guarantee it at whatever cost to the poorest child that breathes the air of our country." In the wake of emancipation, the legal and patriotic doctrine of "free air" had at length come to the United States.

By 1866, a consensus had emerged within the Republican Party that civil equality was an essential attribute of freedom. The Civil War had elevated "equality" to a status in the vocabulary of freedom it had not enjoyed since the Revolution. At Gettysburg, Lincoln spoke of a nation "conceived in Liberty, and dedicated to the proposition that all men are created equal"—an invocation of the Declaration of Independence and a recognition of the inner logic of emancipation. In a remarkable, if temporary, reversal of political traditions, the newly empowered national state now sought to identify and protect the rights of all Americans. The first statutory definition of American citizenship, the Civil Rights Act of 1866, declared all persons born in the United States (except Indians) national citizens and spelled out rights they were to enjoy equally without regard to race. Equality before the law was central to the measure, as were free labor values: no state could deprive any citizen of the right to make contracts, bring lawsuits, or enjoy equal protection of the security of person and property.[20]

But it was the Fourteenth Amendment, approved by Congress in 1866 and ratified two years later, that for the first time enshrined in the Constitution the ideas of birthright citizenship and equal rights for all Americans. The amendment prohibited states from abridging "the privileges and immunities of citizens" or denying them "the equal protection of the law." This broad language opened the door for future Congresses and the federal courts to breathe meaning into the guarantee of legal equality, a process that has occupied the courts for much of the twentieth century. Although most immediately intended to raise the former slaves to the status of equal citizens, the amendment's language did not apply only to blacks. The principle of equality before the law affected all Americans, including, as one congressman noted, "the millions of people of foreign birth who will flock to our shores . . . to find here a land of liberty." Soon afterward, the Fifteenth Amendment, ratified in 1870, barred the states from making race a qualification for voting. "What humbug to call this a free government," wrote a New Yorker, "when you will not allow a man to vote, if he happens to be black." Strictly speaking, suffrage remained a privilege rather than a right, subject to numerous regulations by the states. But by the time Re-

An 1874 lithograph celebrating the promise of black freedom centers on a famous speech by Robert B. Elliott, congressman from South Carolina, in favor of the bill that became the Civil Rights Act of 1875. The print illustrates the centrality of military service to black claims to citizenship, and the linkage of the ideals of freedom and equality during Reconstruction. (Chicago Historical Society)

construction legislation had run its course, the federal government had redefined freedom to embody civil and political equality, regardless of race.[21]

The amendments and civil rights laws reflected the intersection of the two products of the Civil War era—the newly empowered national state and the idea of a national citizenship enjoying equality before the law. They established not only a new definition of freedom but a new mode for its enforcement. Rather than a threat to liberty, the federal government, declared Charles Sumner, had become "the custodian of freedom." Transcending boundaries of race and region, what Carl Schurz called "the great Constitutional revolution" of Reconstruction transformed the federal system, and with it, the discourse of rights so central to American freedom. Before the Civil War, disenfranchised groups laying claim to their rights were far more likely to draw inspiration from the Declaration of Independence than the Constitution. (The only mention of equality in the original Constitution, after all, had occurred in the clause granting each state an equal number of senators.) But the rewriting of the Constitution during Reconstruction not only promoted a sense of the document's malleability, but suggested that the rights of the individual citizen were intimately connected to federal power.

The Bill of Rights had linked civil liberties and the autonomy of the states. Its language—"Congress shall pass no law"—reflected the belief that concentrated power was a threat to freedom. The Reconstruction amendments assumed that rights required political power to enforce them. They authorized the federal government to override state actions that deprived citizens of equality, and each ended with a clause empowering Congress to "enforce" the amendment with "appropriate legislation." Thus began the process of requiring the states to abide by the protections of civil liberties inscribed in the Bill of Rights. The Reconstruction amendments transformed the Constitution from a document primarily concerned with federal-state relations and the rights of property to a vehicle through which members of vulnerable minorities could stake a claim to substantive freedom and seek protection against misconduct by all levels of government.[22]

It is tempting to view the expansion of citizens' rights during Reconstruction as the logical fulfillment of a vision articulated by the founding fathers but for pragmatic reasons not actually implemented when the Constitution was drafted. Yet boundaries of exclusion had long been intrinsic to the meaning of American freedom. Reconstruction represented less a fulfillment of the Revolution's principles than a radical repudiation of the nation's actual practice for the previous seven decades. Indeed, it was precisely for this reason that the era's laws and constitutional amendments aroused such bitter opposition. The underlying principles—that the federal government possessed the power to define and protect citizens' rights, and that blacks were equal members of the body politic—were striking departures in American law. President Andrew Johnson, who vetoed bill after bill only to see them reenacted by Congress, claimed with some justification that federal protection of blacks' civil rights, together with the broad conception of national power that lay behind it, violated "all our experience as a people." "We are not of the same race," insisted Senator Thomas Hendricks of Indiana. "We are so different that we ought not to compose one political community."[23]

Reconstruction Republicans rejected this reasoning, but their universalism too had its limits. In his remarkable "Composite Nation" speech of 1869, Frederick Douglass condemned prejudice against immigrants from China, insisting that America's destiny was to serve as an asylum for people "gathered here from all corners of the globe by a common aspiration for national liberty." Any form of exclusion, he insisted, contradicted the essence of democracy. A year later, Charles Sumner moved to strike the word "white" from naturalization requirements. Senators from the western states objected vociferously. They were willing to admit blacks to citizenship but not persons of Asian origin. At their insistence, the naturalization law was amended to add Africans to the "whites" already eligible to obtain citizenship when migrating from abroad. The ban on Asians remained intact; the racial boundaries of nationality had been redrawn, but not eliminated. The juxtaposition of the Fourteenth Amendment and the 1870 naturalization law created a strange anomaly: Asian immigrants remained ineligible for citizenship, but their nativeborn children automatically became Americans.[24]

Advocates of women's rights likewise encountered the limits of Reconstruction egalitarianism. Like the Revolution, the Civil War unleashed a "contagion of liberty." Given the era's intense focus on equality, the movement for women's suffrage, which had more or less suspended operations during the war to join in the fight for Union and abolition, saw Reconstruction as a golden opportunity to claim for women their own emancipation. Antebellum rhetoric equating the condition of women with slavery took on new value as a vocabulary of protest. No less than blacks, proclaimed Elizabeth Cady Stanton, who had organized the Seneca Falls Convention nearly twenty years earlier, women had arrived at a "transition period, from slavery to freedom." Many believed that women should follow the same path to freedom trod by the slaves. The rewriting of the Constitution, declared suffrage leader Olympia Brown, offered the opportunity to sever the blessings of freedom from race and sex— two "accidents of the body" that did not deserve legal recognition—and to "bury the black man and the woman in the citizen." The "modern theory of individual rights" so powerfully reinforced by the war and Reconstruction, declared the prolific feminist writer Jane Croly, "demands that a woman shall be free to live her life" as she and she alone determined. Suffrage, insisted a third feminist writer, would secure for women "the freedom of an American citizen" and release her from "political bondage."[25]

So, too, women should now enjoy the economic opportunities of free labor. The Civil War had propelled many women into the wage labor force and left many others without a male provider, adding increased urgency to the antebellum argument that the right to work outside the home was essential to women's freedom. Women, wrote Susan B. Anthony, desired an "honorable independence" no less fully than men, and working for wages was no more "degrading" to one sex than the other. To be sure, the racially and sexually segmented labor market fundamentally contradicted the idea that paid work offered a route to female independence. To the end of the century, the largest employment categories for women remained domestic service and low-wage industrial work, hardly paths to economic autonomy. Feminists searched for ways to make real for women the promise of free labor. Every issue of Mary Livermore's new women's rights journal, *The Agitator*, carried stories lamenting the limited job opportunities and unequal pay that confronted females entering the labor market. In *The New Northwest*, editor Abigail Scott Duniway (whose writings supported her six children and husband after his business failed) went even further, insisting that "liberty for married women" required remuneration for housework and an equal share in family property.[26]

At feminism's most radical edge, emancipation inspired demands for the liberation of women from the "slavery" of marriage. The same "law of equality that has revolutionized the state," declared Stanton, was "knocking at the door of our homes." Property in slaves had been abolished, but "the right of property in women" remained intact, and if "unpaid" labor was now illegitimate on southern plantations, how could it be justified within free households? In Stanton's writings and speeches, demands for liberalizing divorce laws (which generally required evidence of adultery, desertion, or extreme abuse to terminate a marriage) and recognizing "woman's control over her own body" (including protection against domestic violence and what later generations would call birth control), moved to the center of feminist concerns. These questions, she found, struck a "deeper chord" among her female audience than the right to vote. "Women respond to my divorce speech as they never did to suffrage," Stanton related. "Oh! How they flock to me with their sorrows." "Our rotten marriage institution," one Ohio woman wrote, "is the main obstacle in the way of woman's freedom." Susan B. Anthony, who remained unmarried her entire life, believed that "an epoch of single women" was fast approaching: "the woman who will *not be ruled* must live without marriage."[27]

Even more radical in applying the logic of liberty to personal life was Victoria Woodhull. "This thing we call Freedom," said Woodhull, a magnetic personality and spellbinding orator, "is a large word, implying a good deal more than people have ever yet been able to recognize." Rather than "a collection of different and unrelated principles," Woodhull insisted, freedom was a unitary idea, resting on individual sovereignty in all realms of life. For women, it implied not only the right to vote and full economic equality but "freedom of the affections." "I am a Free Lover," the irrepressible Woodhull declared. "I have an inalienable, constitutional and natural right to love whom I may, to love as long or as short a period as I can; to change that love every day if I please."[28]

Reviled as enemies of civilized society, the era's small band of self-proclaimed free lovers were hardly libertines; even as they exalted "social freedom" and thundered against existing laws for "enslaving" women to loveless marriages, most led conventional domestic lives. But attacks on the institution of marriage by Stanton, Woodhull, and others thoroughly alienated defenders of public morality. Most damaging to the movement, in the short run, was Woodhull's public revelation of the Beecher-Tilton affair, a scandal involving an amorous relationship between Henry Ward Beecher, the nation's preeminent divine, and Elizabeth Tilton, wife of a leading reform editor. Woodhull's "crime" was making matters public that were widely thought to be properly private. That an advocate of "free love" committed the transgression made it appear doubly outrageous. Respectable opinion rallied to Beecher's defense and the resulting furor caused women's rights activists to pull back from public discussion of divorce. The scandal contributed to the passage of the Comstock law of 1873, barring from the mails "obscene" materials, including information on birth control.[29]

But this cause célèbre was not the only reason why forthright calls for "social freedom" waned. Even as Stanton and her followers spoke of liberalizing divorce, former slaves, young and old, flocked to the army, the Freedmen's Bureau, and local authorities to legalize their marriages for the first time. To blacks, the denial of family rights was a basic evil of slavery and the right to form stable families a defining characteristic of freedom. For most white women as well, including many feminists, marriage remained a sacrament and lifetime bond, not a contractual arrangement dissolvable at will. In the *Woman's Journal*, Lucy Stone denounced "this loose, pestiferous talk in favor of *easy divorce*" for weakening an institution that offered emotional intimacy and economic support to women in a world where few were truly able to live independently. The solution to domestic violence against women, Stone insisted, was not divorce but state protection of battered wives and punishment of wife-beaters.[30]

The largest women's organization of the late nineteenth century, the Women's Christian Temperance Union (WCTU), with 150,000 members by 1892, rallied its followers under the slogan, "Home Protection." Although Frances Willard, the organization's president, insisted that the "larger liberty of woman" lay in the freedom to develop individually and to contribute to the social welfare, the WCTU appealed most powerfully to the millions of women who defined their roles as wives and mothers. Determined to ban hard liquor from American life, the WCTU eventually endorsed woman suffrage, but it could never bring itself to favor easier divorce. Nor did other reformers respond favorably to what the labor leader Samuel Gompers called Woodhull's "extreme doctrine." When the New York branch of the International Workingmen's Association came under Woodhull's influence, Karl Marx, then residing in England, himself ordered its expulsion. Labor, Gompers noted, would never support a program "that threw overboard the family institution." Indeed, commented one female opponent of women's suffrage, the greatest barrier to the movement's success was the "intuitive sense," among both men and women, that the "political independence of women would be the wreck of our present domestic institutions."[31]

Those who continued to raise the issue of birth control, moreover, found themselves subject to legal prosecution. Scores of persons were arrested under the Comstock law, among them the anarchist and free lover Ezra Heywood, sentenced to two years in prison for distributing *Cupid's Yokes,* a plea for sexual freedom within and outside marriage. Meanwhile, the WCTU established a Department for the Suppression of Impure Literature. For all these reasons, discussions of the reform of marriage and a woman's right to control her own sexuality retreated from public life. Not until the twentieth century would "social freedom," and the related question of the right to freedom of speech on sexual matters, resurface as significant public issues within the feminist movement and beyond.[32]

All in all, Reconstruction did little to expand the definition of women's freedom. Reconstruction Republicans saw emancipation as restoring to blacks the natural right to family life, in which men would take their place as heads of the household and women theirs in the domestic sphere from which slavery had unnaturally removed them. Restoring the freedman's "manhood" and women's right to raise their children was central to the meaning of freedom. Several congressmen explicitly denied that the Thirteenth Amendment's prohibition of "involuntary servitude" applied to relations within the family. "A husband has a right of property in the service of his wife," said one, which the abolition of slavery was not intended to destroy. Along with the right to "personal liberty," declared Republican John Kasson of Iowa, the male-headed family, embodying the "right of a husband to his wife" and of a "father to his child," comprised the "three great fundamental natural rights of human society." When it came to the suffrage, few in Congress, even among Radical Republicans, responded sympathetically to feminists' demands. Reconstruction, they insisted, was the "Negro's hour" (the hour, that is, of the black male). Even Charles Sumner, the Senate's most uncompromising egalitarian, as the feminist Francis Gage lamented, fell "far short of the great idea of liberty" so far as the rights of women were concerned.[33]

Thus, even as it rejected the racialized definition of freedom that had emerged in the first half of the nineteenth century, Reconstruction left the law of marriage and conventions of gender relations largely intact. When women tried to use the rewritten legal code and Constitution to claim equal rights, they found the courts singularly unreceptive. Myra Bradwell invoked the prerogatives of free labor (including the right to choose one's occupation) in challenging an Illinois statute limiting the practice of law to men, but the Supreme Court in 1873 rebuffed her claim. Free labor principles, the justices declared, did not apply to women, since "the law of the Creator" had assigned them to "the domestic sphere." Soon afterward, Virginia Minor challenged the limitation of voting rights to men on the grounds that denial of the suffrage violated the "perfect freedom" all citizens should enjoy. Chief Justice Morrison Waite responded that citizenship was fully compatible with disenfranchisement; it meant "membership in a nation and nothing more."[34]

The Court's arguments regarding women were harbingers of a more general narrowing of the meaning of citizenship that would soon strip from blacks many of the protections extended by the Reconstruction Congress. Among feminists, disappointment with what they deemed a betrayal by male abolitionists and Radicals contributed to a shift away from "equal rights feminism," grounded in the abolitionist movement's universalist category of "equal citizen," to a feminism of "difference," in which women's claims rested on the unique moral contribution their special nature enabled them to make to American society. It also produced a split in the movement between those who saw the Fourteenth and Fifteenth Amendments as steps toward truly universal suffrage, and others who deemed the enfranchisement of black men a new barrier to women's voting. The latter group concluded that feminists must free themselves from dependence on the antislavery tradition, form fully independent organizations, and locate new allies wherever they could find them.[35]

Despite its palpable limitations, Reconstruction wrote a remarkable chapter in the story of American freedom. Most remarkable of all was the brief moment of Radical Reconstruction in the South (1867–77), during which, as one former slave later put it, "the tocsin of freedom sounded," and black men, for the first time in American history, enjoyed a genuine share of political power. The southern experiment in interracial democracy proved shortlived, succumbing during the 1870s to violent opposition by the Ku Klux Klan and the North's retreat from the ideal of equality. Southern black communities never forgot this injustice. "The Yankees helped free us, so they say," former slave

Thomas Hall told an interviewer in the 1930s, "but they let us be put back in slavery again." But the Reconstruction amendments remained embedded in the Constitution, sleeping giants to be awakened by the efforts of subsequent generations to redeem the promise of freedom for the descendants of slavery. The importance of this accomplishment ought not to be underestimated: repudiating the racialized definition of democracy that had emerged in the first half of the nineteenth century was a major step toward reinvigorating the idea of freedom as a universal entitlement.[36]

Even while it lasted, however, Reconstruction revealed many of the tensions inherent in nineteenth-century definitions of freedom. Efforts to give the former slaves land failed to receive congressional approval. If emancipation, as Douglass had remarked, represented a convergence of the slaves' interests and those of the nation, eventually those interests, and their respective definitions of freedom, were destined to diverge. Only a minority of Republican policymakers, most notably Radical congressman Thaddeus Stevens, sought to resurrect the older view—the view put forward by the ex-slaves—that without ownership of productive property, genuine freedom was impossible. In this respect, the high hopes inspired by emancipation remained unfulfilled.

Soon after the Civil War ended, a group of former slaves on Edisto Island, South Carolina, protested their eviction from land that had been assigned them by General Sherman shortly after his meeting with Savannah ministers. Landless and homeless, they lamented, they would be economically dependent on their former owners: "this is not the condition of really free men." Long after the end of Reconstruction, a sense of disappointment over the failure to distribute land lingered. "I knows I spected a lot different from what I did get from freedom . . . ," William Coleman, an elderly ex-slave, recalled in the 1930s. "Yes, sir, they should have given us part of Master's land as us poor old slaves we made what our Masters had."[37]

In retrospect, Reconstruction emerges as a decisive moment in fixing the dominant understanding of economic freedom as self-ownership and the right to compete in the labor market, rather than propertied independence. The policy of according black men a place in the political nation while denying them the benefits of land reform fortified the idea that the free citizen could be a dependent laborer. Thus, Reconstruction helped to solidify the separation of political and economic spheres, the juxtaposition of political equality and economic inequality, as the American way. Henceforth, it would be left to dissenters—labor radicals, populists, socialists, and the like—to resurrect the older idea of economic autonomy as the essence of freedom.

"Welcome to the Land of Freedom," from *Frank Leslie's Illustrated Newspaper*, 2 July 1887, one of the earliest depictions of the Statue of Liberty as a symbol of welcome for immigrants arriving in New York harbor. (Library of Congress)

6

Liberty of Contract and Its Discontents

An *immense crowd* gathered in New York Harbor on October 28, 1886, for the unveiling of *Liberty Enlightening the World,* a fitting symbol for a nation now wholly free. The idea for the statue originated at a French dinner party in the summer of 1865. It was conceived by Edouard de Laboulaye, an educator and the author of several books on the United States, as a response to the assassination of Abraham Lincoln. The statue, de Laboulaye hoped, would exemplify Franco-American friendship (somewhat tarnished by French machinations in Mexico during the Civil War) and celebrate the triumph, through the Union's victory, of American freedom. Measuring over 150 feet from torch to toe and standing atop a huge pedestal, the edifice was the tallest man-made structure in the western hemisphere, exceeding in height, newspapers noted with pride, the Colossus of Rhodes, a wonder of the ancient world.

In time, the Statue of Liberty, as it came to be called, would take its place as Americans' most revered national icon, a symbol of welcome to immigrants "yearning to breathe free," in the words of Emma Lazarus's poem inscribed on its base, and, more generally, an emblem of freedom and nationhood. In the years since its dedication, the statue's familiar image has been reproduced by folk artists in every conceivable medium, and has been used by advertisers to sell everything from cigarettes and lawn mowers to war bonds. Political cartoonists have invoked the statue to comment on political events and movements, from presidential elections to McCarthyism, feminism, and ethnic and racial intolerance. As its appropriation by Chinese students in the Tiananmen Square protests of 1989 demonstrated, the statue has become a powerful international symbol as well.

In 1886, however, the year of the "great upheaval"—a massive strike wave that touched every part of the nation—those who dedicated the statue, led by President Grover Cleveland, claimed her as an emblem of political stability and social harmony. Not all Americans accepted this message. Among the many boats traversing New York harbor to celebrate the dedication was one chartered by the New York State Woman Suffrage Association, protesting women's exclusion from "political liberty," as well as the fact that of the 600 dignitaries invited to participate in the unveiling on Bedloe's (now Liberty) Island, 598 were men. A few days after the ceremonies, New Yorkers flocked to the polls to elect their mayor. Nearly seventy thousand voted for Henry George, the candidate of the United Labor Party. George's second-place finish—he eclipsed the total of Republican Theodore Roosevelt and came close to defeating Democrat Abram Hewitt—illustrated the deep social divisions that the statue, for all its grandeur, could not conceal.[1]

Freedom in the Gilded Age

Between the Civil War and the end of the nineteenth century, the United States underwent one of the most profound economic revolutions any country has ever experienced, and witnessed some of the most violent struggles between labor and employers in the history of capitalism. Contemporaries marveled at the triumph of a new economy of coal, iron, and steam over a world centered on agriculture and artisanal production. "One can hardly believe," wrote John Dewey, then a professor at the University of Chicago, in 1899, "there has been a revolution in history so rapid, so extensive, so complete." By the early twentieth century, American manufacturing production had surpassed the combined total of Great Britain, Germany, and France. Railroad mileage tripled between 1860 and 1880, and tripled again by 1920, opening vast new areas to commercial farming, creating a national market for manufactured goods, and inspiring a boom in coal mining and steel production. The voracious appetite for capital of the great trunk railroads facilitated the consolidation of the nation's financial market in Wall Street. By 1900, the process of economic concentration had extended into most branches of industry—a few giant corporations dominated steel, oil, sugar refining, meatpacking, and the manufacture of agricultural machinery. The political influence of these enterprises matched their productive power. In the post–Civil War era, or "Gilded Age," as it was called by Mark Twain, the giant corporations powerfully influenced the activities of both major parties and political decision-making at the national, state, and local levels.

In cities like New York and Philadelphia, artisanal production still survived in many trades, and armies of workers, male and female, labored in their own homes or in the households of others as outworkers and domestics. But inexorably, the factory system came to dominate industrial production. By the turn of the century, nearly half the laborers in manufacturing worked in establishments with more than 250 employees. The new factories drew their labor force from displaced artisans, millions of Americans who moved from farm to city, and millions more who emigrated to the United States from abroad. The effort of corporations to exert managerial prerogatives over this new industrial workforce produced bitter and often violent confrontations whose names have entered the lore of American labor—the Great Railroad Strike, Homestead, Pullman, Coeur d'Alene.[2]

Although real wages rose steadily throughout these years, the result of monetary deflation and falling prices, the prolonged depressions of the 1870s and 1890s, coupled with the pervasive insecurity of employment even in flush times, meant that much of the working class remained desperately poor. At the other end of the economic spectrum, the Gilded Age witnessed an unprecedented accumulation of wealth. By 1890, the richest 1 percent of Americans received the same total income as the bottom half of the population and owned more property than the remaining 99 percent. The emergence of a wealthy and powerful industrial class and a proletariat living on the edge of poverty, coupled with the closing of the frontier (announced by the Census Bureau in 1890), posed a sharp challenge to inherited definitions of freedom. It became increasingly difficult to view wage labor as a temporary resting place on the road to economic independence, or the West as a haven for the dispossessed small producers of the East. The power of the new corporations, seemingly impervious to democratic control, raised equally disturbing questions for the definition of freedom as popular self-government. Concentrated wealth degraded the political process, declared Henry Demarest Lloyd in *Wealth Against Commonwealth* (1894), a book that demonstrated how the Standard Oil Company not only manipulated the market to drive out competition but bribed legislators and in other ways made a mockery of political democracy. "Liberty and monopoly," Lloyd concluded, "cannot live together."[3]

For a minority of workers, the burgeoning industrial system created new modes of freedom. In some industries, craftsmen exercised considerable control over the production process, their autonomy resting on skill and collective self-government rather than property ownership as in earlier times. The "miner's freedom" consisted of elaborate work rules that left skilled underground workers free of managerial supervision on the job. Skilled iron- and steelworkers ruled over a "craftsman's empire"; through their union, they fixed output quotas and controlled the training of apprentices in the technique of iron rolling. Such "freedom," however, applied only to a tiny portion of the industrial labor force and had little bearing on the lives of the new army of unskilled factory operatives. The appearance of what the Massachusetts cotton manufacturer Edward Atkinson called "a permanent factory population" challenged assumptions inherited from antebellum political culture: that liberty rested on the widely diffused ownership of productive property, and that the promise of the New World lay in the opportunity it offered the ordinary citizen to achieve economic autonomy. "The great curse of the Old World—the division of society into classes," declared *The Nation* two years after the end of the Civil War, had come to America.[4]

As the United States matured into an industrial economy and the "labor question" replaced the struggle over slavery as the dominant focus of public life, contemporaries struggled to make sense of the new social and political order and to determine its implications for American freedom. Debates over political economy engaged the attention of millions of Americans, reaching far beyond the tiny academic world into the "public sphere" inhabited by self-educated workingmen and farmers, reformers of all kinds, newspaper editors, and politicians. This broad public discussion produced thousands of books, pamphlets, and articles on such technical issues as land taxation, currency reform, and the subtreasury plan, as well as widespread debate over the social and ethical implications of economic change.

Given the vast expansion of the nation's productive capacity, many Americans viewed the concentration of capital as inevitable, natural, and justified by progress. Among economists, social scientists, and captains of industry, ideas like the worker's right to the fruits of his labor increasingly seemed quaint anachronisms, irrelevant at a time when the modern corporation had replaced the independent producer as the driving force of economic change. Gradually, the old idea of the dignity of labor yielded to an emphasis on the contributions of managers, entrepreneurs, and technology itself to economic progress. By the turn of the century, advanced economics taught that wages were determined by the iron law of supply and demand, and that wealth rightly flowed not to those who labored hardest, but to those with entrepreneurial skills, especially the ability to satisfy consumer needs in a mass market. The close link between freedom and equality, forged in the Revolution and reinforced during the Civil War, appeared increasingly out of date. The task of social science, wrote iron manufacturer Abram Hewitt, was to devise ways of making "men who are equal in liberty" content with the "inequality in . . . distribution" inevitable in modern society.[5]

Among the first to take up this challenge were the self-styled "liberal" reformers, an influential group of editors, academics, and professionals who abandoned the wartime equation of freedom with activism by democratic government. In its place, they elevated a "negative" understanding of freedom as the absence of restraint on autonomous individuals into a moral and political dogma. During the Civil War and early Reconstruction, liberal leaders like E. L. Godkin, editor of *The Nation*, Horace White of the *Chicago Tribune*, and the Republican political activist Carl Schurz had fully embraced the principle that the national state had a responsibility to guarantee equal rights to all citizens regardless of race. But once the framework of legal equality had been established, they came to believe, freedom's further progress must occur in the social and economic realms, not the political. In the face of the Republican Party's degeneration into a set of corrupt state organizations, and demands by women, farmers, and laborers that the government use its new powers to address their grievances, these publicists, who claimed to speak for society's "best men," retreated not only from the Civil War's broad assertion of nationalism and egalitarianism but from democracy itself. Echoing white southerners' complaints that Reconstruction violated principles of good government by expelling men of property from power, liberals became persuaded that spoilsmen and demagogues were manipulating gullible lower-class voters throughout the country, producing such travesties of good government as the Tweed Ring of New York City. The democratic state was in danger of becoming a threat to liberty, rather than liberty's handmaiden. The solution was to return to the long-abandoned principle that voting should be limited to men of property.[6]

Among elite thinkers, a retreat from the previous consensus in favor of manhood suffrage was among the most remarkable developments of the late nineteenth century. "Expressions of doubt and distrust in regard to universal suffrage are heard constantly . . . [at] the top of our society," wrote one observer in 1879. Except in the case of blacks, however, proposals for sweeping restriction of the franchise stood little chance of approval, since as one reformer noted, "men will not vote to disfranchise themselves." But while unable to implement their elitist vision of government, liberals played a major role in popularizing an idea that would achieve hegemonic status among the business and professional classes in the last quarter of the nineteenth century—the equation of freedom with limited government and laissez-faire economics.[7]

With some of the nation's leading newspapers and periodicals at their disposal, liberal reformers took it upon themselves to educate the public in the principles of freedom. Central to their social vision was the idea of contract, ostensibly the embodiment of free will and voluntary action, and an all-purpose metaphor for proper social relationships. "The laws of contract," wrote one reformer, "are the foundation of civilization." In 1861, the British historian of the law Sir Henry Maine had made the oft-quoted observation that the history of "progressive societies" could be described as "a movement *from Status to Contract*." Emancipation and the emergence of the freedpeople as workers whose relations with their former owners were governed by labor contracts rather that the sovereignty of mastership offered a perfect example of this dictum. So long as economic processes and labor relations were governed by contracts freely arrived at by autonomous individuals, Americans had no grounds to complain of a loss of freedom.[8]

The man born a laborer, announced the economist David A. Wells in 1877, would "never be anything but a laborer," and government could do nothing to alter this situation. Indeed, demands by workers that the government enforce an eight-hour day or in other ways intervene in the economy struck liberals as a perfect example of how the misuse of political power posed the gravest threat to liberty. "The right of each man to labor as much or as little as he chooses, and to enjoy his own earnings, is the very foundation stone of . . . freedom," wrote Horace White. The market, not democratic politics, Godkin echoed, was the true realm of freedom: liberty meant "the liberty to buy and sell, and mend and make, where, when, and how we please," without interference by the state. In the Gilded Age, slavery continued to shape discussions of freedom, but in new ways. Liberals invoked the ghost of slavery to discredit efforts to influence the market's operations. Laws regulating labor conditions were a form of slavery, since they deprived free agents of the right to dispose of property, including their own labor, as they saw fit. Thus did the idea of free labor, which originated as a celebration of the independent small producer in a broadly egalitarian society, metamorphosize into a defense of the unfettered operations of the capitalist marketplace.[9]

Just as the idea of the natural superiority of some races to others had earlier been invoked to justify slavery in a free society, social theorists in the Gilded Age called upon science to explain the success and failure of individuals and social classes. Analogies to the natural world pervaded the era's thinking. The growing use of language borrowed from Charles Darwin (often by way of the British social philosopher Herbert Spencer), such as "natural selection," "the struggle for existence," and "the survival of the fittest," became part and parcel of the era's laissez-faire outlook. In the hands of Spencer and his American disciples, what came to be called Social Darwinism offered a powerful critique of all forms of state interference with the "natural" workings of society. Unlike Burkean conservatives, whose politics was rooted in a reverence for tradition, Social Darwinists embraced the idea of constant social change. History, they believed, was a narrative of progress in which, as in nature, simpler forms evolved into more complex ones. The corporation was one of these more advanced forms, more efficient because better adapted to its environment than earlier modes of production. To restrict its operations by legislation would reduce society to an earlier, more primitive level.[10]

Even the severe depressions of the 1870s and 1890s, each of which lasted half a decade and threw millions of Americans out of work, did not shake the general middle-class view that the poor were essentially responsible for their own dire conditions. Charity workers and local governments spent much time and energy distinguishing the "deserving" poor (those destitute through no fault of their own) from the "undeserving," but the former were always defined as exceptions to a general rule. Failure to advance in society bespoke moral incapacity, a lack of "character" (a key term in social discourse on both sides of the Atlantic), the absence of self-reliance, perseverance, and courage in the face of adversity. As late as 1900, half the nation's largest cities offered virtually no poor relief except to those residing in poorhouses. The way for workers to improve their lot was not to form unions—coercive institutions that held their members in "absolute subjection," according to one group of manufacturers—but to practice personal economy, keep out of debt, and educate their children in the principles of the marketplace.[11]

Spencer's most prominent American disciple and the era's most influential Social Darwinist was Yale professor William Graham Sumner, who strove to disabuse Americans of their highly confused notions of freedom. Cries of "wage slavery," and the misguided equation of liberty with a share in political power, Sumner insisted, reflected a dangerous belief that individuals were entitled to a certain standard of living provided, if necessary, by the government. For Sumner, freedom properly understood meant the "abnegation of state power" and a frank acceptance of inequality. Society faced two and only two alternatives: "liberty, inequality, survival of the fittest; not-liberty, equality, survival of the unfittest." Sumner's vision offered as thoroughgoing a defense of laissez-faire individualism as the nineteenth century produced. For him, politics was less a vehicle for expanding freedom than a mode by which individuals defended preexisting liberties against encroachments by others. In 1883, he published an influential work, *What Social Classes Owe to Each Other.* His answer, essentially, was nothing: "in a free state," no one was entitled to claim "help from, and cannot be charged to [offer] help to, another." Government, Sumner believed, existed only to protect "the property of men and the honor of women," not to upset social arrangements decreed by nature.[12]

Laissez-faire conservatism, in one sense an oxymoron given that the unfettered market is not only an agent of constant change but a powerful solvent of traditional values and institutions, sank deep roots in corporate boardrooms and at the most elite universities such as Harvard and Yale. But in elevating unfettered liberty of contract from one element of freedom to its very essence, the courts played perhaps the most significant role. The memory of slavery played a large role in the era's judicial discourse. Yet the courts seemed to understand slavery not as a complex system of economic, political, social, and racial power, but as little more than the denial of the laborer's right to choose his livelihood and bargain for compensation. The identification of freedom of labor with freedom of contract was enshrined in successive decisions of state and federal courts, which struck down state laws regulating economic enterprise as an interference with the right of the free laborer to choose his employment and working conditions and of the entrepreneur to utilize his property as he saw fit.

This line of thinking was pioneered by Justice Stephen J. Field's famous 1873 dissent in the *Slaughter-House* cases, in which he insisted that a butchering monopoly established by Louisiana violated "the right of free labor." An "essential part of liberty . . . in the American sense of the term," Field argued, involved the right to pursue any lawful employment without state interference and to enjoy the fruits of one's labor. The Supreme Court's majority opinion in *Slaughter-House,* which rejected Field's argument and in so doing severely limited the definition of citizenship rights entitled to federal protection, formed a key step in the Court's abandonment of Reconstruction. But Field pointed the way to subsequent decisions that would offer entrepreneurs (if not former slaves) federal protection for the rights secured by the Civil War. "Liberty of contract," not equality before the law for blacks, came to be defined as the meaning of the Fourteenth Amendment.[13]

By the 1880s and for decades thereafter, the courts consistently viewed state regulation of business enterprise—especially interventions in contractual labor relations such as laws establishing maximum hours of work and safe working conditions—as a paternalistic insult to free labor, a throwback to the thinking characteristic of slavery. (Field's belief that freedom also involved the right to the fruits of one's labor was by now lost sight of.) In 1885, the New York Court of Appeals invalidated a state law prohibiting the manufacture of cigars in tenement dwellings on the grounds that such legislation deprived the worker of "liberty"—the right, that is, to work "where he will." Free labor, declared the West Virginia Supreme Court in 1889, meant "not only freedom from servitude . . . but the right . . . to pursue any lawful trade or avocation," which no state law could restrict. In a perverse assertion of equality between the sexes, women were increasingly understood to possess the same economic "liberty," defined in this way, as men. On the grounds that it violated women's contractual freedom, the Illinois Supreme Court in 1895 declared unconstitutional a state law, written by the feminist and labor reformer Florence Kelley, that outlawed production of garments in sweatshops and established a forty-eight-hour working week for women and children. Freedom of contract jurisprudence, however, did not prevent the use of the courts to impede labor organization. Between 1880 and 1931, by one count, nearly two thousand injunctions were issued prohibiting strikes and labor boycotts.[14]

On those occasions when it was persuaded that legitimate health and safety grounds existed for the regulation of working conditions, the Supreme Court upheld legislative interference with unimpeded liberty of contract, such as Utah's law establishing an eight-hour day for miners or statutes requiring that businesses close on Sunday. But most decisions involving labor relations went in the opposite direction. In a 1905 case that became almost as notorious as the *Dred Scott* decision and gave the name "Lochnerism" to the entire body of liberty of contract decisions, the Court in *Lochner* v. *New York* voided a state law establishing maximum hours of work for bakers. By this time, jurists were invoking "liberty" in ways that could easily seem absurd. In one case, the Supreme Court overturned a Kansas law prohibiting "yellow-dog" contracts, which made non-membership in a union a condition of employment, as a violation of "the right of personal liberty." In another, it struck down state laws requiring payment of coal miners in money rather than scrip. The Court seemed to define "the workman's liberty," quipped union leader John L. Mitchell, as the right "to accept merchandise in lieu of money." Workers, Mitchell observed, could not but feel that "they are being guaranteed the liberties they do not want and denied the liberty that is of real value to them."[15]

Labor and the Republic

As Mitchell's remark suggests, more than at almost any other moment in American history, public discourse in the late nineteenth century fractured along class lines. And from the labor movement arose a sustained assault on the understanding of freedom grounded in Social Darwinism and liberty of contract. Caught between nostalgia for the era of small production and frank acknowledgment of the triumph of the factory and the wage labor system, labor reformers of the Gilded Age were attracted to a wide array of programs, from the eight-hour day to public employment in hard times, currency reform, anarchism, socialism, and the creation of a vaguely defined "cooperative commonwealth." But uniting these various plans and panaceas was an "ideology of disinheritance," the conviction that new social conditions amounted to a loss of Americans' birthright of freedom. In the course of its campaigns, labor developed a full-blown critique of the prevailing definition of liberty. Americans, declared Terence V. Powderly, head of the era's largest labor organization, the Knights of Labor, were not "the free people that we imagine we are."[16]

Emancipation cast a long shadow over labor reform discourse in the Gilded Age. Like the courts and Social Darwinists, labor spoke the language of free labor and claimed the mantle of the struggle against slavery—partly as a continuation of prewar rhetoric and partly because the slavery metaphor offered an effective way of appealing to the reform-minded middle class. "The laborer," wrote eight-hour reformer Ira Steward, "instinctively feels that something of slavery still remains, or that something of freedom is yet to come." Although, by and large, the labor movement did little to address the problems of the former slaves or to identify with them as dispossessed laborers, it adopted and expanded the Reconstruction language of equal citizenship. "Under the guise of republican freedom," claimed Florence Kelley in 1889, "we have degenerated into a nation of mock citizens." Only when the "social structure" conformed to the egalitarian ideals embodied in Jefferson's Declaration of Independence, proclaimed a Boston labor newspaper, could genuine freedom be secured. Labor spokesmen referred to the Thirteenth Amendment as a "glorious labor amendment" that enshrined the dignity of labor in the Constitution and whose prohibition of involuntary servitude was violated by court injunctions undermining the right to strike. Reaching back across the divide of the Civil War, labor defined employers as a new "slave power," called for the "emancipation and enfranchisement of all who labor," and spoke of an "irrepressible conflict between the wage system of labor and the republican system of government." Concentrated capital, warned George E. McNeill, a shoe-maker and woolmill operative who became one of the movement's most elo-quent writers, had become "a greater power than that of the State." The remedy was not to return to the days of the small-scale craftsman, but to "engraft re-publican principles into our industrial system," by guaranteeing a basic set of economic rights for all Americans.[17]

Through the 1880s, the "abolition of the wage system" remained the stated goal of labor organizations. When congressional committees in the late 1870s and early 1880s traveled the country taking testimony on "the relations of cap-ital and labor," they encountered a steady stream of complaints from labor lead-ers and ordinary workers—low wages, the power of monopolies, grinding poverty—summarized in the reinvigorated language of "wage slavery." One correspondent of a labor newspaper presented American development as a saga of successive forms of slavery: feudalism, chattel slavery, and wage labor, all members of the same "species."

The growing number of women working for wages in dire circumstances were also described as suffering from a new form of slavery. In 1888, the *Chicago Times* published a remarkable series of articles by reporter Nell Cusack under the title "City Slave Girls," exposing wretched working conditions in the city's factories and sweatshops. The articles unleashed a flood of letters to the edi-tor from women workers themselves, many of whom employed the language of liberty. Domestic service was especially singled out as "a slave's life," as one woman put it, with "long hours, late and early, seven days in the week, bossed and ordered about as niggers before the war." Many complained about sexual abuse on the job—another analogy to chattel slavery—while rejecting the widespread opinion that work outside the home inevitably injured a woman's virtue. The problem, "A Working Woman" observed, was not immorality, but insufficient pay and inadequate job opportunities. Why, she wondered, "in this free country have not women the right to choose their own avocations?" So widespread, on both sides of the Atlantic, was the rhetoric of wage slavery that when the English economic historian John K. Ingram published his *His-tory of Slavery and Serfdom* in 1895, he felt compelled to include an appendix on the "lax" uses of the word "slavery," foremost among them its application to wage workers.[18]

But more than reiterating the venerable idea that wage labor was incompat-ible with freedom, labor offered a powerful critique of a contract ideology that justified increasing inequality in the name of liberty. In *Capital*, Karl Marx, whose works were now beginning to circulate in the United States, had ridiculed the essence of liberty of contract thought—the assumption of equality in the labor market. The "sale and purchase of labor power," he waxed sardonically, occurred in "a very Eden of the innate rights of man," a world of "freedom, because both buyer and seller . . . are constrained only by their own free will." Marx's themes—that the market in labor embodied its own none too subtle coercions and that gross economic inequalities made a mockery of the ostensible equality of employer and employee—were echoed throughout the American labor press. "Competitive freedom, in a scramble for the interests of mere self," one writer insisted, was a "rankly anti-American" definition of liberty, yet "this freedom has obtained such prominent, and almost unquestioned propriety, as to stand and rule." Labor leaders challenged the individualist premises of Gilded Age social thought. Solidarity among all who toiled for a living was the motto of the Knights of Labor, a broadly inclusive social movement that sought to unite the skilled and unskilled, immigrant and native, male and female wage earners (their platform called for "equal pay for equal work for both sexes"), and even black workers (although not the despised Chinese). The labor movement, wrote George McNeill, embodied the principle that "mutualism is preferable to individualism," that no contradiction existed between demands for rights as individuals and an understanding of freedom as a collective attribute of a class.[19]

Most profoundly, labor raised the question whether meaningful freedom could exist in a situation of extreme economic inequality. On July 4, 1886, the Federated Trades of the Pacific Coast rewrote Jefferson's Declaration to list among mankind's inalienable rights "Life and the means of living, Liberty and the conditions essential to liberty." Freedom required certain kinds of social arrangements, not simply liberty of contract. No one was more effective at appropriating the language of American freedom for labor's cause than Eugene V. Debs, the head of the American Railway Union, whose jailing in 1894 as a result of a strike against the Pullman Company made him a symbol of how concentrated economic power, now aligned with federal authority, was undermining traditional notions of freedom. On his release from prison, over one hundred thousand people greeted Debs at a railroad depot in Chicago. Hailing the crowd of well-wishers as "lovers of liberty," Debs went on to offer a discourse on how corporate control of politics and the economy endangered "American liberty."[20]

Even as labor unrest crested, a different kind of uprising was ripening in the South and the Great Plains, a response to falling agricultural prices and growing economic dependency in rural areas. Farmers experienced the spread of sharecropping in the South and mortgage debt in the West not simply as economic deprivation but as a loss of freedom. Through the Farmers Alliance, with its program of cooperative financing and marketing of crops, they sought to restore their beleaguered economic autonomy. The farmers' alternatives, said J. D. Fields, a Texas Alliance leader, were "success and freedom, or failure and servitude." In the early 1890s, the Alliance would evolve into the People's, or Populist, Party—the era's greatest political insurgency. Though strongest in the cotton and wheat belts, the party sought to speak for all the "producing classes" and achieved some of its greatest successes in states like Colorado and Idaho, where it became a vehicle for embattled miners and industrial workers.[21]

In the familiar language of nineteenth-century radicalism, Populists condemned the "new slavery" that kept not only farmers but "sewing women, coal miners, and iron workers" in thrall to "millionaire slavemasters." Their 1892 platform, adopted at the party's Omaha convention, cited a litany of grievances—governmental corruption, denial of the right to organize unions, the rise of "colossal fortunes . . . unprecedented in the history of mankind"—all of which "endanger[ed] liberty." The party's specific demands included government ownership of the railroads, a national currency to end bankers' control of finance, a graduated income tax, and a system of low-cost public financing to enable farmers to market their crops. "The power of government," declared the Omaha platform, must be brought to bear to eliminate "oppression, injustice, and poverty" from American life, thereby creating the social conditions of freedom.[22]

Here was the last great political manifestation of the nineteenth-century vision of America as a commonwealth of small producers. "Two great classes—tramps and millionaires," the Populist platform claimed, had arisen on the American scene, threatening the stability of the republic. Between lay the vast middle ground of the producing classes, inheritors of definitions of freedom and citizenship linked to the ownership of productive property and respect for the dignity of labor. Drawing on both traditional aspirations for economic autonomy and local self-government, and a sense that only the national state could curb the power of the corporations and make American society a "united brotherhood of free men," Populists sought to rethink the meaning of freedom to meet the exigencies of the 1890s. To the heritage of "individual freedom," once "the pride of our system," said a Nebraska Populist newspaper, Americans needed to add "industrial freedom," for "what is life and so-called liberty" if millions were denied "the means of subsistence?" Like the labor movement, Populists rejected the era's laissez-faire orthodoxy ("survival of the fittest," said Governor Lorenzo Lewelling of Colorado, was "the philosophy of brutes"). Populists hardly envisioned the massive programs of state-sponsored social provision that the Progressive era and the New Deal would come to see as the antidote to economic inequality. Yet a generation would pass before a major party offered so sweeping a plan for governmental action on behalf of economic freedom as the Omaha platform.[23]

Dissatisfaction with social conditions in the Gilded Age was not confined to aggrieved workers and farmers. Alarmed by the specter of class warfare and the growing power of concentrated capital, social thinkers of the period offered numerous prescriptions for reclaiming the nation's heritage of freedom. Of the many books proposing remedies for the unequal distribution of wealth, the most popular were *Progress and Poverty* (1879) by Henry George, and Edward Bellamy's *Looking Backward* (1888). Both were among the century's greatest bestsellers, their extraordinary success testifying to what George called "a wide-spread consciousness . . . that there is something *radically* wrong in the present social organization." Both writers sought to restore an imagined golden age of freedom and social harmony. Their solutions, however, pointed in opposite directions: George toward a society in which self-directed individuals controlled their own destiny within a laissez-faire market, Bellamy to a collectivist future in which personal autonomy had been subordinated to a socially determined common good.

No one knows how many of Henry's George's readers actually believed that the single tax on land—his panacea for the nation's social ills—would usher in an egalitarian future, "the City of God on earth." But millions responded to his jargon-free exposition of economic relationships and his stirring explication of how the "social distress" long thought to be confined to the Old World had made its appearance in the New. Freedom lay at the heart of George's analysis. The "proper name" for the political movement spawned by his book, he once wrote, was "freedom men," who would "do for the question of industrial slavery" what the Republican Party had recently done for the slavery of blacks. Political liberty, George wrote at the conclusion of *Progress and Poverty,* was meaningless without its economic counterpart. If George rejected the traditional equation of freedom with ownership of land (since the single tax in effect made land the "common property" of the entire society), in other ways, his definition of freedom was thoroughly in keeping with mainstream thought. George believed fervently in the justice of the free market; the problem was that land monopoly had enabled non-producers to enrich themselves at the expense of laborers and manufacturers alike. Despite calling for a single massive public intervention in the economy, George saw government as a "repressive power," whose functions in the "cooperative society" of the future would be limited to enhancing the quality of life—building "public baths, museums, libraries, gardens," and the like. Genuine laissez-faire, George wrote, would solve the problem of social injustice: "freedom [is] the synonym of equality."[24]

If George's vision of freedom rested on the familiar foundation of the sovereign individual, Bellamy questioned whether freedom was not, in the end, a social condition, resting on interdependence, not autonomy. In *Looking Backward, 2000–1887*, Bellamy's protagonist falls asleep in the late nineteenth century only to awaken in the year 2000, in a world where inequality has been banished and with it the idea of liberty as a condition to be achieved through individual striving free of governmental restraint. From the vantage point of the late twentieth century, Bellamy's utopia—with citizens obligated to labor for years in an Industrial Army controlled by a single Great Trust, and a police force ready to discipline slackers and nonconformists—seems a chilling blueprint for a world of coerced uniformity. Yet the book inspired the creation of hundreds of Nationalist clubs devoted to bringing into existence the world of 2000, and left a profound mark on a generation of reformers and intellectuals, from Debs to John Dewey. For Bellamy held out the hope of retaining the material abundance made possible by industrial capitalism while social inequalities were eliminated and harmony restored to nation and society.

In proposing that the state guarantee adequate annual incomes to all, Bellamy put forward a far-reaching expansion of the notion of citizenship and its entitlements. His utopia, moreover, offered women economic autonomy and political rights, complete with the replacement of private housekeeping and childrearing arrangements by public kitchens and nurseries. It thus helped to popularize the notion, still quite radical at the time, that married women should consider work outside the home a regular feature of their lives. And in suggesting that the idea of the autonomous, self-directing individual was hopelessly out of date in the complex organism of modern society, Bellamy gave expression to a widespread sense that genuine freedom could only be secured by the collective action of the community. "I am aware that you called yourself free in the nineteenth century," a resident of the year 2000 tells Bellamy's Rip Van Winkle. But "the meaning of the word could not then, however, have been at all what it is at present," or it could never have been applied to a society in which so many lived in a state of "galling personal dependence upon others as to the very means of life." For Bellamy, the unfettered market had failed to guarantee freedom; the only alternative was to turn to the state.[25]

By 1888, when *Looking Backward* appeared, Social Darwinism and the laissez-faire definition of freedom were under attack from many quarters, including not only the labor and Populist movements but clergymen shocked by the inequities in the emerging industrial order and a new generation of social science intellectuals proposing to unleash state activism in the service of social equality. If most of the era's Protestant preachers concentrated on attacking individual sins like drinking and sabbath-breaking and saw nothing immoral about the pursuit of wealth, the lineaments of a social gospel were taking shape in the writings of Walter Rauschenbusch, a Baptist minister in New York City, and others, who insisted that freedom and spiritual self-development required an equalization of wealth and power, and that unbridled competition mocked the Christian ideal of brotherhood.[26]

Challenges to prevailing ideas of freedom also sprouted in the academic world, reflected in the establishment in 1885 of the American Economic Association (AEA), whose express purpose was to combat both Social Darwinism and "laissez-faire orthodoxy." "We regard the state," wrote AEA founder Richard T. Ely, "as an educational and ethical agency whose positive assistance is one of the indispensable conditions of human progress." Once the basis of liberty, many younger economists believed, private property had become a means of depriving others of their freedom, and poverty posed a far graver danger to the republic than an activist state. The paradox of liberty in the modern world, wrote the sociologist Lester Ward, was that "individual freedom can only come through social regulation." Here was a reminder that the power of the democratic state spawned by the Civil War could be employed to address issues other than slavery, and a harbinger of the transformation of the idea of freedom by social scientists, politicians, and social reformers in the soon-to-dawn Progressive era. But before this came to fruition, the nation would face its gravest crisis since the Civil War, and the boundaries of freedom would once more be redrawn.[27]

Redrawing the Boundaries

The 1890s was a decade of social turmoil. It witnessed the century's most severe economic depression; the rise and fall of the People's Party; and continued labor unrest highlighted by the 1892 strike at the giant steel mill in Homestead, Pennsylvania, in which strikers fought pitched battles against the Carnegie Corporation's private police, and the railroad strike of 1894 against the Pullman Company, in which federal troops occupied Chicago. Simultaneously, the sources of immigration shifted from Northern and Western Europe to Southern and Eastern. Of the 3.5 million immigrants who entered the United States during the decade, over half hailed from Italy and the Russian and

Austro-Hungarian empires. Among middle-class nativeborn Americans, these events inspired an abandonment of the egalitarian vision of citizenship spawned by the Civil War, and the revival of definitions of American freedom based on race.

By the turn of the century, the language of "race"—race conflict, race feeling, race problems—had assumed a central place in American public discourse. The putative inborn capacity of one or another "races" was commonly invoked to explain everything from the standard of living of various groups of workers to the ability or inability of various peoples to participate in American democracy. Just as individual character was thought to explain personal success or failure in the economic marketplace, the idea of "national character" took on a larger and larger role in explaining historical outcomes. Even as orthodox economic and legal thought spoke of society as a collection of self-directed individuals, nativists resuscitated an older vision of competing races and nations, each occupying a place within a worldwide hierarchy. Immigration, it was claimed, weakened the fiber of American society by allowing "inferior" races to outnumber the Anglo-Saxons best fitted for national and worldwide hegemony. The new immigrants, wrote the economist Francis Amasa Walker in 1890, were "beaten men from beaten races, representing the worst failures in the struggle for existence." American cities, said an Ohio newspaper, were being overrun by foreigners who "have no true appreciation of the meaning of liberty."[28]

The new situation was most evident in the condition of black Americans. By the early twentieth century, a new system of racial subordination had come into being in the South. In the words of the historian Rayford Logan, blacks occupied a "separate wing" of the "edifice of national unity," and "on the pediments . . . were carved Exploitation, Disfranchisement, Segregation, Discrimination, Lynching, Contempt." The disenfranchisement of southern blacks (along with a considerable number of poor white voters), which began in Mississippi in 1890, not only halted and reversed the long trend toward expanding political freedom, but transformed Deep South states into political rotten boroughs whose representatives in Congress would long wield far greater power on the national scene than their tiny electorates warranted. But southern whites did not create their new system of white supremacy alone. The effective nullification of the Fourteenth and Fifteenth Amendments occurred with the full acquiescence of the North. By 1900, the ideals of color-blind citizenship and freedom as a universal entitlement had been repudiated.

The retreat from the ideals of Reconstruction went hand in hand with the resurgence of an Anglo-Saxonism that united patriotism, xenophobia, and an ethnocultural definition of nationhood in a renewed rhetoric of racial exclusiveness. Derogatory iconography depicting blacks and other "lesser" groups as little more than savages and criminals filled the pages of popular periodicals, legitimizing and "naturalizing," the new system of political and economic inequality. Scholars like Columbia University's John W. Burgess, a founder of American political science, taught that "a black skin means membership in a race of men which has never of itself succeeded in subjecting passion to reason, and has never, therefore, created any civilization of any kind." Granting blacks the right to vote had been a ghastly mistake, and the "failure" of Reconstruction was invoked again and again to demonstrate that the former slaves and their descendants were unfit for freedom as whites understood it. "Unpracticed in liberty . . . excited by a freedom they did not understand," the former slaves and their descendants, insisted Woodrow Wilson, then a Princeton professor of political science, were not ready for participation in American public life.[29]

Many of the nation's black leaders, quite understandably, felt, as Douglass put it, that the promise of emancipation had been betrayed. Blacks, he lamented, remained "only half free," standing in "the twilight of American liberty." Ida B. Wells, driven out of Memphis after her newspaper, *Free Speech*, exposed abysmal conditions in black schools and the horror of lynching, bluntly rejected the notion that the United States had a right to call itself the "land of the free." "Freedom is to us a mockery, and . . . liberty a lie," W. E. B. Du Bois would write in 1903, in *The Souls of Black Folk*. Central to blacks' vision of freedom remained the Reconstruction principle of egalitarian citizenship. When the black leadership of New Orleans banded together to challenge the state's 1890 law requiring the segregation of railroad passengers by race, they called themselves the Citizens Committee. They fought the case of Homer Plessy, evicted from a whites-only railroad carriage, all the way to the Supreme Court, insisting that in the United States, "citizenship is national and knows no color." But in 1896, in *Plessy* v. *Ferguson*, the culmination of a series of decisions restricting the rights protected by the Fourteenth Amendment, the Court decreed that state-mandated racial segregation did not violate the Constitution's equal protection clause. The lone dissenter, John Marshall Harlan, hurled at the majority the oft-quoted dictum: "our Constitution is color-blind."[30]

More than merely an interpretation of the Constitution's equal protection clause, Harlan's dissent was a disquisition on the meaning of freedom in a democracy. His target was not so much racial separation as racial domination. Whites' talk of inborn "racial instincts" and their self-proclaimed status as the "dominant race" (phrases employed by the eight-man majority), he insisted, contradicted the principle of equal liberty spawned by the Civil War. To Harlan, freedom for the former slaves meant the right to participate fully and equally in American society. As he predicted, the *Plessy* decision was quickly followed by state laws mandating racial segregation in every aspect of life, from schools to hospitals, waiting rooms to toilets, pay windows to cemeteries. Despite the "thin disguise" (Harlan's phrase) of equality mandated by the Court's "separate but equal" doctrine, facilities for blacks were always inferior. A century later, Americans would look back on segregation as a relic of an era of crude prejudice. When installed, however, the system was justified by political, religious, and scientific leaders as a forward-looking solution to a seemingly intractable problem—the presence of a race that posed a danger to white America and its democratic institutions.[31]

Slowly, the boundaries of nationhood, expanded so dramatically in the aftermath of the Civil War, contracted. While ruling that the Fourteenth Amendment awarded citizenship to children of Chinese immigrants born on American soil, the Supreme Court also affirmed the right of Congress to set racial restrictions on immigration, and to expel without due process foreigners who had not been naturalized (as Chinese could not be). Beginning in 1882, Congress excluded immigrants from China from entering the country altogether. Exclusion profoundly shaped the experience of Chinese Americans, long stigmatizing them as unwanted and unassimilable, and justifying their isolation from mainstream society. (Whether America would truly achieve "liberty and greatness," opined a Chinese-American writer, would in the future depend on "whether this statute against the Chinese or the statue to Liberty will be the more lasting monument.") Congress for the first time also excluded classes of white aliens from naturalization, beginning in 1875 with prostitutes and convicted felons and adding in 1882 "lunatics" and those likely to become a "public charge." "Are we still an asylum for the oppressed of all nations?" wondered James B. Weaver, the Populist candidate for president in 1892.[32]

As the economist Simon Patten noted in 1896, American society seemed to be fracturing along interpenetrating lines of class and race, as universalistic definitions of citizenship and freedom were replaced by an obsession with strictly demarcating the borders of the "imagined community":

> Each class or section of the nation is becoming conscious of an opposition between its standards and the activities and tendencies of some less developed class. The South has its negro, the city has its slums. . . . The friends of American institutions fear the ignorant immigrant, and the workingman dislikes the Chinese. Every one is beginning to differentiate those with proper qualifications for citizenship from some other class or classes which he wishes to restrain or exclude from society.[33]

Wracked by fears that the economic and ethnic unity of American society were in danger of disintegrating, government and private organizations in the 1890s promoted a unifying, coercive patriotism. These were the years when rituals like the Pledge of Allegiance and the practice of standing for the playing of "The Star-Spangled Banner" came into existence. Americans had long honored the Stars and Stripes, but the "cult of the flag," including an official Flag Day, dates to the 1890s.[34]

On the eve of the twentieth century, America's triumphant entry onto the world stage as an imperial power in the Spanish-American War tied nationalism and American freedom ever more closely to notions of Anglo-Saxon superiority, displacing, in part, the earlier identification of the nation with democratic political institutions (or defining those institutions in a more explicitly racial manner). Having demonstrated their special aptitude for liberty and self-government on the North American continent, Anglo-Saxons would now spread these institutions and values to less fortunate peoples throughout the world. As in the South, the domination of non-white peoples by whites was part of the progress of civilization, a fulfillment, not a violation, of American freedom. Anti-imperialists, many of them veterans of the antislavery crusade, wondered whether democracy and empire were truly compatible. A "republic of free men," the Anti-Imperialist League declared, should assist the people of Puerto Rico and the Philippines, acquired by the United States as a result of the war, in their own "struggles for liberty," rather than subjecting them to colonial rule.[35]

But without any sense of contradiction, proponents of an imperial foreign policy also adopted the language of freedom. Anti-imperialists were the real "infidels to the gospel of liberty," claimed the diplomat and historian Albert Beveridge, because America ventured abroad not for material gain or national power but to bring "a new day of freedom" to Cuba, Puerto Rico, and the Philippines. True, raising Filipinos to the condition where they could appreciate "what Anglo-Saxon liberty is" might take a century, the islands' first American governor, William Howard Taft, opined. But the alternative to American rule was "anarchy and barbarism"—although the long and brutal war by which the United States pacified the islands and crushed the indigenous movement for independence seemed barbaric enough. In fact, successive American colonial administrators did try to democratize Philippine politics and prepare the islands for nationhood (achieved in 1946, rather sooner than Taft had anticipated). But, like the victorious North after the Civil War, their policies left intact the land-based power of the local oligarchy, bequeathing enduring poverty to the mass of the rural population.[36]

With black disenfranchisement, Chinese exclusion, the final suppression of Indian resistance, the rigid segmentation of the job market along racial and ethnic lines, and the emergence of an imperial policy toward non-white peoples overseas, the polity and economy were more thoroughly racialized at the dawn of the twentieth century than at any other point in American history. Confronted with seemingly unassailable corporate power and the wholesale repudiation of the universalist definition of American nationhood, even the social movements that had helped to expand the nineteenth-century boundaries of freedom now redefined their objectives so that they might be realized within the new institutional and intellectual framework. Prominent black leaders took to emphasizing economic self-help and individual advancement into the middle class as an alternative to popular political agitation. Symbolizing this shift was the juxtaposition, in 1895, of the death of Frederick Douglass with Booker T. Washington's widely praised speech at the Atlanta Cotton Exposition urging blacks to adjust to segregation and forego agitation for civil rights and the suffrage. The path to racial advancement, Washington asserted, lay in acquiring skills and property. Given economic freedom, political freedom would eventually follow, a notion compatible with both the era's business culture and the restricted practice of freedom being institutionalized in the South. During the 1890s, prominent white educators and reformers gathered at Lake Mohonk, New York, for conferences on the "Negro Question." They concluded that blacks' problem was deficient "personal conduct and character," and that self-help, not national assistance or political agitation, offered the best route to racial progress.[37]

Within the labor movement, the demise of the Knights of Labor and the ascendancy of the American Federation of Labor (AFL) during the 1890s reflected a shift toward the judgment that workers must frankly accept their status as wage earners and seek higher wages and better working conditions rather than pursuing the utopian dream of economic autonomy or the "abolition of the wage system." For Samuel Gompers, the AFL's founder and president, free labor was wage labor and should organize as such. The AFL's acknowledgment that freedom based on ownership of productive property lay beyond the reach of the mass of workers marked both a realistic assessment and a strategic retreat, an accommodation to the economic realities and dominant political language of the time. Indeed, rather than denouncing the equation of freedom with marketplace liberty, Gompers embraced "freedom of contract" as the "whole gospel" of the labor movement, shrewdly turning it into an argument against interference by courts and legislators with workers' right to organize unions. Abandoning the Knights' rhetoric of solidarity, the AFL restricted membership to skilled workers—a small minority of the labor force—effectively excluding the vast majority of blacks, women, and new European immigrants. Only nativeborn white men possessed the requisite skill, character, and sense of manhood to confront employers; the "lower standards of life and work" of the unskilled, the non-white, the female, and the new immigrant led them to accept a level of wages incompatible with what was beginning to be called the "American standard of living."[38]

Meanwhile, the women's movement increasingly focused on the vote rather than broader social issues, speaking far less than in the past about sexual inequality in the home and workplace. It also made its peace with nativism and racism. The earlier "feminism of equal rights," which claimed the ballot as part of a larger transformation of women's status in public and private life, was never fully repudiated. The movement continued to argue for women's equality in employment, education, and politics even while maintaining that women bore a special responsibility for the family, and would bring their unique moral qualities to bear on public life. But the center of gravity shifted toward a feminism more in keeping with prevailing racial and ethnic norms. With disturbing frequency, a new generation of suffrage leaders, like Carrie Chapman Catt, suggested that educational and other suffrage qualifications did not conflict with the movement's aims so long as they applied equally to men and women. Believing that immigrants and former slaves had been enfranchised with "ill-advised haste," Catt suggested that extending the franchise to nativeborn white women would counterbalance the growing power of the "ignorant foreign vote" in the North and the dangerous potential for a second Reconstruction in the South.[39]

Even more than its growing hostility to immigrant voting, the women's movement's changing stance regarding the "Southern question" reflected the eclipse of egalitarian feminism. Despite the fact that black disenfranchisement in the South undermined the argument for women's suffrage by reinforcing the idea that society could limit the vote as it saw fit, leaders of the national suffrage movement said virtually nothing about it. In 1895, the same year that Booker T. Washington delivered his famous Atlanta address, the National American Woman Suffrage Association held its annual convention in the city, symbolizing how the suffrage movement had made its peace with the nation's new racial order. Indeed, one Mississippi delegate told the assembly that the North, its civilization threatened by the influx of foreigners, would be forced to "look to the South for redemption" because of "the purity of its Anglo-Saxon blood." At a time when political liberty was increasingly being linked to political capacity, the nativeborn, middle-class women who dominated the suffrage movement claimed the vote as educated members of a "superior race." Even in as staunch an egalitarian as the feminist editor Abigail Scott Duniway, unconscious racial and class prejudices sometimes rose to the surface. Throughout these years, Duniway struggled to keep alive the equal rights tradition, claiming for women the right to control their reproductive and sexual lives during marriage, and insisting to the end of her long life that the battle for suffrage was another chapter in the "irrepressible conflict between freedom and slavery." Yet Duniway also devised a plan for increased Asian immigration so that white women could "hire a Chinaman" to liberate themselves from the burden of housework.[40]

In 1893, in his famous lecture on how the frontier had shaped American development, the historian Frederick Jackson Turner concluded that the "first period" of American history—the period that had nurtured individualism, democracy, and widespread opportunity for economic autonomy—had come to an end. He might have added that with the re-racialization of American freedom, the long era of the Civil War, when political debate revolved around the future of slavery and the fate of the former slaves, had also passed into history. Yet the questions central to nineteenth-century debates over freedom—the relationship between personal, political, and economic liberty, the role of the state in creating the conditions of freedom, and the boundaries of the "imagined community"—had not been permanently answered. The era's "violent unrest," the novelist William Dean Howells observed in 1895, suggested that a new definition of liberty was in order, one offering the mass of the population "more power, more ease, more freedom." Here was the challenge bequeathed by the nineteenth century to the first generation of the twentieth.[41]

"Where the Mother's Vote is Needed," a cartoon from a women's suffrage magazine, invokes an image of child labor to suggest that exploited workers do not enjoy freedom. (*Maryland Suffrage News*, 15 May 1915)

7

Progressive
Freedom

In 1902, the monthly magazine *The Independent* organized a forum
on economic inequality in the United States. On one side stood
staunch defenders of laissez-faire Social Darwinism, convinced that
vast disparities of wealth were the natural consequence of individual
freedom. Riches, declared the Wall Street financier Russell Sage, whose
personal fortune reputedly exceeded $70 million, were the reward for
superior intelligence, honesty, and thrift—"to rail against the accumulation of wealth is to rail against the decrees of justice." William
Graham Sumner, nearing the end of his long career at Yale, insisted
that economic inequality was not only inevitable but violated no "law
of nature, religion, ethics, or the State." To this, the labor economist
John R. Commons responded that monopolistic control of industry
stifled competition, the lifeblood of economic progress, and Ernest H.
Crosby, a longtime advocate of Henry George's single tax, declared
that an economic aristocracy had arisen, powerful enough to endanger republican government. Henry Demarest Lloyd, the author of
Wealth Against Commonwealth, boldly called for a "new democracy of industry" requiring the creation of unions and cooperatives, perhaps
even socialism.[1]

Clearly, deep disagreements over the political and social consequences of economic change had survived from the nineteenth century
into the twentieth. If Sage and Sumner represented the mainstream of
respectable opinion at the beginning of the new century, Commons,
Crosby, and Lloyd heralded a fundamental shift in social thinking

over the course of the next two decades, a period that has come to be called the Progressive era.

In the Gilded Age, concern that concentrated economic power endangered freedom had been articulated most forcefully by organized workers and embattled farmers. In the Progressive years that followed, as severe inequality remained the most visible feature of the urban landscape, this fear animated a far broader array of individuals and social movements. When the British writer H. G. Wells visited the United States soon after the turn of the century, he found that "the steady trend towards concentration" had become "the cardinal topic of thought and discussion in the American mind." Everywhere, the signs of economic and political consolidation were apparent—in the power of a small directorate of Wall Street bankers and corporate executives, the manipulation of democracy by political machines, the rise of new systems of hierarchical control in workplaces, even the ability of national mass-circulation monthlies like *The Independent* to shape public discourse. In these circumstances, wrote Benjamin P. DeWitt in *The Progressive Movement* (1915), "the individual could not hope to compete. . . . Slowly, Americans realized that they were not free."[2]

"Freedom" was not the most prominent word in the vocabulary of Progressivism. So tainted had it become by association with Social Darwinism and liberty of contract jurisprudence that many reformers preferred to speak instead of democracy and its discontents. Progressive commentators were far more concerned with finding concrete ways to rejuvenate democratic citizenship than with abstract discussions of freedom. Yet much public discussion continued to revolve around the question of whether traditional definitions of liberty were still valid. "The rise of modern freedom," wrote the German sociologist Max Weber in 1906, "presupposed unique constellations which will never repeat themselves." Many Americans shared Weber's fear that the increasingly bureaucratic organization of life eroded the foundations of individualism and with them nineteenth-century ideas of freedom. Some Progressives proposed to restore individual opportunity by returning to a competitive marketplace populated by small producers; others accepted the permanence of the large corporation and looked to the government to protect the interests of workers and consumers. Still others would relocate freedom from the economy and polity to a private world of consumption or a psychic realm of personal fulfillment. But nearly all Progressives agreed that freedom must be infused with new meaning. The task was to find a moral and social equivalent for the widespread property ownership once deemed the foundation of liberty. How, asked Herbert Croly, editor of the bible of Progressive intellectuals, *The New Republic*, could Americans be "free men" in a modern, industrial economy?[3]

The Varieties of Economic Freedom

Inspired by the sense that traditional understandings of democracy and liberty were obsolete in the new century, the Progressive era produced a remarkable outpouring of social commentary and a complex array of movements aimed at addressing economic inequality and finding common ground in a society racked by labor conflict and experiencing massive immigration from abroad. The quest took Progressives down many paths. The era witnessed the use of political power to expand economic freedom, and the restriction of other kinds of liberty, such as the consolidation of racial segregation in the South and the legislative triumph of prohibition. A fluid and complex set of beliefs, Progressivism occupied a broad political spectrum that ranged from socialists who advocated state control of the economy to forward-looking businessmen who realized that workers must be accorded a voice in economic decision-making. But at its core stood a coalition of middle-class reformers, male and female, often linked to trade unions, who sought to humanize capitalism by making it more egalitarian and to reinvigorate democracy by restoring political power to the citizenry and civic harmony to a fractured society. The "old democracy," wrote Walter E. Weyl, *The New Republic's* associate editor, provided no answer to the problems of a world in which the "chief restrictions upon liberty" were "economic," not political.[4]

In Progressive America, the terms "industrial freedom" and "industrial democracy," which had entered the political vocabulary during the Gilded Age, assumed a central place in political discourse. Their very indeterminacy allowed them to be employed by socialists and antisocialists, forward-looking businessmen and trust-busting reformers, labor organizers seeking the right to collective bargaining and industrial relations experts hoping to promote harmony between employer and employee. All could agree that lack of "industrial freedom" stood at the root of the widely discussed "labor problem." At stake were not simply the living conditions of workers but the foundations of American democracy. "Political freedom," wrote Basil Manly, director of research for the Commission on Industrial Relations, established by Congress in 1912, "can exist only where there is industrial freedom."[5]

To many Progressives, the key to industrial freedom lay in empowering workers to participate in economic decision-making via strong unions freed from managerial hostility and court injunctions. The era's massive strikes among immigrant workers, notably the "uprising of twenty thousand" in New York's garment industry in 1909, the Lawrence, Massachusetts, textile strike of 1912, and the Paterson, New Jersey, silk strike the following year, attracted nationwide attention and placed labor's demand for the right to bargain collectively at the forefront of the reform agenda. Unions, wrote Croly, allowed "the condition of freedom" to be introduced "into the wage system itself." Yet nothing was more stubbornly resisted by entrepreneurs, courts, and conservative middle-class opinion. Louis D. Brandeis, an active ally of the labor movement whom President Wilson appointed to the Supreme Court in 1916, maintained that unions embodied an essential principle of freedom—the right of people to govern themselves. The contradiction between "political liberty" and "industrial slavery," Brandeis insisted, was America's foremost social problem, and workers were entitled to a voice not only on wages and working conditions but such managerial prerogatives as the relocation of factories, layoffs, and the distribution of profits. Restoring economic freedom, Brandeis insisted, would equip working people to become full and active citizens—"self-respecting members of a democracy." Without such "freedom in things industrial," the United States would be "a nation of slaves."[6]

Like Brandeis, many Americans in the Progressive era still invoked the venerable dichotomy between freedom and slavery to describe working conditions and employers' hostility to collective bargaining. In their periodic and often violent struggles for union recognition, for example, miners appealed to the American heritage of freedom against the coal companies that dominated local and state government and employed private police forces to suppress efforts at union organization. The motto "Mountaineers are Free" was emblazoned on the West Virginia capitol; but, as the fiery organizer Mary ("Mother") Jones insisted, miners needed to be emancipated just as the slaves had been. Born in 1830, Mother Jones was a living link to the days and the language of the irrepressible conflict. "We forever wiped out chattel slavery," she told a group of striking miners. "Now, industrial slavery is the battle you are in." (Indeed, Jones urged white miners to solicit black support; more than most union leaders, she appreciated that because of slavery, "the black man . . . knows what liberty is.")[7]

But it was not only miners living under the despotic rule of corporate power who believed themselves deprived of freedom. The great increase in the number of white-collar workers—the new army of bookkeepers, salespeople, salaried professionals, and corporate managers that sprang up with the new system of bureaucratic management—also undermined the sense of personal autonomy. For although they enjoyed far greater social status and higher incomes than manual workers, many, wrote one commentator, were the kind of individuals who "under former conditions, would have been . . . managing their own businesses." Likewise, skilled factory workers experienced the spread of scientific management—the system pioneered by efficiency expert Frederick W. Taylor whereby the work process was subjected to minute control in the name of increased productivity—as a loss of freedom. To work under the constant supervision of a manager and a stopwatch, said one skilled worker, was "getting down to slavery." Scientific management, declared Samuel Gompers, was incompatible with democracy: "Men and women cannot live during working hours under autocratic conditions, and instantly become sons and daughters of freedom as they step outside the shop gates."[8]

Economic freedom was also a rallying cry of American socialism, which reached its greatest influence during the Progressive era. Freedom was central to the Marxian conception of history at the heart of socialist ideas. Socialism, in the oft-quoted words of Friedrich Engels, would propel mankind from "the kingdom of necessity," where human relations (including those in the ostensibly "free" market) were governed by coercion into "the kingdom of freedom." In the nineteenth century, most advocates of socialism in the United States were European immigrants. By the turn of the century, the Americanization of socialism was proceeding apace, spurred by the same sense of economic injustice that inspired Progressive reform.

In 1912, the Socialist Party had 150,000 dues-paying members, published hundreds of newspapers, enjoyed substantial support in the American Federation of Labor (AFL), and had elected scores of local officials. Socialism flourished on the Lower East Side of New York City, where it fed on the economic exploitation of immigrant workers and Judaism's reform tradition, and in old Populist regions of the Midwest, where it spoke the traditional language of land ownership as the basis of freedom. No one was more important in spreading the socialist gospel or linking it to ideals of equality, self-government, and freedom than Eugene V. Debs, who crisscrossed the country preaching that capitalism reduced workers to "slavery" while control of the economy by the democratic state held out the hope of "political equality and economic freedom." It was the task of socialism, said the western labor leader John O'Neill, to "gather together the shards of liberty" scattered by a government controlled by capitalist millionaires.[9]

If the idea of economic freedom recalled the great battles of the Gilded Age, its specific meaning was subtly altered in Progressive America in response to the inexorable maturation of an industrial economy. As late as 1919, an article in *The Carpenter* defended the use of the term "wage slavery" as an accurate description of laborers forced to toil "under conditions to which they do not consent." By this time, however, that venerable metaphor had been largely eclipsed by a vocabulary more in keeping with the reality that the vast majority of the employed population would spend its life working for wages. To the Progressive social commentator David Phillips, "the basis of freedom" now required expanding the notion of citizenship to ensure that "every American" could find, "as his right," a job at a decent wage. Here was a definition of economic freedom for the industrial age. New concepts—a "living wage" and an "American standard of living"—offered a language for criticizing the inequalities of wealth and power in Progressive America while recognizing that the wage system was here to stay. Father John A. Ryan's influential book, *A Living Wage* (1906), described the American standard of living as a "natural, and absolute" right of citizenship, underpinned by the Christian principle that economic relationships should be governed by moral standards. Ryan, who had grown up in Minnesota in a family sympathetic to Henry George, the Knights of Labor, and the Populists, sought to translate into American terms Pope Leo XIII's powerful encyclical of 1894, *Rerum Novarum,* which denounced the divorce of economic life from ethical considerations, endorsed the right of workers to organize unions, and repudiated liberal individualism in favor of an organic vision of the good society.[10]

The idea that social and moral considerations, not simply the law of supply and demand, should determine the level of wages, became a staple of Progressive thought. In the Clayton Act of 1914, Congress itself proclaimed that "the labor of a human being is not a commodity." A wonderfully malleable concept, the living wage was "constantly invading new realms," in the words of Jane Addams, perhaps the era's most renowned social reformer. By the 1920s, it would include the ability to purchase labor-saving devices for the home and mass-produced consumer goods, and to enjoy new forms of entertainment such as motion pictures. Yet even as it rejected the market definition of wages, the idea of the living wage suggested that a just social order could, in fact, be grounded in the wage system. The level of wages, not economic autonomy, became the index of economic freedom, and, increasingly, "slave wages" supplanted "wage slavery" as a description of economic servitude. (Simultaneously, "white slavery," a term widely applied to wage earners in the nineteenth century, was appropriated by campaigners for social purity to describe prostitution.)[11]

In the nineteenth century, while male workers had stigmatized working for wages as a form of servitude, many feminists had seen labor outside the home as a source of autonomy. In the Progressive era, advocates of the living wage, by and large, viewed it as a male prerogative. The labor movement made some effort to organize women workers, but for the most part it clung to the nineteenth-century idea of the family wage. The living wage, said a spokesman for the AFL, was an emblem of manliness, "the right to be a man and to exercise freely and fully the rights of a free man," including the ability to protect one's wife and children from the necessity of engaging in paid work. The man obliged to send his wife and children into the factories to make ends meet, said John Mitchell, president of the United Mine Workers of America, was "not really free." Father Ryan stood out for his insistence that women "forced" to support themselves were entitled to the same remuneration as men. Many advocates of a living wage assumed that wage differentials between men and women were not unjust, since women workers did not have to support families and were accustomed to a lower "standard of life."[12]

Yet no matter how pervasive the ideology of domesticity, the stark reality was that more and more women were working for wages at the dawn of the twentieth century, and that such work was no longer, as in the past, almost entirely confined to young, unmarried women (at least among the white population). For nativeborn white women, the kinds of jobs available expanded enormously, with the opening of clerical, retail, teaching, and social work positions. By 1920, only 20 percent of employed women worked in domestic service, the largest female job category of the nineteenth century. If the slave woman had served nineteenth-century feminists as an emblem of all women's oppression, the working woman—both working-class and professional—became, for a new generation, the symbol of female emancipation. The growing number of younger women desirous of a lifelong career, wrote Charlotte Perkins Gilman, offered evidence of a "spirit of personal independence" that portended a transformation of both economic and family life. Gilman's turn-of-the-century writings reinforced the claim that the road to woman's freedom lay through the workplace, and offered the most uncompromising critique of domesticity in the history of feminist thought. The home, she argued, was the site not of woman's fulfillment but of oppression, and the housewife not the guardian of the republic or protector of social virtue but an unproductive parasite. By condemning woman to a life of domestic drudgery, prevailing gender norms rendered her "a social idiot," incapable of contributing to society or enjoying freedom in any meaningful sense of the word.[13]

Influenced by nineteenth-century Owenite communities and by Edward Bellamy's utopia, Gilman devised plans for communal nurseries, cafeterias, and laundries. Only the complete abolition of women's individualized domestic sphere would allow women to attain "domestic liberty" and "stand free as economic agents." Gilman's critique had special resonance among the era's small but growing numbers of professional women. In 1907, Harriot Stanton Blatch, daughter of the great nineteenth-century feminist Elizabeth Cady Stanton and an activist strongly influenced, like Florence Kelley, by contact with socialism during a residence in Europe, founded the Equality League of Self Support-ing Women. Ideologically, the group aimed to unite the women's movement's nineteenth-century natural rights legacy with notions of economic freedom common in the Progressive era. In practical terms, the league hoped educated women and the new army of female wage earners could join in a struggle both for the vote and for the right of all women to combine marriage, motherhood, and paid labor. Another organization of middle-class and society women, the Feminist Alliance, tried to implement Gilman's ideas by constructing apartment houses with communal kitchens and day-care centers, and campaigning for maternity leaves for employed married women.[14]

Given the realities of the labor market, as Emma Goldman pointed out, working for wages offered most women "the merest subsistence," not genuine freedom. "How much independence is gained," she wondered, "if the narrow-ness and lack of freedom of the home is exchanged for the narrowness and lack of freedom of the factory, sweat-shop, department store, or office?" Among the army of young immigrant women who entered the urban labor market in these years, paid work was first and foremost a contribution to family survival, not a quest for independence. Yet even for those who handed their paychecks over to their families, wages still signified a form of autonomy. Almost in spite of themselves, union leader Abraham Bisno remarked, working daughters of im-migrants developed a sense of independence: "they acquired the *right to a per-sonality,*" something alien to the highly patriarchal family structures of the old country. "We enjoy our independence and freedom" was the assertive statement of the Bachelor Girls Social Club, a group of female mail-order clerks in New York.[15]

The wrenching intrafamily battles between immigrants and their self-consciously "free" children, especially daughters, over employment, leisure ac-tivities, and sexual mores have been chronicled in remarkably similar accounts of virtually every immigrant group, from Jews to Mexicans. Contemporaries, na-tive and immigrant, noted, often in a tone of disapproval, the penchant of young working women for "the novelties and frivolities of fashion," and the growing number who spent part of their meager wages at dance halls and other places of entertainment. In their sociological study of Muncie, Indiana, that produced the classics *Middletown* and *Middletown in Transition* in the 1920s and 1930s, Robert and Helen Lynd attributed the rise of work among women to the hope of catching "the rear platform of the speeding 'American standard of living.'"[16]

The Lynds' pregnant quotation marks testified to the widespread popular-ity that the idea of an American standard of living achieved during the Pro-gressive era—a development that reflected a subtle shift in understandings of economic freedom. In these years a consumer definition of freedom—access to the cornucopia of goods made available by modern capitalism—began to supplant an older version centered on economic and political sovereignty. There was, of course, nothing new in the idea that the promise of American life lay, in part, in the democratization of consumption, the enjoyment by the masses of citizens of goods available, in Europe, only to the well-to-do. Nineteenth-century American economists like Henry C. Carey and labor advocates of the eight-hour day had argued that the material well-being of the mass of citizens was the surest measure of national greatness and that rising wages and a re-duction in working hours would produce more leisure, more consumption, and more prosperity.

Scholars have dated the origins of consumer society in America to the early nineteenth century, or even earlier, when goods like china, glassware, and fash-ionable clothing became objects of common use. Not until the Progressive era, however, did the consolidation of the national market and the advent of huge department stores in central cities, chain stores in urban neighborhoods, and retail mail-order houses for farmers and small town residents make available to consumers throughout the country the vast array of goods now pouring from the nation's factories. By 1910, Americans could purchase electric sewing ma-chines, washing machines, vacuum cleaners, and phonographs; by 1920, there were 8 million automobiles on American roads. Low wages and the highly un-equal distribution of income limited the consumer economy; not until after World War II would it fully come into its own. But it was in Progressive Amer-ica that the promise of mass consumption became the foundation for a new de-finition of freedom to supplant the now obsolete ideal of economic autonomy.[17]

As economic production shifted from capital goods (steel, railroad equip-ment, etc.) to consumer products, the new advertising industry perfected ways of increasing exponentially the "wants" of mankind. It also hammered home the message that freedom would now be enjoyed in the marketplace, not the workplace. Numerous products took "liberty" as a brand name or used an image of the Statue of Liberty as a sales device. Consumption was a central el-ement of freedom, an entitlement of citizenship—"every free-born American," said advertising executive Kenneth Goode, has a "right to name his own ne-cessities." Consumerism was also, according to the department store magnate Edward Filene, a "school of freedom," since it required individual choice on basic questions of living. By this definition, as opposed to older ones center-ing on economic autonomy and political sovereignty, freedom was available to women as fully as men. The "woman of today," announced an ad for Piggly

Wiggly supermarkets in 1928, was "free to choose" among the multitude of products offered for sale in its emporiums.[18]

Eventually, a new "culture of abundance" would come to define the "American way of life" and the values of thrift and self-denial, central to earlier notions of "character," would be supplanted by an ethos of personal fulfillment through the acquisition of material goods. Later social critics would see mass consumption as a diminished, depoliticized utopia, which abandoned older foundations of freedom such as active participation in public affairs in favor of passive citizenship and privatized aspirations. Yet the promise of abundance could galvanize political activism as well as promote self-absorption. Exclusion from the world of mass consumption (and unequal access to department stores, restaurants, and other sites where consumption occurred) would come to seem almost as great a denial of the entitlements of citizenship as exclusion from voting once had been. Workers' increasing "wants" inspired struggles for a "living wage," while the desire for consumer goods led many workers to join unions. "We find ourselves simply swamped by our desires," wrote the wife of one worker, in a classic statement of the dilemma of a market society. "Without the union earning power, we would not have had the money to buy the radio or countless other things." The argument that monopolistic corporations artificially raised prices at the expense of consumers would become a weapon against the trusts. "Consumers' consciousness," wrote Walter Lippmann, who emerged in these years as one of the nation's most influential social commentators, was growing more rapidly than class consciousness, with the "high cost of living" emerging as its rallying cry.[19]

A new collective actor, "the consumer," now stepped onto the stage of social reform. In the Gilded Age, Helen Campbell had brilliantly exposed the contradiction of a market economy in which fashionable women wore clothing produced by poor women in wretched sweatshops. "Emancipation on the one side," she pointedly observed, "has meant no corresponding emancipation for the other." A generation later, under the leadership of Florence Kelley, the National Consumers' League became the nation's most important advocate of laws governing the working conditions of women and children. Their very freedom of choice in the marketplace, Kelley insisted, enabled socially conscious consumers to "unite with wage-earners" by taking cognizance of the exploitative conditions under which goods were produced.[20]

OPPOSITE. One of numerous advertisements of the early twentieth century that invoked the Statue of Liberty to market consumer goods, in this case a brand of crackers. (Library of Congress)

THE SATURDAY EVENING POST

93

Armed with New KNOWLEDGE

—sure of her new skill

*The Woman of Today has made
This Plan of Household Buying a
Nation-Wide Vogue*

Because they want to be free to choose for themselves, 2,000,000 women are daily using Piggly Wiggly.

THE woman of today! So self-reliant now in all her shopping—so sure of her new skill!

Only yesterday her mother depended almost wholly on the advice of salesmen when she bought food-stuffs. Needed to be persuaded and convinced.

The woman of today with her new, wide knowledge of real values has blazed a trail of her own. That she may be entirely *free to choose for herself*, she has made this special plan of household buying a nation-wide vogue.

There are no clerks to persuade her in the Piggly Wiggly Store.

The choice foods of five continents

On the open shelves with all prices plainly marked, you find the choice foods of the world at Piggly Wiggly.

Out of the countless brands and grades on the market today, the experienced men in charge of Piggly Wiggly have selected the finest varieties of every food for you to choose from.

You take what you please in your hands, examine it, make comparisons, arrive at your own decision *purely on merit*. No clerks to wait for—no delays—no hurry, at the Piggly Wiggly Store. What useful ideas you get for dishes and menus!

And with every article you see a big square price tag, the celebrated "swinging" tag of the Piggly Wiggly Store.

Finer foods—less expense

How easily you save money at Piggly

From the ice box as well as from the shelves, you simply help yourself at the Piggly Wiggly Store

Wiggly! Week in and week out you cut your expenses for groceries. Consistently low prices are assured by Piggly Wiggly's special plan of operation.

To serve more tempting meals at lower cost—that is why two million women are now daily using this new plan of household buying. Today there are over 2800 Piggly Wiggly Stores serving the country from coast to coast.

To give your husband pleasant surprises both at the table and with your savings, try this modern method of shopping. Visit the Piggly Wiggly Store in your neighborhood.

More tempting foods at lower cost! Dishes that give new pleasure to their families—that is what Piggly Wiggly is supplying to more than 2,000,000 women

From a single store a few years ago to a nation-wide system of over 2800 stores today! Here is the amazing record of this new plan of shopping—Piggly Wiggly

PIGGLY WIGGLY
STORES
The finest kinds of each food
selected for you to choose from

Unusual opportunity to own and operate a profitable local business with the merchandising co-operation of a national organization—exclusive Piggly Wiggly franchises available in cities where stores have not been established. Open only to men who command sufficient capital to finance a number of stores. Address Piggly Wiggly Corporation, Memphis, Tennessee.

A S E R V I C E N O W O F F E R E D I N O V E R 800 C I T I E S A N D T O W N S

For the first time in American history, mass consumption came to occupy a central place in descriptions of American society and its future. In the Gilded Age, social theorists had wondered why economic progress simultaneously produced increased wealth and abject misery. The Progressive generation was strongly influenced by the more optimistic writings of Simon W. Patten, a "prophet of prosperity and progress," as the economist Rexford Tugwell would later call him. Patten taught that mass consumption offered an antidote to class warfare as well as the prospect of improving the lives of the poor, whose degradation resulted from a low standard of living rather than moral failings. In language that recalled both Adam Smith and Karl Marx, Patten proclaimed the end of the "reign of want" and the advent of a society of abundance and leisure, spurred by the rising material aspirations of the mass of citizens. Without abandoning capitalism, Americans in the dawning "new civilization" would enjoy both market liberty and the benefits promised by the socialists—personal fulfillment, economic equality, a world in which "every one is independent and free."[21]

In 1928, André Siegfried, a Frenchman who had visited the United States four times since the beginning of the century, commented that a "new society" had come into being, in which Americans considered their "standard of living" a "sacred acquisition, which they will defend at any price." In the *Atlantic Monthly,* the journalist Samuel Straus called this new society "consumptionism" and identified advertising and motion pictures as its distinctive forms of communication. In Muncie, the Lynds found that new leisure activities and a new emphasis on consumption had supplanted politics as the focus of public concern. Elections were no longer "lively centers" of public attention as in the nineteenth century and voter turnout had fallen dramatically. National statistics bore out their point; the turnout of eligible voters, over 80 percent in 1896, had dropped to less than half of those registered by 1924. There were many reasons for this decline, including the consolidation of one-party politics in the South, the enfranchisement of women (who for many years voted in lower numbers than men), and the long period of Republican dominance in national elections. But the consumerist shift from public to private concerns undoubtedly played a part. "The American citizen's first importance to his country," declared a Muncie newspaper, "is no longer that of a citizen but that of a consumer."[22]

OPPOSITE. In a Piggly Wiggly supermarket, proclaims this 1928 advertisement from the *Saturday Evening Post,* the "woman of today" is "entirely *free to choose for herself*" from the cornucopia of goods in the consumer marketplace. (Reprinted by permission of Piggly Wiggly Company, 1998)

Freedom and the Progressive State

Citizenship, nonetheless, remained central to the Progressive idea of freedom. Drawing on the heritage of the Civil War era and the reform programs of the Gilded Age, a broad coalition—reform-minded intellectuals, a resurgent women's movement, unionists, and socialists—emerged to reinvigorate the idea of an activist national state, and bring to its support a large urban middle-class and labor constituency. The old idea that "a minimum of State regulation" meant a "maximum of . . . freedom," wrote Father John A. Ryan, no longer could claim "any considerable number of adherents." Whether the aim was to regulate or destroy the power of the trusts, protect consumers, civilize the marketplace by eliminating cutthroat competition, or guarantee "industrial freedom" at the workplace, Progressives assumed that the modern era required a fundamental rethinking of the functions of government. The national state, noted one Progressive commentator, was "a moral agent," which should set the rules under which society conducted its affairs.[23]

Most of the era's reform legislation, including changes in voting requirements, regulation of corporations, and the overseeing of safety and health conditions in factories, was enacted at the municipal and state levels. But the most striking development of the early twentieth century was the rise of the nation-state, complete with administrative agencies, independent commissions, and laws establishing the parameters for labor relations, business behavior, and financial policy, and acting as a broker among the disputatious groups whose conflicts threatened to destroy social harmony. These were the years when the Federal Reserve Board, the Federal Trade Commission, and other agencies came into existence, and when the federal government, through measures like the Pure Food and Drug Act (1906), sought to set basic rules for market behavior and protect citizens from market abuses.

To most Progressives, the tradition of localism and states' rights seemed an excuse for parochialism, an impediment to a renewed sense of national purpose. Poverty, economic insecurity, and lack of industrial democracy were national problems that demanded national solutions. As for laissez-faire, this, observed the Progressive social scientist Horace Kallen, had become "anathema among lovers of liberty." Many Progressives believed that economic evolution, rather than the misconduct of capitalists, had produced the large corporation acting nationally and even internationally. The same kind of process, they concluded, had made the national state the natural unit of political action. Only energetic government could create the social conditions for freedom. The democratic state, wrote Herbert Croly, embodied an alternative to control of Americans' lives by narrow interests that manipulated politics or by the all-powerful corporations. To achieve the "Jeffersonian ends" of democratic self-determination and individual freedom, he insisted, it was now necessary to employ the "Hamiltonian means" of a government-directed economy.[24]

Progressives could reject the traditional assumption that a powerful government posed a threat to freedom because their understanding of freedom was itself in flux. In a lecture in 1880 that would exert a powerful influence on Progressive social thought, the British philosopher T. H. Green had argued that freedom was a positive concept, a matter, ultimately, of "power." Green's call for a new definition of freedom was taken up throughout Progressive America. "Effective freedom," wrote John Dewey, who pondered the question from the 1890s until his death in 1952, was far different from the "highly formal and limited concept of liberty" as a preexisting possession of autonomous individuals that needed to be protected from outside restraint. It meant "effective power to do specific things," and as such was a function of "the *distribution* of powers that exists at a given time." Thus, freedom was "always a *social* question" and inevitably also a political issue. Freedom—and the individual endowments, powers, and desires it embodied—was constructed by and enjoyed through social institutions and democratic citizenship. "Freedom," wrote Dewey's brilliant young admirer Randolph Bourne, "means a democratic cooperation in determining the ideals and purposes and industrial and social institutions of a country."[25]

What the nineteenth century had called autonomy appeared to Progressives like Dewey and Croly mere isolation; real freedom, they believed, involved the constant growth entailed by a lifetime of interaction with others. In seeing freedom as an ongoing process of self-realization, to be sure, they harked back to the Emersonian notion of personal fulfillment and even to Jefferson's natural right to "the pursuit of happiness." But to traditional notions of individualism and autonomy, Progressives wedded the idea that such freedom required the conscious creation of the social conditions for full human development. To Croly, this suggested that the state must become responsible for "a morally and socially desirable distribution of wealth." For Dewey, it meant equipping Americans with the intellectual resources required to understand the modern world, and empowering the state to combat economic deprivation and disempowerment. Progressivism, said the social scientist William F. Willoughby, "looks to state action as the . . . only practicable means now in sight, of giving to the individual, all individuals, not merely a small economically strong class, real freedom."[26]

Yet while Progressive intellectuals developed a new conception of the national state, their "new democracy" (the title of Walter Weyl's influential book) had a highly ambiguous relationship to the inherited definition of political freedom as democratic participation in governance. Enhancing the power of the state made it all the more important to identify the boundaries of political participation. During the Progressive era, a host of changes were implemented in the electoral process and political arena, many seemingly contradictory in purpose. The electorate was simultaneously expanded and contracted, empowered and removed from direct influence on many functions of government. The era witnessed the massive disenfranchisement of blacks in the South (a process begun in Mississippi in 1890 and completed in Georgia in 1908), and a constitutional amendment enfranchising women—the largest expansion of democracy in U.S. history. It saw the adoption of measures like the initiative, referendum, and recall, designed to allow the electorate to propose and vote directly on legislation and remove officials from office, and the widespread replacement of elected mayors by appointed city managers. It saw literacy tests (increasingly common in the North as well as the South) expanded, and new residency and registration requirements implemented in the hope of limiting the franchise among the poor.[27]

Taken as a whole, the electoral changes of the Progressive era represented a significant and ironic reversal of the nineteenth-century trend toward manhood suffrage and a rejection of the venerable idea that voting was an inalienable right of American citizenship. To most Progressives, the "fitness" of voters, not their absolute numbers, defined a functioning democracy. In the name of improving democracy, millions of men—mostly blacks, immigrants, and other workers—were eliminated from the voting rolls, even as millions of white women were added. The more egalitarian Progressives, like Dewey, believed that given the necessary opportunities and resources, all citizens were capable of mastering the spirit of disinterested inquiry and of applying themselves to finding pragmatic, "scientific" solutions to social problems. Thus, government could safely be removed from the control of trusts and machines and placed in the hands of "the people." Yet most Progressive thinkers were highly uncomfortable with the real world of politics, which seemed to revolve around the pursuit of narrow class, ethnic, and regional interests. Indeed, one reason for many Progressives' support for women's suffrage was the belief—encouraged by feminists—that as an independent, non-partisan force, women voters could help rescue politics from politicians and partisanship and reorient it toward the pursuit of the common good.[28]

"He didn't believe in democracy; he believed simply in government." H. L.

Mencken's quip about Theodore Roosevelt came uncomfortably close to the mark for many Progressive advocates of an empowered national state. The government could best exercise intelligent control over society through a "democracy" run by impartial experts and in many respects unaccountable to the citizenry. This technocratic impulse toward order, efficiency, and centralized management—all, ostensibly, in the service of social justice—was an important theme of Progressive reform. The title of Walter Lippmann's influential work of social commentary, *Drift and Mastery* (1914), posed the stark alternatives facing the nation. "Drift" meant continuing to operate according to the outmoded shibboleth of individual autonomy; "mastery," recognition that society could be remade by the application of rational inquiry to social problems and conflicts. "The scientific spirit," Lippmann wrote, was "the outlook of a free man." But, Lippmann feared, ordinary citizens, attached to antiquated ideas and parochial concerns, were ill-prepared to embrace it (an augury of his full-fledged repudiation of the idea of popular democracy during the 1920s). The new generation of corporate managers and educated professionals could be trusted to address creatively and efficiently America's deep social problems. For Lippmann, political freedom was less a matter of direct participation in governance than of proper policy outcomes.[29]

But alongside this elitist administrative politics arose a more democratic Progressive vision of the activist state. As much as any other group, organized women reformers were its midwives. In the first two decades of the century, as women's suffrage for the first time became a mass movement, it moved beyond the elitism of the 1890s to engage a broad coalition, ranging from middle-class club women to unionists, socialists, and settlement house workers, and its rhetoric became more democratic and less nativist. Among the reasons for the movement's expanding base was that it became linked to the broad demand for state intervention on behalf of economic freedom. The immediate catalyst was a growing awareness of the plight of the immigrant poor among women involved in the settlement house movement, and the emergence of the condition of women and child laborers as a major focus of public concern.

Still barred from political participation in most states, women nonetheless were central to the era's political history. The effort of middle-class women to uplift the poor, through clubs, settlement houses, and other agencies, and of laboring women to uplift themselves, helped shift the center of gravity of political discourse toward activist government. Well-educated middle-class women not only found a calling in providing social services and education to poor families, but discovered the severe limitations of laissez-faire orthodoxy as an explanation for urban poverty and the failure of even well-organized social work

A women's suffrage parade. (*Suffragist*, 10 Aug. 1918)

to alleviate the problems of inadequate housing, income, and health. Out of the settlement houses came not only Jane Addams and Florence Kelley but also Julia Lathrop, the first woman to head a federal agency (the Children's Bureau, established in 1912 to investigate the conditions of mothers and children and advocate their interests), and Frances Perkins, secretary of labor during the 1930s. In turning for assistance to the state, Progressive women helped to launch a mass movement for governmental regulation of working conditions and direct state assistance to improve the living standards of the poor.[30]

"We need the ballot," said labor leader Leonora O'Reilly, "to do justice to our work as home-keepers. Children need pure milk and good food, good schools and playgrounds, sanitary homes and safe streets." What historians have called "maternalist" reform—based on the assumption that the state had an obligation to encourage women's unique capacity for childbearing and child-rearing—inspired many of the era's experiments in governmental policy. Ironically, those who sought to exalt women's role within the home helped to inspire the state-building process during the Progressive era.[31]

By the time the United States entered World War I in 1917, Progressives had succeeded in bringing governmental power to bear in seeking to enhance the conditions of women's freedom, at work and at home. Laws providing for mothers' pensions (state aid to mothers of young children who lacked male support) spread rapidly after 1910. Although the pensions tended to be meager and local eligibility requirements opened the door to discrimination in application (white widows were always the primary beneficiaries, single mothers were widely discriminated against, and only 3 percent of the recipients nationally were black), the laws recognized the government's responsibility to enable women to devote themselves to their children and be economically independent at the same time. Both "egalitarian" and "difference" feminists favored mothers' pensions—the former in the hope that they would subvert women's traditional economic dependence on men, the latter as a way of strengthening traditional families and the mother-child bond. "The only way we can keep mothers free," said the feminist Crystal Eastman, was to compensate the raising of children as "a service to society." Laws prohibiting child labor, a major issue at a time when an estimated 2 million children under the age of fifteen were gainfully employed, represented another "maternalist" reform (although these laws were often opposed by poor families for whom income earned by children was essential for family survival).[32]

Other Progressive legislation recognized that large numbers of women did in fact work outside the home, but defined them as a dependent group (analogous to children) in need of state protection in ways male workers were not. In 1908, in the landmark case of *Muller v. Oregon,* the Supreme Court unanimously upheld the constitutionality of a maximum hours law for women. In his famous brief supporting the Oregon measure, Louis Brandeis invoked a battery of scientific and sociological studies to demonstrate that because they had less strength and endurance than men, long hours of labor were especially dangerous for women, while their unique ability to bear children gave the state a legitimate interest in their working conditions. Thus, three years after the notorious *Lochner* decision invalidating a state law limiting the working hours of bakers, the Court created the first large breach in liberty of contract orthodoxy. But the cost was high: at the very time that women in unprecedented numbers were entering the labor market and earning college degrees, Brandeis's brief and the Court's opinion solidified the idea that women workers were weak, dependent, and incapable of enjoying the same economic freedom as men. By 1914, twenty-seven states had enacted laws limiting the hours of labor of female workers.[33]

While the maternalist agenda built gender inequality into the early foundations of the welfare state, the very use of government to regulate working conditions called into question basic assumptions concerning laissez-faire and the sanctity of the labor contract. State regulation of the labor market began with the family, but programs based on the needs of women and children coexisted with those based on the rights of all workers. Although not all reformers were willing to take the step, it was easy to extend the idea of protecting women to demand that government better the living and working conditions of men by insuring them against the vagaries of unemployment, old age, ill health, and disability. Brandeis himself insisted that a broad definition of social welfare formed part of the "liberty" protected by the Fourteenth Amendment and that government should concern itself with the health, income, and future prospects of all its citizens. John A. Ryan's prescription for state action to secure economic freedom began with the protection of women and child laborers, and moved on to legal support for union activities, an eight-hour day, municipal housing, public ownership of utilities, and a progressive income tax. All these measures, he insisted, were necessary "to safeguard individual liberty" in an industrial society.[34]

Brandeis and Ryan envisioned a different welfare state from that of the maternalist reformers, one rooted less in the social work tradition and visions of healthy motherhood than in the idea of universal economic entitlements, including the right to a decent income and protection against unemployment and injury on the job. This vision, too, enjoyed considerable support in the Progressive era. By 1920, nearly all the states had enacted workmen's compensation laws, the entering wedge for broader programs of social insurance. But state minimum wage laws and most laws regulating working hours applied only to women. The provision of a basic living standard and a set of working conditions beneath which no individual should fall would await the coming of the New Deal.[35]

All the cross-currents of Progressive-era thinking about what *McClure's Magazine* called "the problem of the relation of the State and the corporation" came together in the presidential campaign of 1912. A "year with supreme possibilities," as Eugene V. Debs put it, 1912 witnessed a four-way contest between Republican president William Howard Taft, former president Theodore Roosevelt, now running as candidate of the Progressive Party, Democrat Woodrow Wilson, and Debs himself, representing a Socialist Party at the height of its influencε. The campaign became an extended national debate on the relationship between political and economic freedom in the age of the large corporation. At one end of the political spectrum stood the president, a bona fide Progressive, although in 1912 he stressed that economic individualism could remain the foundation of the social order so long as government and private entrepreneurs cooperated in addressing social ills. At the other end was Debs, the only candidate to demand a complete change in the economic structure to propel the nation "from wage slavery to free cooperation, from capitalist oligarchy to industrial democracy." Relatively few Americans adhered to the party's goal of abolishing the "capitalistic system" altogether, but its immediate demands—including public ownership of the railroads and banking system, government aid to the unemployed, legislation establishing shorter hours and a minimum wage, and a graduated income tax—summarized the most forward-looking Progressive thought.[36]

But it was the battle between Wilson and Roosevelt over the meaning of freedom and the role of the state in securing it that galvanized public attention in 1912. The two differed on many issues, notably the dangers of governmental power and the inevitability of economic concentration, but both believed increased state action was necessary to preserve individual freedom. Though representing a party thoroughly steeped in states' rights and laissez-faire ideology, Wilson was deeply imbued with Progressive ideas. "Of course, we want liberty," he had declared in 1911, "but what is liberty?" "Old words . . . consecrated throughout many generations," he insisted, needed to be "translated into experience," and as governor of New Jersey, he had presided over the implementation of workmen's compensation and state regulation of utilities and railroads. Nonetheless, Wilson's 1912 "program of liberty," or the "New Freedom," as he came to call it, was heavily indebted to traditional Democratic ideology. Government, he insisted, was the antagonist of freedom: "the history of liberty is a history of the limitation of governmental power, not the increase of it." Yet freedom, Wilson maintained, meant more than in Jefferson's time, and government had a responsibility to promote it: "freedom today is something more than being let alone. The program of a government of freedom must in these days be positive, not negative merely." Strongly influenced by Brandeis, with whom he consulted frequently during the campaign, Wilson insisted that freedom was "an economic idea" as well as a political one, and that the way to reinvigorate democracy was to restore market competition by freeing government from subservience to big business. Freedom could only thrive in a decentralized economy that bred independent citizens and restored self-government to local communities—goals the federal government could pursue by strengthening antitrust laws, protecting the right of workers to unionize, and actively encouraging small entrepreneurs.[37]

In retrospect, it seems clear that Wilson had little understanding of the myriad sources of corporate hegemony in a modern economy. But his warning that consolidated economic power might join with concentrated political power to the detriment of ordinary citizens was remarkably prescient, especially given the confidence of so many Progressives that the state could be counted upon to act as a disinterested arbiter of the nation's social and economic purposes. To Roosevelt's supporters, however, Wilson seemed a relic of a bygone era, whose program served the needs of small businessmen but ignored the interests of professionals, consumers, and labor. The New Freedom, wrote Lippmann, meant "freedom for the little profiteer, but no freedom for the nation from the narrowness, the . . . limited vision of small competitors." Wilson and Brandeis spoke of the "curse of bigness"; what the nation actually needed, Lippmann countered, was frank acceptance of the inevitability and benefits of bigness, coupled with the active intervention of government to counteract its abuses while guiding society toward common goals. Lippmann was articulating the core of the New Nationalism, Theodore Roosevelt's alternative vision of 1912. Wilson's statement that limits on governmental power formed the essence of freedom, Roosevelt pointedly remarked, "has not one particle of foundation in the facts of the present day." It was a recipe for "the enslavement of the people by the great corporations who can only be held in check by the extension of governmental power"; only the "regulatory, the controlling, and directing power of the government" could represent "the liberty of the oppressed."[38]

Where Wilson opposed extensive social welfare programs for making citizens dependents of the state, the Progressive Party platform offered a myriad of proposals to promote social justice. Inspired by a group of settlement house feminists, labor reformers, and Progressive social scientists, the platform laid out a blueprint for a modern, democratic welfare state, complete with women's suffrage, federal supervision of corporate enterprise, national labor and health legislation for women and children, an eight-hour day and a "living wage" for all workers, the right of workers to form unions, and a national system of social insurance covering unemployment, medical care, and old age. Roosevelt called it the "most important document" since the end of the Civil War, and the platform brought together many of the streams of thought and political experience that flowed into Progressivism. Roosevelt, of course, lost the election (although once in office, Wilson often seemed to act as a New Nationalist). But his campaign helped give freedom a modern social and economic content and established an agenda that would continue to define political liberalism for much of the rest of the century.[39]

Indeed, by 1916, writers like Herbert Croly were consciously attempting to redefine the venerable term "liberalism," previously shorthand for limited government and laissez-faire economics, to describe belief in an activist, socially conscious state.[40] This would become the word's meaning for most of the twentieth century. Modern liberalism, however, has other features conspicuously absent from the Progressive agenda: an overriding preoccupation with civil liberties, including the right to personal privacy and the free expression of ideas, and a pluralist concern for the rights of racial and ethnic minorities. With its impulse toward social cohesiveness and homogeneity, and its exaltation of the national state as the embodiment of democracy, mainstream Progressivism was not attuned to these understandings of freedom. Their origins lay elsewhere— among the radicals and cultural bohemians of Progressive America.

The Wanderer finds Liberty in America

A 1919 Americanization pageant in Milwaukee, in which
immigrants encounter Abraham Lincoln and the Statue of
Liberty. The actress dressed as Liberty is probably Golda Meir,
future prime minister of Israel. (State Historical Society of
Wisconsin)

8

The Birth of
Civil Liberties

SO CENTRAL has freedom of expression become to Americans' understanding of liberty that it is difficult to recall how fragile were its legal defenses in the early twentieth century. As a practical matter, one scholar has written, "no genuinely effective, legally enforceable right to freedom of speech" existed in the United States before the 1920s. Free speech claims rarely came to court, and when they did, judges generally allowed authorities wide latitude in determining which speech had a "bad tendency" and therefore could be suppressed. The only prewar organization devoted to the defense of civil liberties was the tiny Free Speech League, founded in 1902 by the era's leading scholarly commentator on the subject, Theodore Schroeder. Convinced that absolute freedom of speech was a necessary complement to individual autonomy in all realms of life, Schroeder avidly defended the right to free expression across the political spectrum, but won few legal victories. When Zechariah Chaffee, Jr., a professor at Harvard Law School, wrote his landmark study *Freedom of Speech*, published in 1920, he searched the judicial record in vain for a tradition of free speech jurisprudence.

Vigorous public debate, of course, was a longstanding feature of democratic politics. But it coexisted with stringent restrictions on speech deemed radical or obscene. Nor was the First Amendment yet regarded as the cornerstone of American freedom. The fiftieth anniversary and centennial (in 1841 and 1891) of the Bill of Rights passed virtually unremarked. Until the Supreme Court in the twentieth century began to "incorporate" the Bill of Rights (that is, require the states to abide by its provisions), it had little bearing on the lives of most Americans.[1]

Between 1900 and 1915, more free speech cases were brought to court than in the previous century. The litigants included advertisers seeking to avoid government regulation and the fledgling motion picture industry demanding an end to local censorship.[2] But it was the struggle of workers for the right to strike, of socialists and labor radicals against restraints on open-air speaking, and of cultural modernists and feminists for an end to the broad regulation of "obscenity" that made free speech a significant public issue. By and large, the courts rejected their claims. But these battles laid the foundation for the rise of civil liberties as a central component of freedom in twentieth-century America.

State courts in the Progressive era regularly issued injunctions prohibiting strikers from speaking, picketing, or distributing literature during labor disputes. Like the abolitionists, the labor movement developed a "Constitution of Freedom," an alternative legal outlook that, in the name of liberty, demanded the right to assemble, organize, and strike. Dozens of state laws were, in fact, enacted to limit the scope of antilabor injunctions, but most were invalidated by the courts. The investigations of the Commission on Industrial Relations, established by Congress in 1912, revealed an abysmal state of civil liberties in many industrial communities, with labor organizers prohibited from speaking freely under threat of violence from private police or suppression by local authorities. "I don't think we live in a free country or enjoy civil liberties," labor lawyer Clarence Darrow told the commission.[3]

Even more than the fight against injunctions, the battle for the right to public expression by the Industrial Workers of the World (IWW) breathed new meaning into the idea of free speech. Part trade union, part advocate of a workers' revolution that would seize the means of production and abolish the state, the IWW sought to mobilize the migrants, new immigrants, and racial minorities excluded from existing labor organizations. Lacking union halls, its organizers relied on street-corner gatherings to spread their message and attract support. In response to IWW activities, officials in Los Angeles, Spokane, Denver, and more than a score of other cities limited or prohibited outdoor meetings. The IWW responded by insisting, in the words of labor radical Elizabeth Gurley Flynn, that in "Free America," authorities could not require those who sought to speak in public to "submit a schedule of our thoughts for official approval."

To arouse popular support, the IWW filled the jails with members who defied local law by speaking in public. Sometimes, prisoners were treated with wanton brutality, as in Spokane, where three died and hundreds were hospi-

Metamorfosi

1776   1909

"Metamorfosi," from the Italian-American journal *L'Internazionale*, 15 January 1909.
Inspired by governmental efforts to repress the anarchist movement, the cartoon
transforms the Statue of Liberty into a belligerent President Theodore Roosevelt.
(Immigration History Research Center, Collection of Rudolph J. Vecoli)

talized after being jailed for violating an ordinance requiring prior approval of
the content of public speeches. The longest, bloodiest, and most publicized battle took place in San Diego in 1911, where IWW members, after being arrested
for violating a ban on downtown public speaking, were handed over to vigilante
groups for punishment. Like the abolitionists eighty years earlier, the IWW
succeeded in arousing a broad debate on the acceptable limits of public speech.
In nearly all the free speech battles it eventually forced local officials to give way.
"Whether they agree or disagree with its methods or aims," wrote one journalist, "all lovers of liberty everywhere owe a debt to this organization for . . .
[keeping] alight the fires of freedom."[4]

Second only to labor's claim to freedom of expression and access to public space, the battle over obscenity regulation—especially the right to disseminate information about birth control—exposed the limits on free speech in Progressive America. The open discussion of sexuality was intimately tied to the rise of a self-conscious radical bohemia. But the free speech issues raised by the challenge to conventional sexual mores extended far beyond its confines, and added a new dimension to the meaning of personal freedom.

The story of prewar Greenwich Village and its counterparts in San Francisco, Chicago, and other cities has often been told. Amid a flowering of experimental theaters, discussion clubs, art galleries, and little magazines, a "lyrical left" came into being, to preside, it confidently claimed, over the emancipation of the human spirit from the traditions and prejudices of the nineteenth century. One symbol of the new era was Isadora Duncan, who brought from California a new, expressive dance based on the free movement of a body liberated from the constraints of traditional technique and costume. At the famed salon in heiress Mabel Dodge's New York living room, a remarkable array of talented radicals—anarchists, socialists, Progressive reformers, feminists, artists—gathered to discuss with equal passion labor unrest, modernism in the arts, and sexual liberation. Here, it seemed, was Dewey's "community of free inquiry" at last made flesh. Though many Progressives frequented the Dodge salon, there was a world of difference between the exuberant individualism of the lyrical left and the Progressive obsession with order and efficiency. "We are free who live in Washington Square," proclaimed a poem by John Reed. And the lyrical left made freedom the key to its vision of society. In so doing, it elevated free speech to a central place in the language of liberty, and expanded it from a defense of unimpeded political debate to a demand for free expression, unrestrained by the state, on matters economic, artistic, and sexual.[5]

During the Progressive era, as the journalist William M. Reedy jested, it struck "sex o'clock" in America. Issues of intimate personal relations previously confined to private discourse blazed forth in popular magazines and public debates. For the generation of women who adopted the newly minted word "feminism" to express their demands for greater autonomy, free sexual expression and reproductive choice emerged as critical definitions of women's emancipation. Feminism, wrote one young woman, had two "dominating ideas: the emancipation of woman both as a human-being and as a sex-being." "What [women] are really after," explained Crystal Eastman, was *"freedom."* But for Eastman, freedom went beyond the vote, beyond "industrial freedom," to encompass "emotional freedom" and sexual self-determination.[6]

Greenwich Village before World War I became a center of sexual experimentation. Among others, the aura of tolerance attracted many homosexuals to the area. Organized demands for gay rights lay far in the future, but by the 1920s, with its tearooms, speakeasies, and dances, the gay community had become an important element of the Village's reputation and lifestyle. But new sexual mores spread far beyond bohemia; they flourished among the era's much-publicized young, unmarried, self-supporting women, who made sexual freedom a hallmark of their oft-proclaimed personal independence. No single factor did more to promote challenges to conventional sexual mores than the massive entrance of women into the labor market. Their presence reinforced the importance of the demand for access to birth control both to prewar feminism and to the growing consciousness of limits on freedom of speech in America.[7]

In effect, the issue of birth control gave political expression to the new sexual mores, uniting avowed proponents of women's rights with what Crystal Eastman called "the millions of unconscious feminists" who sought ways of separating sex from reproduction. In the nineteenth century, the right to "control one's body" generally meant the ability to refuse sexual advances, including those of a woman's husband. Now, it suggested the right to enjoy an active sexual life without necessarily bearing children. For the new feminists, as Eastman put it, "freedom of any kind for women" was impossible unless they "know how to control the size of their families." Emma Goldman, one of the era's most indefatigable speakers (she toured the country lecturing on subjects from anarchism to the need for more enlightened attitudes toward homosexuality), regularly included the right to birth control in her speeches on women's rights, and distributed pamphlets with detailed information about various contraceptive devices. An uncompromising advocate of "unlimited freedom of expression" as well as "freedom in love and freedom in motherhood," Goldman constantly ran afoul of the law. By one count, she was arrested more than forty times for seditious or "obscene" statements or simply to keep her from speaking.[8]

No one did more to place birth control at the heart of the new feminism than Margaret Sanger, one of eleven children born to an Irish-American working-class family, who directly challenged the laws banning contraceptive devices and information as obscene. At the outset, Sanger was part of New York's left-wing bohemia, and her campaign was closely linked to political radicalism. In 1911, she began a column on sex education, "What Every Girl Should Know," for *The Call*, a New York socialist newspaper. The ever-vigilant public censor Anthony Comstock ordered one issue, containing a column on venereal disease, barred from the mails. The following week, the *Call* published a blank column with the headline: "What Every Girl Should Know—Nothing; by order of the U.S. Post Office."

By 1914, the intrepid Sanger was openly advertising birth control devices in her own journal, *The Woman Rebel*. Freedom was Sanger's watchword. "No woman can call herself free," she proclaimed, "who does not own and control her own body. . . . No woman can call herself free until she can choose consciously whether she will or will not be a mother." Indicted under the Comstock Law for sending obscenity through the mails (an offense for which the maximum sentence was forty-five years in prison), Sanger fled to England. When she returned to America in 1915, the charges were dropped, and Sanger embarked on a nationwide speaking tour that made her name synonymous with the early birth control movement. In 1916, she opened a clinic in a working-class neighborhood of Brooklyn and began distributing contraceptive devices to poor Jewish and Italian women, an action for which she was sentenced to a month in prison. Few Progressives rallied to her defense. But Sanger became a hero among the radical intelligentsia. For a time, birth control and the free speech issues associated with it became a crossroads where the paths of labor radicals, cultural modernists, and feminists intersected. The IWW and the Socialist Party distributed her writings, and Eugene V. Debs strongly endorsed her efforts.[9]

Like the IWW free speech fights and Goldman's persistent battle for the right to lecture, Sanger's travail was part of a rich history of dissent in the Progressive era that helped to focus enlightened opinion on the ways local authorities and national obscenity legislation made a mockery of freedom of expression. But it was World War I that made civil liberties a major public issue in America. The war produced the empowered, purposeful national state Progressives had so long desired. The actions of that state, and the popular frenzy its policies unleashed, not only destroyed the Progressive impulse but propelled civil liberties to the forefront of discussions of American freedom.

World War I and the Crisis of Freedom

Looking back on American participation in the European conflict, Randolph Bourne summed up its lesson: "War is the health of the state." But what Bourne saw as a danger struck most Progressives as a golden opportunity. To them, the war offered the possibility of rationalizing American society, instilling a sense of national unity and self-sacrifice, and imposing justice in labor relations. That American power could now disseminate Progressive values around the globe heightened the war's appeal. Almost without exception, Progressive intellectuals and reformers, joined by many socialists and labor leaders, rallied to what President Wilson in 1917 called the war to make the world safe for democracy. The roster included intellectuals like John Dewey, journalists such as Walter Lippmann and Herbert Croly, AFL head Samuel Gompers, and prominent feminist social reformers like Jane Addams, Florence Kelley, and Charlotte Perkins Gilman. In *The New Republic,* Dewey urged Progressives to recognize the "social possibilities of war." The crisis, he wrote, offered the prospect of "the more conscious and extensive use of science for communal purposes," and of attacking the "immense inequality of power" within the United States, thus laying the foundations for "effective freedom."[10]

Like the Civil War, World War I, albeit temporarily, created a national state with unprecedented powers and administrative capacities. The War Industries Board presided over manufacturing, while seeking to cultivate a popular taste for "rational types of consumption." The War Labor Board mediated labor disputes. The Food Services Administration instructed farmers on modern methods of cultivation and promoted the more efficient preparation of meals. Once peace arrived, the wartime state quickly withered away. But for a time, the federal government seemed well on its way to fulfilling the task set for it by Progressives of promoting social reconstruction and economic justice.[11]

During the Civil War, it had been left to private agencies—Union Leagues, the Loyal Publication Society—to mobilize prowar public opinion. But the Wilson administration decided that patriotism was too important to leave to the private sector. American participation was vehemently opposed by the IWW and the Socialist Party (whose 1917 convention condemned the declaration of war as "a crime against the people of the United States"), and by many Americans of Irish and German descent. There was considerable skepticism outside these groups about whether democratic America should enter a struggle between rival empires. In April 1917, shortly after the American declaration of war on Germany, the Wilson administration created the Committee on Public Information (CPI) to explain to Americans and the world, as its director, George Creel, put it, "the cause that compelled America to take arms in defense of its liberties and free institutions."

Enlisting academics, journalists, artists, and advertising men, the CPI flooded the country with pro-war propaganda, using every available medium from pamphlets (of which it issued 75 million) to posters, newspaper advertisements, and motion pictures. It trained and dispatched across the country seventy-five thousand Four Minute Men, who delivered brief standardized talks (sometimes in Italian, Yiddish, and other immigrant languages) to audiences in movie theaters, schools, and other public venues. Some of the nation's most distinguished historians produced pamphlets to government specifications explaining, for example, the "common principles" shared by Jean-Jacques Rousseau, Oliver Cromwell, and Thomas Jefferson, to illustrate the historical basis of the Franco-British-American alliance. Never before had an agency of the federal government expressly attempted the "conscious and intelligent manipulation of the organized habits and opinions of the masses," in the words of young Edward Bernays, a member of Creel's staff who went on to create the modern profession of public relations.[12]

The idea of freedom, it seems, requires an antithesis, and the CPI found one in the German kaiser and, more generally, the German nation and people. Government propaganda whipped up hatred of the wartime antagonist by portraying it as a nation of barbaric Huns. Overall, however, the CPI's appeal was couched in the more positive Progressive language of social cooperation and expanded democracy. Abroad, this meant a peace based on the principle of national self-determination; at home, protecting and improving democracy. A Progressive journalist, Creel believed the war would accelerate the movement toward solving the "age old problems of poverty, inequality, oppression, and unhappiness." And the CPI directed much of its attention to persuading labor and the new immigrants that "our interest in democracy and justice begins at home." Creel took to heart a warning from the historian Carl Becker that a simple contrast between German autocracy and American democracy would not seem plausible to this audience: "You talk to him of our ideals of liberty and he thinks of the shameless exploitation of labor . . . and of the ridiculous gulf between wealth and poverty." The CPI distributed pamphlets foreseeing a peacetime social order based on "industrial democracy," complete with a "universal eight-hour day" and a living wage for all. By the war's end, it was widely believed that what Herbert Hoover called "a new industrial order" was imminent in America.[13]

While democracy served as the keyword of wartime mobilization, freedom, a subordinate theme in mainstream Progressive thinking, suddenly took on new significance. The war, a CPI ad proclaimed, was being fought in "the great cause of freedom." The most common visual motif in wartime propaganda was the Statue of Liberty, employed to urge Americans to subscribe to Liberty Loans and especially to rally support among immigrants. "You came here seeking Freedom," stated a caption on one Statue of Liberty poster. "You must now help preserve it." Buying Liberty bonds became a demonstration of patriotism. Wilson's speeches cast the United States as a land of liberty, fighting alongside a "concert of free people" to secure self-determination for the oppressed peoples of the world.[14]

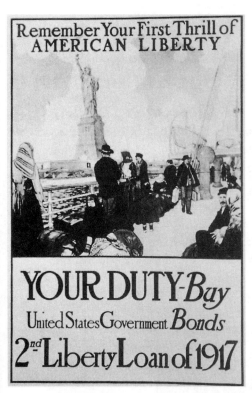

During World War I, the government produced numerous patriotic posters, including many that invoked the Statue of Liberty in an effort to appeal to newly arrived immigrants. The Italian-language poster proclaims, "Food will win the war!", urging those who came to the United States "to look for liberty" not to waste bread. (Library of Congress; Poster Collection, Hoover Institution)

The enlistment of "democracy" and "freedom" as ideological war weapons, qualities that set the country apart from German authoritarianism, inevitably inspired demands for their expansion at home. In 1916, Wilson had cautiously endorsed women's suffrage and, indeed, carried ten of the twelve states where women enjoyed the franchise. When America entered the war, Carrie Catt and the traditional women's suffrage organizations enthusiastically enlisted in the effort. Simultaneously, a new generation of college-educated activists, led by Alice Paul and organized in the National Women's Party, pressed for the vote with militant tactics many older suffragists found scandalous. Paul compared Wilson to the kaiser, burned the president's speeches, and with a group of followers chained herself to the White House fence, resulting in a seven-month prison sentence. The combination of women's patriotic service and widespread outrage over the mistreatment of Paul and her fellow prisoners pushed the administration toward full-fledged support for women's suffrage. In 1920, the decades-long struggle ended with the ratification of the Nineteenth Amendment (making the United States the twenty-seventh country to allow women to vote).[15]

But it was among black Americans that the wartime language of freedom inspired the most exalted hopes. Blacks subject to disenfranchisement and segregation were understandably skeptical of the nation's professions of freedom and fully appreciated the ways the symbols of liberty could coexist with brutal racial violence. In one of hundreds of lynchings in these years, a white mob in Springfield, Missouri, in 1906 took three black men falsely accused of rape, hanged them from an electric light pole, and burned their bodies in a public orgy of violence. Atop the pole stood a replica of the Statue of Liberty.[16]

Black leaders had struggled to find a strategy to rekindle the national commitment to equality that had flickered brightly, if briefly, during Reconstruc-

In a cartoon commenting on the 1906 lynching of three black men in Springfield, Missouri, the shadow cast by the Statue of Liberty forms a gallows on the ground. (*St. Louis Post-Dispatch*, 17 April 1906)

tion. No one thought more deeply, or over so long a period, about the problem of black freedom and the challenge it posed to American democracy than the scholar and activist W. E. B. Du Bois. "All my life," Du Bois later wrote, "I have been painfully aware of the dichotomy between American freedom for whites and the continuing subjection of Negroes." In 1906, Du Bois helped to organize the Niagara movement, which sought to reinvigorate the traditions of abolitionism and Reconstruction. "We claim for ourselves," Du Bois wrote in the group's manifesto, "every single right that belongs to a freeborn American, political, civil, and social; and until we get these rights we will never cease to protest and assail the ears of America." Five years later, he joined with a group of white reformers in creating the National Association for the Advancement of Colored People (NAACP), which launched a long legal struggle for the enforcement of the Fourteenth and Fifteenth Amendments.[17]

With the notable exception of the militant Boston editor William Monroe Trotter, most black leaders saw American participation in World War I as an opportunity to make real the promise of freedom. To Trotter, much-publicized German atrocities were no worse than American lynchings; rather than making the world safe for democracy, the government should worry about "making the South safe for the Negroes." Yet the black press rallied to the war, insisting that the service of black soldiers would result in the dismantling of racial inequality (even though the Civil War's black troops were being viciously caricatured in movie theaters throughout the country in the film *Birth of a Nation*). Du Bois himself, in a widely reprinted editorial in the NAACP's monthly magazine, *The Crisis*, called on black Americans to "Close Ranks" and enlist in the segregated army, to help "make our own America a real land of the free." Such hopes echoed in the segregated South, where the war inspired a campaign for democracy that anticipated the larger and better organized "Double-V" crusade of World War II. If blacks closed ranks, said a preacher in the Texas hamlet of Kildare, they must demand "another war for democracy, right here at home."[18]

The war unleashed social changes that altered the contours of American race relations. The combination of increased wartime production and the cutoff of immigration from Europe opened thousands of industrial jobs to black laborers, inspiring a massive migration from South to North. By 1920, nearly half a million blacks had left the South. Many motives sustained the Great Migration—higher wages in northern factories (even if blacks remained confined to menial and unskilled positions), opportunities for educating their children, escape from the threat of violence in the South and the backbreaking work of sharecropping, the prospect of exercising the right to vote. All of these and more were understood as components of freedom, interpreted through the lens of black Americans' distinctive historical experience. James Reese moved from Florida to Chicago in 1917, "looking for a free state to live in." The biblical story of Exodus was firmly fixed in black consciousness. Migrants spoke in apocalyptic terms of a Second Emancipation, of Crossing over Jordan or leaving the realm of pharaoh for the Promised Land. One group of emigrants from Mississippi stopped when their train crossed the Ohio River to sing, "I am bound for the land of Canaan."[19]

The black migrants, mostly young men and women, carried with them "a new vision of opportunity, of social and economic freedom," as Alain Locke explained in the preface to his influential book, *The New Negro* (1925). Even after the bloody Chicago race riot of 1919, when blacks were asked what they most prized about life in the North, nearly all of those interviewed by the city's Commission on Race Relations answered, "Freedom." Yet that riot, the worst of several violent confrontations that shattered cities throughout the country, also exposed the vast disappointments that migrants encountered: severely restricted employment opportunities, exclusion from unions, rigid housing segregation, and machine control of urban politics that limited the impact of the right to vote. The last year of the war witnessed an orgy of violence (there were eleven lynchings in Georgia alone in May 1918) and a wave of repression that drove the NAACP out of local communities throughout the South. Meanwhile, the Paris Peace Conference of 1919 sacrificed the principle of self-determination—ostensibly the Allies' major war aim—on the altar of imperialism, so far as the world's non-white peoples were concerned. Nation-states were created for the peoples of Eastern Europe, but not for what Wilson's adviser Colonel Edward House, called the "backward countries" of Asia and Africa. In the end, the Allies left the British empire intact, while dividing up German and Turkish colonies among the victorious British and French.[20]

The result was a feeling of deep betrayal that affected everyone from Du Bois, who had traveled to Paris to plead the cause of colonial independence, to ordinary black Americans. Du Bois was forced to conclude that Wilson had "never at any single moment meant to include in his Domocracy" black Americans or the non-white peoples of the world. In the new black ghettoes of the North, the disappointed hopes of World War I kindled widespread support for the separatist movement launched by Marcus Garvey, a recent immigrant from Jamaica. Freedom for Garveyites meant national self-determination; they demanded for blacks the same internationally recognized identity now enjoyed by Poles, Czechs, and the Irish. "Everywhere we hear the cry of freedom," Garvey proclaimed in 1921. "We desire a freedom that will lift us to the common standard of all men . . . freedom that will give us a chance and opportunity to rise to the fullest of our ambition and that we cannot get in countries where other men rule and dominate." To Du Bois and other established black leaders, Garvey was little more than a demagogue. But the massive following his movement achieved in the early 1920s offered the best testimony to the sense of betrayal the war and its aftermath kindled in black communities. No one, said Arnold E. Gregory, a Savannah minister, believed "more whole-heartedly in democracy than the Negro does." Would the nation, he wondered, ever satisfy blacks' "longings after American liberty?"[21]

Among aggrieved workers, the official language linking patriotism with democracy and freedom inspired hopes that an era of social justice and economic empowerment was at hand. In 1917, Wilson had told the AFL, "while we are fighting for freedom, we must see to it among other things that labor is free." Labor took him seriously—more seriously, it seems, than Wilson intended. The government itself, as one machinist put it, had "proclaimed to the World that the freedom and democracy we are fighting for shall be practiced in the Industries of America." During the war, union membership doubled, to over 5 million workers, and millions more rallied around the demand for an end to "industrial slavery." "One can hear the footsteps of the Deliverer," wrote garment union leader Sidney Hillman, one of those caught up in the utopian dreams inspired by the war and reinforced by the Russian Revolution of 1917. "Labor will rule and the World will be free."[22]

In the first month of American involvement in the war, Walter Lippmann had declared that the struggle for democracy would not end with the "overthrow of Prussian autocracy." America must turn its attention "to our own tyrannies—to our Colorado coal mines, our autocratic steel industries, our sweatshops, and our slums." The armistice was followed, in 1919 and 1920, by the greatest wave of labor unrest in American history. Throughout the country, workers appropriated the imagery and rhetoric of the war, parading in army uniforms with Liberty buttons, denouncing their employers and foremen as "kaisers" and demanding "freedom in the workplace." In the tightly controlled textile districts of the North Carolina Piedmont, workers flocked to the tiny United Textile Workers union and in a series of strikes beginning in 1919 demanded "industrial emancipation at home." American workers, said one union newspaper, were "hungry for freedom," while employers had "blotted that grand word 'Liberty' from our dialect," the "very thing" the nation had been fighting for in Europe.

In the West Virginia coalfields, a company manager warned in 1918, wartime propaganda had raised unrealistic expectations among workers, who took the promise of "an actual emancipation" too "literally." When the war ended, miners demanded an end to company absolutism. The struggle for the union, one miner wrote, was a "struggle for freedom and liberty." Kansas, where a 1920 law prohibited strikes in key industries, substituting the resolution of labor disputes by an "industrial court," witnessed a four-month protest strike by ten thousand miners. Here, where pro- and antislavery forces had battled in the 1850s, the strikers' language—"involuntary servitude," "half-slave and half-free"—linked the ideals of World War I back to the irrepressible conflict.[23]

The wartime language of nationalism, economic democracy, and freedom helped to inspire the era's greatest labor uprising, the steel strike of 1919–20, which at its peak involved some 365,000 mostly immigrant workers. Like their nineteenth-century predecessors, the new immigrants had arrived imagining the United States as a "land of freedom," where men were equal before the law, could worship as they pleased, enjoyed economic opportunity, and had been emancipated from the oppressive social hierarchies of Europe. "American is a free country," one Polish immigrant wrote home. "You don't have to be a serf to anyone." Work in the steel industry belied these expectations. Before the war, the steel mills were miniature autocracies, where workers, according to one study, confronted "an irresistible power" that arbitrarily established wages and working conditions and suppressed all efforts at union organizing. During the war, workers flooded into the Amalgamated Association, the steel union that had been all but moribund since its catastrophic defeat at Homestead a generation earlier. By the end of 1918 they had won an eight-hour day. The armistice was quickly followed by a drop in production and employment and by the resumption of employers' anti-union activities. "For why this war?" asked one immigrant steelworker at a union meeting. "For why we buy Liberty bonds? For the mills? No, for freedom and America—for everybody. No more [work like a] horse and wagon. For eight-hour day." If the steel strike illustrated the aspirations galvanized by the war in the name of freedom, its crushing defeat marked the beginning of an era of retreat for organized labor and for the idea of industrial freedom.[24]

The beating back of demands for fundamental change in economic relations was a devastating rebuke to the hopes with which so many Progressives had enlisted in the war effort. In 1917, Randolph Bourne had shrewdly remarked that their enthusiasm for the war exposed the underside of the Progressives' outlook. Their talk of reconstructing society masked a set of managerial attitudes in which democratic values were "subordinated to technique." Bourne ridiculed the naïveté of intellectuals who believed they could mold the conflict according to their own "liberal purposes." The war, he predicted, would empower not Progressive reformers, but the "least democratic forces in American life." Bourne's prescience soon become apparent. For all the administration's exalted rhetoric, the war inaugurated the most intense repression of civil liberties the nation has ever known. It laid the foundation not for the triumph of Progressivism but for one of the most conservative decades in American history.[25]

Perhaps the very nobility of wartime rhetoric contributed to the massive suppression of dissent, for in the eyes of Wilson and many of his supporters, America's goals were so self-evidently benevolent that disagreement could only bespeak treason to the ideas of democracy and freedom. For the first time since the Alien and Sedition Acts of 1798, the federal government enacted statutes to restrict freedom of speech. The Espionage Act of 1917 prohibited not only spying and interfering with the draft but also "false statements" that might impede military success. Although Congress denied Wilson the authority he requested to censor the press, it granted extremely broad powers to the Postmaster General to bar antiwar publications from the mails. In the following year, the Sedition Act criminalized spoken or printed statements intended to cast "contempt, scorn, contumely or disrepute" on the "form of government" or that advocated interference with the war effort. Soon afterward, Congress authorized the deportation of anarchist aliens. More than two thousand persons were charged with violating these statutes and over one thousand were convicted, among them Eugene V. Debs, sentenced to ten years in prison for an antiwar speech. (Before his sentencing, Debs gave the court a lesson in the history of American freedom, tracing the tradition of dissent from Tom Paine to the abolitionists and women's suffrage leaders, and pointing out that the nation had never engaged in a war without internal opposition.) Numerous publications, including virtually the entire socialist press and many foreign-language newspapers, were denied the use of the mails, often for their "general tenor" rather than specific violations of the law.[26]

Many private groups seized upon the atmosphere of repression as a weapon against domestic opponents. Employers cooperated with the government in crushing the Industrial Workers of the World, a move long demanded by business interests in the West. In September 1917, operating under one of the broadest warrants in American history, federal agents swooped down on IWW offices throughout the country, arresting hundreds of leaders and seizing files and publications. The repression of dissent reached its climax with the Red Scare of 1919–20, a response, in part, to social tensions generated by the Russian Revolution and the massive strike wave that followed the war. Thousands of radicals were arrested and hundreds deported, including Emma Goldman. "The word 'Liberty,' " declared an Italian-American newspaper, "has become a myth."[27]

Even more extreme repression took place at the hands of state governments. During the war, thirty-three states outlawed the possession or display of red or black flags (symbols, respectively, of communism and anarchism), and twenty-three adopted laws creating the crime of "criminal syndicalism," the advocacy of unlawful acts to accomplish political change or "a change in industrial ownership." (Thus, patriotism became linked to support for the economic status quo as well as for the war). John White, an Ohio farmer, was sentenced to twenty-one months in prison for saying that the murder of innocent women and children by German soldiers was no worse than what the United States had done in the Philippines. The use of the German language became a particular target of pro-war organizations. In Iowa, Governor William L. Harding issued a proclamation restricting oral communication in schools, public places, and over the telephone to the English language. Freedom of speech, he declared, did not include "the right to use a language other than the language of the country." Minnesota, home to a large German-American population and an active labor movement, prohibited virtually all union activity during the war and established a Commission of Public Safety to root out disloyalty from the state. Throughout the country, the playing of German music was prohibited, school curricula were scrutinized to ensure their patriotism, and teachers were required to sign loyalty oaths.[28]

If the war and its aftermath proved anything, Lippmann wrote in 1919, it was that "the traditional liberties of speech and opinion rest on no solid foundation." But while some pro-war Progressives protested individual excesses, most, including Lippmann himself, acquiesced in the broad suppression of civil liberties. More was involved here than the familiar tendency to equate wartime dissent with disloyalty. Civil liberties, by and large, had never been a major concern of Progressivism, which had always viewed the national state as the embodiment of democratic purpose and insisted that freedom flowed from participating in the life of society, not standing in isolated opposition. Many Progressives viewed broad claims for individual rights as symptoms of the excessive individualism they blamed for many of society's ills. Strong believers in the active use of governmental power to improve social conditions, and sharp critics of the courts' penchant for overturning enactments of democratically elected legislatures in the name of "liberty," Progressives were ill-prepared to develop a coherent defense of minority rights against majority or governmental tyranny. From the AFL to New Republic intellectuals, moreover, supporters of the war saw the elimination of socialists and alien radicals as a necessary prelude to the integration of labor and immigrants into an ordered society, an outcome they hoped would emerge from the war.[29]

American involvement in World War I lasted barely nineteen months, but it cast a long shadow over the ensuing decade. The idealistic goals with which the war began, commented the young minister Reinhold Niebuhr, seemingly had been abandoned: "we are rapidly becoming the most conservative nation on earth." Under the heading "Sweet Land of Liberty," *The Nation* in 1923 detailed recent examples of the degradation of American freedom: lynchings in Alabama, Arkansas, and Florida; the beating by Columbia University students of an undergraduate who had written a letter defending freedom of speech and the press; the arrest of a union leader in New Jersey; the refusal to allow a socialist to speak in Pennsylvania. The repression eased somewhat over the next few years, but the reason, commented one civil libertarian, was "that there is little to repress." Americans, commented the British writer D. H. Lawrence in 1923, prided themselves as being the "land of the free," but "the free mob" had destroyed the right to dissent. "I have never been in any country," he wrote, "where the individual has such an abject fear of his fellow countrymen."[30]

With the defeat of the labor upsurge of 1919 and the dismantling of the wartime regulatory state, business seized on the rhetoric of democracy, Americanism, and "industrial liberty" as weapons against collective bargaining. Some corporations during the 1920s implemented a new style of management, complete with private pension and medical insurance plans and the promise of job security. But at the core of their American Plan stood the open shop, a workplace free of unions. Collective bargaining, declared one group of employers, represented "an infringement of personal liberty and a menace to the institutions of a free people." The open shop embodied "the principles of individual liberty and freedom," and prosperity depended on giving business free rein, unimpeded by unions or government regulation. In case workers failed to understand the message, it was reinforced in a massive propaganda campaign linking unionism and socialism as threats to freedom and examples of the sinister influence of foreigners on American life.[31]

During the 1920s, labor lost over 1 million members and unions conceded demand after demand to employers in an effort to stave off complete elimination. In cities like Minneapolis and Seattle, until recently centers of thriving labor movements with their own cooperatives and consumer organizations, unions and their institutional infrastructure all but ceased to exist. Uprisings by the most downtrodden workers occurred sporadically throughout the decade. The imposition of scientific management in southern textile mills led to desperate strikes by workers who believed employers were "making slaves out of the men and women" who labored there. "The most damnable system ever put on a free people," was how one worker described the new regime, but facing the combined opposition of employers, local politicians, and the courts, these uprisings were doomed to defeat.[32]

In the postwar years, the Progressive ideals of industrial freedom and a socially conscious national state were eclipsed by a resurgence of doctrinaire laissez-faire economics. The Supreme Court reasserted the primacy of freedom of contract, striking down a federal child labor law as an invasion of states' rights and even repudiating *Muller v. Oregon* in a 1923 decision overturning a minimum wage law for women in Washington, D.C. Now that women enjoyed the vote, the justices declared, they were entitled to the same workplace freedom as men. "This," lamented Florence Kelley, "is a new *Dred Scott* decision," which, in the name of liberty of contract, "fills those words with the bitterest and most cruel mockery."[33]

Even as Kelley wrote, the women's movement was dissolving into its component parts, partly because the achievement of suffrage eliminated the bond of unity between various kinds of activists each "struggling for her own conception of freedom," in the words of labor reformer Juliet Stuart Pyntz. Black women insisted the movement must now demand enforcement of the Fifteenth Amendment in the South, but won little support from white feminists. A few prominent feminists, most notably Harriot Stanton Blatch, joined the rapidly diminishing Socialist Party, convinced that with suffrage achieved, women should support an independent electoral force that would promote state protection of all vulnerable workers, not just women. The longstanding division between two competing definitions of woman's freedom—one based on motherhood, the other on the right to work—now crystallized in the debate over an Equal Rights Amendment (ERA) to the Constitution proposed by Alice Paul and the National Women's Party. To Paul, the elimination of all legal distinctions "on account of sex" was the logical sequel to enfranchisement. Having achieved political equality, women no longer needed special legal protection. To supporters of mothers' pensions and protective legislation, which the ERA would sweep away, the proposal represented a giant step backward. In the end, both "egalitarian" and "difference" feminists suffered reverses. The ERA campaign failed, and in 1929 Congress repealed the Sheppard-Towner Act of 1921, a major achievement of the maternalist reformers that had provided federal assistance to programs for infant and child health.[34]

Where the prewar feminist demand for personal freedom survived was in the vast consumer marketplace and the actual behavior of the decade's much-ballyhooed "New Woman." Moribund as a political issue, female liberation resurfaced as a lifestyle, the stuff of advertising and mass entertainment, denuded of any connection to political or economic radicalism. Sexual freedom now meant an assertion of individual autonomy or personal rebellion, an emblem of free choice, not one element of broader social reform. What had been scandalous a generation earlier—women's self-conscious pursuit of sexual pleasure—now became a device to market goods from cigarettes to automobiles. (Edward Bernays, who masterminded the public relations campaign to persuade women to smoke, dubbed cigarettes women's "torches of freedom.") As depicted in advertising and motion pictures, the New Woman—young, single, independent—typically smoked, drank, wore revealing attire, and engaged in a far freer sex life than her mother or grandmother. Once married, however, she found contentment within the home, "liberated," according to advertisements, from "cooking slavery" and household drudgery by labor-saving appliances.[35]

In 1924, the social scientist Horace Kallen remarked that the United States had just passed through "one of the most critical ten-year periods" in its history. Among the changes was the disintegration of Progressivism as a political movement and body of thought. The wartime belief in the conscious creation of a new world order died in Paris, and the government's success in whipping up mass hysteria and xenophobic hatreds seemed to undermine the very foundation of democratic thought—the idea of the self-directed citizen. By the 1920s, the idea of "the people" as a rational collective entity, invented during the American Revolution, appeared to have been rendered obsolete. Freudians emphasized the unconscious, instinctual motivations of human behavior; scientists pointed to wartime IQ tests allegedly demonstrating that large numbers of Americans were mentally unfit for self-government. "The great bulk of people are stupid," one advertising executive commented, explaining why ads played on the emotions rather than providing actual information.[36]

During the 1920s, Walter Lippmann published two of the most penetrating indictments of democracy ever written, *Public Opinion* and *The Phantom Public*, valedictories to Progressive hopes for the application of "intelligence" to social problems via mass democracy. Instead of acting out of careful consideration of the issues or even individual or collective self-interest, the American voter, Lippmann claimed, was ill-informed, myopic, and prone to fits of enthusiasm. Not only were modern problems beyond the understanding of ordinary men and women (a sentiment that had earlier led Lippmann to favor administration by experts), but in an age of mass communications the independent citizen was nothing but a myth. The government, like advertising copywriters and journalists, had perfected the art of creating and manipulating public opinion—a process Lippmann called the "manufacture of consent"—while at the same time consumerism was sapping Americans' concern for public issues. Dewey, who struggled to defend the idea of an engaged citizenry as

A 1920s advertisement for the Excel Electric Cooker. (Library of Congress)

the basis of social betterment, ceded ground before Lippmann's critique. "The public," Dewey wrote, "seems to be lost; it is certainly bewildered."[37]

Another casualty of the war and its aftermath was Progressivism's blithe faith in the federal government as the embodiment of national purpose. Not only wartime repression but the constitutional amendment prohibiting the manufacture and sale of intoxicating liquors, passed by Congress in 1917 and ratified two years later, offered to many urban Progressives and Greenwich Village bohemians a notable illustration of how public power, in the wrong hands, could go grievously awry. Building on prewar struggles for freedom of expression by labor, socialists, and birth control advocates, some Progressives now acquired a new appreciation for civil liberties—rights an individual may assert against government—as essential elements of American freedom. In effect, they rediscovered Madison's warning that democratic government itself could endanger freedom. The result was the beginning of a subtle shift from the language of majority rule and effective democracy to a discourse of rights, checks on state power, and individual autonomy. In the name of a "new freedom for the individual," the 1920s saw the birth of a coherent concept of civil liberties, and with it, the beginnings of meaningful legal protection for freedom of speech against the actions of the state.[38]

During World War I, the prolific pacifist minister John Haynes Holmes later recalled, "there suddenly came to the fore in our nation's life the new issue of civil liberties." The arrest of antiwar dissenters under the Espionage and Sedition Acts inspired the formation in 1917 of the Civil Liberties Bureau, which in 1920 became the American Civil Liberties Union (ACLU). Over the next decades, the ACLU would take part in most of the landmark cases that precipitated a "rights revolution" that gave substantive meaning to traditional civil liberties, such as freedom of speech and the press, and invented new ones, like the right to privacy. At its inception, however, the ACLU was a small, beleaguered organization. A coalition of pacifists, Progressives like Dewey shocked by wartime repression, and lawyers outraged at what they deemed egregious violations of Americans' rights, it saw its own pamphlets defending free speech barred from the mails by postal inspectors. The dominant figure in the organization's early history was Roger Baldwin, a prewar pacifist. Baldwin was "antistatist in the extreme." His profound distrust of governmental power set him apart from most Progressive reformers and did much to ground the defense of free speech in an exaltation of the autonomous individual's right to unrestrained self-expression.[39]

Slowly, the Supreme Court was forced to address the question of the permissible limits on political and economic dissent. In its initial decisions, it dealt the concept of civil liberties a series of devastating blows. In 1919, the justices upheld the constitutionality of the Espionage Act and the conviction of Charles T. Schenck, a socialist who had distributed antidraft leaflets through the mails. Speaking for the Court, Justice Oliver Wendell Holmes declared that the First Amendment did not prevent Congress from prohibiting speech that presented a "clear and present danger" of inspiring illegal actions. For the next half century, Holmes's doctrine would remain the basic test in First Amendment cases. Since the justices usually allowed public authorities wide latitude in deciding which speech was in fact "dangerous," it hardly provided a stable foundation for the defense of free speech in times of crisis. A week after *Schenck*, the Court unanimously upheld the conviction of Debs, even though his speech condemning the war had not urged resistance to the draft or government. It also affirmed the wartime jailing of the editor of a German-language newspaper whose editorials had questioned the constitutionality of conscription.

Also in 1919, the justices upheld the conviction of Jacob Abrams and five other men for distributing pamphlets critical of the American intervention in Russia after the Bolshevik Revolution. This time, however, Holmes and Louis Brandeis dissented, marking the emergence of a Court minority committed to a broader defense of free speech. Six years after Abrams, Brandeis (who had come to regret voting with the majority in *Schenck* and *Debs*) and Holmes again dissented when the Court upheld the conviction of Benjamin Gitlow, a Communist whose *Left-wing Manifesto* calling for revolution led to his conviction under New York's criminal anarchy law. "The only meaning of free speech," Holmes declared, was that advocates of every set of beliefs, even "proletarian dictatorship," should have the right to convert the public to their views in the great "marketplace of ideas" (an apt metaphor for a consumer society). Brandeis had already called for the application of the First Amendment to the states. "I cannot believe," he wrote, "that the liberty guaranteed by the Fourteenth Amendment includes only liberty to acquire and to enjoy property." Now, although Gitlow was convicted, the Court majority observed that the Fourteenth Amendment obligated the states to refrain from unreasonable restraints on freedom of speech and the press. The comment marked a major step in the process by which the Bill of Rights was transformed from an often ineffective statement of principle into a significant protection of civil liberties.[40]

Slowly, the tide of civil liberties jurisprudence began to turn. Although explaining judicial voting is a notoriously inexact science, it seems likely that the extent of wartime and postwar repression shocked at least some members of the Supreme Court into a greater sensitivity to civil liberties questions. By the end of the 1920s, the Court had voided the criminal syndicalism law of Kansas and a Minnesota statute allowing for censorship of the press. The new regard for free speech was not confined to political expression, the ACLU's dominant concern in these years. In 1930, the Court reversed the conviction under the Comstock Law of Mary Ware Dennett for sending a sex education pamphlet, *The Sex Side of Life*, through the mails. Three years later a federal court overturned the Customs Service's ban on James Joyce's *Ulysses*, a turning point in the battle against the censorship of works of literature.[41]

Meanwhile, Brandeis was crafting an intellectual defense of civil liberties on grounds somewhat different from Holmes's model of a competitive market in ideas. In 1927, Brandeis concurred on procedural grounds when the Court upheld the conviction of Anita Whitney, a prominent California socialist and women's rights activist, for attending a convention of the Communist Labor Party, which advocated violent revolution. But he issued a powerful defense of freedom of speech as essential to active citizenship in a democratic polity: "Those who won our independence believed . . . that freedom to think as you will and to speak as you think are indispensable to the discovery and spread of political truth. . . . The greatest menace to freedom is an inert people." A month after the decision, the governor of California pardoned Whitney, terming freedom of speech the "indispensable birthright of every free American." The intrepid Mrs. Whitney was soon back in court for violating a California statute making it a crime to display a red flag. This time, she had greater success. In 1931, the Supreme Court overturned the law as "repugnant to the guaranty of liberty contained in the Fourteenth Amendment." Slowly, a judicial defense of civil liberties was being born.[42]

Who Is an American?

Even as the slow growth of civil liberties during the 1920s expanded the substance of American freedom, the implementation of severe restrictions on immigration narrowed the definition of those entitled to enjoy its blessings. Rather than a repudiation of Progressivism, the triumph of a nativist definition of Americanism drew on crucial elements of prewar thought. We are accustomed to thinking of Progressivism as a precursor to major developments of the twentieth century—the New Deal, the Great Society, the empowered national state. But it is important to remember how in so many ways Progressives still bore the marks of their nineteenth-century origins. The idea of "race" as a permanent, defining characteristic of individuals and social groups retained a powerful hold on their thinking. Consciously or not, it circumscribed the "imagined community" of Progressive America.

African-Americans were excluded from nearly every Progressive definition of freedom. In some ways, the disenfranchisement of southern blacks was a typical Progressive reform, a step, its advocates claimed, toward "upgrading" the electorate and allowing for a broader democracy among remaining voters. Indeed, in Mississippi, the first state to revise its constitution to eliminate black suffrage, disenfranchisement was soon followed by the direct election of judges, the initiative and referendum, and other measures that placed the state in the mainstream of Progressive reform. Women's suffrage was achieved by a constitutional amendment that left the states free to limit voting on other grounds, and thus did nothing for the vast majority of the country's black women. Barred from joining most unions and from skilled employment, black workers had little access to "industrial freedom." A majority of adult black women worked outside the home, but for wages that offered no hope of the independence work ostensibly provided, and their occupations—overwhelmingly domestic and agricultural—remained unaffected by laws regulating the hours and conditions of female labor. Nor could blacks, the majority desperately poor, participate fully in the emerging consumer economy, either as employees in the new department stores (except as janitors and cleaning women) or as purchasers of the consumer goods now flooding the marketplace.

Progressive intellectuals, social scientists, labor reformers, and suffragists all displayed a remarkable indifference to the black condition. Walter Weyl waited until the last fifteen pages of The New Democracy to introduce the "race problem." Though he acknowledged that "white democracy" was a contradiction in terms, he offered no concrete proposal for moving toward a more egalitarian standard. Some settlement house reformers tried to address the problems of the urban black poor, but few understood the innumerable disabilities under which blacks labored. Most accepted segregation as natural and equitable, assuming there should be white settlements for white neighborhoods and black settlements for black.[43]

Theodore Roosevelt's ingrained belief in Anglo-Saxon racial destiny (he called Indians "savages" and blacks "wholly unfit for the suffrage") did nothing to lessen the Progressive intellectuals' enthusiasm for his New Nationalism. Even Jane Addams, one of the few Progressives to take a strong interest in black rights, and a founder of the NAACP, acquiesced when the Progressive Party convention of 1912 rejected a civil rights plank in its platform and barred contested black delegates from the South. Woodrow Wilson, a native of Virginia, could speak without irony of the South's "genuine representative government" and its exalted "standards of liberty." His administration imposed full racial segregation in Washington and hounded from office considerable numbers of black federal employees. "Have you a 'new freedom' for white Americans and a new slavery for your African-American fellow citizens?" William Monroe Trotter asked the president during a contentious audience in 1914.[44]

The status of blacks, however, was only one strand in what Progressives called the era's "race problem." The *Dictionary of Races of Peoples*, published in 1911 by the U.S. Immigration Commission, listed the immigrant "races" within a hierarchy ranging from Anglo-Saxons at the top down to Hebrews, Northern Italians, and, lowest of all, Southern Italians—allegedly violent, undisciplined, and incapable of genuine assimilation. Popular bestsellers like *The Passing of the Great Race*, published in 1916 by Madison Grant, president of the New York Zoological Society, warned that the influx of new immigrants and the low birthrate of native white women threatened to obliterate the foundations of American civilization. If democracy could not flourish in the face of vast inequalities of economic power, neither, most Progressives believed, could it survive in a nation permanently divided along racial and ethnic lines. Somehow, the very nationalization of politics and economic life served to heighten awareness of ethnic and racial difference, and spurred demands for "Americanization"— the conscious creation of a more homogenous national culture.[45]

The task of Americanizing the new immigrants was taken up by public and private bodies of all kinds—educators, employers, labor leaders, social reformers, and public officials. Americanization was not necessarily incompatible with respect for immigrant subcultures and the right of individuals to retain Old World loyalties. At Jane Addams's Hull House in Chicago, teachers encouraged immigrants to value their European heritage, teaching English through tales of the struggles for independence of Italians, Greeks, and Poles. Other versions of Americanization were more coercive. The Ford Motor Company's famed sociology department entered the homes of immigrant workers to evaluate their clothing, furniture, and cuisine according to American standards. Until the United States entered World War I, however, efforts at Americanization were largely conducted by private organizations. It was the war that transformed Americanization into a government-sponsored campaign to instill undivided loyalty in immigrant communities and gave the concept "American" a deeply conservative new meaning.[46]

The wartime obsession with "100 per cent Americanism" not only led the federal and state governments to unprecedented restrictions on freedom of expression but demanded that immigrants demonstrate their unwavering devotion to the United States. No longer, declared Theodore Roosevelt in September 1917, was there room for "divided loyalty." Patriotism now meant absolute support for the government and the war, while labor radicalism, sympathy for the Russian Revolution, and a desire to retain elements of foreign culture, including immigrants' native language, were stigmatized as "un-American." By 1919, the vast majority of the states had enacted laws restricting the teaching of foreign languages. In 1922, Oregon became the only state ever to require all students to attend public schools—a measure deemed necessary, said the state's attorney general, to alleviate "religious suspicions" by abolishing parochial institutions and to prevent "bolshevists, syndicalists and communists" from organizing their own schools. The campaign intensified during the 1920s—a decade of citizenship education programs in public schools and vigorous efforts by employers to teach immigrants English and instill an appreciation for "American values." Only "an agile and determined immigrant," commented the *Chicago Tribune*, could "hope to escape Americanization by at least one of the many processes now being prepared for his special benefit."[47]

No matter how coercive, Americanization programs assumed that the new immigrants (and especially their children) could adjust to the conditions of American life, embrace "American ideals and ideas," and become productive citizens, enjoying the full blessings of American freedom. Yet simultaneously, the war strengthened the conviction that certain kinds of immigrants ought to be excluded altogether from American life. The new immigrants, one advocate of restriction declared in 1919, were far less attuned to the values of democracy and freedom than "the Anglo-Saxon," as evidenced by their attraction to "extreme political doctrines" such as anarchism and socialism. Intelligence tests administered to recruits by the army seemed to confirm "scientifically" that blacks, Irish Americans, and the new immigrants stood far below native white Protestants on the IQ scale.[48]

Perhaps the most menacing reflection of the renewed association between racialism, citizenship, and ideas of freedom was the spectacular resurgence of the Ku Klux Klan in the early 1920s. By mid-decade, the Klan claimed over 3 million members, nearly all white nativeborn Protestants, mostly respectable members of their communities. Unlike the Klan of Reconstruction days, the organization in the 1920s sank deep roots in parts of the North. For a time, it was the largest private organization in the state of Indiana. In the 1920s, the Klan insisted, civilization faced a broader array of enemies than during Reconstruction—not only blacks but immigrants (especially Jews and Catholics), and all the forces (feminism, labor radicalism, even, on occasion, the giant corporation) that endangered "individual liberty." Despite its extremism, in demanding that control of the nation be returned to "citizens of the old stock," the Klan reflected a sentiment widely accepted in 1920s America.[49]

The linkage of Americanism, intelligence, and "race" helped to inspire a fundamental change in immigration policy, the implementation of a new answer to the venerable question, "Who is an American?" In 1924, in a repudiation of the tradition of open entry for whites except for specifically designated classes of undesirables, Congress imposed the first sharp limits on European immigration, establishing a nationality quota system that sought to ensure that descendants of the old immigrants would forever outnumber children of the new. "America must be kept American," declared President Calvin Coolidge in signing the 1924 statute; his secretary of labor, James J. Davis, commented that immigration policy, once based on the ideal of asylum and the need for labor, now must rest on a biological definition of the ideal population. Although enacted by a highly conservative Congress, the 1924 immigration law reflected, among other things, the Progressive desire to improve the "quality" of democratic citizenship and employ scientific methods to rationalize public policy. Simultaneously, it revealed how these aims were overlain with pseudoscientific assumptions about the superiority and inferiority of particular "races" and influenced by the political power of descendants of the old immigrants and the pragmatic need for immigrant labor. The result was less a rational definition of the boundaries of nationhood than a hodgepodge of contradictory policies.[50]

The 1924 law severely restricted immigration from Southern and Eastern Europe and barred the entry of all those ineligible for naturalized citizenship—that is, the entire population of Asia. With women now recognized as part of the political nation, Congress also overturned a 1907 law requiring American women who married foreigners to assume the citizenship of the husband—except in the case of those who married Asians, who still forfeited their nationality. At the same time, to satisfy the demands of large farmers in California, who relied heavily on seasonal Mexican labor, no quotas at all were established for nations of the western hemisphere. The seemingly "scientific" calculation of the new nationality quotas—based on the "national origins" of the American population dating back to 1790—involved a highly speculative analysis of past census returns, with the results, as in the case of Irish-Americans, sometimes altered to increase allowable immigration. Meanwhile, non-whites were excluded altogether when calculating the origins of the American population—otherwise African nations would have received a far higher quota than the tiny numbers they were eventually allotted. But then, the entire concept of race as a basis of public policy lacked any rational foundation. The Supreme Court admitted as much in 1923 when it rejected the claim to naturalization of Bhagat Singh Thind, an Asian Indian and World War I veteran who asserted that as a "pure Aryan," he was actually white. "White," the Court declared, was part of "common speech, to be interpreted with the understanding of the common man" (a forthright affirmation of what a later generation would call the "social construction" of race).[51]

Only a handful of Progressives seriously questioned the massive Americanization efforts of the World War I era. Horace Kallen, who coined the phrase "cultural pluralism," insisted that the country should glory in its ethnic and cultural diversity rather than attempting to suppress it. Toleration of difference was itself part of the "American Idea," Kallen wrote. The United States was and always would be a "federation of nationalities" in which groups retained their separate identities while cooperating as citizens toward common goals. Louis Brandeis, like Kallen a Zionist, insisted that "True Americanism" required not coerced assimilation, but that "each race or people, like each individual" should enjoy the right to unfettered development.

Probably the most penetrating critique issued from the prolific pen of Randolph Bourne, whose 1916 essay, "Trans-National America," pointedly linked demands for Americanization to the Progressive obsession with forging "an integrated and disciplined America." "There is no distinctive American culture," Bourne pointed out, exposing the fundamental flaw in the Americanization model. The nation's music, poetry, philosophy, and other cultural expressions were produced by the interaction between individuals and groups. Rather than a threat to a preexisting culture, continued immigration was essential to cultural vitality. The alternative was "stagnation." Whereas Kallen seemed to view group identities as primordial and never-changing, Bourne posited a democratic, cosmopolitan society, in which the parochial loyalties of immigrants and natives alike were submerged in a "trans-national" culture freed from the Americanizers' uniformity. Meanwhile, the idea that Southern and Eastern Europeans were unfit to become citizens, or could only do so by abandoning their traditions in favor of Anglo-Saxon ways, was being challenged from another source. Anthropologists Franz Boas, Alfred Kroeber, and Ruth Benedict insisted that no scientific basis existed for theories of racial superiority or for the prevailing notion that societies and races inhabited a fixed spectrum running from "primitive" to "civilized."[52]

Whatever their differences in emphasis, Kallen, Bourne, Boas, and others planted the seeds of a pluralist vision of Americanism that would eventually become a "touchstone of liberal enlightenment." At the time, however, their writings had little impact on public policy. In the 1920s, the most potent defense of pluralism emanated from the new immigrants themselves, who in the face of immigration restriction, prohibition, a revived Ku Klux Klan, and widespread anti-Semitism and anti-Catholicism reasserted the validity of cultural diversity and identified toleration of difference—religious, cultural, and individual—as the essence of American freedom. In effect, they reinvented themselves as "ethnic" Americans, claiming an equal share in the nation's life but, in addition, the right to remain in many respects culturally distinct. The

Roman Catholic Church urged immigrants to learn English and embrace "American principles," but strenuously insisted on the right to maintain a separate system of schools and other institutions. In 1924, the Catholic Holy Name Society brought ten thousand marchers to Washington to challenge the Klan and nativism and to affirm the loyalty of Catholics to the nation. Throughout the country, organizations like the B'nai B'rith and the National Catholic Welfare Council lobbied for laws prohibiting discriminatory practices by employers, colleges, and government agencies. The Americanization movement, declared a Polish newspaper in Chicago, had "not the smallest particle of the true American spirit, the spirit of freedom, the brightest virtue of which is the broadest possible tolerance."[53]

Time would reveal that in a society increasingly knit together by mass culture and a consumer economy, few could escape the gravitational pull of assimilation. The department store, dance hall, and motion picture theater were as much agents of Americanization as the school and workplace. In the 1920s, however, every major city still harbored self-contained ethnic enclaves, with their own civic institutions, theaters, churches, and foreign-language newspapers, and a sense of separate identity heightened by the emergence of independent nation-states in Eastern Europe after the war. It would be wrong, to be sure, to view ethnic communities as either homogeneous or as wholly united in opposition to assimilation. From the perspective of many women, the voyage to the New World marked an escape, as one female Italian emigrant put it, from "fear" and "servility." In these circumstances, Americanization often seemed less an assault on an inherited culture than a loosening of patriarchal bonds and an expansion of freedom. "All women have to be free a little," said one Polish-American woman, hardly a ringing claim to autonomy, but a fruit, nonetheless, of Americanization.[54]

The efforts of immigrant communities to resist coerced Americanization and of the Catholic Church to defend its alternative system of schools broadened the definition of liberty for all Americans. In landmark decisions of the 1920s, the Supreme Court struck down Oregon's law requiring all students to attend public schools and Nebraska's prohibiting teaching in a language other than English (including, according to the letter of the law, Latin). "The protection of the Constitution," the Nebraska decision declared, "extends to all, to those who speak other languages as well as to those born with English on the tongue," a startling rebuke to enforced Americanization. In these cases, the Court expanded the Fourteenth Amendment's guarantee of equal liberty to embrace the right to "marry, establish a home and bring up children," and practice religion as one chose, without governmental interference. The decisions gave pluralism a constitutional foundation and paved the way for the Court's elaboration, two generations later, of a constitutional right to privacy.[55]

In 1927, the New School for Social Research in New York City organized a series of lectures on the theme of "Freedom in the Modern World." Founded eight years earlier as a place where "free thought and intellectual integrity" could flourish in the wake of wartime repression, the school's distinguished faculty included Dewey and historian Charles Beard (who had resigned from Columbia to protest the dismissal of antiwar professors). The lectures depicted a country in which nineteenth-century values had lingered into the modern world, where they were increasingly inappropriate. "The idea of freedom," declared the economist Walton H. Hamilton, had become "an intellectual instrument for looking backward. . . . Liberty of contract has been made the be-all and end-all of personal freedom . . . the domain of business has been defended against control from without in the name of freedom." The free exchange of ideas, moreover, had not recovered from the crisis of World War I. Dissenting views, declared Max Eastman, editor of the defunct *Masses*, once the journalistic voice of prewar bohemia, were widely considered "un-American," and in the popular mind, belief in liberty had been replaced by "the complex of national efficiency." The "sacred dogmas of patriotism and Big Business," said Horace Kallen, who had been forced to leave the University of Wisconsin for defending the rights of pacifists, dominated teaching, the press, and public discourse. Never before, he added, had "the unity of the social structure and the social purpose . . . so clamped down upon the individual."

As the comments of Eastman and Kallen suggested, the lectures offered, among other things, a valedictory for Progressivism. For what was more central to Progressive thought than belief in "national efficiency" and "social purpose"? That state and private efforts to produce social cohesion could seriously threaten freedom had been one of the unpleasant surprises of World War I. As a result, observed Kallen, the meaning of freedom had become "a paramount topic of liberal discussion." In that discussion, the seeds had been planted for a new conception of freedom, which combined two disparate elements in a sometimes uneasy synthesis. One was the Progressive belief in a socially conscious state making what Dewey called "positive and constructive changes" in economic arrangements. The other centered on respect for civil liberties and cultural pluralism, and declared realms of life such as group identity, personal behavior, and the free expression of ideas outside legitimate state concern.[56]

For the moment, however, a different understanding of freedom reigned supreme, one that reveled in the unimpeded reign of economic enterprise, yet tolerated the coercive surveillance of private life and individual conscience. The prosperity of the 1920s and the elimination of "widespread poverty" (or so President Herbert Hoover claimed in his inaugural address of 1929) seemed to vindicate this definition of freedom.[57] When the economic crash came, it would be swept aside, making way for the consolidation of modern liberalism and its remapping of American freedom.

In the realist style characteristic of 1930s art on both sides of the Atlantic, a sculpture by Attilio Piccirilli, commissioned by the Works Progress Administration for the Whitman, Massachusetts, post office, depicts two muscular laborers as ringers of the Liberty Bell. (National Archives)

9

The New Deal and the Redefinition of Freedom

THE STOCK MARKET CRASH of 1929 plunged the United States into the greatest economic and social crisis in its history. By 1932, the gross national product had fallen by one-third, prices by nearly half, and over 15 million Americans—25 percent of the labor force—could not find work. For those who retained their jobs, wages fell precipitously; not until 1940 would they regain the level of 1929. One-third of the nation, said Franklin D. Roosevelt when he assumed the presidency in 1933, was ill-housed, ill-clothed, and ill-fed. Hungry men and women lined the streets of major cities; thousands more inhabited the ramshackle shanty towns called Hoovervilles that sprang up in parks and on abandoned land. With the future shrouded in uncertainty, the birth rate fell to the lowest level in the nation's history.[1]

No part of American society was left untouched by the crisis. The Depression spawned a political revolution, sweeping from power the Republicans who had controlled the presidency since 1896 except for Woodrow Wilson's two terms, and inaugurating a long period of Democratic hegemony. Under Roosevelt's guidance, the Democratic Party was transformed from a bastion of localism and states' rights into a broad coalition of farmers, industrial workers, the reform-minded urban middle class, liberal intellectuals, and, somewhat incongruously, the white-supremacist South, all committed to federal intervention to reconstruct the economy and provide Americans with social security.

Southern power in Congress meant that the boundaries of American freedom would continue to be defined by race. But the empowering of the new immigrants through their active participation in a resurgent labor movement and the New Deal's political coalition went a long way toward recasting the definition of American nationality.

The Great Depression made inevitable, in the words of one historian, a "reckoning with liberty." For too many Americans, Roosevelt proclaimed, "life was no longer free; liberty no longer real; men could no longer follow the pursuit of happiness." The "American Way of Life," that ebullient slogan of the consumer culture of the 1920s, took on a hollow ring. Americans, the Lynds discovered when they revisited Muncie, Indiana, in the mid-1930s, still believed themselves "the freest people in the world." But the Depression discredited the idea that social progress rested on the unrestrained pursuit of wealth and transformed expectations of government, reinvigorating the Progressive conviction that the national state must protect Americans from the vicissitudes of the marketplace. It elevated "social citizenship"—a broad public guarantee of economic security—to the forefront of American discussions of freedom. When Irwin Edman, a popular writer on philosophy and aesthetics, in 1941 published a survey of democratic thought from the ancient world to the twentieth century, he concluded that what distinguished his own time was its awareness of "the social conditions of freedom." Thanks to the Depression, "economic security" had "at last been recognized as a political condition of personal freedom."[2]

Security and Freedom

Like the Civil War, the New Deal recast the idea of freedom by linking it to the expanding power of the national state. But now, economic security, not the civil and political rights of the former slaves and their descendants, dominated discussions of freedom. "Our democracy," wrote John A. Ryan, "finds itself . . . in a new age where not political freedom but social and industrial freedom is the most insistent cry."[3] During the 1930s, the federal government took up this responsibility, laying the foundations, in the name of greater freedom, for a broadly based American welfare state. The pathbreaking legislation of the 1930s arose from the historical conjuncture of an unprecedented economic crisis, the coming to power of men and women long committed to government-sponsored reform, and a popular mobilization demanding far-reaching economic and social change.

Many Americans reacted to the Depression with resignation or blamed themselves for economic misfortune. Others responded with protests at first spontaneous and uncoordinated, since unions, socialist organizations, and other groups that might have provided disciplined leadership had been decimated during the 1920s. Armed farmers blocked roads to protest low farm prices and to prevent foreclosures by banks. Twenty thousand unemployed World War I veterans descended on Washington, D.C., in the spring of 1932 to demand early payment of a bonus due in 1945, only to be driven away by federal soldiers. Throughout the country, the unemployed demonstrated for jobs and public relief, an early indication of a shift in attitudes toward the government's responsibility for underwriting economic freedom.[4]

Franklin D. Roosevelt's election as president in 1932 did much to rekindle hope among those who called themselves, in the words of a worker writing to Secretary of Labor Frances Perkins, "slaves of the depression." Indeed, Roosevelt's inauguration unleashed a flood of poignant letters to the federal government describing what a Louisiana sugar laborer called the "terrible and inhuman condition" of many workers. "We have no freedom nor rights," wrote an employee of an Alabama textile mill. "Truly," a Detroit brass worker wrote the president, "there is such a thing as economic slavery." Roosevelt, declared another correspondent, should "be another Lincoln and free us from the slavery that we are in." "I believe that this country owes a living to every man, woman, and child," a New York City woman wrote to Harry Hopkins, administrator of the Works Progress Administration (WPA), one of the New Deal's public works agencies. "If it can't give us this living thru private industry it *must* provide for us thru government means. [This is] an inalienable right of every person living under this government."[5]

The 1930s produced a plethora of books and essays on freedom. The large majority took for granted that individualism as a coherent philosophy was outmoded and that the Depression had made a new definition of liberty imperative. Influenced by Ryan, the National Catholic Welfare Conference in 1935 abandoned the church's traditional hostility to federal intervention in the economy, declaring that "social justice" required a government guarantee of continuous employment and a "decent livelihood and adequate security" for all Americans. A number of works bore the title *Land of the Free*, often employed ironically. In one such volume, Archibald MacLeish juxtaposed Farm Security Administration photographs of migrants, refugees, and impoverished sharecroppers with his own poetry to question the reality of freedom in desperate times. "We told ourselves we were free," he wrote. Now, "we wonder if the liberty is done . . . or if there's something different men can mean by Liberty."

In this 1930 cartoon from the *Chicago Defender*, a black weekly, the Brotherhood of
Sleeping Car Porters awakens a worker to the promise of economic freedom. (*Chicago
Defender*, 25 Jan. 1930)

Americans, declared a writer in the journal *Christian Century*, had been "so busy
defending a traditional . . . concept of freedom from governmental control" that
they had forgotten that liberty can be protected "*by* the state" rather than need-
ing protection from it. Such views were widely shared. A 1935 survey by *Fortune*
magazine found that among poor respondents, 90 percent believed that the government should guarantee that "every man who wants work has a job." Freedom, John Dewey insisted in 1935, needed once more to be reconceptualized:
"today, it signifies liberation from material insecurity."[6]

   In the quest for economic freedom, the most striking development of the
1930s was the mobilization of millions of workers in the Congress of Industrial Organizations (CIO), founded in 1935 to organize laborers in mass pro-

duction industries ignored by the AF of L. The mid- and late thirties were an era of heroic labor militancy. Aided by a federal government for the first time openly taking the side of labor, the CIO wrested contracts from the nation's most powerful corporations, finally winning the decades-long battle for union-ization in basic industries. In tightly controlled industrial towns scattered across the nation, CIO organizers spread the message that the "political liberty for which our forefathers fought" had been "made meaningless by economic in-equality" and "industrial despotism." With the National Industrial Recovery Act of 1933 and the Wagner Act two years later offering statutory recognition of workers' right to collective bargaining, the union became an emblem of cit-izenship. "We are free Americans," declared the Steel Workers' Organizing Committee. "We shall exercise our inalienable rights to organize into a great in-dustrial union."

Building on the idea, so prominent in the 1920s, that an American standard of living based on mass consumption was the key to prosperity, CIO leaders explained the Depression as the inevitable result of an imbalance of wealth and income. One-tenth of 1 percent of the population in 1929 earned as much as the bottom 42 percent, making it impossible for society to absorb the products that rolled off modern assembly lines. The role of unions, in cooperation with the government, was to "create a consumer's demand" by raising wages and re-distributing wealth, thus stimulating production and lifting the nation back to prosperity. Indeed, the pathbreaking 1937 agreement between the auto workers' union and General Motors spoke of a "rate of pay commensurate with an American standard of living." By mid-decade, the "underconsumptionist" ex-planation of the Depression was widely accepted among New Dealers, who drew from it the conclusion that the government must act to raise dramatically wage earners' share of the national income.[7]

But even more than the struggle for a living wage, the overriding concern of the labor uprising, as garment union leader Sidney Hillman declared, was the "quest for security." "The most marked trait of present life, economically speaking, is insecurity," Dewey wrote in 1930. The vast economic transforma-tions of the past half century had woven insecurity into the fabric of working-class life, a situation the Depression greatly exacerbated. In the face of pervasive economic uncertainty and widespread resentment over the arbitrary and capri-cious authority of employers, union activists resurrected the Progressives' lan-guage of "economic freedom" and "industrial democracy," as well as an older vocabulary equating oppressive working conditions with "slavery." "Libera-tion" meant not only higher wages but stable and steady employment, an end to management's "dictatorship" on the shop floor, and recognition of the right to collective bargaining. Workers, declared one union newspaper, had "rights in the workshop as well as at the polls. . . . Can you really be free if they are not recognized and respected?" The Depression had brought in its wake the collapse of the "welfare capitalism" of the 1920s and a sharp increase in arbitrary discipline and dismissals. The coming of the union, said a member of New York City's transport workers' organization, enabled workers "to go to our bosses and talk to them like men, instead of . . . like slaves." The implementation in 1930s contracts of impartial grievance procedures and seniority systems governing hiring, firing, and promotions marked a major accomplishment of the CIO unions, stabilizing a chaotic employment situation and offering members a sense of dignity and freedom by ending what one union organizer called the "total submissiveness of worker to boss." "People were longing for some kind of security in their work," declared a local organizer for the auto workers union, and the CIO went a long way toward providing it.[8]

Throughout the nation's industrial heartland, the labor upsurge altered the balance of political and economic power and propelled to the forefront of politics labor's grievances—economic insecurity and pervasive inequality—and its goal of a fairer, freer, more egalitarian America. Unlike the AFL, with its traditional aversion to government intervention in labor-management relations, the CIO put forward an ambitious program for federal action to shield Americans from economic and social insecurity, complete with public housing, universal health care, and unemployment and old age insurance. Other mass movements of the mid-1930s also placed the question of economic justice, not just economic recovery, on the political agenda. In 1934, Huey Long, heir to Louisiana's populist and socialist traditions as well as the state's heritage of undemocratic politics, launched his Share-Our-Wealth movement. Long called for confiscatory taxes on the wealthy to finance an immediate grant of $5,000 and a guaranteed minimum annual income for all Americans. In the same year, the "radio priest," Charles E. Coughlin, attracted millions of listeners by his attacks on Wall Street bankers and rapacious capitalists and his call for expanded public works and other measures to combat unemployment. (Coughlin's crusade would later shift to anti-Semitism and support for European fascism.) Meanwhile, Dr. Francis Townsend, a California physician, won wide support for a proposal that unemployed older Americans receive a monthly payment of $200 from the government, with the requirement that they spend it immediately to stimulate the economy.[9]

Franklin D. Roosevelt did not enter office with a blueprint for dealing with the Depression or enhancing the social welfare. As the historian Richard Hofstadter pointed out, one searches Roosevelt's record in vain for a consistent intellectual vision. Campaigning in 1932, he spoke of the government's responsibility to guarantee "every man . . . a right to make a comfortable living," yet simultaneously called for a balanced budget and offered few specific plans for economic recovery. A master improvisor and brilliant political tactician, Roosevelt shifted course many times during his presidency. In 1933 and 1934, the New Deal concentrated on promoting agricultural and industrial recovery, reforming the banking system and securities industry, and providing emergency relief and public employment. Spurred by the failure of his initial policies to pull the country out of the Depression (and the Supreme Court's invalidation of some of these early measures), and the growing popular clamor for more sweeping measures, Roosevelt in 1935 launched the "second New Deal," with greatly expanded relief programs and a highly publicized tax on concentrated fortunes. The centerpieces, however, were the Wagner Act, which threw the government's support behind the right to collective bargaining, and Social Security, a complex system of unemployment insurance, old age pensions, and aid to the disabled and to dependent children. These were soon followed by appropriations for the construction of public housing and by the Fair Labor Standards Act of 1938, which established a national minimum wage and limits on hours of work.[10]

Compared with the welfare states of social democratic Europe, the American version was far more decentralized and involved lower levels of public spending. It represented a dramatic departure, however, from the traditional functions of government in the United States. Taken together, these measures transformed the relationship of the federal government to the economy and citizenry and established much of the agenda of modern American liberalism. The federal government assumed a responsibility, which it has never wholly relinquished, for guaranteeing Americans a living wage and protecting them against economic and personal misfortune. The second New Deal forged a close and long-lasting marriage between the Democratic Party, organized labor, and the federal government, all committed to enhancing mass consumption and taming the power of big business. "Laissez-faire is dead," wrote Walter Lippmann, "and the modern state has become responsible for the modern economy [and] the task of insuring the continuity of the standard of life for its people."[11]

Along with being a consummate politician, Roosevelt was a master of political rhetoric. The first president to employ the radio to bring his message directly into American homes, he was particularly adept at appealing to traditional values in support of new departures. Thus, in urging passage of the wages and hours law, he invoked the rights of "free labor." Roosevelt consciously abandoned the term "progressive" and chose instead to employ "liberal" to de-

Signs carried by striking cotton mill workers in Lumberton, North Carolina, in 1937, illustrate the survival of the rhetoric of wage slavery. (Highlander Research and Educational Center)

scribe himself and his administration. In so doing, he transformed "liberalism" from a shorthand for weak government and laissez-faire economics into belief in an activist, socially conscious state, an alternative both to socialism and to unregulated capitalism. He also reclaimed the word "freedom" from conservatives and made it a rallying cry for the New Deal. "Freedom," declared the journalist Dorothy Thompson in a speech to the American Woman's Club in 1935, "has not been the word of our generation. We have talked instead of prosperity, of high standards of living, of recovery. . . . In the name of freedom every sort of injustice has been practiced." But as early as 1934, in his second "fireside chat," Roosevelt juxtaposed his own definition of "liberty" as "greater security for the average man" to the older notion of freedom of contract, which served the interests of "the privileged few." Henceforth, Roosevelt would consistently link freedom with economic security and identify entrenched economic inequality as its greatest enemy. At the height of the second New Deal, he made the election of 1936 a crusade against "economic royalists" and pledged that the federal government would establish a "democracy of opportunity for all the people." The "right to work" and the "right to live" were no less central to citizenship than "the right to vote," and the same federal government that protected "political freedom" had an obligation to act against "economic slavery." "The liberty of a democracy," he declared in 1938, was not safe if citizens were unable to "sustain an acceptable standard of living."[12]

In the mid-1930s, with urban working-class voters providing massive majorities for the Democratic Party and business large and small bitterly estranged from the New Deal, politics reflected class divisions more completely than at any other time in American history. Conceptions of freedom were sharply divided as well. Americans, wrote George Soule, editor of *The New Republic*, were confronted with "two opposing systems of concepts about liberty," reflecting "the needs and purposes of two opposing aggregations of the population." One was the old shibboleth of "freedom for private enterprise," the other a "socialized liberty" based on "an equitably shared abundance."

If Roosevelt invoked the word to sustain the New Deal, "liberty"—in its Gilded Age sense of limited government and laissez-faire economics—became the fighting slogan of his opponents. The principal concervative critique of the New Deal, which emanated from wealthy conservatives and from "populists" like Father Coughlin, was that it restricted American freedom. When conservative businessmen and politicians in 1934 formed an organization to mobilize opposition to the New Deal, they called it the American Liberty League. Robert Taft, leader of the Republican bloc in Congress, accused Roosevelt of leading the country down the road to communism by sacrificing "individual freedom" in a misguided effort to "improve the conditions of the poor." Increasingly, the New Deal's opponents rallied around the slogan "freedom of enterprise" and opposed not only economic planning but all regulation of employment relations by the federal government.[13]

As the 1930s progressed, opponents of the New Deal invoked the language of liberty with greater and greater passion, convinced that the New Deal constituted the greatest threat to individual freedom in American history. Herbert Hoover launched ever more strident attacks on his successor for endangering "fundamental American liberties." Freedom, Hoover insisted, meant unfettered economic opportunity for the enterprising individual. Far from being an element of liberty, the quest for economic security was turning Americans into "lazy parasites" dependent on the state. For the remainder of his life, Hoover continued to call himself a "liberal," even though, he charged, the word had been "polluted and raped of all its real meanings." The fight for possession of the "ideal of freedom," the *New York Times* reported, was the central issue of the presidential campaign of 1936. Opposition to the New Deal planted the seeds for the later flowering of an antistatist conservatism bent on upholding the free market and dismantling the welfare state. But as Roosevelt's landslide reelection indicated, most Americans by 1936 had come to accept the view that freedom must encompass economic security, guaranteed by the government.[14]

Within a year of Roosevelt's reelection, the Supreme Court gave its imprimatur to this epochal shift in the meaning of freedom. Having earlier invalidated numerous pieces of New Deal legislation, major and minor, in the name of freedom of contract and states' rights, the Court in 1937 executed an astonishing about-face, spurred in no small measure by Roosevelt's sweeping reelection victory and his plan (rejected by Congress) to "pack" the Court with sympathetic judges. Beginning with a decision upholding the constitutionality of a state minimum wage law, the Court exhibited a remarkable new deference to economic regulation by both the states and the federal government. In ensuing decisions, it affirmed federal power to regulate wages, hours, child labor, agricultural production, and numerous other aspects of economic life. Heralding the advent of a new judicial definition of freedom, Chief Justice Charles Evans Hughes remarked that the words "freedom of contract" did not appear in the Constitution. "Liberty," however, did, and, Hughes continued, this required "the protection of law against the evils which menace the health, safety, morals, and welfare of the people."[15]

Roosevelt conceived of the second New Deal, and especially Social Security, as expanding the meaning of freedom by extending assistance to broad groups of needy Americans—the unemployed, elderly, and dependent—as a universal right of citizenship, not charity or special privilege. His goal, according to Frances Perkins, was a broadly inclusive cradle-to-grave system of social provision that guaranteed every American a measure of economic security. But as enacted, New Deal measures were far from universal. Political realities—especially the enduring power of urban political machines in the North and black disenfranchisement in the South—powerfully affected the drafting of legislation. The result was a two-tiered system that offered generous, nationally established benefits to some Americans, primarily white and male, while leaving others with lesser entitlements or none at all.

The Social Security Act of 1935 encompassed a series of programs with divergent structures and target populations. The most generous—old age pensions and unemployment insurance—provided aid automatically and without the stigma of dependency. By linking benefits to taxes paid by eligible wage workers, these programs identified assistance as a right rather than charity. The payroll taxes were harshly regressive, but Roosevelt believed they gave contributors "a legal, moral, and political right to collect their pensions and their unemployment benefits," which no future Congress could rescind. But this link to paid work eliminated most women, and the exclusion of agricultural, domestic, and casual laborers left uncovered the large majority of the employed black population.

Social Security also included public assistance programs, notably aid to dependent children and to the impoverished elderly. These were open to all Americans, regardless of race, who met a means test. But they set benefits at extremely low levels and authorized the states to determine eligibility standards, which in some instances included moral behavior as determined by local authorities. As a result, public assistance programs allowed for widespread discrimination in the distribution of benefits. Because recipients did not pay Social Security taxes, they soon came to bear the humiliating stigma of dependency on government handouts. The gap between the two programs widened in 1939, when wives, elderly widows, and dependent survivors of covered male workers were moved from general public relief into the Social Security system, leaving single mothers and the non-white poor to dominate what would come to be called "welfare."[16]

Designed to alleviate poverty and economic insecurity, the Social Security law of 1935 established the key elements of federal social policy for the next half century. From the system's inception, boundaries of gender and race circumscribed the new definition of economic freedom. White male (and some female) workers were covered by different programs and benefits from non-white men and poor women and children. These boundaries of inclusion and exclusion reflected prevailing social norms and political realities. The Depression had inspired widespread demands for married women to remove themselves from the labor market to make room for unemployed men. Indeed, many states and localities prohibited the hiring of women whose husbands earned a "living wage," and employers from banks to public school systems adopted rules barring married women from jobs. Although the CIO organized women workers, it too adhered to the family wage tradition. "The working wife whose husband is employed," said a vice president of the United Auto Workers, "should be barred from industry." The Social Security Act institutionalized the assumption that in normal circumstances, the man was household head and economic provider, and the wife a homemaker. The large number of women still employed as domestics also enjoyed no benefits under Social Security. "Those who need protection most are completely overlooked," the sister of a household worker complained to Secretary of Labor Perkins. "What about the poor domestics, both in private homes and private institutions. What have you done for them? Nothing."[17]

Even more dramatic was how the power of the solid South helped to mold the New Deal welfare state into an entitlement of white Americans. Roosevelt spoke of the system's universality, but the demand for truly comprehensive coverage came from the political left and black organizations. Representing Minnesota's Farmer-Labor Party, Congressman Ernest Lundeen in 1935 introduced a bill establishing a federally controlled system of old age, unemployment, and health benefits (illness being a major cause of economic hardship completely ignored by Social Security) for all categories of wage workers, plus support for female heads of households with dependents. Recognizing the long-term dangers of relegating blacks to "welfare" programs, black organizations like the Urban League and NAACP supported the Lundeen bill and lobbied strenuously for a Social Security system that enabled agricultural and domestic workers to receive unemployment and old age benefits and that established national relief standards. The Social Security Act, however, not Lundeen's proposal, became law, and its limitations, complained the *Pittsburgh Courier*, a black newspaper, reflected the power of "reactionary elements in the South who cannot bear the thought of Negroes getting pensions and compensations," and who feared that the inclusion of black workers would disrupt the region's low-wage, racially segmented labor system.[18]

Despite his great personal popularity and political power, Roosevelt preferred to work within the Democratic Party's prevailing power structure and felt he could not frontally challenge the power of southern Democrats, who during the 1930s chaired about half the committees of Congress. In 1938, with many southern congressmen turning against the New Deal (in large part out of fear that continued federal intervention in their region would upset race relations), Roosevelt tried to persuade voters to replace recalcitrant congressmen with more cooperative ones. The South's truncated electorate dealt him a stinging rebuke. In the end, because of the "Southern veto," non-white workers were confined to the weakest, least generous, and most vulnerable wing of the new welfare state. The National Resources Planning Board presciently noted in 1942 that because of their exclusion from programs "which give aid under relatively favorable conditions," blacks were becoming disproportionately dependent on "general relief," a program widely viewed with popular "disfavor." The situation, the report concluded, seemed certain to stigmatize blacks as recipients of "welfare," and welfare as a program for minorities, thus dooming it forever to inadequate "standards of aid."[19]

Overall, the Great Depression and the New Deal had a contradictory impact on black Americans. Hit hardest by the Depression, blacks benefited disproportionately from federal relief measures. Although Roosevelt seems to have had little personal interest in race relations or civil rights, he appointed Mary McLeod Bethune, a prominent black educator, as a special adviser on minority affairs and a number of other blacks to important federal positions. Key members of his administration, including his wife Eleanor and Secretary of the Interior Harold Ickes, directed national attention to the injustices of segregation, disenfranchisement, and lynching. These developments contributed to a historic shift in black voting patterns. In the North and West, where they enjoyed the franchise, blacks in 1934 and 1936 abandoned their historic allegiance to the party of Lincoln in favor of Democrats and the New Deal. A "new day" had dawned, Bethune proclaimed, when blacks would finally reach "the promised land of liberty."[20]

But hopes for broader changes in the nation's race system were quickly disappointed. Despite a massive lobbying campaign, a southern filibuster prevented passage of a federal antilynching law. Federal relief and public works employment were implemented in a blatantly discriminatory manner. In the South, many New Deal works projects refused to hire blacks. "They give all the work to white people and give us nothing," a black resident of Mississippi wrote the president in 1935. The New Deal began the process of modernizing southern agriculture, but tenants, black and white, footed much of the bill. Tens of thousands of sharecroppers were driven off the land as a direct result of the Agricultural Adjustment Administration's policy of supporting crop prices by paying landowners to reduce cotton acreage. Landlords were supposed to share federal payments with their tenants, but many failed to do so. Eventually, support for civil rights would become an acid test of liberal credentials. But in the 1930s, there was no correlation between support for Roosevelt's economic program and support for antilynching legislation or moves to incorporate black workers within Social Security. Roosevelt gave no assistance to the antilynching initiative, and Theodore Bilbo, the notoriously racist senator from Mississippi, was one of the New Deal's most loyal supporters.[21]

Nowhere were the limits of New Deal freedom more evident than in the evolution of federal housing policy, which powerfully reinforced residential segregation. Owning one's home had long been a widely shared ambition in American society. "A man is not a whole and complete man," Walt Whitman had written in the 1850s, "unless he owns a house and the ground it stands on." Although the renter is, in some ways, "freer" than the owner, in the industrial age homeownership increasingly replaced ownership of productive property as an economic measure of freedom. More than an investment, a home was a mark of middle-class respectability, and, for workers, a form of economic security at a time of low wages, erratic employment, and limited occupational mobility. In the early twentieth century, immigrants invested heavily in ethnic building and loan associations in order to purchase homes. Indeed, on the eve of World War I, a considerably higher percentage of immigrant workers than the nativeborn middle class were homeowners.[22]

The Depression devastated the American housing industry. The construction of new residences all but ceased and banks and savings and loan associations that had financed homeownership collapsed or, to remain afloat, foreclosed on many homes (a quarter of a million in 1932 alone). In 1931, President Hoover convened a Conference on Home Building and Home Ownership to review the housing crisis. Owning a home, the president proclaimed, was a "birthright" essential to "the national well-being," the embodiment of the spirit of "enterprise, of independence, and of . . . freedom." Rented apartments, Hoover pointed out, did not inspire "immortal ballads like *Home, Sweet Home,* or *The Little Gray Home in the West.*" The conference revealed that millions of urban families lived in overcrowded, unhealthy slums, and millions of other Americans resided in ramshackle rural dwellings. Private enterprise alone, it seemed clear, was unlikely to solve the nation's housing crisis.[23]

Despite Hoover's aversion to federal economic intervention, his administration established a federally sponsored bank to issue home loans. Not until the New Deal, however, did the government systematically enter the housing market. Roosevelt spoke of "the security of the home" as a fundamental right akin to "the security of livelihood, and the security of social insurance." In 1933 and 1934, his administration moved energetically to protect homeowners from foreclosure and to stimulate new construction. The Home Owners Loan Corporation and Federal Housing Administration (FHA) insured millions of long-term mortgages issued by private banks. At the same time, the federal government itself constructed thousands of units of low-rent housing. Like Social Security, New Deal housing policy represented a remarkable departure from previous government practice. Thanks to the FHA and, later, the Veterans Administration, homeownership was brought within the economic reach of tens of millions of families. It became cheaper for most Americans to buy single-family homes than to rent.[24]

Also like Social Security, housing policy was put into practice by local officials, who established a two-tiered system that reinforced existing racial boundaries. Many municipalities opted out of public housing altogether; nearly all, North as well as South, insisted that such housing be racially segregated. (In Texas, some communities financed three sets of housing projects—for whites, blacks, and Mexicans.) The FHA, moreover, had no hesitation about insuring, and sometimes insisted upon, mortgages with racially restrictive covenants, and resolutely refused to channel money into any but segregated neighborhoods. It declared entire areas, mostly in central cities, ineligible for loans. In some cases, the presence of a single black family on a block led the agency to declare the entire block off-limits for federal mortgage insurance. Along with discriminatory practices by private banks and real estate companies, federal policy was a major factor in institutionalizing housing segregation in America. In housing as in other matters, the New Deal greatly expanded the definition of American freedom while leaving intact or even reinforcing the racial barriers to the full enjoyment of freedom's benefits.[25]

"A New Conception of America"

But if the New Deal failed to dismantle the impenetrable boundary that barred non-whites from full participation in American life, the 1930s witnessed the absorption of other groups into the social mainstream. With Catholics and Jews occupying prominent posts in the Roosevelt administration and new immigrant voters forming an important part of its electoral support, the New Deal made ethnic pluralism a living reality in American politics. Thanks to the cutoff of Eastern European immigration in 1924, the increasing penetration of movies, chain stores, and mass advertising into ethnic communities, and the common experience of economic crisis, the 1930s witnessed an acceleration of cultural assimilation. But in the transformed political environment, the process had a different character from the nativist upsurge and corporate-sponsored American plans of the preceding years. For the children of the new immigrants, labor and political activism were themselves agents of a different kind of Americanization. The thirties proved that one could participate fully in the broader society without surrendering one's ideals and ethnic identity. "Unionism is Americanism" became a CIO rallying cry. "I'm in the U.S.A.," a Minnesota iron miner wrote Secretary of Labor Perkins, complaining of low wages and management hostility to unions, but "the Mesabi range isn't Americanized yet."[26]

In the mid-1930s, for the first time in American history, the left enjoyed a shaping influence on the nation's politics and culture. The CIO and the Communist Party became focal points of a broad social and intellectual impulse, a "cultural front" that helped to redraw the boundaries of American freedom. An obscure, faction-ridden organization when the Depression began, the party experienced remarkable growth during the 1930s. Its membership never exceeded one hundred thousand, but several times that number passed through its ranks, some to suffer bitter disillusionment and turn sharply to the right, others to become anti-Communist leftists, still others to emerge as independent radicals willing to work in Communist-affiliated activities. At the height of its influence, the Communist Party's militant antifascism attracted the support of numerous New Deal liberals, while its commitment to socialism resonated with a widespread belief that the Depression had proved the bankruptcy of capitalism and that Marxism offered the only comprehensive vision of a better future. As Dewey, hardly a supporter of Joseph Stalin, put it, liberalism would have to adjust itself to the realization that "the liberty of individuals" required planned action to "socialize the forces of production."

But it was not so much the party's ideology as its vitality and activism—its involvement in a mind-boggling array of activities, including demonstrations of the unemployed, epochal struggles for industrial unionism from Kentucky's Harlan County to the auto factories of Detroit, and the renewed movement for black civil rights—that for a time made it the center of gravity for a broad democratic upsurge. It is one of the era's ironies that an organization so authoritarian in structure and so tied—at least at its upper echelons—to Stalin's Russia should have contributed so much to the expansion of freedom in the United States. But men and women joined the party or cooperated with it not only to defend the world's first "workers' state" overseas, but in the hope of building unionism, fighting racial injustice, and democratizing life at home. In the end, the party did not create a new form of American socialism, but it helped to invigorate New Deal liberalism, to imbue it with a more militant spirit and a more pluralistic understanding of Americanism.[27]

Politically, the era of the Popular Front, when the Communist Party actively sought to ally itself with liberals, socialists, and independent radicals in broadly based movements for social change, lasted only a few years. Launched in 1935, it was shattered four years later by the Nazi-Soviet Pact. Even before then, the Moscow Trials of 1937, in which former revolutionaries were condemned to death as Western agents, had led numerous former allies, especially among the intelligentsia, to dissociate themselves from the party. But at the height of the Popular Front, Communists gained an unprecedented respectability, working closely with church, academic, and civil rights groups, and with the Democratic Party in many local elections. Earl Browder, the party's leader, even appeared on the cover of *Time*.[28]

The left's impact was felt far beyond the Communist Party, among intellectuals, artists, and social activists. In literature, theater, film, and dance, the Popular Front vision of American society sank deep roots and survived much longer than the political moment from which it sprang and the New Deal agencies like the federal arts and theater projects that briefly gave it an outlet. In this broad left-wing culture, social and economic radicalism, not support for the status quo, defined true Americanism; ethnic and racial diversity was the glory of American society; and "the American Way of Life" meant unionism and social citizenship, not the unbridled pursuit of wealth. The American "people," declared obsolete by Lippmann in the 1920s and viewed by many intellectuals in that decade as a repository of mean-spirited fundamentalism and crass commercialism, was suddenly rediscovered as the embodiment of democratic virtue. Museum exhibitions, murals sponsored by the Works Progress Administration, the federally sponsored "people's theater," and Hollywood films all rediscovered the American people and expanded its definition to include the new immigrants and their children, and even non-whites. Art about the people—such as Dorothea Lange's photographs of migrants and sharecroppers and documentary films like *The Plow That Broke the Plains*—and art of the people such as folksongs and black spirituals came to be seen as expressions of genuine Americanism. Painters, sculptors, photographers, and choreographers eagerly took up the task of depicting the daily routines, the work lives and leisure activities, of farmers and urban dwellers. "The heart and soul of our country," Roosevelt proclaimed, was "the heart and soul of the common man."[29]

"A new conception of America is necessary," wrote the immigrant labor radical Louis Adamic in 1938. Despite bringing "ethnic" and northern black voters into the Democratic coalition, the New Deal devoted little explicit attention to ethno-cultural issues, fearful of rekindling the divisive battles of the 1920s. It was the Popular Front, not the mainstream Democratic Party, that forthrightly sought to popularize the idea that the country's strength lay in diversity and tolerance, a love of equality, and a rejection of ethnic prejudice and class privilege. Depicting itself as an uprising of ordinary Americans who had set aside prejudice to struggle for the common good, the CIO avidly promoted the idea of ethnic and racial inclusiveness. Breaking decisively with the AFL's tradition of exclusionary unionism, it made cultural pluralism—an idea previously associated with intellectuals like Randolph Bourne and Horace Kallen and with the self-defense of ethnic and Catholic enclaves—an article of faith of a mass movement. The Communist Party, a meeting ground for nativeborn Protestant radicals, blacks, and new immigrants (especially Jews), insisted that racial and ethnic prejudice was incompatible with the country's democratic tradition. Party membership offered one road to acculturation, bringing second-generation immigrants who had grown up in ethnic ghettos into contact with indigenous regional and folk cultures, and, through self-education in literature and the fine arts, with a broadly cosmopolitan culture. At least partly because of the party, for example, young Jews from New York's Lower East Side, weaned on the Yiddish theater, came to embrace modern dance, cubism, and the plays of Ibsen and O'Neill.[30]

Later critics on the left would chide the Popular Front for unquestioning allegiance to Roosevelt, the Democratic Party, and the national state, and for a sentimental glorification of all things American. Viewed in light of the subsequent Cold War, it seems highly ironic that the Communist Party claimed to be the inheritor of "the traditions of Jefferson, Paine, Jackson, and Lincoln." The Young Communist League in 1937 even organized a celebration of the anniversary of Paul Revere's ride, and chided the Daughters of the American Revolution for failing to mark the occasion. But Popular Front culture also disseminated a more critical reading of the country's past and present. Communist historians produced pathbreaking scholarly studies of African-American and labor history, fields then ignored at mainstream universities, which shed a less than flattering light on the national past. Martha Graham's modern dance masterpiece, *American Document* (1938), an embodiment of Popular Front aesthetics with its emphasis on America's folk traditions and multi-ethnic racial heritage, centered its account of history on the Declaration of Independence and the Gettysburg Address. Yet Graham did not neglect what the narrator called "things we are ashamed of," including the dispossession of the Indians and the plight of the unemployed. Attempting to answer Crèvecoeur's old question, "What is an American?", Graham answered, in effect, not only middle-class Anglo-Saxons but also blacks, immigrants, and the working class. Earl Robinson's "Ballad for Americans," a quintessential expression of Popular Front culture that invoked the religious, racial, and ethnic diversity of American society, became a national hit and was performed at the Republican National Convention of 1940.[31]

It was fitting that "Ballad for Americans" reached the top of the charts in a version performed by the magnificent black actor and singer Paul Robeson. For where Popular Front culture moved well beyond New Deal politics was in condemning racism as a malignant set of beliefs and practices, incompatible with true Americanism. In the 1930s, groups like the American Jewish Committee and the National Conference of Christians and Jews actively promoted ethnic and religious tolerance. But whether in Harlem or East Los Angeles, the Communist Party was the era's only predominantly white organization to make fighting racism a top priority. "The communists," declared Charles H. Houston, chief legal strategist of the NAACP, "have made it impossible for any aspirant to Negro leadership to advocate less than full economic, political and social equality."

Communist influence spread even to the South, where the party helped to create the Southern Conference for Human Welfare. Founded in 1938, it brought together a new generation of homegrown radicals—New Dealers, black activists, organizers of the sharecroppers union and other labor leaders, even a few elected officials—to work for unionization, unemployment relief, and racial justice. The Communist-influenced International Labor Defense, whose origins lay in the defense of civil liberties after World War I, mobilized popular support for black defendants enmeshed in a racist criminal justice system. It helped make the Scottsboro Case, in which nine young black men were unjustly convicted of rape in Alabama, an international cause célèbre. Despite the patent implausibility of the evidence against the "Scottsboro boys," Alabama authorities three times put them on trial during the 1930s and three times won convictions. The first two verdicts were overturned by landmark Supreme Court decisions that established legal principles greatly expanding the definition of civil liberties: defendants have a constitutional right to effective counsel and states cannot systematically exclude blacks from juries. (The third set of convictions, which led to long prison sentences for five of the defendants, was allowed to stand.)[32]

Throughout the country, despite considerable resistance from white workers determined to preserve their historic monopoly of skilled positions and access to promotions, the CIO, and especially its Communist-influenced unions, welcomed blacks as members and advocated the passage of antilynching laws and the enfranchisement of southern black voters. The CIO brought black industrial workers into the labor movement for the first time in significant numbers. The Depression's devastating impact in black communities had propelled economic survival to the top of the agenda for black organizations. In this atmosphere, black workers, many of them traditionally hostile to unions because of their long experience of exclusion, responded with enthusiasm to CIO organizing efforts. The union offered not only the promise of higher wages but dignity in the workplace and an end to the arbitrary power of often racist foremen. Blacks understood the rise of the CIO through their own historical experience. Unionization, said A. Philip Randolph, head of the Brotherhood of Sleeping Car Porters and the era's most prominent black union leader, was part of the "unfinished task of emancipation." Ed McRea, a white CIO organizer in Memphis, reported that it was not difficult to persuade black workers why a union was necessary: "You didn't have any trouble explaining this to blacks, with the kinds of oppression and condition they had. It was a question of freedom."[33]

Another central element of Popular Front public culture was its mobilization for civil liberties, especially the right of labor to organize. The struggle for industrial unions encountered sweeping local restrictions on freedom of speech, as well as repression by private and public police forces. Nationwide publicity about the wave of violence directed against the Southern Tenant Farmers Union in the South and the CIO in industrial communities in the North elevated the rights of labor to a central role in discussions of civil liberties. The ACLU, primarily concerned in the 1920s with governmental repression, by 1934 had concluded that "the masters of property" posed as great a danger to freedom of speech and assembly as public authorities. "The crucial struggle for civil liberty today," declared *Social Action*, a left-wing periodical, "is among tenant farmers and industrial workers, fighting for economic emancipation and security." Beginning in 1936, a Senate subcommittee headed by Robert M. La Follette, Jr., of Wisconsin exposed the methods used by employers to combat unionization, including a vast array of spies and private police forces. Workers had "no liberties at all," an employee of General Motors wrote the committee from Saginaw, Michigan. The extensive violence unleashed against strikers in California's cotton and lettuce fields and canneries made that state, the committee report concluded, seem "more a fascist European dictatorship than part of the United States."[34]

Labor militancy and the related efforts of Communists to organize throughout the country helped produce an important shift in the understanding of civil liberties. Previously conceived as individual rights that must be protected against infringement by the state, the concept was now expanded to include violations of free speech and assembly by concentrated power in private hands. As a re-

Ben Shahn's 1939 mural, sponsored by the Section of Fine Arts of the Public Buildings Administration, depicts various aspects of American freedom, including freedom of speech, religion, and the press, and the rights to petition the government and to vote, all surrounding the hand and torch of the Statue of Liberty. The text at the center is that of the First Amendment, reflecting the central place civil liberties had assumed in the New Deal conception of freedom. (Ben Shahn. Jamaica Post Office Mural, 1939. Oil on canvas. © Estate of Ben Shahn/Licensed by VAGA, New York, NY.)

sult, just as the federal government was emerging as a guarantor of economic security, it also became a protector of freedom of expression. With its restrictions on employers' anti-union activities and explicit recognition of the right of unionists to assemble and organize, the Wagner Act, the young sociologist David Reisman observed in 1942, was one of the "essential pillars for civil liberty in our time."

Even more portentous for the future course of free speech, the same Supreme Court that had relinquished its role as a "censor" of economic legislation moved to expand its authority over civil liberties. While deferring to legislative judgments on economic issues, the justices insisted that constitutional guarantees of free thought and expression were essential to democratic governance and "nearly every other form of freedom," and therefore deserved special protection by the courts. Thus, civil liberties replaced liberty of contract as the foundation of freedom. In 1937, the justices overturned on free speech grounds the conviction of Angelo Herndon, a Communist organizer jailed in Georgia for "inciting insurrection." Three years later, they invalidated an Alabama law that prohibited picketing in labor disputes. Since 1937, the large majority of state and national laws overturned by the courts have been those that, in the justices' view, infringed on civil liberties.[35]

By the eve of World War II, civil liberties had assumed a central place in the New Deal understanding of freedom. In 1939, Attorney General Frank Murphy established a Civil Liberties Unit in the Department of Justice. "For the

first time in our history," Murphy wrote the president, "the full weight of the Department will be thrown behind the effort to preserve in this country the blessings of liberty." In 1941, the administration celebrated with considerable fanfare the 150th anniversary of the Bill of Rights. It embodied, said Roosevelt, the "freedoms that are inherent in the right of free choice by free men and women." The new appreciation of free thought and expression was hardly universal. In 1938, the House of Representatives established the Un-American Activities Committee to investigate disloyalty. Its expansive definition of the term "un-American" included Communists, labor radicals, and the left wing of the Democratic Party—in sum, the constellation of forces represented by the Popular Front—and its hearings led to the dismissal of dozens of federal employees on charges of subversion. Two years later, Congress enacted the Smith Act, which made it a federal crime to advocate the overthrow of the government. A similar pursuit of unorthodox views took place at the state level. The New York legislature's Rapp-Coudert Committee held sweeping hearings in-

vestigating "subversive" influences in New York City's public colleges, resulting in the firing in 1941 of some sixty faculty members charged with Communist sympathies.[36]

By then the New Deal, as an era of far-reaching social reform, had reached
its peak and begun to recede. In the fall of 1938, in the face of a severe economic
recession, the electorate not only rebuked Roosevelt's effort to purge conservative southerners but increased Republican congressional representation. A
long period of political stalemate followed, in which a conservative coalition
of southern Democrats and northern Republicans dominated Congress. Increasingly, the administration's energies came to focus on the storm gathering
in Europe. Even before December 1941, when the United States entered World
War II, "Dr. Win-the-War," in Roosevelt's celebrated phrase, had replaced "Dr.
New Deal." Yet, as the left's influence in Washington receded, the Popular
Front ideal of Americanism gained even wider dissemination as the official version of American society. During World War II, the new immigrants would be
fully reconfigured as loyal ethnic Americans, black Americans' lack of freedom
would assume, for the first time since Reconstruction, a prominent place on the
national political agenda, and freedom would become the nation's rallying cry
in the struggle against fascism.[37]

10

Fighting for Freedom

$\mathbf{F}_{EW\ EVENTS}$ have transformed American life as broadly and deeply as World War II. From the development of the Sun Belt to the modern struggle for black equality, the economic trends and social movements we associate with the postwar world had their roots in the war years. As during the Civil War and World War I, but on a far larger scale, wartime mobilization expanded the size and scope of government. The gross national product nearly doubled and unemployment disappeared as war production finally conquered the Depression. The insatiable demand for industrial labor sent a vast tide of migrants from rural America to the industrial cities of the North and West, permanently altering the nation's social geography. Between 1940 and 1947 some 25 million Americans, over one-fifth of the population, moved in search of new economic opportunities. The war justified a new and permanent role for the United States as a world power and created a close link between corporate-dominated business and a militarized federal government—a "military-industrial complex," President Dwight D. Eisenhower would later call it—that long survived the cessation of hostilities.[1]

In contrast to the ambiguous outcome of the Korean War and the unprecedented divisiveness spawned by Vietnam, World War II came to be remembered as the Good War, a time of national unity in pursuit of indisputably noble goals. But as in any war, acceptance of sacrifice required the conscious mustering of patriotic public opinion. By the 1940s, "to sell *goods,* we must sell *words*" had become a credo of the

1778 1943

AMERICANS
will always fight for liberty

One of numerous patriotic posters issued by the Office of
War Information during World War II. (Library of Congress)

advertising industry. And words helped to "sell" World War II. If the rallying cry of World War I had been democracy, that of World War II was freedom. It echoed in the claim of refugees from Nazism to speak for a "free Europe," talk of a wartime alliance of "freedom-loving nations," and the rhetorical division of the globe into a "free world" and a fascist realm of slavery. Wartime mobilization drew on values deeply rooted in the American experience. The portrait of the United States holding aloft the torch of liberty in a world overrun by oppression reached back as least as far as the American Revolution, and the description of a political universe half-slave and half-free recalled the irrepressible conflict and the Great Emancipator. Most dramatically, Franklin Delano Roosevelt linked the defense of American traditions with a widespread longing for a better future in what became the official statement of the war's purposes—the Four Freedoms.[2]

The Four Freedoms

Well before the Japanese attack on Pearl Harbor brought the United States into World War II, those who believed that the country must intervene to stem the rising tide of European fascism invoked the language of freedom. To awaken a reluctant country to prepare for war, interventionists popularized slogans that would become central to wartime mobilization. In June 1941, émigrés from Germany and the occupied countries of Europe joined with Americans to form the Free World Association, which sought to bring the United States into the war against Hitler. The same year saw the formation of the Fight for Freedom Committee, soon to be renamed Freedom House, a self-proclaimed "beacon lighting the struggle for a free world." With a prestigious membership that included university presidents, writers, prelates, businessmen, and labor leaders, Freedom House cast the war raging in Europe as an ideological struggle between authoritarianism and democracy, with German defeat "essential to insure man's freedom." In October 1941, it sponsored a Fight for Freedom rally at New York's Madison Square Garden, complete with an entertainment program, "It's Fun to be Free"—a somewhat incongruous name for a patriotic variety show that ended with the demand for an immediate declaration of war against Germany.[3]

But it was Roosevelt himself who formulated what would become the nation's wartime rallying cry, appealing to the defense of freedom as justification for the country's ever-expanding military assistance to beleaguered Britain. During 1940, the president experimented with various ways of describing what was

Walt Disney's program cover for the October 1941 "Fight for Freedom" rally at New York's Madison Square Garden, a gathering that demanded American entry into the European War. (Freedom House)

at stake in the world conflict. Finally, in his State of the Union Address of January 6, 1941, he spoke eloquently of a world order founded on four "essential human freedoms": freedom of speech, freedom of worship, freedom from want, and freedom from fear. In the future, he vowed, the Four Freedoms would be enjoyed "everywhere in the world."[4]

Although most of the address was drafted by speechwriters, Roosevelt himself wrote the concluding section on the Four Freedoms. And until his death in 1945, on the eve of Allied victory, he would portray the worldwide military conflict as a battle "between human freedom and human slavery." In August 1941, Roosevelt spoke of how Americans must shoulder the burden of defending "the great freedoms against the encroachment and attack of the dark forces of despotism which would enslave the globe." Once the United States entered the war four months later, the Four Freedoms became Roosevelt's favored statement of Allied aims. At various times, he compared them with the Ten Commandments, the Magna Carta, and the Emancipation Proclamation. The Four Freedoms, he declared in a 1942 radio address, embodied the "rights of men of every creed and every race, wherever they live," and they identified "the crucial difference between ourselves and the enemies we face today."[5]

Confronted with the task of preserving national unity in the face of a titanic struggle, and forced to work with an increasingly conservative Congress, Roosevelt preferred to describe freedom in general terms. He rarely discussed the mundane problems of balance-of-power diplomacy, or, until late in his presidency, the specific domestic policies that might give substantive meaning to the Four Freedoms. Together, however, the Four Freedoms had an unmistakably liberal cast. Embodying principles associated with the New Deal, they suggested that Roosevelt's policies of the 1930s were an expression of deeply held American values worthy of being spread worldwide. Freedom from fear appealed not only to a longing for peace but to a more general desire for security in a world that appeared to be out of control. Freedom of speech and religion scarcely required detailed elaboration, although they received increased attention during the war as defining characteristics of American life as opposed to Nazism. Their prominent place among the Four Freedoms accelerated the process by which the Bill of Rights, and especially the First Amendment, moved to the center of Americans' definition of liberty. In 1943, the Supreme Court reversed a 1940 ruling and, on First Amendment grounds, upheld the right of Jehovah's Witnesses to refuse to salute the American flag in public schools. The decision, a repudiation of the coercive patriotism of World War I, affirmed the sanctity of individual conscience even in times of crisis as a bedrock of freedom and

An Office of War Information poster invoking the words of Abraham Lincoln for the struggle against Nazi tyranny. (Library of Congress)

explicitly contrasted the American system of constitutional protection for un-popular minorities with Nazi tyranny.[6]

The "most ambiguous of the Four," *Fortune* magazine remarked, was freedom from want. Yet this "great inspiring phrase," as a Pennsylvania steelworker wrote to the president in 1942, seemed to strike the deepest chord in a nation just emerging from the Great Depression. Initially, Roosevelt had meant it to refer to the elimination of barriers to international commerce. But he quickly came to link freedom from want to economic aspirations more relevant to the aver-age citizen—the preservation of the "standard of living of the American worker and farmer" and a guarantee that the Depression would not resume when the war ended. "There can be no real freedom for the common man," the president declared a month before Pearl Harbor, "without enlightened social policies." Even *Fortune*, a zealous advocate of unfettered market capitalism, ad-mitted that the desire for economic security was so strong that the government must guarantee freedom from want by shouldering the "unequivocal responsi-bility for maintaining employment" and establishing a minimum standard of living in the postwar world.[7]

Talk of freedom permeated wartime America. The war witnessed an out-burst of books, pamphlets, and advertisements intended to arouse patriotic sen-timent, market war bonds ("a symbol of the Four Freedoms we are fighting for," according to the Treasury Department), and give concrete meaning to wartime ideals. *Life* magazine offered a survey of American history that iden-tified "the historic ideal of freedom" as the nation's heritage. Artists took up the theme with enthusiasm. In 1942, Hugo Ballin unveiled an enormous mural, *The Four Freedoms*, in the Burbank, California, city council chambers. Hailed as "the greatest work of art ever to come out of Pacific Palisades," it was crowded with imagery ranging from American Indians to the pope. The following year, composer Robert Russell Bennett produced a symphony of four movements, each dedicated to one of the freedoms. But by far the most widely circulated representations of the Four Freedoms were paintings by the popular artist and magazine illustrator Norman Rockwell.[8]

"Words like *freedom* or *liberty*," declared one wartime advertisement, "draw close to us only when we break them down into the homely fragments of daily life," an insight that helps to explain Rockwell's astonishing popularity. Draw-ing on the lives of his Vermont neighbors, Rockwell translated the Four Free-doms into images of real people situated in small-town America. Each of the four paintings focuses on an instantly recognizable situation: a workingman rises to speak at a town meeting; members of different religious groups are seen at prayer; a family enjoys a Thanksgiving dinner; a mother and father stand over

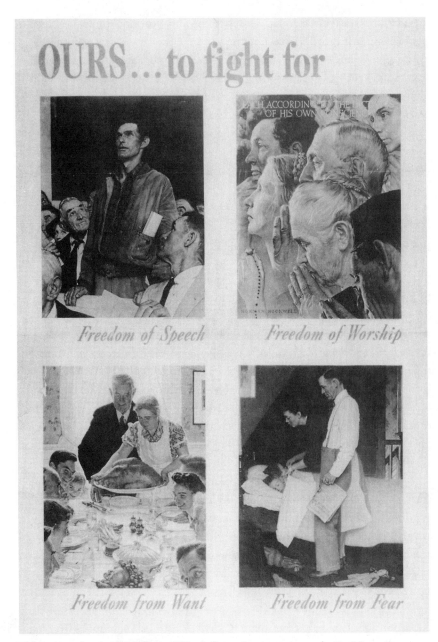

The immensely popular Office of War Information poster reproducing Norman Rockwell's paintings of *The Four Freedoms*. (Library of Congress)

a sleeping child. The works elicited an enormous response. Millions of reprints were sold and the paintings toured the country as the centerpiece of the highly successful "Four Freedoms War Bond Show." With the notable exception of *Freedom of Speech*, which depicts civic democracy in action, the paintings' message seemed to be that the freedoms Americans were fighting to preserve were private entitlements, enjoyed individually or within the family. Indeed, only one painting actually referred to the war: *Freedom from Fear*, in which the father holds a newspaper whose headline refers to the bombing of London.

The paintings first appeared in the *Saturday Evening Post* early in 1943, accompanied by brief essays emphasizing that the values Rockwell depicted were both quintessentially American and antithetical to those of the Axis powers. Three were by celebrated authors—Stephen Vincent Benét, Booth Tarkington, and Will Durant. For *Freedom from Want*, the editors chose an unknown Filipino poet, Carlos Bulosan, who had emigrated to the United States at the age of sixteen. Bulosan's essay showed how the Four Freedoms could inspire hopes for a better future as well as a nostalgic retreat into Rockwell's imagined small-town past. Bulosan wrote of those Americans still outside the social mainstream— migrant workers, cannery operatives, black victims of segregation—for whom freedom meant having enough to eat, sending their children to school, and being able to "share the promise and fruits of American life."[9]

The Four Freedoms' very imprecision left them open to divergent interpretations, reflecting the still bitter political divisions spawned by the New Deal. This was evident in the history of the Office of War Information (OWI), established in 1942 to mobilize public opinion. The liberal Democrats who dominated the OWI's writing staff sought to make the conflict "a 'people's war' for freedom," defined as a worldwide expansion of the New Deal. Concerned that Americans' understanding of the war's purposes were vague and inconsistent, and that the populace seemed more fervently committed to paying back the Japanese for their attack on Pearl Harbor than ridding the world of fascism, the OWI utilized radio, film, the press, and other media to impart a coherent ideological meaning to the war, while seeking to avoid the nationalist hysteria of World War I. Its publications criticized "reactionaries" like former president Hoover and publicized statements by officials like Undersecretary of State Sumner Welles, who promised that the postwar world would tackle the problem of the unequal distribution of economic resources at home and abroad. The federal government, one of the first OWI pamphlets insisted, must assume "a certain responsibility for the solution of economic problems," mentioning as elements of freedom from want the rights to a job at fair pay, and to adequate food, clothing, shelter, and medical care.[10]

In this recruiting poster for the Boy Scouts, a svelte Miss Liberty prominently displays the Bill of Rights, widely celebrated during World War II as the centerpiece of American freedom. (Library of Congress)

Such publications aroused the ire of conservatives. Freedom of speech and religion were fine, one New Yorker complained, but freedom from want and fear were "New Deal Freedoms," not "American Freedoms," since they encouraged individuals to become dependent on the government. The advertising executives who dominated the OWI's leadership had a somewhat different objection to its activities. Most were not only uncomfortable with liberal rhetoric but believed, in keeping with the best wisdom of their profession, that the most effective messages were simple slogans, endlessly reiterated. Freedom, they believed, should be promoted but not explained. In June 1943, after the ad men moved to rein in the writers, a group of the latter resigned in protest, charging that the OWI was controlled by "high-pressure promoters who prefer slick salesmanship to honest information." Soon afterward, concerned that the OWI was devoting as much time to promoting New Deal social programs as the war effort, Congress eliminated most of the funding for its domestic activities.[11]

The OWI's fate was symbolic of the general trend of wartime politics. Dominated by a conservative alliance of Republicans and southern Democrats, Congress left intact core New Deal programs like Social Security, but eliminated agencies thought to be controlled by leftists, including the Civilian Conservation Corps, the National Youth Administration, and the Works Progress Administration. The relationship between the federal government and big business changed dramatically from the days of the second New Deal, as corporate executives flooded into federal agencies concerned with war production. Roosevelt jettisoned his strictures against "economic royalists" and offered vast pecuniary incentives—low-interest loans, tax concessions, risk-free contracts—to spur production. The great bulk of federal spending went to the one hundred largest corporations, furthering the long-term trend toward economic concentration. The astonishing achievements of wartime manufacturing—the tens of thousands of aircraft, tanks, and armored cars that poured off American assembly lines—coupled with rising incomes as unemployment all but disappeared did much to resurrect the reputation of business and businessmen, which had reached a low ebb during the Depression.[12]

For labor, the war was an experience filled with ambiguity. The vast majority of workers supported the war effort, many viewing it, as the CIO repeatedly proclaimed, as a crusade for freedom and democracy, a "people's war" that would expand economic and political democracy at home and abroad and accord labor a major voice in industrial management. During the war, organized labor in effect entered a tripartite arrangement with government and business that allowed union membership to soar to historic levels. By 1945, 15 million workers, one-third of the non-farm labor force, were unionized, the highest proportion in American history. Because of wage and price controls, the disappearance of unemployment, and the strength of unions, the war witnessed a significant redistribution of income in favor of ordinary workers. But if labor was a partner in government, it was very much a junior partner, and its influence on Congress and the administration was considerably reduced since the heyday of the New Deal.[13]

Especially after the OWI's demise, the "selling of America" became overwhelmingly a private affair. Under the watchful eye of the War Advertising Council, private companies joined in the campaign to promote wartime patriotism, while positioning themselves and their brand names for the postwar world. Alongside ads urging Americans to grow victory gardens, purchase war bonds, and guard against revealing military secrets, the war witnessed a burst of messages marketing advertisers' definition of freedom. Without directly criticizing Roosevelt, they repeatedly suggested that he had overlooked a central element of freedom—"free enterprise." One Republican member of Congress, Edith N. Rogers of Massachusetts, even introduced a joint resolution to recognize officially "Freedom of Private Enterprise" as a "Fifth Freedom" without which the "four annunciated [sic] by the President of the United States are meaningless." The National Association of Manufacturers (NAM) and individual companies bombarded Americans with press releases, radio programs, and advertisements attributing the amazing feats of wartime production to "free enterprise." "Hardly a speech is made today," Robert Gaylord, the NAM's president, boasted in 1944, "unless it starts out by extolling free enterprise. All bow to its marvelous war record." Businessmen depicted a postwar world filled with consumer goods, with "freedom of choice" among abundant possibilities assured if only private entrepreneurs were liberated from government controls. One ad for Royal typewriters, entitled "What This War Is All About," explained that its purpose was to "hasten the day when you . . . can once more walk into any store in the land and buy anything you want." Certainly, the war did not imply any alteration in American institutions. "I'm fighting for freedom," said a soldier in an ad by the Nash-Kelvinator Corporation. "So don't anybody tell me I'll find America changed."[14]

Like Rockwell's paintings, these wartime discussions of freedom simultaneously looked forward to a day of material abundance and backward to a time when the family stood as the bedrock of society. At a time when consumer goods were rationed and the memory of the Depression still very much alive, the advertisers' "world of tomorrow" rested on a vision of family-centered abundance. In terms of gender relations, men at the front would come home to a world with which they were familiar and resume the traditional family life they had known. The emphasis on hearth and home was in one sense ironic, in that simultaneously the nation engaged in an unprecedented mobilization of "womanpower" to fill industrial jobs vacated by men. OWI publications en-

In this advertisement by the Liberty Motors and Engineering Corporation, published in the February 1944 issue of *Fortune*, a rather bellicose-looking Uncle Sam offers the Fifth Freedom—"free enterprise"—to war-devastated Europe. (Library of Congress)

couraged women to go to work, Hollywood films glorified the independent woman, and private advertising celebrated the achievements of Rosie the Riveter, the emblematic female industrial laborer.[15]

The war experience did broaden many women's aspirations and made them more self-reliant. Women workers forced unions like the United Auto Workers to confront issues like equal pay for equal work, maternity leaves, and childcare facilities for working mothers. Having enjoyed what one wartime worker called "a taste of freedom"—doing "men's" jobs for men's wages—many women desired to remain in the labor force once peace returned. Yet working outside the home was still depicted by government, employers, and unions as a temporary necessity, not an expansion of women's freedom. Advertisements gave women's work a patriotic sanction it had never before enjoyed, assuring those working in factories that they too were "fighting for freedom." But the rhetoric was of sacrifice and military victory, not rights and autonomy, and "freedom" meant not the feminists' vision of self-determination through labor, but the American way of life, with "a little house of your own, and a husband to meet every night at the door." In one wartime radio program, a young man described his goal for peacetime: "Having' a home and some kids, and breathin' fresh air out in the suburbs . . . livin' and workin' *decent*, like free people."[16]

The promise of an affluent future provided a point of unity between New Dealers and conservatives, business and labor. Advertising's images of economic security and celebration of mass-produced abundance were echoed in Rockwell's *Freedom from Want* painting, which depicted a well-stocked Thanksgiving table so bountiful that some observers considered it in poor taste, given the sufferings of war-torn Europe. (Rockwell himself later wrote that he feared it depicted "overabundance.") The promise of consumer prosperity underpinned and in some ways united two of the most celebrated wartime blueprints for the postwar world. One was *The American Century* (1941), publisher Henry Luce's effort to mobilize the American people for the coming war and for a new era of postwar dominance. Americans, Luce insisted in his essay, must embrace the role history had thrust upon them as the "dominant power in the world" and seize the opportunity to spread their understanding of "freedom and justice" throughout the globe. In the future, American power and American values would underpin a previously unimaginable prosperity—"the abundant life," Luce called it—produced by "free economic enterprise."[17]

With its anticipation of a new world role for the United States and its shrewd observation that mass culture—"our jazz, movies, slang, technology, products"—was as much a source of international power as the country's military might, Luce's essay anticipated important aspects of the postwar world. But its bombastic rhetoric and a title easily interpreted as a call for an American imperialism aroused immediate opposition among liberals and the left. Their answer was offered by Vice President Henry Wallace in "The Price of Free World Victory," an address delivered in May 1942 to the Free World Association. In contrast to Luce's American Century, a world of business hegemony no less than American power, Wallace predicted that the war would usher in a "century of the common man," based on a global extension of the New Deal. The "march of freedom," said Wallace, would continue in the postwar world. That world, however, would be marked by international cooperation, not any single power's dominance, with hunger, illiteracy, and poverty eliminated by the actions of governments to "humanize" capitalism and redistribute economic resources. Hundreds of thousands of copies of Wallace's address were distributed by government agencies, making him a hero of the left-liberal antifascist alliance, a wartime resurrection of the old Popular Front.[18]

Luce and Wallace both spoke the language of freedom. If Luce's vision reflected the "confident chauvinism" of global free enterprise, Wallace's rested on

a worldwide guarantee of the Four Freedoms. But as the left-wing political essayist Dwight Macdonald shrewdly observed, in an essay whose title, "The
(American) People's Century" succinctly linked the two, Luce and Wallace had
more in common than either was prepared to admit. Whether in the guise of
universal free enterprise or a global New Deal, the war had produced an imperial vision of America's role in the postwar world, a vision inextricably tied
to the promise of economic abundance.[19]

Wallace's speech nonetheless helped to establish the parameters of the era's
social liberalism. Even as Congress moved to dismantle much of the New
Deal, liberal Democrats and their left-wing allies proposed plans for a postwar
world in which federal economic policy would allow all Americans to enjoy
freedom from want. In 1942 and 1943, the reports of the National Resources
Planning Board (NRPB) offered a blueprint for a peacetime economy based on
full employment, a greatly expanded welfare state, and a widely shared "American Standard of Living." Economic security and full employment were the
board's watchwords. The NRPB's 1943 report called for a "new bill of rights"
that would guarantee all Americans an expanded Social Security system, greater
access to education, health care, and adequate housing, and work for all able-
bodied adults. Here was a "vision of freedom" for the postwar world. Labor
and farm organizations, church and civil rights groups, and liberal New Dealers hailed the reports as designs for fulfilling the goals of the Four Freedoms.
The NRPB's plan for a "high-income, full-employment economy," with a "fair
distribution of income," said The Nation, epitomized "the way of life of free
men."[20]

As the historian Alan Brinkley has argued, the reports exemplified a subtle
shift in economic thinking during the war. A decade earlier, many New Dealers had followed Louis D. Brandeis in seeking to rid the economy of "the
curse of bigness," while others, influenced by socialism, had favored the nationalization of business enterprise or a "mixed economy" in which
government-controlled economic activity coexisted with the modern corporation. Now, rather than seeking to reform the institutions of capitalism, liberals would rely on government spending and fiscal policy to secure full
employment, social welfare, and mass consumption, while leaving the prerogatives of employers intact and the operation of the economy in private hands.
The government's job was to stimulate economic growth and create a floor
below which no American would fall. As the journalist Max Lerner noted in
The New Republic, the reports appeared to reflect the views, just becoming popular in economic circles, of the British economist John Maynard Keynes. Yet
Lerner also noted that in calling for massive spending on public works—urban

redevelopment, rural electrification, an overhaul of the transportation system, and the like—the NRPB went well beyond Keynes's emphasis on fiscal policy and deficit spending as the means of promoting economic growth. Certainly, it went well beyond what the majority of congressmen were willing to countenance, and funding for the planning board was quickly eliminated.[21]

Roosevelt had done virtually nothing to publicize or promote the NRPB reports of 1942 and 1943, although in transmitting them to Congress he endorsed the idea that translating "freedom into modern terms" meant adding "new freedoms," such as those the board proposed. Yet as his 1944 campaign for reelection approached, mindful that public opinion polls showed a large majority of Americans favoring a guarantee of employment for those who could not find work, Roosevelt embraced the NRPB's call for an "Economic Bill of Rights." "We have come to a clear realization," Roosevelt declared, "of the fact that true individual freedom cannot exist without economic security and independence." Invoking an aphorism first used in the eighteenth century—"necessitous men are not free men"—Roosevelt went on to call for a broad government guarantee of a remunerative job, a decent standard of living, medical care, education, and adequate protection from the ravages of old age, sickness, accident, and unemployment.[22]

Already ill and preoccupied with winning the war, Roosevelt spoke only occasionally of the Economic Bill of Rights during the 1944 campaign. The replacement of Wallace by Harry S. Truman as his running mate, moreover, suggested that the president was not prepared to do battle with Congress over economic policy. Nonetheless, the Economic Bill of Rights not only enhanced public expectations about the kind of life that would follow the war but also put the issue of social citizenship on the political agenda. Spearheaded by the CIO's new political action committee, the liberal-left coalition rallied around a social democratic vision of a revitalized and expanded postwar New Deal and an economy of consumer abundance and full employment. The People's Program of 1944 would remain the essential liberal social agenda for the next thirty years, a "substantial down payment," as the United Steel Workers Union described it, "on the Four Freedoms."[23]

As the war drew to a close, the goal of full employment prosperity (often couched in terms of avoiding a recurrence of the Depression) dominated political discussion. "Employment," Wallace had declared in 1944, would be "the one great test of statesmanship after the war." During 1945, unions, civil rights organizations, and religious groups urged Congress to enact the Full Employment bill, introduced by Senator James E. Murray of Montana, which established a "right to employment" for all Americans and required the federal government to adjust its level of spending to compensate in case the economy failed to generate enough jobs. Full employment, said Robert Wagner, senator from New York, was the linchpin of "the America of the future—an America of ever-increasing social and economic progress." In September, a special issue of *The New Republic* spoke of the "tremendous opportunity" to raise living standards, rebuild cities, and expand education and health services. The "participation of democratic government in the economic process," the magazine insisted, extended the "sphere of freedom" rather than endangering it. In the modern world, government was liberty's "protector" and full employment "a milestone on the road to freedom."[24]

The conservative majority in Congress showed little enthusiasm for the Full Employment bill or other elements of the left-liberal program. The target of an intense business lobbying campaign, the bill, before being passed in 1946, was shorn of its commitment to full employment and its connection with government social and economic policies to create jobs and promote the social welfare. In the GI Bill of Rights, Congress did offer a vast array of health and educational benefits and low-cost mortgage loans to veterans, helping to underwrite postwar prosperity, but these were not extended to the general public.[25]

Given conservative domination of Congress, these limitations were not surprising. They confirmed the political stalemate that had begun with the elections of 1938. More revealing was the renewed intellectual respectability of the idea that economic planning constituted a threat to liberty. When *The New Republic* spoke of full employment as the "road to freedom," it subtly acknowledged the impact of *The Road to Serfdom*, a surprise bestseller published in 1944 by Friedrich A. Hayek, a previously obscure Austrian-born British economist. Hayek claimed that even the best-intentioned governmental efforts to direct the economy posed a threat to individual liberty. His message was simple: "planning for freedom" was an oxymoron, since "planning leads to dictatorship."

As the historian H. Stuart Hughes noted a decade later, the publication of *The Road to Serfdom* was "a major event in the intellectual history of the United States." It was one thing for self-interested contemporaries like Eric A. Johnson, president of the U.S. Chamber of Commerce, to repeat the familiar litany that "too much government" endangered American freedom. But coming at a time when the miracles of war production had reconciled many liberals to the virtues of capitalism, and with the excesses of Stalin and the confrontation with Nazism highlighting the danger of consolidated economic and political power, Hayek offered a new intellectual underpinning for opponents of active government. If his definition of liberty as "freedom from coercion" echoed a theme rooted in classical liberalism, Hayek's argument was in other respects quite modern. In a complex economy, he insisted, no single person or group of experts could possibly possess enough knowledge to direct economic activity intelligently. A spontaneous social order based on the free market could mobilize the fragmented and partial knowledge scattered throughout society far more effectively than a planned economy. Hayek outraged New Deal liberals by equating indirect interventions like the establishment of employment targets and measures to boost consumer spending with comprehensive governmental direction of the entire range of economic activities. All planning, he insisted, inevitably restricted individual liberty. And without "freedom in economic affairs," political and personal freedom were impossible.[26]

Unlike many of his disciples, Hayek was not a doctrinaire advocate of laissez-faire. His book endorsed measures that later conservatives would denounce as tantamount to socialism—minimum wage and maximum hours laws, antitrust enforcement, and a social safety net guaranteeing all citizens a basic minimum of food, shelter, and clothing. (When the *Reader's Digest* published a condensed version of Hayek's work in 1945, it omitted all references to such measures.) Hayek, moreover, chastised traditional conservatives for nostalgia for a long-lost hierarchical society antithetical to economic experimentation and free market progress, and a fondness for authoritarianism. "I am not a conservative," he would later write. But in effectively equating fascism, socialism, and the New Deal, and identifying economic planning with a loss of freedom, he helped lay the foundation for the rise of modern conservatism, offering a powerful weapon with which to attack liberalism and the left and inspiring a revival of classic economic thought. Among other things, Hayek's book was a clarion call for conservatives to reclaim the word "freedom," which, he charged, had been usurped and distorted by socialists, New Dealers, and liberals. Thus, as the war drew to a close, the stage was set for a renewed battle over the meaning of American freedom.[27]

Patriotic Assimilation

The unprecedented attention to freedom as the defining characteristic of American life had implications that went far beyond wartime mobilization. World War II reshaped Americans' understanding of themselves as a people. The struggle against Nazi tyranny and its theory of a master race gave new emphasis to the civic definition of American nationality and discredited ethnic and racial inequality. In public and private pronouncements, the pluralist vision of

American society pioneered during the 1930s now became part of official rhetoric. What set the United States apart from its wartime foes was not only dedication to the ideals of the Four Freedoms, but the resolve that Americans of all races, religions, and national origins could enjoy those freedoms equally. Racism was the enemy's philosophy; Americanism rested on toleration of diversity and equality for all. By the end of the war, the new immigrant groups had been fully accepted as ethnic Americans, rather than members of distinct and inferior "races," and the contradiction between the putative American Creed and the actual status of blacks had come to the forefront of national life.[28]

Among other things, World War II created a vast melting pot. Millions of Americans were uprooted from urban ethnic neighborhoods and isolated rural enclaves and thrust into the army and industrial plants, where they came into contact with countrymen of very different backgrounds. But what the historian Nelson Lichtenstein has called "patriotic assimilation" was far different from the coercive Americanization of World War I. If the Wilson administration had established Anglo-Saxon culture as a national norm, Roosevelt promoted a pluralistic acceptance of cultural diversity as the only real source of harmony in a heterogeneous society. The essence of the American way of life, wrote the novelist Pearl Buck in an OWI pamphlet, was brotherhood: the principle that "persons of many lands can live together . . . and if they believe in freedom they can become a united people."[29]

Government and private agencies avidly promoted group equality as the definition of Americanism. Officials rewrote history to establish racial and ethnic tolerance as the American way and freedom as a universal entitlement. To be an American, declared the president, had always been a "matter of mind and heart," and never "a matter of race or ancestry"—a statement more effective in mobilizing support for the war than in accurately describing the nation's past. "We have always believed—and we believe today," echoed Secretary of State Cordell Hull, "that all peoples, without distinction of race, color, or religion, who are prepared and willing to accept the responsibilities of liberty are entitled to its enjoyment." Mindful of the intolerance spawned by World War I, the OWI highlighted the contributions to American life of nearly every group, including even Italian and German immigrants and their descendants (who represented, of course, a large pool of potential draftees). Not infrequently, the message was contradicted by cartoons depicting the German and Japanese foes as demonic and subhuman. But the central idea was clear: ethnic and racial prejudices were not only detrimental to the war effort but antithetical to American traditions.[30]

Arthur Poinier's cartoon for the *Detroit Free Press*, 19 June 1941, graphically illustrates how during World War II, white ethnics were incorporated within the boundaries of American freedom. (Reprinted by permission of the *Detroit Free Press*)

Private efforts at mobilization also embraced the notion that the country's strength lay in diversity and the image of Americans casting aside old enmities to unite as a single people in a common struggle. Originally popularized by the Popular Front in the 1930s, these ideas now moved to the center stage of mass culture. To be sure, in the interest of wartime unity the Depression-era focus on the people was shorn of some of its critical edges. In 1942, the Museum of Modern Art in New York mounted a major exhibition, "Road to Victory." A heartwarming patriotic endeavor, it featured photographs of a diverse populace at work, at play, and at war, but studiously avoided the downbeat social realist images so prominent during the 1930s. When Martha Graham revived *American*

Document that same year, she excised some of the work's more critical comments on the country's history.[31]

But if social celebration, not social criticism, was the order of the day, what was celebrated was the resiliency of a people united in respect for diversity. Americanism meant toleration, and bigots were portrayed as a fifth column more dangerous than spies and saboteurs. *Parents* magazine warned that the "intolerances" of adults had done great harm to children and the nation. "The four freedoms," it concluded, "will have little meaning for anyone who is not convinced of the inherent dignity of every human being of every race, color, and creed." Horrified by the uses to which the Nazis put the idea of inborn racial difference, physical and social scientists retreated wholesale from the idea of race, only recently central to their disciplines. The writings of Franz Boas, Ruth Benedict, and other anthropologists critical of the link between race, culture, and ability now for the first time reached a mass audience. Benedict's *Races and Racism,* published in 1942, described racism as "a travesty of scientific knowledge." In the same year, Ashley Montagu's *Man's Most Dangerous Myth: The Fallacy of Race* became a bestseller. By the war's end, racism and nativism had been stripped of intellectual respectability and equated with pathology and irrationality.[32]

Hollywood too did its part, portraying fighting units whose members represented the various regional, ethnic, and religious groups—typically a Jew, a southerner, and a sprinkling of Italians, Poles, Irish, and Scandinavians— putting aside parochial loyalties and prejudices for the common cause. In the 1943 film *Bataan,* the ethnically balanced celluloid platoon included a black soldier, even though the real U.S. Army was still racially segregated. The war's most popular film, *This Is the Army,* starring, among others, future president Ronald Reagan, offered a vision of postwar society in which the Four Freedoms were linked to celebration of the ethnic diversity of the American people.[33]

Intolerance, of course, hardly disappeared from American life. T. C. Upham, a theatrical director from New Jersey, complained to Norman Rockwell that in his *Freedom of Worship* painting, too many of the faces were "foreign-looking." But the war made millions of ethnic Americans, especially the Jewish and Catholic children of the new immigrants, feel fully American for the first time. If the pluralism of the CIO and the Popular Front had begun the process of forging the new immigrants into a white working class, the war greatly accelerated the process. They benefited enormously from wartime fair employment policies (more so than blacks, for whom such rules were initiated). During the war, one New York "ethnic" recalled, "the Italo-Americans stopped being Italo and started becoming Americans." But the event that inspired this comment, the Harlem race riot of 1943, suggested that such assimilation stopped at the color line.[34]

Despite the abhorrence of Nazi racism, the war's meaning for non-white groups was far more ambiguous than for whites. On the eve of Pearl Harbor, racial barriers remained deeply entrenched in American life. The vast majority of blacks were locked within the rigid caste system of the segregated South. Asians were still barred from emigrating to the country or becoming naturalized citizens. Mexican-Americans, historically considered "white" by the U.S. Census Bureau, had been reclassified as a non-white race in 1930 and during the early years of the Depression over 400,000 had been "voluntarily" repatriated by local authorities in the Southwest. Most of the adults "encouraged" to leave the country were recent immigrants, but perhaps 200,000 were American-born (and therefore citizen) children.[35]

The war set in motion changes that would reverberate in the postwar years. Thanks to the Bracero program agreed upon by the Mexican and American governments, large-scale immigration from Mexico resumed as tens of thousands of contract laborers crossed into the United States. Designed as a temporary measure to meet the wartime labor shortage in the agricultural fields of the Southwest, the program lasted into the 1960s and stimulated a far broader movement of Mexican men, women, and children into the United States. Congress in 1943 ended decades of exclusion by establishing a nationality quota for immigrants from China, now an ally in the Pacific War, although the annual limit of one hundred and five Chinese hardly suggested a desire for large-scale immigration. Nonetheless, the image of Chinese as gallant allies called into question anti-Asian stereotypes.[36]

Far different was the experience of Japanese-Americans. Longstanding racial animosities and the shocking attack on Pearl Harbor combined to produce an unprecedented hatred of Japan. "In all our history," according to the historian Allan Nevins, "no foe has been detested as were the Japanese." Government propaganda and war films demonized the Japanese as rats, dogs, gorillas, and snakes—bestial and subhuman. Japanese aggression was said to stem from innate racial characteristics or national character, not, as in the case of Germany and Italy, from tyrannical rulers. Even Frank Sinatra's popular short film, *The House I Live In,* based on a Popular Front song that celebrated the United States as a land of "all races and religions," consistently used the word "Japs."[37]

As the Pacific conflict took on overtones of a race war, the Japanese-American community could not remain unaffected, even though a considerable majority were American citizens. The federal government bent over backward to include German-Americans and Italian-Americans in the war effort and examined the loyalty of nationals of its European foes on a case-by-case basis. But it assumed that every person of Japanese origin was a potential spy. Inspired by fears of an impending Japanese invasion of California, and by covetous eyes cast by many whites on Japanese-American property holdings, the military persuaded the Roosevelt administration to order the removal of persons of Japanese descent from the West Coast. In the spring and summer of 1942, nearly 120,000 men, women, and children, more than two-thirds of them American citizens, were removed to internment camps far from their homes.[38]

One searches the wartime record in vain for public protests among non-Japanese. In Congress, only Senator Robert Taft spoke out against the greatest violation of civil liberties since the end of slavery. Groups publicly committed to fighting discrimination, from the Communist Party to the NAACP and the American Jewish Committee, either defended the internment or remained silent. The ACLU promised to represent Gordon K. Hirabayashi, who challenged a West Coast curfew applying only to Japanese-Americans, but soon withdrew from the case. In 1943, the Supreme Court unanimously rejected Hirabayashi's plea, and in the following year, in the *Korematsu* decision, the justices rejected the appeal of a Japanese-American citizen against the internment policy. Speaking for the 6–3 majority, Justice Hugo Black, usually an avid defender of civil liberties, managed to persuade himself that an order applying only to persons of Japanese descent was not based on race. In the fall of 1944, the Court did order to release of a Japanese-American woman whose loyalty had been definitively established. But it never examined the constitutionality of the incarceration program as a whole. Somewhat incongruously, the government marketed war bonds to the internees and recruited soldiers from among them. One of the main activities in the camps was the education of Japanese-American children. "One of our basic subjects was American history," Peter Ota, imprisoned at a desolate internment center in Amache, Colorado, later recalled. "They talked about freedom all the time."[39]

If the treatment of Japanese-Americans revealed the stubborn hold of racism in American life, the wartime message of freedom and tolerance portended a major transformation in the status of blacks. "There never has been, there isn't now, and there never will be," Roosevelt declared, "any race of people on the earth fit to serve as masters over their fellow men." Yet Nazi Germany cited American segregation as proof of its own race theories, and the Japanese (who during the war ruled tyrannically over Koreans, Chinese, and other Asians) cast themselves as defenders of the rights of non-white peoples against a racist United States. In 1940 and 1941, even as Roosevelt called for aid to the free peoples of Europe, there were thirteen lynchings in the United States. Given the message of the war and the nation's vulnerability to charges of hypocrisy, the condition of black Americans became increasingly difficult to justify. In 1942, a public opinion survey sponsored by the army's Bureau of Intelligence showed that the vast majority of white Americans were "unaware that there is any such thing as a 'Negro problem,' " and believed that blacks were well satisfied with their social and economic conditions. They would soon discover their mistake.[40]

What David Riesman called the "wide disparities between the words of promise in our Constitution and the actual lack of freedom" of black Americans spawned a renewed movement for black equality even before Pearl Harbor. Angered by the almost complete exclusion of African-Americans from employment in the rapidly expanding war production industries (of 100,000 aircraft workers in 1940, fewer than 300 were black), labor leader A. Philip Randolph in July 1941 called for a March on Washington to demand not only defense jobs but an end to segregation in government departments and the armed forces. Hurling Roosevelt's rhetoric back at the president, Randolph declared racial discrimination "undemocratic, un-American, and pro-Hitler."[41]

The prospect of thousands of angry blacks descending on Washington, remarked Joseph L. Rauh, then a lawyer for the Lend-Lease administration, "scared the government half to death." To persuade Randolph to call off the march, Roosevelt issued an executive order banning discrimination in defense employment and establishing a Fair Employment Practices Commission (FEPC) to monitor compliance. The black press hailed the order as a new Emancipation Proclamation, a promise of "economic freedom." Essentially an investigative agency, the FEPC had few enforcement powers. But its very existence marked a significant shift in public policy, and its hearings exposed patterns of racial exclusion so ingrained that firms at first freely admitted that their want ads asked for "colored" applicants for porters and janitors, and "white" ones for skilled manufacturing jobs, or that they allowed black women to work only as laundresses and cooks. The first federal agency since Reconstruction to campaign for equal opportunity for black Americans, the FEPC played an important role in obtaining jobs for black workers in industrial plants and shipyards, an enormous step forward for migrants from the rural South. By 1944, over 1 million blacks held manufacturing jobs, 300,000 of them women. ("My sister always said that Hitler was the one that got us out of the white folks' kitchen," recalled one black woman.) Other egalitarian steps soon followed. The National War Labor Board banned racial wage differentials. In 1944, the

Supreme Court outlawed all-white primaries, one of many mechanisms by which blacks were deprived of the franchise in the South.[42]

Far more than in the 1930s, federal officials during the war spoke openly of the need for change in race relations. When Congress considered a bill outlawing the poll tax, Senate majority leader Alben W. Barkley of Kentucky said the issue involved the principle that government must rest on the consent of the governed, "the very basis of democracy and freedom." Yet the bill's defeat demonstrated that southern Democrats more intransigent than Barkley on racial matters retained their hold on the levels of power. Indeed, one reason for the demise of the OWI was southern outrage that in appealing for black support for the war, its publications condemned racism as un-American and candidly acknowledged that many blacks were "free" only "in name." Throughout the conflict, Washington remained a rigidly segregated city, the army continued to fight a segregated war, and the Red Cross refused to mix blood from blacks and whites in its blood banks (thereby, critics charged, tacitly accepting Nazi race theories).

The black migrants who poured out of the South into the industrial heartland on what they called "liberty trains" encountered hostility, sometimes violent, from white residents in the North and West. Detroit in June 1943 experienced a race riot that left thirty-four persons dead and a "hate strike" of twenty thousand auto workers protesting the upgrading of black workers in a plant manufacturing aircraft engines. In the same year, the Zoot Suit riots, in which club-wielding soldiers, sailors, and policemen attacked Mexican-American youths on the streets of Los Angeles, also illustrated the limits of the wartime commitment to pluralism and tolerance. Nor did the war produce an end to lynching. Isaac Simmons, a black minister, was murdered in 1944 after refusing to sell his land to a white man who believed it might contain oil. The perpetrators went unpunished. This took place in Liberty, Mississippi.[43]

Nonetheless, official rhetoric helped to inspire a new black militancy. Racism, a black steelworker declared in 1944, was "an evil characteristic of our fascist enemies," and when the president "said that we should have the Four Freedoms," he meant to include "all races." Banks, insurance companies, public transportation systems, and numerous other employers who had previously refused to hire blacks found themselves the targets of wartime demonstrations. "People were in a belligerent mood," a civil rights activist from Louisiana later recalled. In February 1942, the *Pittsburgh Courier* coined the phrase that came to epitomize black attitudes during the war: the "double-V." Victory over Germany and Japan, it insisted, must be accompanied by victory over segregation at home. While most of the white press supported the war as an expression of American ideals, black newspapers persistently pointed to the gap between those ideals and reality. Side by side with ads for war bonds, *The Crisis* insisted that "a jim crow army cannot fight for a free world." Surveying wartime public opinion, the political scientist Horace Gosnell concluded that "symbols of national solidarity" had very different meanings to white and black Americans. To blacks, freedom from fear meant, among other things, an end to lynching; freedom from want included an end to "discrimination in getting jobs." If in whites' eyes, freedom was a "possession to be defended," Gosnell observed, to blacks and other racial minorities it remained a "goal to be achieved." "*Our* fight for freedom," said a black veteran returning from Pacific combat, "begins when we get to San Francisco."[44]

During the war, a broad political coalition centered on the left but reaching well beyond it called for an end to racial inequality in America. The NAACP and the American Jewish Congress cooperated closely in denouncing racial and religious intolerance and advocating laws to outlaw discrimination in employment and housing. The simultaneous fight against anti-Semitism and racism broadened the perspective of both Jews and blacks, while subtly obscuring how much more deeply racism was embedded in American law and social custom than religious intolerance. The war gave birth to the fabled black-Jewish alliance that would enjoy its heyday during the civil rights era. ("Doesn't anybody have any trouble except Jews and the colored people?" asked one disgruntled subscriber to the left-wing New York newspaper *PM.*) Freedom House gave the NAACP office space in its New York headquarters, condemned the treatment of blacks in the armed forces, and called for federal legislation to outlaw employment discrimination as "evidence of good faith on the part of a government which is asking [blacks] to fight for such ideals as the Four Freedoms."[45]

Despite considerable resistance from rank-and-file white workers, CIO unions, especially those where left-liberal and Communist influence was strong, made significant efforts to organize black workers and win them access to skilled positions. A racial job ceiling persisted in most industrial plants, and AFL craft unions by and large continued their long tradition of excluding black workers. But during the war, the CIO was probably more racially integrated than any labor organization since the Knights of Labor. As a result, unions for the first time (with the exception of the all-black Brotherhood of Sleeping Car Porters) became important forces in black communities across the country.[46]

An uncompromising demand for political, economic, and civil equality provided the unifying theme of *What the Negro Wants*, a book of essays by fourteen prominent black leaders edited by the historian Rayford Logan and published in 1944. Virtually every essay called for the enfranchisement of black voters in the South, the dismantling of segregation, and access to "the accepted American standard of living." "The Negro," A. Philip Randolph insisted in the book's most impatient essay, "is not free. . . . He is not free because he is not equal to other citizens." Reflecting how the war had inspired among black Americans an intense identification with the struggles for independence of the "subject peoples" of the colonial world, several essays also insisted that with peace must come an end to European imperialism. "We want the Four Freedoms," wrote Logan, "to apply to black Americans as well as to the brutalized peoples of Europe and to the other underprivileged peoples of the world."[47]

What the Negro Wants also revealed that southern white liberalism was facing a crisis. The book had been commissioned by W. T. Couch, a founder of the Fight for Freedom Committee, who as director of the University of North Carolina Press had published pathbreaking works on lynching, unionism, and southern poverty. But when he read the manuscript, Couch was stunned. "If this is what the negro wants," he told Logan, "nothing could be clearer than what he needs, and needs most urgently, is to revise his wants." In the end, Couch published the text as submitted, but added a highly unusual introduction of his own, in effect repudiating the book. His response was typical of a generation of white southern liberals who, during the 1930s, had pressed for incremental improvements in race relations. They now saw their forward-looking middle ground evaporating as blacks demanded an end to segregation while white demagogues took up the cry of defending white supremacy (sometimes invoking the wartime language of freedom to mean the right to shape their region's institutions without outside interference). "The highest casualty rate of the war," quipped Walter White of the NAACP, "seems to be that of Southern white liberals."[48]

In the rest of the country, however, the war saw the status of black Americans propelled to the forefront of enlightened liberalism. After touring the world to demonstrate American unity and rally support for the Allies, Wendell Willkie, Roosevelt's 1940 electoral opponent, published *One World*, which became the leading bestseller of 1943. Priced at one dollar, it sold 1 million copies faster than any non-fiction work in American history. His travels persuaded Willkie that what would soon come to be called the Third World would play a pivotal role in the postwar era, and he called for a new age of international cooperation based on independence for all peoples and respect for their desire to be "free in their own way" (a subtle rebuke to Luce's notion of an Ameri-

can Century). But the book's great surprise came in Willkie's attack on "our im-
perialisms at home." His candid message was that unless the United States addressed the "mocking paradox" of racism, its claim to world leadership would
lack moral authority. "If we want to talk about freedom," Willkie wrote, "we
must mean freedom for others as well as ourselves, and we must mean freedom
for everyone inside our frontiers."[49]

No event exemplified the new concern with race more clearly than the publication in 1944 of *An American Dilemma*, a sprawling account of the country's
racial past, present, and future written at the request of the Carnegie Foundation by the Swedish social scientist Gunnar Myrdal. Myrdal's conclusion was
unambiguous: "there is bound to be a redefinition of the Negro's status as a
result of this War." The book offered an uncompromising account of the long
history of racial injustice and a candid analysis of the economics of inequality. Part of its appeal lay in Myrdal's success in combining this sobering analysis with admiration for what he considered core American ideals. The basis for
the country's "peculiar brand of nationalism," Myrdal wrote, was "the American Creed"—belief in equality, justice, equal opportunity, and freedom. The
war had made Americans more aware than ever of the contradiction between
this creed and the reality of racial inequality. As a result, enlightened men and
women were abandoning racial prejudice, which was now confined to "poor and
uneducated" inhabitants of the "isolated and backward" rural South. Thus, the
nation was well positioned to rise to the challenge of living up to its professed
ideals.[50]

Myrdal's notion of a conflict between American values and American racial
policies was hardly new—Frederick Douglass and W. E. B. Du Bois had said
much the same thing. But in the context of a worldwide struggle against Nazism
and rising black demands for equality at home, his book struck a chord. If it
identified a serious national problem, it also seemed to offer a solution through
a combination of moral suasion and planned, peaceful change in which the federal government would take the lead in outlawing discrimination and guaranteeing to all Americans a "decent living standard." Sociologist Robert Lynd
called it "the most penetrating and important book on our contemporary
American civilization that has been written." Despite the book's title, Myrdal's
demonstration of how deeply racism was entrenched in law, politics, economics, and mores suggested that racial inequality was far more than a moral
dilemma or conflict in the minds of white Americans and would require government intervention to solve. This coupling of an appeal to American principles with advocacy of federal social engineering established a liberal
orthodoxy on race relations that would survive for many years.

By 1945, support for racial justice had become a test of liberal credentials, a central element in the liberal conception of American freedom. In *While You Were Gone*, a book of essays intended to inform returning soldiers how the country had changed in their absence, the writer Carey McWilliams reported that the "race problem" had moved to the forefront of public consciousness. It could only be resolved by guaranteeing a "state of universal civic freedom" for all, coupled with "special ameliorative measures" to combat the lasting legacy of discrimination in housing, education, and employment.[51]

McWilliams spoke for a left-liberal political movement on whose agenda racial justice had finally taken its place alongside full employment, individual civil liberties, and the expansion of the New Deal welfare state, all as expressions or logical extensions of the Four Freedoms. What had happened was less the eclipse of New Deal economic liberalism by a "rights-based" outlook than the rise of a new awareness of the interconnection between the partially overlapping, partially distinct problems of race and class. Full employment and fair employment became the watchwords of the progressive coalition that formed during the war. In the campaign of 1944, Roosevelt himself insisted that his Economic Bill of Rights knew no racial boundaries and called for making the FEPC permanent (a proposal blocked by Congress). Many liberals went even further, insisting that racial discrimination must be confronted head-on, through federal antilynching legislation, the extension of unionism into the South, an end to employment discrimination and segregated housing and schools, and the expansion of Social Security and other New Deal programs to cover agricultural and domestic workers. Here was a vision of a racially integrated full employment economy, a bridge between the New Deal and the Great Society of the 1960s. Such policies, CIO official Willard S. Townsend wrote in his contribution to *What the Negro Wants*, would lead to a "practical realization of the Four Freedoms" by making them applicable to all Americans.[52]

With Japan's surrender in August 1945, World War II came to an end. The world, said Truman, who had assumed the presidency when Roosevelt died four months earlier, would enjoy a "new beginning in the history of freedom on this earth." Over the next few weeks, he reiterated again and again that the war's meaning lay in the triumph of the "spirit of liberty." But the euphoria of victory would soon be followed by the Cold War, and with it, new contests over the meaning of American freedom.[53]

"Fire!"

Cartoonist Herbert Block's 1949 comment on the danger to freedom posed by the anti-Communist crusade that would come to be known as McCarthyism. ("Fire!—" from *The Herblock Book* [Beacon Press, NY, 1952])

11
Cold War
Freedom

O*N SEPTEMBER 16, 1947*, the 160th anniversary of the signing of the Constitution, the "Freedom Train" opened to the public in Philadelphia. A traveling exhibition of some one hundred thirty-three historical documents, the train, bedecked in red, white, and blue, soon embarked on a sixteen-month tour that took it to over three hundred American cities. Never before or since have so many cherished pieces of Americana—among them the Mayflower Compact, the Declaration of Independence, and the Gettysburg Address—been assembled in one place, although the low lighting (not to preserve the documents, but to create the atmosphere of a religious shrine) made the contemplation of individual items nearly impossible. After leaving the train, visitors were exhorted to rededicate themselves to American values by taking the Freedom Pledge and adding their names to a Freedom Scroll.

The idea for the Freedom Train, perhaps the most elaborate peacetime patriotic campaign in American history, originated in 1946 with the Department of Justice. President Truman endorsed it as a way of contrasting American freedom with "the destruction of liberty by the Hitler tyranny." Since direct government funding smacked of propaganda, however, the project was turned over to the non-profit American Heritage Foundation, whose board of trustees, dominated by leading bankers and industrialists, was headed by Winthrop W. Aldrich, chairman of Chase Manhattan Bank. Private donations financed the Freedom Train as well as the accompanying advertising campaign designed to "re-sell America to Americans."

By any measure, the Freedom Train was an enormous success. It attracted over 3.5 million visitors, and millions more took part in the civic activities that accompanied its journey, including labor-management forums, educational programs, and patriotic parades. Unlike later celebrations such as the 1986 Statue of Liberty Centennial, the Freedom Train did not succumb to crass commercialism—there were no product endorsements or brand-name sponsorships. The powerful grassroots response to the train, wrote *The New Republic,* revealed a deep popular hunger for "tangible evidence of American freedom." Behind the scenes, however, the Freedom Train demonstrated that the meaning of freedom remained as controversial as ever. The liberal staff members at the National Archives who proposed the initial list of documents had included the Wagner Act and Roosevelt's Four Freedoms speech, but these were eliminated by the more conservative American Heritage Foundation. Also omitted were the Fourteenth and Fifteenth Amendments and Roosevelt's order establishing the Fair Employment Practices Commission, which Congress had recently allowed to expire. In the end, nothing on the train referred to organized labor or twentieth-century social legislation and the only documents relating to blacks were the Emancipation Proclamation, the Thirteenth Amendment, and a 1776 letter by South Carolina patriot Henry Laurens criticizing slavery.[1]

Black Americans, indeed, had virtually no voice in planning the exhibit and many were initially skeptical about it. "I want freedom itself, not a Freedom Train," said Paul Robeson. On the eve of the train's unveiling, the poet Langston Hughes expressed the hope that there would be "no Jim Crow on the Freedom Train." When it stopped in Mississippi, Hughes wondered, "will it be made plain/ Everybody's got a right to board the Freedom Train?" In fact, with the Truman administration about to make civil rights a major priority, the train's organizers announced that they would not permit segregated viewing. A reconditioned baggage car containing the Confederate constitution and other southern documents did accompany the train in Georgia. But in an unprecedented move, the American Heritage Foundation canceled visits to Memphis and Birmingham when local authorities insisted on separating visitors by race. The Freedom Train visited forty-seven other southern cities without incident and was hailed in the black press for breaching, if only temporarily, the unbreachable walls of segregation.[2]

If the Freedom Train reflected a growing sense of national unease about overt expressions of racial inequality, its journey also revealed the impact of the Cold War. Conceived in the wake of World War II to underscore the contrast between American freedom and Nazi tyranny, the Freedom Train quickly became caught up in the emerging ideological struggle with communism (even

ON GUARD IN THE FREEDOM TRAIN, A MARINE KEEPS AN EYE ON THE DOCUMENTS. ALL ARE PROTECTED BY BULLETPROOF GLASS AND SPECIAL PLASTIC CASES INSIDE

FREEDOM TRAIN

Traveling museum begins yearlong,
33,000-mile tour of the country

On Sept. 17, after a solid hour of oratory and the smashing of a quart of champagne against its side, the Freedom Train was dedicated in Philadelphia. It then set off on a 33,000-mile tour of the U.S. with a cargo of 128 historical American documents, including the original Bill of Rights and George Washington's private copy of the Constitution. During the coming year the train will stop in 300 communities where citizens will have a chance to examine the documents that form the spiritual and political basis of their way of life.

Seven cars long, and painted red, white and blue, the train and its contents are guarded by a detachment of Marines wherever it goes. The idea was conceived by Attorney General Clark, and is being promoted by the nonprofit American Heritage Foundation. But diverse organizations all over the country are also giving a helpful push. These range from the National Association of Manufacturers to the C.I.O. and from M-G-M to the Girl Scouts.

IN PHILADELPHIA'S BROAD STREET STATION, PART OF THE OPENING DAY'S CROWD OF 10,000 WAITS TO GO THROUGH THE RED, WHITE AND BLUE STREAMLINER

A page from *Life* magazine reporting on the Freedom Train. At the top, a Marine stands guard over historic documents. (*Life*, 29 Sept. 1947; courtesy, Time-Life Syndication)

though its closest precedent was the Lenin Train of 1918, which brought Bolshevik books, newspapers, films, and avant-garde posters to the Russian countryside). In the spring of 1947, a few months before the train was dedicated, President Truman had committed the United States to the worldwide containment of Soviet power. Soon, Attorney General Tom C. Clark was praising the Freedom Train as a means of preventing "foreign ideologies" from infiltrating the United States and of "aiding the country in its internal war against subversive elements," and the FBI began compiling reports on those who found the train objectionable. Thus, if the Freedom Train inaugurated a period when the language of freedom suffused American politics, culture, and society, it also revealed how the Cold War subtly reshaped freedom's meaning and practice, identifying it with anticommunism, "free enterprise," and the defense of the social and economic status quo.[3]

The Free World

In retrospect, it seems inevitable that the Soviet Union and the United States, the two major powers to emerge from World War II, would come into conflict. Born of a common foe rather than common long-term interests, values, or history, their wartime alliance began to unravel almost from the day that peace was declared. Early in 1946, in his famous Long Telegram from Moscow, American diplomat George Kennan advised the Truman administration that no modus vivendi was possible because the Soviets were determined to expand their power throughout the globe. Two weeks later, in a speech at Fulton, Missouri, Britain's wartime prime minister, Winston Churchill, declared that an "iron curtain" had descended across Europe, partitioning the free West from the Communist East. But it was not until March 1947, in his speech announcing what came to be known as the "Truman Doctrine," that the president officially embraced the Cold War as the foundation of American foreign policy and cast it as a worldwide struggle over the future of freedom.[4]

The immediate occasion for this epochal decision was Britain's announcement that it could no longer supply financial aid to the beleaguered governments of Greece, threatened by a Communist-led rebellion, and Turkey. The time had come, Truman concluded, for the United States to assume the global responsibility for containing communism. Conscious, as speechwriter Joseph M. Jones later recalled, that a "major turning point in American history" was at hand," Truman's advisers produced nine drafts of the address. The early versions stressed the economic needs of war-torn Europe. Dry and factual, they made "the whole thing sound like an investment prospectus," the president complained. Later drafts were far more ideological. Truman had been told by Senate leader Arthur Vandenberg that the only way a reluctant public and Congress would support a permanent role overseas was for the president to "scare hell" out of the American people. To rally popular support, Truman rolled out the heaviest weapon in his rhetorical arsenal—the defense of freedom. As the leader of the "free world," the United States must now shoulder the responsibility of supporting "freedom-loving peoples" wherever they were threatened by communism. Twenty-four times in the eighteen-minute speech, Truman used the words "free" or "freedom."[5]

Building on the wartime division of the globe into free and enslaved worlds, and invoking a far older messianic vision of America's mission as defending liberty against the forces of darkness, the Truman Doctrine created the language through which most Americans came to understand the postwar world. More than any other statement, Senator J. William Fulbright would later write, it established "the guiding spirit of American foreign policy." As the Cold War intensified in the next few years, with the Berlin blockade, the advent of a Communist government in China, the establishment of NATO, and the Korean War, so too did the rhetoric. The aim of the Soviet Union, declared *Life* magazine in 1950, was "slavery . . . for all the world, including the people of the United States." In that year, another seminal Cold War document, NSC 68, issued a clarion call for a permanent military buildup to enable the United States to engage in a global crusade against communism. Drafted for the National Security Council by State Department officer Paul Nitze, this manifesto described the Cold War as a conflict between "the idea of freedom" and the "idea of slavery under the grim oligarchy of the Kremlin." This rhetoric established the framework within which Truman understood the historical meaning of his presidency. "I have hardly had a day in office," he observed on retiring in 1953, "that has not been dominated by this all-embracing struggle between those who love freedom and those who would lead the world back into slavery and darkness."[6]

As a number of contemporary critics, few of them sympathetic to Soviet communism, pointed out, casting the Cold War in the stark terms of a worldwide battle between freedom and slavery had certain unfortunate consequences. Kennan, whose Long Telegram had inspired the policy of "containment," observed that the sweeping language of the Truman Doctrine made it impossible to view international crises on a case-by-case basis, or to determine which genuinely involved either freedom or American interests. In a penetrating critique of Truman's policies, Walter Lippmann objected to turning foreign policy into an "ideological crusade." Lippmann supported aid to Greece and Turkey. But, he pointed out, the world outside Europe was being swept by a tide of revolutionary nationalism, an upheaval in which Communists were bound to play an important role. To view every challenge to the status quo through the lens of Soviet power, he correctly predicted, would require the United States to recruit and subsidize "a heterogeneous array of satellites, clients, dependents and puppets," as well as to intervene continuously in the affairs of nations whose politics did not emanate from Moscow and could not be easily subsumed in the dichotomy between freedom and slavery. Henry Wallace, speaking for those who believed the spread of freedom could better be promoted by economic cooperation than military confrontation, also condemned Truman's policies and in 1948 ran for president as an independent, with support from the now much-reduced Communist Party as well as many disillusioned New Dealers. His crushing defeat inaugurated an era when public criticism of the foundations of American foreign policy became all but impossible.[7]

In practice, America's role in the world was often less messianic than Cold War rhetoric implied. Geopolitical and economic interests shaped foreign policy as much as the idea of freedom. But the language of a crusade for freedom remained unchanged, invoked to justify a proliferation of national security bodies immune from democratic oversight such as the Atomic Energy Commission and Central Intelligence Agency (established, respectively, in 1946 and 1947), and American actions in the rest of the world that had little to do with freedom by almost any definition. The CIA in the early 1950s organized military coups in Guatemala and Iran that replaced elected officials deemed to threaten foreign investments with dictators attuned to American interests. These events were then hailed as examples of the "progress of freedom."[8]

Cold War freedom was a circular concept. If a nation was part of the worldwide anti-Communist military alliance led by the United States, it automatically became a member of the "free world." This usage produced such anomalies as Fascist Spain being praised by President Eisenhower for its devotion to freedom, and the Republic of South Africa being included within the "free world" even though its white minority had deprived the black population of nearly all their rights. The most Eisenhower would say about apartheid was that it was "a touchy thing," and he called the soldiers defending the tottering French empire in Vietnam upholders of "the cause of human freedom" and "the survival of the free world." Was there not some way, one commentator asked, that the United States could accept "the aid of tyrants" on pragmatic grounds "without corrupting our speeches by identifying tyranny with freedom?"[9]

If the Cold War produced unsavory alliances overseas, it also helped to legitimize a serious assault on civil liberties at home. Dividing the world between liberty and slavery automatically made those who could be linked to communism enemies of freedom. Despite the celebration of liberty as the foundation of the American way of life, the right to dissent inevitably came under attack as the Cold War intensified. Less than two weeks after announcing the Truman Doctrine, the president established a loyalty review system in which government employees were forced to demonstrate their patriotism without being allowed to confront their accusers or, in some cases, know the specific charges against them. Soon, congressional committees and counterparts on the state level were calling individuals to testify about their past and present political activities and beliefs. Membership in organizations with Communist influence, or even participation in campaigns in which Communists had taken part, such as the defense of Loyalist Spain ten years earlier, suddenly took on sinister retrospective implications. Throughout the country, loyalty oaths proliferated and "subversives" were driven from their jobs. The academic world suffered a "collective failure of nerve," with universities firing teachers who claimed the constitutional privilege against self-incrimination or refused to testify against others. Such actions, said Lewis W. Jones, president of Rutgers University, were necessary so that institutions of higher learning could maintain their role as "guardians of the Western tradition of freedom."[10]

By 1950, the anti-Communist crusade had engendered a pervasive atmosphere of fear. Writing from Washington, the historian Howard K. Beale described a city rife with "spying, suspicion, defamation by rumor," with "democratic freedoms" at risk as power slipped into the hands of those "whose values are the values of dictatorship and whose methods are the methods of the police state." Four years later, as mainstream a publication as *Life* magazine commented that the attack on nonconformity had made Americans reluctant to speak their minds. "Freedom," it observed, might be in greater danger from "disuse" than from Communist subversion.[11]

At its height, from the late 1940s to around 1960, the anti-Communist crusade powerfully structured American politics and culture. Yet there is something mysterious about the era that came to be named for Senator Joseph McCarthy of Wisconsin, whose Senate subcommittee aired charges of Communist membership or sympathies against government employees, army officers, and leading Democrats. The tiny Communist Party hardly posed a threat to American security and many of the victims of the Red Scare had little or nothing to do with communism. The anti-Communist crusade had many faces and purposes. It was a popular mass movement, especially strong in ethnic enclaves with roots in Eastern European countries now dominated by the Soviet Union and in communities (such as the Irish) where the influence of the Catholic Church was strong. It was also a weapon that individuals and groups wielded in battles unrelated to defending the United States against subversion.

For McCarthy and his Republican followers, the target was often not so much Stalin but Roosevelt, and anticommunism became a potent tool in the long battle to overturn the New Deal. For many Democrats, anticommunism was a form of self-defense against Republican charges of disloyalty and a weapon in a struggle for the party's future, a way of redrawing the boundaries of acceptable liberalism to exclude Communists and all those willing to cooperate with them as in the days of the Popular Front. Indeed, "sympathetic association" with Communists—past or present—was grounds for dismissal under the government's loyalty program. For business, the anti-Communist crusade became part of a campaign to tar government intervention in the economy with the brush of socialism. Anticommunism became a tool wielded by white supremacists against black civil rights, employers against unions, and upholders of sexual morality and traditional gender roles against homosexuality, all allegedly responsible for eroding the country's fighting spirit. (Homosexuals and members of nudist colonies were among those now barred from government service.)[12]

There undoubtedly were Soviet spies in the United States. It is equally certain that the vast majority of those jailed or deprived of their livelihoods during the McCarthy era were guilty of nothing more than holding unpopular beliefs and engaging in totally legitimate political activities. As they had during World War I, the courts acquiesced in the political repression, demonstrating once again Madison's dictum that popular hysteria would override "parchment barriers" to the limitation of freedom. During the 1950s, wrote the civil libertarian John Frank, "the First Amendment . . . went into hibernation." In 1951, the Supreme Court upheld the jailing of eleven Communist Party leaders under the Smith Act. Evidently, wrote Justice Hugo Black in a stinging dissent, only "safe" opinions were protected by the Bill of Rights. Even many liberals retreated from the idea that freedom of expression was a birthright of all Americans. The ACLU refused to defend the indicted Communist leaders, and in an influential 1950 article, "Heresy Yes, Conspiracy, No," the philosopher Sidney Hook, a former Marxist, declared that normal protections of academic freedom did not apply to Communists. Hook was a key figure in the American Committee for Cultural Freedom, which sought to mobilize American intellectuals as foot soldiers in the Cold War even as it denounced the Soviets for subordinating culture and intellectual life to politics. The committee's leadership soon made its peace with McCarthyism. (The group, quipped

Dwight Macdonald, should call itself the American Committee for Cultural Freedom in Russia.)[13]

The Cold War could not but affect the domestic political agenda. In 1950, NSC 68 coyly referred to the need to defer "certain desirable programs" in order to finance military preparedness. Although calls for domestic reform hardly disappeared, and could even be justified as a way of strengthening America's hand in the battle for freedom, the range of political debate narrowed considerably. In the early years of the Truman administration, the United States confronted what some scholars have called a "social democratic" moment. As the CIO launched "Operation Dixie" in the hope of bringing unionization to the South and shattering the hold of white supremacists on politics in the region, Truman pressed for the enactment of FDR's Economic Bill of Rights. But with the failure of Operation Dixie, conservative control of Congress remained intact, and Truman's proposals stood little chance of enactment. The president's reelection in 1948 demonstrated that the electorate had no desire to dismantle the New Deal. Indeed, during the 1950s, the number of people covered by Social Security, the emblematic New Deal program, was greatly expanded. Among those included for the first time were domestic and agricultural workers.[14]

But the Cold War gave powerful ammunition to opponents of further change. In the largest public relations campaign in American history, the American Medical Association (AMA) successfully invoked the specter of "socialized medicine" to discredit Truman's proposal for national health insurance. The real estate industry likewise mobilized against public housing, terming it "socialized housing," part of a continuum that stretched all the way to Moscow. As the idea of expanding the welfare state faded, private welfare arrangements proliferated. The labor contracts of unionized workers established health insurance plans, automatic cost of living wage increases, paid vacations, and supplemental unemployment payments, benefits not enjoyed by the majority of the population.[15]

Every political and social organization had to make its peace with the anti-Communist crusade or face destruction, a wrenching experience for movements, such as labor and civil rights, in which Communists had been some of the most militant organizers. After the passage of the Taft-Hartley Act of 1947, which withdrew bargaining rights and legal protection from unions whose leaders failed to swear under oath that they were not Communists, the CIO expelled numerous left-wing officials and eleven Communist-led unions, representing nearly 1 million workers.[16] The civil rights movement also underwent a metamorphosis. In the early years of the Truman administration, the status of black Americans enjoyed an almost unprecedented salience in national affairs.

Between 1945 and 1951, eleven northern states established fair employment practices commissions and numerous cities legislated against job discrimination and
bias in access to public accommodations, measures inspired by a broad civil
rights coalition involving labor, church, and black organizations. In October
1947, *To Secure These Rights,* the report of Truman's Commission on Civil Rights,
offered a devastating indictment of racial inequality in America and called for
government intervention to abolish segregation and ensure equal treatment in
housing, employment, education, and the criminal justice system. The report,
said Truman, was "an American charter of human freedom." He added that if
the United States were to offer the "peoples of the world" a "choice of freedom or enslavement," it must "correct the remaining imperfections in our practice of democracy." In 1948, liberals at the Democratic National Convention
placed a strong civil rights plank in the national platform, prompting a walk-
out by several southern delegations.[17]

At first, mainstream black organizations like the NAACP and the Urban
League protested the Truman administration's loyalty program and wondered
aloud why congressional committees defined communism but not racism as
"un-American." But while a few prominent black leaders, notably Paul Robeson and W. E. B. Du Bois, became outspoken critics of the Cold War, most
eventually felt they had no choice but to go along. The NAACP launched a
purge of Communists from its local branches, and when the government deprived Robeson of his passport and implausibly indicted Du Bois for failing
to register as an agent of the Soviet Union, few prominent Americans, white
or black, protested. (The charge against Du Bois was so absurd that even at the
height of the anti-Communist hysteria, a jury acquitted him.) One result was
a subtle shift in thinking and tactics among civil rights groups. Organizations
like the National Negro Congress and the Southern Conference for Human
Welfare, in which Communists and non-Communists had cooperated in linking racial equality with labor organizing and economic reform, had been crucial to the struggles of the 1930s and war years. Their demise left a gaping hole
that the NAACP, with its narrowly legalistic strategy, was ill-prepared to fill.[18]

Black organizations now embraced the discourse of the Cold War, while
using it to advance their own aims, thus complicating the idea of freedom
while helping to cement Cold War ideology as the foundation of the political
culture. Both civil rights groups and the Truman administration insisted that
racial inequality, an aberration in an otherwise free society, damaged the American image abroad and thus played into the Russians' hands. Indeed, in its am-
icus brief in *Brown v. Board of Education,* the case in which the Supreme Court in
1954 declared school segregation a violation of the Fourteenth Amendment, the

administration urged the justices to consider "the problem of racial discrimination . . . in the context of the present world struggle between freedom and tyranny," and spoke of segregation's "adverse effect" on America's standing in the world.[19]

Even so, the height of the Cold War was an inauspicious time to raise questions about the imperfections of American freedom. It is revealing that two months after the Truman Doctrine speech, Undersecretary of State Dean Acheson chose a meeting of the Delta Council, an organization of Mississippi planters, bankers, and merchants, to deliver a major address defending the president's pledge to aid "free peoples" seeking to preserve their "democratic institutions." Acheson seemed unaware that he had ventured into what the historian David Oshinsky would later call the "American Siberia" to make the case for the Cold War. Had he glanced outside the meeting place, he would have discovered large numbers of citizens deprived of the very liberties supposedly endangered by communism. The black 70 percent of the delta's population not only had no voice in choosing their government, but lived in wretched poverty and faced the persistent threat of legal and extralegal violence. "I call it slavery," one sharecropper later observed of conditions on the region's plantations. In his memoirs, published in 1969, Acheson recalled the day's activities as "thoroughly American" and the delta as a "lush and prosperous agricultural area." After all, the Mississippi delta was part of the Free World.[20]

Aside from the integration of the armed forces, ordered by the president in 1948, little came of the Truman administration's civil rights flurry. The new state and local laws banning discrimination in employment and housing remained largely unenforced. In 1952, the Democrats' nomination of Adlai Stevenson, a candidate with little interest in civil rights, who chose a southern segregationist, John Sparkman, as his running mate, revealed how quickly the issue had faded. Even liberals, the historian Richard Hofstadter noted, were becoming "far more conscious of those things they would like to preserve than they are of those things they would like to change." In 1953, Hortense Gabel, director of the "eminently respectable" New York State Committee Against Discrimination in Housing, reported that the shadow of "fear" hung over the movement, with the result that "a great many people are shying away from all activity in the civil liberties and civil rights fronts." Time would reveal that the waning of the civil rights impulse was only temporary. But it came at a crucial historical juncture, just as the greatest housing and employment boom in American history was reconfiguring the society, opening vast new opportunities for whites while leaving blacks locked in the rural South or the decaying urban ghettos of the North.[21]

By the end of the 1950s, the idea that the love of freedom was the defining characteristic of American society had become fully incorporated into the popular consciousness. So overwhelmingly did Americans respond to statements about freedom, reported a study of public opinion polls, that "a far-reaching consensus" on its value had been achieved. Every domestic political initiative, it seemed, from John F. Kennedy's decision to send a man to the moon to more mundane proposals for manpower development or highway construction were promoted in the fulsome language of freedom. Freedom emerged as the "masterword" in critical writing on American culture, linking the spontaneous "action painting" of Jackson Pollock, John Cage's musical compositions incorporating chance, and the "graceful freedom" of George Balanchine's ballerinas to the nature of American life. American modern art, commented the critic Meyer Schapiro, cultivated the "surest world of freedom—the interior world of [the] fancies, sensations, and feelings." American writing, declared the historian Perry Miller, could appeal to "free men everywhere" because it was "a literature of freedom."[22]

During the 1950s, freedom became an inescapable theme of academic research, popular journalism, mass culture, and official pronouncements. In ways overt and subtle, the Cold War established the framework for this discussion. Probably the most ambitious study of freedom produced in these years was conducted by the Institute for Philosophical Research in San Francisco. More than twenty scholars pored over the works of Western authors, beginning with the ancients, to ascertain their understandings of freedom. The findings were synthesized in a massive two-volume tome, *The Idea of Freedom* (1958–61), by the project's director, philosopher Mortimer Adler. A founder of the "Great Books" course of study at the University of Chicago in the 1930s, Adler exemplified a new type in American popular culture—the celebrity intellectual (or "egghead," as they were called). He appeared regularly on television and radio shows to explain philosophy and sell his great books idea. Convinced that he could bring order to twenty-five centuries of thought, Adler monomaniacally tried to squeeze the ideas of hundreds of writers into three categories: freedom as self-realization (the ability to become what one wishes); freedom as self-perfection (a moral state achieved by acquiring wisdom and virtue); and freedom as self-determination (the ability to decide upon one's own wishes and actions). Adler's aim was to make sense of the ongoing discussion of freedom, not choose sides. But his system encouraged the idea that freedom was essentially an inner quality rather than a social one. Political liberty was mentioned, but as a "special variant" of self-realization. Notably slighted were issues that had historically shaped American debates over freedom, such as its relationship to economic structures and racial and gender inequality. The exclusion of non-Western thinkers, moreover, seemed to reinforce the notion that freedom was a unique possession of the West.[23]

Other than students of philosophy, it is unlikely that many readers actually waded through Adler's dense volumes. More accessible and influential was "Two Concepts of Liberty," an elegant essay published in 1958 by the Russian-born British philosopher, Isaiah Berlin. "Negative liberty," Berlin wrote, meant the absence of external obstacles to the fulfillment of one's desires; "positive liberty" the condition in which an individual transcends internal obstacles to freedom such as uncontrollable wants and false needs, and reaches genuine self-fulfillment. Berlin's positive liberty was an inner state, not a form of social organization or public policy. But in the atmosphere of the 1950s, his deceptively simple distinction was seized upon as another weapon against communism. Negative liberty represented the West, with its constitutional safeguards for individual choice; positive liberty the Soviet Union, where the state imposed its vision on society. To his annoyance, Berlin's essay was widely interpreted to brand any governmental action that interfered with economic decision-making as "positive" freedom and therefore akin to communism. Berlin's aim was not to delegitimize the welfare state, but to force its supporters to defend the ideal of economic equality on its own terms rather than as a form of freedom. Indeed, when he reissued the essay in 1969, Berlin took pains to point out that negative liberty has often been a license for exploitation and that economic inequality deprives mankind of the social conditions of freedom.[24]

Along with freedom, the Cold War's other great "mobilizing and unifying concept" was "totalitarianism," an idea that reinforced the sharp division of the world into opposing camps. The term originated in Europe between the world wars to describe Fascist Italy and Nazi Germany—aggressive, ideologically driven states that sought to subdue all of civil society to their controlling grasp and thus left no room for individual rights and alternative values. By 1950, the year the McCarren Internal Security Act barred "totalitarians" from entering the United States, it had become a shorthand for those on the other side in the Cold War. Some of its chief adherents, like the historian Arthur Schlesinger, Jr., would come to regret the "mystical" description of the Soviet Union as a totalitarian state impervious to change. But the term's widespread use reflected the prevailing view that freedom required shielding a private realm of belief and action against the interference of the state, and that the greatest danger to liberty lay in too much government.[25]

Thus, just as the confrontation with the Nazis had shaped wartime understandings of American freedom, the Cold War reshaped them once more. Russia had already conquered America, Archibald MacLeish complained in 1949, since politics was conducted "under a kind of upside-down Russian veto"—whatever Moscow stood for was by definition the opposite of freedom. Freedom meant the constitutional and legal system and democratic political structure, which distinguished the American way of life from communism. Ironically, even as McCarthyism punished those who overstepped the boundaries of acceptable political discourse and personal behavior, the right to express one's views without fear of government reprisal was exalted as a quintessential element of Western freedom. This definition united defenders of McCarthyism (although they denied its benefits to "enemies of freedom" and "sexual perverts") and those who opposed the anti-Communist purges, for whom the lone dissenter became the standardbearer of liberty and the right to express unpopular ideas the sine qua non of a free society.[26]

In 1950, Freedom House began assessing the status of freedom in the world's nations. Its criteria were entirely political, emphasizing citizens' right to participate in open elections and to speak out on public issues. Freedom House candidly acknowledged the imperfections of parts of the free world. But its surveys explicitly rejected the idea that freedom had any substantive economic content. Considering employment, housing, education, medical care, and the like as part of the definition of freedom was "a materialist mistake." Here was an apt illustration of Louis Hartz's observation in *The Liberal Tradition in America* (1955) that as a result of the Cold War, prevailing ideas had become so rigid and narrow that they could no longer "appreciate nonpolitical definitions of 'freedom' and hence are baffled by their use."[27]

The Triumph of Consumer Freedom

In fact, however, Cold War freedom did have a strong economic content. In the 1950s, freedom became fully identified with consumer capitalism, or, as it was now universally known, "free enterprise." More than political democracy or freedom of speech, which many allies of the United States lacked, what united the nations of the free world was an economic system resting on private ownership. Freedom from want, with its vaguely socialistic implications, all but dropped out of public discourse. A week before his Truman Doctrine speech, the president, in a major address on economic policy, reduced Roosevelt's Four Freedoms to three. Freedom of speech and worship remained, but freedom from want and fear had been superseded by freedom of enterprise, "part and parcel," said Truman, "of what we call American." Thus, "free enterprise" took its place as a fundamental freedom, part of the official definition of the American way of life.[28]

During the Cold War, the "selling of free enterprise" became a major industry, involving corporate advertising, school programs, newspaper editorials, and civic activities. Even more than during World War II, paeans to the virtues of free enterprise became ubiquitous in Americans' daily lives. Convinced that advertising was "a new weapon in the world-wide fight for freedom," the Advertising Council invoked cherished symbols like the Statue of Liberty and the Liberty Bell in the service of "competitive free enterprise," while business journals incessantly promoted the message that freedom meant economic activity unhampered by government controls. To be sure, the free enterprise campaigners were hardly of one mind on every issue. Representing what might be called business's more liberal wing, the Advertising Council preached both free enterprise and government-business cooperation, and, in its million-dollar "American Economic System" ad campaign of 1949, reaffirmed labor's right to collective bargaining. The underlying message, however, was that the existing economic order, responsible for the "highest standard of living and the greatest freedom in the world," was sacrosanct. By 1958, a public opinion survey revealed that 82 percent of respondents (and 87 percent of "influentials") believed that "our freedom depends on the free enterprise system."[29]

As the German-born sociologist Norbert Elias pointed out, market competition had become "a kind of archetype of the freedom of the individual." Free enterprise seemed an odd way of describing an economy whose key sectors were dominated by a few large corporations. In the 1950s, moreover, the glorification of free enterprise did not necessarily preclude support for labor's right to organize or for the kinds of governmental intervention pioneered by the New Deal. Liberals spoke of free enterprise as enthusiastically as conservatives. To be sure, the linkage of free enterprise with Cold War freedom served to legitimate a group of conservative writers who defined free enterprise in strict laissez-faire terms. Their moment of greatest influence, however, lay in the future. In the 1950s, the definition of free enterprise had less to do with either the structure of economic power or the legacy of the New Deal than with the existence of a flourishing marketplace, especially in consumer products. "Without a free exchange of goods," declared an advertisement by the Brand Names Foundation, "you cannot have a free people."

As consumer culture reached its apotheosis during capitalism's "golden age," so too did paeans to consumerism as an embodiment of freedom. Americans, wrote David Lilienthal, chairman of the Atomic Energy Commission, in 1952, must abandon the emotional repugnance to "big business" so prominent in the

Progressive era and second New Deal, and with it the fear that concentrated economic power endangered "our very liberties." Large-scale production was not only necessary to fighting the Cold War but enhanced freedom by multiplying consumer goods. "By freedom," wrote Lilienthal, "I mean essentially *freedom to choose* to the maximum degree possible. . . . It means a maximum range of choice for the consumer when he spends his dollar." This idea, of course, antedated the 1950s, but now for the first time the full benefits of the consumer economy were within reach of the majority of the population.[30]

Virtually all Americans reaped the rewards of an era of unprecedented economic expansion and rising living standards. The gross national product more than doubled between 1946 and 1960, and in every measurable way—diet, housing, wages, education, recreation—most Americans lived better than their parents and grandparents had. Providing the engine of economic growth were residential construction and spending on consumer goods, as the postwar baby boom fueled demands for housing, television sets, home appliances, and cars. In the new suburbs that sprang up across the landscape, the dream of homeownership came within the reach of the majority of Americans. By 1960, suburban residents of single-family homes outnumbered both urban and rural dwellers and the detached house had become the physical embodiment of hopes for a better life. Even more than in the past, homeownership became an American creed. For beneficiaries of postwar prosperity like Rica Kartides, a maintenance man who made heroic sacrifices to move his family to the suburbs of Boston, the home became "the center of freedom." Even though the rapid expansion of the suburban middle class owed much to federal tax subsidies, mortgage guarantees for home purchases, highway construction, military spending, and benefits under the G.I. Bill, Cold War affluence greatly expanded the constituency that identified freedom with free enterprise.[31]

Americans, declared a 1953 article in *House Beautiful*, had achieved a new level of freedom and given new meaning to the pursuit of happiness and the timeless goal of individual self-fulfillment, with "a greater chance to be yourself than any people in the history of civilization." In a consumer culture, the measure of freedom was the ability to gratify market desires, not, as in the nineteenth century, the social relations of labor. Industrial society, wrote Clark Kerr, president of the University of California at Berkeley, in 1960, might undermine freedom "in the workplace," but the compensation was the greater range of "alternatives in goods and services," and thus "a greater scope of freedom" in Americans' "personal lives." Public opinion surveys revealed that Americans were more preoccupied with the level of wages and time off from work than with working conditions and production processes.[32]

For millions of city dwellers, the suburban utopia fulfilled the aspiration, postponed by depression and war, for homeownership and middle-class incomes. The move to the suburbs was also a great agent of Americanization, severing urbanites from ethnic communities and bringing them fully into the world of middle-class mass consumption. An array of services—central heating, indoor plumbing, telephones, refrigerators, washing machines—that within living memory had been enjoyed only by the solidly middle class now became aspects of common life. In the face of abundance, who could deny that the capitalist marketplace was the preeminent embodiment of individual freedom? "It was American Freedom," proclaimed *Life*, "by which and through which this amazing achievement of wealth and power was fashioned." Economic prosperity not only demonstrated the superiority of the American way of life to communism but virtually redefined the nation's historic mission. "We supposed that our revelation was 'democracy revolutionizing the world,'" commented the historian David Potter, "but in reality it was 'abundance revolutionizing the world.'"[33]

"The concept of freedom," wrote one commentator in 1959, "has become as familiar to us as an old hat or a new Ford." Hats aside, a new Ford now seemed as essential to the enjoyment of freedom's benefits as the right to vote or workplace autonomy once had been. Along with a home and a television set, the car became part of what sociologists called "the standard consumer package" of the 1950s. The proliferation of automobiles, the pivot on which suburban life turned, vaulted car manufacturers and oil companies to the top echelons of corporate America and transformed the nation's social landscape and daily life. As early as 1933, the President's Committee on Recent Social Trends had identified the automobile as "a dominant influence in the life of the individual." But it was not until after World War II that car ownership came within the reach of the majority of Americans. By 1959, the country's 44 million families owned 56 million cars. The car symbolized the identification of freedom with individual mobility and private choice. On the road, Americans were constantly reminded in advertising, television shows, and popular songs, they were truly "free," modern versions of western pioneers or Huckleberry Finn on his Mississippi River raft, able to leave behind urban crowds and workplace pressures for the "open road."[34]

The emergence of suburbia as a chief site of American freedom placed all the more pressure on the family—and especially women—to live up to freedom's promise. The war's end brought a sharp drop in the employment of women outside the home and a reversion to the pattern whereby women who did work were concentrated in low-paid clerical, sales, and service jobs. Although the number employed soon began to rise, the nature and aim of women's work had changed. The modern woman, said *Look* magazine, worked part time, to help buttress the family's middle-class suburban lifestyle, not to pull it out of poverty or to pursue personal fulfillment or an independent career. Despite the increasing numbers of wage-earning women, the suburban dream meant a father who went to work and a mother devoted to her children (an average of 3.2 per family), husband, and home. The idea of domestic life as a refuge and full-time motherhood as a woman's "sphere" had a long history in the United States. But only in the postwar suburbs did it come close to realization, with the spatial separation of family life from work, relatives, and the web of social organizations typical of cities. Like everything else, the family became a weapon in the Cold War. The ability of women to remain at home, outside the labor force, declared James O'Connell, undersecretary of labor in the Kennedy administration, was one of those things "that separates us from the Communist world," where a high percentage of women worked.[35]

During the 1950s, American men and women engaged in an astonishing reaffirmation of the virtues of domesticity. They married younger and divorced less frequently than in the 1940s. The family life exalted at the height of the Cold War was not the frugal, patriarchal household of old, but a modernized relationship in which both partners reconciled family obligations with personal freedom through shared consumption, leisure activities, and sexual pleasure. The personal freedom once associated with working women, in other words, could now be found within marriage and the family. Thanks to modern conveniences, women enjoyed their greatest "hope for freedom" at home. Frozen and prepared meals, exulted food writer Poppy Cannon in 1953, offered the modern housewife "freedom from tedium, space, work, and [her] own inexperience"—quite a change from the Four Freedoms of World War II.[36]

If the suburbs offered a new locale for the enjoyment of American freedom, they retained at least one familiar characteristic: rigid racial boundaries. Suburbia was never as uniform as both its celebrants and its critics claimed. There were upper-class suburbs, working-class suburbs, industrial suburbs, and "suburban" neighborhoods within city limits. But if the class homogeneity of suburbia has been much exaggerated, its racial homogeneity was all too real. As late as 1993, nearly 90 percent of suburban whites lived in communities with nonwhite populations of less than 1 percent—the legacy of conscious decisions by government, real estate developers, banks, and initial residents.[37]

If homeownership was an element of freedom, declared the Commission on Civil Rights' report *To Secure These Rights*, then "equality of opportunity" to purchase a home "should exist for every American." But during the postwar suburban boom, federal agencies continued to insure mortgages with racially re-strictive provisions, thereby financing housing segregation. Even after the Supreme Court in 1948 declared such covenants unenforceable, banks and pri-vate developers continued to bar non-whites from the suburbs and federal lending agencies refused to subsidize mortgages for blacks except in segregated enclaves. The vast new communities built by the developer William Levitt, which epitomized the suburban revolution, refused to allow blacks to rent or purchase homes. In 1957, not a single black family resided among the sixty thousand inhabitants of Levittown, Pennsylvania. (Only in 1960, in response to a lawsuit, did Levitt agree to sell homes to blacks.) Meanwhile, under the slo-gan of "urban renewal," cities used their power of eminent domain to remove the poor from urban areas slated for redevelopment, frequently replacing them with all-white middle-income complexes like New York's Stuyvesant Town, which opened in 1947 and only agreed to admit a handful of black families as tenants after years of protests and lawsuits.[38]

With black migration from the rural South to the urban North reaching un-precedented levels (3 million blacks moved from South to North between 1940 to 1960, followed by another 1.4 million in the following decade), the process of racial exclusion became self-reinforcing and self-justifying. As industrial jobs fled the central cities of the industrial heartland for suburbs and the South—a process soon to be known as deindustrialization—more and more poor blacks remained trapped in urban ghettos, associated in the white mind with crime and welfare. Suburbanites, for whom the home served not only as an emblem of freedom but also as the family's major accumulation of capital, became increasingly fearful that any non-white influx would lower the quality of life and destroy property values. "Freedom is equal housing too," became a slogan in the campaign for residential integration. But suburban homeowner-ship long remained a white entitlement, with the freedom of non-whites to rent or purchase a home where they desired overridden by the potent mixture of pri-vate property, the right to privacy, and "freedom of association." Thus, even as the old divisions between white ethnic Americans faded in the suburban melt-ing pot and a black movement arose in the South to challenge institutionalized segregation, racial barriers in housing and therefore in public education and jobs were being reinforced. To many black Americans, the boundary between the free and unfree worlds seemed to run along the color line, not the iron curtain. Speaking of the street that marked the entrance to an all-white Los Angeles neighborhood, a black resident of the city later recalled, "we used to say that Alameda was the Berlin Wall."[39]

Cold War affluence coexisted with urban decay and racism, the seeds from which bitter protest would soon flower. Yet to many observers in the 1950s it seemed that the problems of American society had been solved. In contrast to the turmoil of the thirties and the immediate postwar years, the fifties appeared a placid time, partly because of widespread affluence, partly because of the narrowing of the permissible boundaries of political debate. The boom-and-bust cycles, mass unemployment, and economic insecurity of capitalism seemed largely to have disappeared. Problems remained, but their solution required technical, piecemeal adjustments, not structural change or aggressive political intervention. Despite the excesses of McCarthyism, scholars celebrated the "end of ideology," the triumph of a democratic, capitalist "consensus" in which all Americans, except malcontents and fanatics, shared the same liberal values. In a homogenous suburban society, class no longer constituted a salient feature of American life or provided an adequate language of social analysis. The United States, not Russia, declared *Fortune* magazine, had achieved the Marxist goal of a classless society. Rediscovering Madison, writers of the fifties stressed that the best security for liberty lay in the multiplication of interest groups so that no single one could ever control the state. Indeed, in the finely tuned American polity, with everyone (except those deemed subversive) free to pursue their own ideas, goods, and politics, excessive power automatically called forth its own "countervailing" opposite, "resulting in greater freedom and equity all around."[40]

As for religious differences, the source of persistent tension in American history, these were elided under the rubric of a common Judeo-Christian heritage, a notion that became central to the cultural and political dialogue of the 1950s. This "invented tradition" sought to demonstrate that Catholics, Protestants, and Jews shared the same history and values and had all contributed to the evolution of American freedom. In the era of McCarthyism, ideological pluralism may have been un-American, but group pluralism reigned supreme, with the free exercise of religion yet another way of differentiating the American way of life from life under communism. To highlight the contrast with atheistic Russia and "strengthen our national resistance to communism," Congress in the 1950s invoked the deity as an ally in the Cold War, adding the words "under God" to the Pledge of Allegiance and declaring "In God We Trust" the nation's official motto. If the idea of a Judeo-Christian tradition trivialized the long history of hostility between religious denominations, it reflected both the decline of anti-Semitism and anti-Catholicism and the ongoing secularization of American life. As Will Herberg argued in his influential work, *Protestant—Catholic—Jew* (1955), religion now had less to do with devotional activities or sacred values than personal identity and group assimilation. Society's "common religion," he argued, was the American way of life, a combination of democratic values and material prosperity—in a word, "free enterprise."[41]

Occasionally, dissenting voices could be heard, wondering whether the celebration of affluence and the either-or mentality of the Cold War obscured the extent to which the United States fell short of its ideal of freedom. In 1957, the political scientist Hans J. Morgenthau noted that free enterprise had "engendered new accumulations of power, as dangerous to the freedom of the individual as the power of the government had ever been." Echoing thinkers of the Progressive era and New Deal, Morgenthau concluded that the abdication of government made possible "the unhindered growth of private power," and that the state needed to be "called back" to act as a "champion of freedom." Morgenthau believed that in a democratic society, the government *could* act as an agent of the common good. More radical in pointing to the problem of unequal power in American society and more pessimistic about prospects for meaningful change was the sociologist C. Wright Mills, whose work challenged the self-satisfied vision of democratic pluralism that dominated mainstream social science in the 1950s. Authority was not, Mills insisted, diffused among a multiplicity of social groups, but concentrated in a "power elite"—an interlocking directorate of corporate leaders, politicians, and military men who dominated government and society, rendering political democracy obsolete. Freedom, Mills insisted, meant more than "the chance to do as one pleases." It required "the chance to formulate the available choices," and this most Americans were effectively denied.[42]

Did modern Americans truly enjoy freedom? Ironically, even as the government and media portrayed the United States as a beacon of liberty locked in a titanic struggle with its opposite, a powerful strain of social analysis in the 1950s contended that Americans did not even desire freedom. Generally, the culprit was not, as for Mills, the unequal structure of power, but modernity itself and its psychological and cultural discontents. "Western man in the middle of the twentieth century," Arthur Schlesinger, Jr., proclaimed at the opening of his influential book, *The Vital Center* (1949), "is tense, uncertain, adrift." Modern life inevitably produced loneliness and anxiety, causing mankind to crave stability and authority. In Europe, according to *Escape from Freedom* (1941), Erich Fromm's account of the rise of Nazism that reached a broad popular audience in the Cold War years, this alienation had led men willingly to sacrifice their own freedom.

In the United States, too, modern bureaucratic structures seemed to have rendered the idea of the free individual obsolete. Americans, as David Riesman put it in his book *The Lonely Crowd* (1950), were "other-directed" conformists, who lacked the inner resources to lead truly autonomous lives. Other social critics charged that corporate enterprises had transformed independent-minded employees into "organization men," and that mass culture reduced intellectual life and artistic expression to the lowest common denominator. A new subfield of sociological investigation, the study of mass communication, found that the economic powers-that-be had substituted a "subtler type of psychological exploitation"—the shaping of tastes, perceptions, and consciousness—for the "direct exploitation" of an earlier stage of capitalism's development. Suburbia was a bastion of uniformity, the antithesis of individualism, and even consumer freedom was a myth, since advertisers had perfected the technique of "engineering consent," manipulating a passive public to multiply its desires.[43]

Together, these portraits of American society came perilously close to reproducing the definition of totalitarianism, in which individuals were controlled in the name of freedom. Some commentators even feared that the Russians had achieved a greater ability to sacrifice for common goals than the United States. Americans' obsession with "negative" liberty, George Kennan argued, in words reminiscent of the old Christian definition of freedom, deprived the country of a sense of moral purpose. Indeed, Kennan seemed almost to view the Cold War as a providential opportunity for Americans to rededicate themselves to a goal more meaningful than ever-expanding consumption. What kind of society, the economist John Kenneth Galbraith asked in *The Affluent Society* (1958), slighted investment in schools, parks, and public services while producing ever more goods to fulfill desires created by advertising? Was the spectacle of millions of educated middle-class women seeking happiness in suburban dream houses a reason for celebration or a waste of precious "womanpower" at a time when the Soviets trumpeted the accomplishments of their female scientists, physicians, and engineers?[44]

In his *Letter to the New Left*, published in 1960, Mills called for the birth of a radicalism appropriate to the changed conditions of American society and the world. Distrustful of mass politics, however, most social critics simply threw up their hands, despairing even to suggest how the idea of freedom might be reinvigorated. Inadvertently, books like William Whyte's *The Organization Man* (1956) and Vance Packard's *The Hidden Persuaders* (1957), with their critique of the monotony of modern work, the role of bureaucracies, and the emptiness of suburban life, created the vocabulary for an assault on the nation's political institutions and social values that lay just over the horizon. In the 1950s, however, while criticism of mass society became a minor industry among intellectuals, it failed to dent the ebullient optimism generated by affluence and widespread complacency about the American way. At any rate, calls for a rejection of consumerism struck many observers as unpatriotic. Americans, declared M. C. Patterson, a vice president of the Chrysler Corporation, were not prepared to give up "material things," to "go without that new powerboat—[to] stop planning that new modernized kitchen." Unsheathing the Cold War's most potent rhetorical weapon, Patterson charged that "economic Spartanism" was akin to socialism, a direct threat to "our free enterprise system." Consumer products provided the best propaganda for the United States, insisted Joseph Barry, a reporter for *House Beautiful.* Unlike "some of our own intellectuals," Barry claimed, foreign visitors to exhibitions of American goods appreciated "the freedom offered by washing machines and dishwashers, vacuum cleaners, automobiles, and refrigerators."[45]

Indeed, it was at one of the era's numerous expositions of American consumer products that a classic Cold War confrontation over the meaning of freedom took place. This was the famous "kitchen debate" between Vice President Richard Nixon and Soviet premier Nikita Khrushchev, at the 1959 American National Exhibition in Moscow. A showcase of consumer goods and leisure equipment, complete with hi-fi sets, a movie theater, home appliances, and twenty-two different cars, the exhibit was intended, as *Newsweek* observed, to demonstrate the superiority of "modern capitalism with its ideology of political and economic freedom." But the exhibit's real message was not freedom but consumption—or, to be more precise, the conflation of the two. When Nixon prepared for his trip to Moscow, a former ambassador to the USSR urged him to emphasize American values: "we are idealists; they are materialists." But the events of the opening day seemed to reverse these roles. Nixon's address, given the title "What Freedom Means to Us," when reprinted in *Vital Speeches of the Day,* was devoted not to freedom of expression or differing forms of government but to the "extraordinarily high standard of living" in the United States, with its 56 million cars and 50 million television sets. The United States, he declared, had achieved what Soviets could only dream of—"prosperity for all in a classless society."

Twice during the first day, Nixon and the Soviet leader engaged in unscripted debate about the merits of capitalism and communism, first in the kitchen of a model suburban ranch house, later in a futuristic "miracle kitchen" complete with a mobile robot that swept the floors. Supposedly the home of an average steelworker, the ranch house was the exhibition's centerpiece. It epit-

Vice President Richard Nixon and Soviet premier Nikita Khrushchev during the "kitchen debate," a discussion, among other things, of the meaning of freedom, which took place at the 1959 American National Exposition in Moscow. (Wide World Photos)

omized, Nixon proclaimed, the mass enjoyment of American freedom within a suburban, family-oriented setting—freedom of choice among colors, styles, and prices, freedom from drudgery for "our housewives." It also implied a particular role for women. Throughout the exchange, Nixon used the words "women" and "housewives" interchangeably. Pointing to an automatic floor-sweeper, the vice president remarked, "you don't need a wife." (In planning the exhibit, one designer had proposed including a photograph of a man sweeping the kitchen floor, but the idea was rejected as unrepresentative of American life.)

Nixon's decision to make a stand for American values in the setting of a suburban kitchen was a brilliant stroke. In reply, Khrushchev ridiculed the American obsession with household gadgets. "Don't you have a machine," he quipped, "that puts food in the mouth and pushes it down?" In his inimitable style, Khrushchev offered an appraisal of consumer culture not unlike that of American critics. Many of the items on display at the exposition, he maintained, were "interesting" but had "no useful purpose." Yet, in a sense, the Soviet leader conceded the debate when he predicted that within seven years, his country would surpass the United States in the production of consumer goods. Henceforth, it seemed, the competition between the two systems would be joined not so much in the realm of political ideals or military might but over which could provide the greater material abundance. If this was to be the battlefield of freedom, it was one chosen by the United States.[46]

In March 1965, in conjunction with the struggle for voting rights in the South, students organized a 52-hour sit-in at the Liberty Bell to demand federal protection for civil rights workers. "The Liberty Bell," declared a broadside distributed by the demonstrators, "again serves as a national focal point in the struggle for freedom." (National Park Service)

1 2
Sixties Freedom

O<small>N DECEMBER 1, 1955,</small> Rosa Parks, a veteran of civil rights activities in Montgomery, Alabama, was arrested for refusing to surrender her seat on a city bus to a white rider, as required by municipal law.
The incident sparked a year-long bus boycott, the beginning of the
greatest mass movement in modern American history. Within a decade,
the civil rights revolution had overturned the edifice of de jure segregation and won the ballot for black citizens in the South. But more
than bringing down the curtain on a particularly unhappy chapter in
the story of American freedom, the movement shattered what David
Riesman called the "bi-partisan deep freeze" that had come close to
reducing freedom to a sterile propaganda slogan.[1] Challenging the received orthodoxy of the Cold War, it redirected national attention to
the unfinished business of freedom at home.

Today, with the birthday of Martin Luther King, Jr., a national holiday and the struggles of Montgomery, Little Rock, Birmingham, and
Selma celebrated as heroic episodes in the history of freedom, it is easy
to forget that at the time, the civil rights revolution came as a great surprise. In retrospect, its precipitants seem clear: the destabilization of
the racial system during World War II; the migration out of the segregated South that made black voters a major part of the Democratic
Party coalition; and the Cold War and rise of independent states in
Africa, both of which made the gap between American rhetoric and
the reality of American race relations an international embarrassment.
Yet the mass movement for civil rights was hardly inevitable. With

blacks' traditional allies on the left decimated by McCarthyism, union leaders, by and large, unwilling to challenge racial inequalities within their own ranks, and the NAACP concentrating almost entirely on court battles, new constituencies and tactics were sorely needed. The movement found in the black church the organizing power for a militant, non-violent assault on the edifice of segregation. Then, beginning with the sit-ins of 1960, college students, black and white, propelled the struggle to a new level of mass activism and civil disobedience. By the end of 1960, some seventy thousand people had participated in civil rights demonstrations. The sit-ins launched a decade of "great dreams" when, for the first time in American history, the young became active agents of social change.

More than elevating blacks to full citizenship, declared the writer James Baldwin, the movement challenged the United States to rethink "what it really means by freedom." When the journalist Sally Belfrage prepared to write her book *Freedom Summer*, chronicling the events of 1964, a friend urged her to choose another title, since " 'freedom' has such dreadful CIA connotations." With their freedom rides, freedom schools, freedom songs, freedom marches, and the insistent cry "freedom now," black Americans and their white allies reappropriated the central term of Cold War discourse and rediscovered its radical potential. And the courage of thousands of ordinary men and women—maids and laborers alongside teachers, businessmen, and ministers—who risked physical and economic retribution to lay claim to freedom inspired a host of other challenges to the status quo, including a mostly white student movement known as the "New Left," the "second wave" of feminism, and claims by other dispossessed minorities. Together, they restored to freedom the critical edge often lost in Cold War triumphalism, making it once again the rallying cry of the dispossessed.[2]

The Freedom Movement

From the beginning, the language of freedom pervaded the black movement. It resonated in the speeches of civil rights leaders and in the impromptu declarations and hand-lettered placards of the struggle's foot soldiers. On the day of Rosa Parks's court appearance in December 1955, even before the bus boycott had officially been announced, a torn piece of cardboard appeared on a bus shelter in Montgomery's Court Square, advising passengers: "Don't ride the buses today. Don't ride it for freedom."[3]

"None of us knew exactly what it meant," one participant later recalled, "but

A cross burned in front of a Freedom House during the Mississippi Freedom Summer of 1964 was left in place by civil rights workers, emblazoned with the movement's byword. (Tamio Wakayama)

we were saying freedom." During the Freedom Summer of 1964, when the Student Nonviolent Coordinating Committee (SNCC) established "freedom schools" for black children across Mississippi, lessons began with students being asked to define the word. Some answers were specific ("going to public libraries"), some more abstract ("standing up for your rights"). Some youths associated freedom with "having power in the system," others with "hatred of restraint." Some insisted that freedom meant legal equality; others saw it as essentially a "state of mind."[4]

Anne Braden, a white native of the South who took a leading part in Freedom Summer, concluded that to participants freedom meant "an end to all that was wrong." Clearly, blacks did not adhere to standard 1950s assumptions about freedom—Isaiah Berlin's distinction, for example, between "positive" and "negative" liberty. Freedom meant both of these and more—equality, power, recognition, rights, opportunities. It required eradicating a multitude of historic wrongs—segregation, disenfranchisement, exclusion from public facilities, confinement to low-wage menial jobs, harassment by the police, and the ever present threat of extralegal violence. It meant courteous treatment in stores and by public officials, down to the right to be addressed as "Mr.," "Miss," and "Mrs." rather than "boy" and "auntie." Freedom also meant sloughing off relationships of dependency on whites, an idea that drew on the old equation of liberty with personal autonomy but had special resonance in a black community where it was rare to find a person whose relations did not include at least one domestic worker. But ultimately, freedom meant more than the sum of its individual parts. To Ned Cobb, a Georgia sharecropper born not long after the end of Reconstruction, who lived to see the civil rights revolution, "this freedom movement" promised that "the bottom rail would come to the top [and] the poor generation on earth will banish away their toils and snares."[5]

Although they had been "treated in a way that makes mockery of our belief in liberty," commented a white faculty member at a black college in Tennessee, African-Americans believed "wholeheartedly" in the ideal of constitutional equality. The movement invoked the unfulfilled promises of the Declaration of Independence, the Emancipation Proclamation, and the Fourteenth Amendment to demand that the nation live up to the letter of the law and to its professed values. "Seek the Freedom in 1963 promised in 1863," read one banner at the 1963 March on Washington. Like the abolitionists, civil rights activists sought to identify the nation's cherished symbols of freedom with their cause, as when students organized a sit-in at the Liberty Bell in 1965 to support the southern drive for voting rights. The acquisition of material goods weighed less heavily on the movement's understanding of freedom than in the culture at large. Still, it was not surprising that the struggle's most active phrase began with the demand to be served at lunch counters and downtown department stores, central locations of a consumer culture. Business firms, said Franklin McCain, an organizer of the first sit-in, in Greensboro, North Carolina, had no right to "advertise in the public media" yet bar blacks from full participation in the consumer marketplace.[6]

To participants in the struggle, the goals of public and private freedom were inseparable. "Freedom of the mind," insisted SNCC, was the greatest freedom of all. But it was "in the very act of working for the impersonal cause of racial freedom," said James Farmer, a leader of the Congress of Racial Equality (CORE), that "a man experiences, almost like grace, a large measure of private freedom . . . an intuition of the expanding boundaries of his self." The movement itself became an all-consuming experience, which produced what SNCC activists called a "freedom high," a sense of individual purpose and personal fulfillment that encouraged hostility to structure and authority of all kinds. Suspicious of the "Moses-type leader" common in church-based organizations, SNCC insisted that a movement for greater democracy must itself be democratic. Rather than adopting a predetermined agenda, said Ella Baker, a longtime black activist who had a powerful influence on the student activists, "you must let the oppressed define their own freedom."[7]

But it was in the soaring oratory of Martin Luther King, Jr., who more than any single individual came to lead and symbolize the movement, that the protesters' many understandings of freedom fused into a coherent whole. A master at appealing to the conscience of white America without appearing to be dangerous or threatening, King presented the case for black rights in a vocabulary that bridged the gap between the races and fused the black experience with that of the nation. From the beginning of his national prominence as chief spokesman for the Montgomery movement, freedom was central to King's rhetoric. For the title of his first book, relating the history of the bus boycott, King chose the title *Stride Toward Freedom.* His most celebrated oration, the "I Have a Dream" speech of 1963, began by invoking the unfulfilled promise of emancipation ("one hundred years later, the Negro still is not free") and closed with a cry borrowed from a black spiritual: "Free at last! Free at Last! Thank God Almighty, we are free at last!"[8]

Suffused with Christian themes derived from his family background and training in the black church, King's speeches resonated deeply in the broader culture. He repeatedly invoked the Bible to preach justice and forgiveness, even toward those "who desire to deprive you of freedom." Central to his theology was the story of Exodus, a mainstay of black preaching that interpreted the African-American experience as a divinely guided progress toward Canaan, the promised land of freedom. Among other things, Exodus suggested that individual rights and group empowerment were interdependent and reinforcing, a point King drove home when he proclaimed, "we as a people will get to the promised land." Like Frederick Douglass before him, King appealed to white America by insisting that the protesters were motivated by love of country and devotion to national values. "We will reach the goal of freedom," he wrote in his *Letter from Birmingham Jail* (1963), "because the goal of America is freedom." The "daybreak of freedom and justice and equality," King made clear, was a new dawn not just for blacks but for the whole of American society.[9]

At a time when Cold War ideology had highlighted the danger to liberty from excessive government and made respect for the distinction between "civil society" and the realm of politics a cornerstone of liberal thinking, civil rights activists resurrected the vision of federal authority as the custodian of freedom. Despite the long history of federal complicity in segregation, blacks' historical experience suggested that they had more hope for justice from national power than from local governments or the voluntary acquiescence of well-meaning whites, This conviction was reinforced not only by southern resistance to integration but by the failure of northern states to enforce the fair employment laws of the late 1940s. Far from being a bastion of liberty, moreover, the institutions of civil society—businesses, unions, homeowners' associations, private clubs, and the like—were riddled with racism, which only federal power could eradicate.

With Congress and the Eisenhower administration unwilling to address the issue, it fell to the Supreme Court to place civil rights irrevocably on the national agenda. Initially, however, both political parties shrank from embracing the Court's unanimous 1954 mandate outlawing school segregation. In 1955, the justices themselves decreed that compliance need not be immediate, but could proceed "with all deliberate speed." This formulation inadvertently encouraged a campaign of "massive resistance" that paralyzed civil rights progress in much of the South. The refusal of the white South to accede to black demands and to the clear requirements of the federal courts convinced the movement that only Washington's active intervention could assure that citizens obtained their constitutional rights.[10]

Although Eisenhower sent federal troops to Little Rock in 1957 to enforce a court order for school integration, during his administration the federal government generally remained aloof from the black struggle. But in the 1960s, the movement's growing militancy and the violent resistance it encountered created a national crisis that propelled a reluctant federal government to champion the cause of black freedom. John F. Kennedy's inaugural address in January 1961 was an eloquent but familiar paean to Cold War freedom that made no mention whatever of civil rights at home. By June 1963, with demonstrations sweeping the country (in one week, over 15,000 Americans were arrested in 186 cities) and the violence unleashed against black protesters in Birmingham attracting worldwide attention, Kennedy went on television to announce that the nation confronted a "moral crisis." Adopting the movement's own rhetoric, Kennedy declared that until blacks achieved full citizenship, "this nation, for all its hopes and all its boasts, will not be fully free." Two years later, the crisis in Selma—where voting rights marchers were assaulted by the Alabama state police—led Kennedy's successor, Lyndon B. Johnson, to demand legislation securing the right to vote. Appealing to "the outraged conscience of the nation," Johnson called Selma a milestone in "man's unending search for freedom." He closed his speech by quoting the demonstrators' favorite song, "We Shall Overcome." Never before had the movement received so sweeping or powerful an endorsement from the federal government.[11]

By 1965, with court orders having dismantled legal segregation and new fed-

Part of the crowd that gathered at the Lincoln Memorial for the 1963 March on Washington to demand "Jobs and Freedom." (UPI/Corbis-Bettman)

eral laws prohibiting discrimination in public accommodations, employment, and voting, the movement had succeeded in eradicating the legal bases of second-class citizenship. In the same year, inspired in part by the conviction that racism should no longer serve as a basis of national policy, the Hart-Cellar Act abandoned the national origins quota system, substituting "family reunification" and job skills as new, non-racial criteria for immigration. The 1924 immigration law, which had stigmatized Italians, Greeks, Poles, and Eastern European Jews as unworthy of citizenship, seemed increasingly anomalous as the Cold War intensified. The main result of the 1965 measure, however, was to open the door to a flood of newcomers from Latin America, the Caribbean, and Asia. Taken together, the civil rights revolution and immigration reform marked the triumph of a pluralist, civic definition of Americanism. By 1976, a public opinion survey reported that 85 percent of respondents agreed with the statement: "the United States was meant to be . . . a country made up of many races, religions, and nationalities."[12]

Yet even at its moment of triumph, the civil rights movement confronted a crisis as it sought to move from access to schools, public accommodations, and the voting booth to the intractable economic divide separating blacks from other Americans. In its first decade, civil rights activity had not entirely ignored the economic dimensions of black freedom: expanded employment opportunity was one part of the "treaty" that ended the Birmingham crisis of 1963, while "Jobs and Freedom" was the slogan of that year's March on Washington. But the issue had been muted, partly because of the pressing need to challenge the legal and political dimensions of black inequality, and partly because the Cold War had severed the civil rights movement from left-wing groups that linked the black condition to a broad critique of economic inequality. Even as the struggle achieved its greatest successes, however, violent outbreaks in black ghettoes outside the South—Harlem in 1964, Watts in 1965 (just a few days after Johnson signed the Voting Rights Act), other cities in ensuing years—drew attention to the fact that racial justice was a national, not southern problem, and to the inequalities in employment, education, and housing that the dismantling of legal segregation left intact.

In the mid-1960s, economic issues rose to the forefront of the civil rights agenda. With black unemployment two and a half times that of whites and average black family income little more than half the white norm, the movement groped for ways to "make freedom real and substantive" for black Americans. In 1964, King called for a "Bill of Rights for the Disadvantaged" to mobilize the nation's resources to abolish the scourge of economic deprivation. His proposal was directed against poverty in general, but King also insisted that after "doing something special *against* the Negro for hundreds of years," the United States had an obligation to "do something special *for* him now"—an early call for what would come to be termed "affirmative action." In 1966, black unionist A. Philip Randolph and civil rights veteran Bayard Rustin proposed the Freedom Budget, which envisioned spending $100 billion over a ten-year period for a federal program of job creation and urban redevelopment.[13]

Also in 1966, King launched the Chicago Freedom Movement, with demands quite different from its predecessors in the South—upgrading black employment, ending discrimination by employers and unions, equal treatment in granting mortgages, and the construction of low-income housing scattered throughout the region. His aim was nothing less than to dismantle the black ghettos and make Chicago an "open city." Encountering the entrenched power of Major Richard J. Daley's Democratic machine and the ferocious opposition of white homeowners, the movement failed. Southern tactics—marches, sit-ins, mass arrests—proved ineffective in the face of the less overt but no less pervasive structures of racial inequality in the North. And the violent reactions of white residents in Chicago's ethnic enclaves stunned King. Even in the South, he commented, he "had never seen as much hatred." By 1967, when he composed his last book, *Where Do We Go from Here?*, the optimism that had sustained King during the southern phase of the movement had faded. Open housing and equal employment opportunity remained "a distant dream," he wrote, and radical economic reforms—full employment, a guaranteed annual income, "structural changes" in capitalism itself—were necessary to bring blacks fully into the social mainstream. (Ironically, King's white adviser Stanley Levison, whose former ties to the Communist Party led FBI director J. Edgar Hoover to view the entire civil rights movement as a Communist conspiracy, urged King to moderate his rhetoric. The white majority, Levison warned, would never embrace a program to "alter the social structure of America" in order to "free the Negro.")[14]

If the movement's first phase had produced a clear set of objectives, far-reaching accomplishments, a series of coherent if sometimes competitive organizations (SNCC, CORE, King's own Southern Christian Leadership Council), and a preeminent national leader, the second phase witnessed ideological and organizational fragmentation and few significant victories. Even before 1965, an alternative definition of freedom had been articulated by the fiery orator Malcolm X, who drew on the nationalist tradition of Martin Delany and Marcus Garvey to insist that blacks must control the political and economic resources of their own communities and rely on their own efforts, not alliances with whites or federal assistance, to achieve full emancipation. The United States, Malcolm X proclaimed, had never been a "country of freedom."[15]

When he was assassinated in 1965 by members of the Nation of Islam—the nationalist religious group in which he had risen to prominence and had then

abandoned—Malcolm X left neither a consistent ideology nor a coherent organization. But in death, his powerful language and call for blacks to rely on
their own resources struck a chord among younger civil rights activists. More
than any other individual, Malcolm X was the intellectual father of "Black
Power," a slogan that first came to national attention in 1966 when SNCC
leader Stokely Carmichael and other young blacks employed it during a civil
rights march in Mississippi. To King, Black Power was a "cry of disappointment, certain to alienate whites." To its adherents, as one put it, "Black Power
means Black Freedom." "An all-black project is needed," SNCC declared in
1966, "in order for the people to free themselves." In terms of specific content,
the term was hopelessly imprecise. "Black Power" suggested everything from the
election of more black officials (hardly a radical idea, given the long history of
ethnic politics in the United States) to the belief that black Americans were a
colonized people, analogous to inhabitants of the Third World, whose freedom
could only be won through a revolutionary struggle for self-determination.
But however employed, the slogan's prominence marked a subtle shift in the definition of black freedom, identifying it less with integration into the American mainstream than with group self-determination. Although the equation of
freedom and power was hardly new, Black Power gave pluralism a separatist
tinge and helped to inspire similar movements among other racial minorities,
including Native Americans and Chicanos, and a renewed emphasis on ethnic
identity among third-generation whites.[16]

Although the remarkable victories of the early sixties were soon followed by
a period of frustration, the black movement succeeded in placing the question
of economic freedom back on the nation's political agenda. Having swept to a
landslide election victory in 1964 that shattered the conservative stranglehold
on Congress, Johnson not only presided over the legislative triumphs of the civil
rights era—the Civil Rights Act of 1964, the Voting Rights Act of 1965, and
the Fair Housing Act of 1968—but launched the most far-reaching domestic
agenda since the New Deal. Overcoming longstanding hostility to "socialized
medicine," public housing, and intrusive federal power, Johnson's Great Society
programs provided health services to the poor and elderly (in the new Medicaid and Medicare programs) and poured federal funds into education and
housing. The government's reach was felt through new agencies such as the En-
vironmental Protection Agency and the Equal Employment Opportunities
Commission (the latter a fulfillment, under a new name, of the postwar campaign for a permanent FEPC). Taken together, these measures went far toward
completing the social agenda stalled in Congress since 1938 and creating for the
first time an "equal-opportunity welfare state" that brought under its wing

those excluded from New Deal entitlements, especially blacks and working women.[17]

The centerpiece of the Great Society, however, was Johnson's crusade to eradicate poverty. After the complacent talk of universal affluence during the 1950s, widespread deprivation had been rediscovered, thanks in part to Michael Harrington's 1962 book, *The Other America*, and in part because of the civil rights movement (even though Johnson saw the antipoverty initiative as a way of balancing efforts on behalf of blacks with measures aimed at uplifting dispossessed whites, who constituted a large majority of the nation's poor). Under the rubric of the "War on Poverty," the Johnson administration launched a series of initiatives designed to lift the poor into the social and economic mainstream. In a departure from the New Deal, when poverty had been seen as arising from an imbalance of economic power and flawed economic institutions, in the 1960s it was attributed to an absence of skills and opportunity and a lack of proper attitudes and habits. Johnson himself, who could talk with feeling of his experience with poverty in the hills of East Texas, adhered to the venerable notion that dependency on government relief was incompatible with genuine freedom. His hostility toward direct government assistance was widely shared among policymakers—more so than among the general public. In a 1964 public opinion survey, over one-half of the electorate but only one-third of "influentials" believed that the government had a responsibility to ensure that all Americans enjoyed a decent standard of living.

Thus, while the War on Poverty included measures to alleviate suffering, such as providing food stamps to those in need, Johnson rejected the most direct ways of eliminating poverty—establishing a guaranteed annual income for all Americans, creating jobs for the unemployed, actively promoting the spread of unionization, or making it more difficult for businesses to shift enterprises to low-wage centers in the South. Instead, the War on Poverty concentrated on equipping the poor with skills, and rebuilding their spirit and motivation through job training, education, legal services, and community development programs. In an echo of SNCC's philosophy of empowering ordinary individuals to take control of their lives, the War on Poverty required that poor people play a leading part in the design and implementation of local policies, a recipe for persistent conflict with local political leaders accustomed to controlling the flow of federal dollars.[18]

Johnson defended these measures in a vocabulary of freedom derived from the New Deal (when his own political career began), and reinforced by the civil rights movement. Soon after assuming office in 1963, he resurrected the phrase "freedom from want," all but banished from political discourse during the

1950s, as "the fullest measure of social justice." Echoing FDR, Johnson told the 1964 Democratic National Convention, "the man who is hungry, who cannot find work or educate his children, who is bowed by want, that man is not fully free." Within a year, he was declaring that the battle for civil rights had entered a new and "more profound stage." Recognizing that black poverty was fundamentally different from its white counterpart, since its roots lay in "past injustice and present prejudice," Johnson in 1965 announced that it was no longer sufficient to define economic freedom as equality of opportunity:

> Freedom is not enough. You do not wipe away the scars of centuries by saying: Now you are free to go where you want, do as you desire, and choose the leaders you please.
>
> This is the next and more profound stage of the battle for civil rights. We seek . . . not just equality as a right and a theory, but equality as a fact and as a result.

The Great Society, Johnson proclaimed, would enable Americans to move beyond Roosevelt's Four Freedoms to even more expansive meanings—"freedom to learn," "freedom to grow," "freedom to hope," freedom to "live as [people] want to live." To critics who viewed the national state as "a menace to individual liberty," Johnson responded that government was a force for liberation, enabling the individual to rise above "the enslaving forces of his environment."[19]

Johnson's Great Society represented a remarkable reaffirmation of the ideas of social citizenship and racial equality, the most expansive effort in the nation's history to mobilize the powers of the national government to address the needs of the least advantaged Americans. The War on Poverty succeeded in greatly reducing the incidence of poverty, all but wiping it out among the elderly. But the sums expended (a total of a few billion dollars) were far too low to achieve the utopian goal of ending poverty altogether or the more immediate task of transforming the conditions of life in impoverished urban neighborhoods. Together with the civil rights movement itself, government action opened doors of opportunity for black Americans, spurring an enormous expansion of the black middle class. But millions of African-Americans remained trapped in poverty. By the 1990s, the historic gaps between white and black in education, income, and access to skilled employment had narrowed considerably. But the median wealth of white households remained quadruple that of blacks; unemployment was far lower; and nearly a quarter of all black children lived in poverty. Shortly before her death, Fannie Lou Hamer, who had risen from sharecropping obscurity in Mississippi to become a national symbol of the civil rights struggle, remarked to a friend, "Mac, we a'int free yet."[20]

In 1965, Bayard Rustin wondered how political leaders could spend hundreds of billions of dollars on an ever-growing military budget, "yet throw up their hands before the need for overhauling our schools, clearing the slums, and really abolishing poverty." Reflecting the unquenchable optimism of the era's "growth liberalism," Johnson insisted that given an expanding economy, Americans could "afford to make progress at home while meeting obligations abroad." But with the escalation of U.S. military involvement in Vietnam, it became impossible to fight a war on want and a war in Southeast Asia. By 1967, the War on Poverty had ground to a halt. With ghetto uprisings punctuating the urban landscape, the antiwar movement assuming massive proportions, and millions of young people ostentatiously rejecting mainstream values, American society faced its greatest social crisis since the Depression.[21]

The New Left

Like the civil rights revolution, the rise of a protest movement among white youth came as a complete surprise. During the 1950s, students had been a "silent generation," who harbored, one professor lamented, "no great loves, no profound hates, and pitifully few enthusiasms." For most of the century, colleges had by and large been elitist institutions that drew their students from a small, privileged segment of the population. They were also bastions of conservatism—the Harvard undergraduates who took the places of striking Boston policemen in 1919 were far more typical of campus politics than the much-publicized radicals at New York's City College during the 1930s. Indeed, if blacks' grievances were self-evident to anyone with even a passing acquaintance with American life, those of students were in many ways difficult to comprehend. "At 21," wrote Raymond Mungo, a young journalist and antiwar protester in 1968, "I am independent, well read, capable of earning a more than substantial income. . . . I am everything but free. And it is freedom alone that I most cherish and that I must achieve." What persuaded large numbers of white children of affluence that they were "unfree"? In part, the answer lay in a redefinition of the meaning of freedom by what came to be called the "New Left."[22]

What was new about the New Left was that it rejected the intellectual and political categories that had animated both radicalism and liberalism for most of the twentieth century. Instead of material deprivation, class conflict, and social citizenship, students spoke of loneliness, isolation, and alienation, of powerlessness in the face of bureaucratic institutions, of a hunger for authenticity that affluence could not sate. Similar discontents, to be sure, has been voiced by social critics in the 1950s. Now, however, they galvanized a mass movement among what was rapidly becoming a major sector of the American population. In the mid-1950s, there were 2.7 million college students. By 1968, thanks to the coming of age of the baby boom generation and the explosion of institutions of higher learning that accompanied it, the number had risen to over 7 million (more than farmers, miners, or steelworkers). By then, the uprising of young people against both existing institutions and the traditional left had become an international phenomenon, evident in the streets of Paris and Prague as well as New York, Berkeley, and Chicago.[23]

The New Left, to be sure, was not nearly as new as its members or its critics claimed. Its call for a democracy of citizen participation harked back to the republicanism of the Revolution; its moral critique of the contrast between American values and American reality to the abolitionists. In its emphasis on authenticity in the face of conformity, it recalled the bohemians of the years before World War I, and its critique of a suffocating culture of consumption clearly drew inspiration from C. Wright Mills, Dwight Macdonald, and other critics of mass society of the 1950s. But the New Left's greatest inspiration was the black freedom movement. More than any other single event, the sit-ins galvanized white student activism. "For the New Left," one scholar has concluded, "the meaning of *freedom* began with the struggle of African-Americans."

Here was the volatile combination that created the upheaval known as "the sixties"—the convergence of society's most excluded members demanding full access to all its benefits, with the children of the affluent middle class rejecting the social mainstream. The black movement and white New Left shared certain basic assumptions: that the evils to be corrected were endemic to social institutions and that direct confrontation was necessary to persuade Americans of the urgency of change. From the black movement, and especially SNCC, the New Left learned that everyday life is a political arena and that everyday choices have political implications. Both movements shared an optimism (a later, more cynical age would call it utopianism or naïveté) that far-reaching changes in American mores and institutions were not only desirable but eminently possible.[24]

The years 1962 and 1963 witnessed the appearance of pathbreaking books that challenged one or another aspect of the Cold War consensus. James Baldwin's *The Fire Next Time* gave angry voice to the black revolution. Rachel Carson's *Silent Spring* exposed the ecological costs of the heedless growth of production and consumption. Michael Harrington's *The Other America* revealed the persistence of poverty amid plenty. Yet in some ways the most influential critique of all issued in 1962 from the Students for a Democratic Society (SDS), a tiny offshoot of the socialist League for Industrial Democracy, whose origins dated back to the turn of the century. Meeting at Port Huron, Michigan, some sixty college students adopted a document, originally drafted by Tom Hayden of the University of Michigan, that captured the mood and summarized the beliefs of this generation of student protesters.

Four-fifths of the Port Huron Statement was devoted to criticism of the institutions of American life, from political parties to corporations, unions, and the military-industrial complex. But what made the document the guiding spirit of a new radicalism was the remainder, which offered a new vision of social change. "We seek the establishment," Hayden wrote, "of a democracy of individual participation, governed by two central aims—that the individual share in those social decisions determining the quality and direction of his life; that society be organized to encourage independence in men and provide the media for their common participation." To achieve this, the document called for the creation of a new left, "a left with real intellectual skills," consisting of "younger people" who had come of age in the postwar world.

Thus was the language of Jefferson and Emerson, of Garrison, Debs, and Dewey filtered through the experience of the civil rights movement and reborn as a critique of a militarized, bureaucratized society and the organization man. The emphasis on "participatory democracy" announced a new conception of politics, whose function would be to bring Americans "out of isolation and into community." Never defined with any precision, participatory democracy was as much a critique of the undemocratic features of American life as an alternative blueprint. Nonetheless, it soon became a standard by which existing social arrangements—workplaces, schools, government, political parties, and organizations of the Old Left—were judged and found wanting. And although the Port Huron Statement called for the government to promote greater economic equality, construct more schools, and provide universal health care, it also resonated with suspicion of the centralized state. Its call for politics on a "human scale" set the new radicals apart from much of the twentieth-century left. The idea of participatory democracy suggested a rejection of the elitist strain that had marked liberal thinking from the Progressives to postwar advocates of national economic planning, as well as the social science managerialism that reduced citizens to consumers of goods and services whether in the political or the economic arena. "Freedom," Hayden insisted in preparatory notes for the Port Huron meeting, echoing John Dewey, "is more than the absence of arbitrary restrictions on personal development." Ultimately, it meant the power to participate in the decisions that shaped one's life.[25]

By the end of 1962, with the sit-ins galvanizing northern student activism, SDS had grown to eight thousand members. Then, in 1964, events at the University of California at Berkeley suddenly revealed the possibility for a far broader mobilization of students in the name of participatory democracy. The quintessential Cold War "megaversity," Berkeley was an immense, impersonal institution where enrollments in many classes approached one thousand students. The spark that set the Free Speech movement alight was a new administrative rule prohibiting the use of a central area of the campus for disseminating political ideas. There followed months of protests involving thousands of Berkeley students, during which student leaders moved from demanding a change in the new rule to a critique of the entire structure of the university and of an education geared to preparing graduates for white-collar corporate jobs. "We want freedom for all Americans, not just Negroes," said Mario Savio, the most prominent Free Speech leader and a veteran of Mississippi's Freedom Summer. Freedom, defined in the SNCC-SDS language of participatory democracy, became "the banner of the movement." When the university capitulated early in 1965, student activist Barbara Garson proclaimed, "we can take pride in having, for once, reversed the world-wide drift from freedom."[26]

More than any other issue, however, what transformed student protest into a full-fledged generational rebellion was the war in Vietnam. The war was both a logical extension and a reductio ad absurdum of Cold War policies and assumptions. It tragically exposed the dangers of viewing the entire world and every local situation within it through the either-or lens of an anti-Communist crusade. Few Americans had any real knowledge of Vietnam's history and culture (and those who did had been purged from the State Department during the McCarthy era). A complex struggle for national independence, led by indigenous Communists who enjoyed widespread support throughout the country, was reduced in American eyes to a defining battleground of the Cold War. As early as 1949, the Truman administration had cast its lot with French colonialism in the region. By the early 1960s, the United States was committed to the survival of a corrupt and dictatorial South Vietnamese regime, a commitment that led inexorably to the introduction first of military "advisers" and then tens of thousands of ground troops.

Fear that the public would not forgive them for "losing" Vietnam made it impossible for either John F. Kennedy or Lyndon B. Johnson to extricate the United States from an increasingly untenable situation. For Kennedy, the Vietnam War became a test of the commitment, announced in his inaugural address,

to "pay any price, bear any burden" to assure the "survival . . . of liberty." Johnson, too, never abandoned the conviction that the Vietnam War was part of "the
struggle for freedom everywhere." On signing the Civil Rights Act of 1964, he
could not refrain from linking black protesters at home with the "soldiers in
Vietnam, each willing to sacrifice for freedom." By 1967, the number of American troops fighting in Vietnam exceeded half a million.[27]

As casualties mounted and American bombs poured down on North and
South Vietnam, the Cold War consensus in the United States began to unravel.
By 1968, the war had scuttled much of the Great Society; torn families, universities, and the Democratic Party apart; and led Johnson to announce that he
would not seek reelection. With the entire political leadership, liberal no less
than conservative, committed to the war for most of the 1960s, young activists
were radicalized and turned on their erstwhile liberal supporters.

Opposition to the war became the organizing principle around which
doubts, disillusionments, and hidden discontents now coalesced. "We recoil
with horror," said an SNCC position paper in 1965, "at the inconsistency of a
supposedly 'free' society where responsibility to freedom is equated with the responsibility to lend oneself to military aggression." Outrage over the war, and
over the disproportionate number of young black men being drafted to fight
it, contributed significantly to SNCC's embrace of Black Power.[28]

As for SDS, its leaders had long questioned the foundations of Cold War
thinking. At Port Huron, a representative from a student organization linked
to the Communist Party was allowed to participate as an observer. Members
of the League for Industrial Democracy, SDS's parent organization (including
Michael Harrington, then all of thirty-four), objected with a vociferousness
that mystified most of the students. The debate presaged not only SDS's decision to strike out on its own, but the coming breach between student activists
and Cold War liberals. In 1965, a clause barring advocates of "totalitarianism"
from SDS membership was removed as "a relic of a bygone era." When SDS
invited all who opposed American policy in Vietnam (presumably including
Communists) to assemble in Washington in April of that year to protest the
war, Harrington, Bayard Rustin, and others warned people to stay away. The
turnout of twenty-five thousand amazed the organizers, offering the first hint
that the antiwar movement might soon enjoy a mass constituency. In his speech
at the rally, SDS president Paul Potter sought to reclaim the language of freedom from the administration:

> The President says that we are defending freedom in Vietnam. Whose free-
> dom? Not the freedom of the Vietnamese. . . . What has the war done for

freedom in America? It has led to even more vigorous governmental efforts to control information, manipulate the press and pressure and persuade the public through distorted or downright dishonest documents. . . . The President mocks freedom if he insists that the war in Vietnam is a defense of American freedom.[29]

As Potter suggested, the war provided the perfect antithesis to participatory democracy, since American involvement had come through stealth, lies, and elite decision-making, with no semblance of public debate. At the next antiwar rally, in November 1965, SDS leader Carl Ogelsby explicitly linked Vietnam to a powerful critique of foreign policy in general—CIA interventions in Guatemala and Iran, support for South African apartheid, Johnson's dispatch that summer of troops to the Dominican Republic—all rooted in monomaniacal anticommunism. Some might feel, Ogelsby concluded, "that I sound mighty anti-American. To these, I say: Don't blame *me* for *that!* Blame those who mouthed my liberal values and broke my American heart." The speech, observed one reporter, was a "declaration of independence from the traditional thread of American liberalism" and a "call to battle to alter the fundamental social, political, and economic structure."[30]

As divisions over the war deepened, many students found an unlikely guru in Herbert Marcuse, a neo-Marxist refugee from Nazi Germany whose book *One-Dimensional Man* (1964) offered a savage indictment of a society in which tolerance, that liberal value par excellence, was merely a way of reinforcing the repressive status quo. Dulled by an obsession with acquiring consumer goods, the working class, Marcuse insisted, was no longer an agent of change. Only "the outcasts and outsiders"—minorities, the unemployed, the young—were capable of achieving an awareness of their own oppressed condition. Marcuse's work reinforced the belief that American freedom was a myth. Its popularity testified to a growing rift between the New Left and white workers, now viewed as part of the "system." Soon, some white student leaders would be identifying Third World revolutions of every stripe as "struggles for human freedom." By 1969, leadership in SDS had passed to a violent fringe of self-styled revolutionaries, three of whom died the following year when their bombmaking apparatus exploded in the basement of a Greenwich Village town house.[31]

But far more significant than this turn toward "revolution" was the war's broader cultural impact. Although many streams flowed into what came to be known as the "counterculture," the generational rebellion against accepted mores and lifestyles is inconceivable without the war having delegitimized authority. By the late 1960s, millions of young people were openly rejecting the values and behavior of their elders. Their ranks included not only college students but numerous young workers, even though most unions evinced strong hostility to antiwar demonstrations and countercultural displays. For the first time in American history, the flamboyant rejection of "bourgeois" norms in attire, language, sexual behavior, and the use of drugs, previously confined to artists and bohemians, became the basis of a mass movement. Its rallying cry was "liberation."

Here was John Winthrop's nightmare of three centuries earlier made flesh—a massive redefinition of freedom as a rejection of all authority. Cynics might well charge that far from being rebellious, the counterculture in some ways represented the fulfillment of the consumer marketplace, extending into every realm of life its definition of freedom as the right to individual choice. (Indeed, the emblems of rebellion—beards and long hair, colorful clothing, rock music, drugs, even images of black revolution and sexual freedom—were soon being mass-marketed, legally and illegally, as fashions of the day.) The assumption that prosperity would last forever, and that therefore young people who "dropped out" of the world of conventional employment could later drop back in, was built into the counterculture. So too were hedonism and self-destruction. To followers of Timothy Leary, the Harvard scientist-turned-prophet of mind expansion, the psychedelic drug LSD embodied a new "Fifth Freedom"—"the freedom to expand your own consciousness" and thus escape not only the constraints of society but those of rationality itself. But there was more to the counterculture than its colorful surface—the famed triad of sex, drugs, and rock 'n' roll. To millions of young people, personal liberation represented a spirit of creative experimentation, a search for a way of life in which friendship and pleasure eclipsed the single-minded pursuit of accumulation and consumption. It meant a rejection of the world created by their elders, a release from bureaucratized education, stultifying work, hypocritical social conventions, politics manipulated by the mass media, and, above all, from a militarized state that, in the name of freedom, rained destruction on a faraway people.[32]

No one embodied the contradictions of the counterculture, its fusion of serious politics with self-indulgence, more fully than Abbie Hoffman, who cavorted through the 1960s as the crown prince of irreverence. Hoffman struggled to formulate a new radicalism that took into account the realities of modern life—consumerism, mass communications, the alienation of the young. In a sense, he turned Marcuse on his head, arguing that mass culture could be a source of rebellion and that radicals could use the media to alter popular consciousness. He challenged the way the left had traditionally communicated its ideas, introducing humor and theatricality into the repertoire of protest, as when he showered the floor of the New York Stock Exchange with dollar bills, temporarily bringing trading to a halt (something the Old Left had never accomplished) as brokers scrambled to retrieve the bills. Hoffman was a consummate egotist, but he did not even put his name on his 1968 book, *Revolution for the Hell of It*, whose author was identified simply as "Free." But his deepening involvement with drugs also illustrated the pitfalls of making personal liberation the fundament of politics.[33]

Although the counterculture emphasized the ideal of community—establishing little worlds within the larger society in New York's East Village and San Francisco's Haight-Ashbury district and some two thousand communes nationwide—its notion of liberation had a powerful individualist cast. Nowhere was this more evident than in the central place occupied by sexual freedom in the generational rebellion. Here, too, Marcuse served as an inspiration. His *Eros and Civilization*, published in 1955 but discovered a decade later by the rebellious young, portrayed unrestrained sexuality as a subversive challenge to a repressive, conformist society. But one did not need Marcuse to discover that sexual pleasure was the route to freedom. For men, this was the message of *Playboy* magazine, the increasingly popular advocate of a "swinging" lifestyle. In 1962, Helen Gurley Brown showed women as swinging singles in her bestseller, *Sex and the Single Girl*. Avant-garde painters, choreographers, filmmakers, and other artists found in brashly erotic representations of the body a symbol of liberation from traditional moral and artistic conventions. And, starting in 1960, the mass marketing of birth control pills made possible what "free lovers" had long demanded—the separation of sex from procreation.[34]

In the 1950s, C. Wright Mills had ridiculed the "gonad theory of revolution." By the late 1960s, sexual freedom had become as much an emblem of the counterculture as long hair and drugs. The transition from the Mississippi Freedom Summer of 1964 to San Francisco's Summer of Love three years later symbolized how the "erotic revolution" was overtaking the political. Yet in complex ways, the claim to sexual freedom was intrinsic to yet another movement to emerge from the sixties—the "second wave" of feminism.[35]

The public reawakening of feminist consciousness got its start in 1962, with the publication of Betty Friedan's *The Feminine Mystique*. A prolific journalist during the 1940s for *UE News*, published by the United Electrical Workers' union, Friedan had written pioneering articles on pay equity for women workers and racism in the workplace. But like so many other social critics of the fifties and early sixties, she now took as her theme not class or racial inequality, the preoccupations of the Old Left, but the emptiness of consumer culture and the discontents of the middle class. Seeking to apply to the suburban home the definition of freedom as opportunity for personal self-realization, Friedan contended that "the core of the problem for women today" was a set of social values that did not allow them to "grow and fulfill their potentialities as human beings." Barred from the opportunity to "use [her] full capacities," the suburban housewife lacked the "freedom to be [her] self." Friedan's opening chapter, "The Problem That Has No Name," presented a devastating account of talented, educated women trapped in a world where fulfilling their femininity—the "feminine mystique" of the title—meant marriage and motherhood, while those who desired to pursue careers were deemed neurotic and unwomanly. Somehow, after more than a century of agitation for equal access to public life, the kitchen was still the center of women's lives. Three years earlier in Moscow, Richard Nixon had made the suburban home an emblem of American freedom. For Friedan, employing the era's all-purpose symbol of evil, it was a "comfortable concentration camp."[36]

Few books have had as powerful an impact as *The Feminine Mystique.* Friedan was deluged by desperate letters from female readers. The "problem that has no name," it seemed, was widely shared, and for many women the suburban dream had become a nightmare. A resident of a South Carolina suburb described her female neighbors: women dependent on alcohol, tranquilizers, and sleeping pills; victims of domestic abuse; a "compulsive baby-machine"; an obsessive cleaner; a duplicitous housewife with secret lovers. Readers spoke of the home as a "prison," of their "subtle bondage," of *The Feminine Mystique* as women's "Emancipation Proclamation." "Freedom," wrote an Atlanta woman, "was a word I had always taken for granted," but after reading Friedan, she realized that "I had voluntarily enslaved myself." A sense of bitterness—at society, at men, at women themselves—over wasted educations and purposeless lives was palpable in many of the letters. "My feeling of betrayal," wrote one woman from Brookline, Massachusetts, "is not directed against society so much as at . . . those of us who were educated, and therefore privileged, who put on our black organza nightgowns and went willingly, joyfully, without so much as a backward look at the hard-won freedoms handed to us by the feminists (men and women)."[37]

Obviously, Friedan's book struck a deep chord among its intended audience, testifying to pervasive discontent in spite of an affluence unimaginable to previous generations. Yet Friedan's mailbag also contained evidence that reactions to her critique differed strongly along lines of class and religion. Shortly before *The Feminist Mystique* appeared, Friedan had published a summary of her argument in *McCall's*, the mass-circulation women's magazine. The reaction from readers was not favorable. Many found the article insulting or condescending in denying that homemaking was an honorable calling and "satisfying career." A writer from California insisted that for a woman to create "a comfortable, happy home for her family" was "to be what God intended." Among the largely working-class readers of *McCall's*, Friedan's analysis raised issues of class relations her suburban correspondents ignored. Friedan's call for housewives to find work and sources of identity outside the home, wrote one woman from Fargo, North Dakota, appeared to assume the availability of domestic workers to look after their children. "If the care of a house and children is so unrewarding and unfulfilling to a wife and mother," she asked, "why isn't it so to other women, and why should other women do such work?" Friedan, echoed a Tennessee reader, ignored the plight of "the poor thing who must tie herself to the bonds of housekeeping in my place? What of her? We must emancipate her too."[38]

Here was a harbinger of class divisions that would affect the women's movement for many years to come. But the immediate result of Friedan's book was to focus attention on yet another gap between American rhetoric and American reality. Slowly, the law began to address feminist concerns. In 1963, Congress passed the Equal Pay Act, barring sex discrimination among holders of the same jobs. The Civil Rights Act of 1964 prohibited inequalities based on sex as well as race—a provision proposed by conservatives hoping to scuttle the bill but embraced by liberal and female members of Congress as a way to broaden its scope. The result was to make the Equal Employment Opportunity Commission a major force in breaking down barriers to the employment of women. The year 1966 saw the formation of the National Organization for Women (NOW), with Friedan as president. Modeled on traditional civil rights organizations, it was devoted to obtaining full equality for women in public life, including employment, education, and political participation.[39]

If NOW grew out of the resurgence of middle-class feminism, a different female revolt was brewing within the civil rights and student movements. "How will we convince our daughters," a New Jersey housewife had asked Friedan, "not to make the same mistakes?" By the mid-1960s, it was clear that millions of daughters were learning the lesson of sexual inequality for themselves.

Like abolitionism, the civil rights and student movements became the seedbeds of feminist revolt. Young women who had absorbed an ideology of social equality and personal freedom, and learned the methods of political organizing, simultaneously encountered rampant inequality and sexual exploitation. They found themselves excluded from positions of leadership and prominence in civil rights organizations, often relegated to typing, cooking, and cleaning for male coworkers, and pressured to engage in sexual liaisons. What-

A 1970 women's rights demonstration at the Statue of Liberty. (UPI/Corbis-Bettman)

ever their differences, male civil rights leaders like King, Malcolm X, and many SNCC activists agreed that one of racism's most debilitating effects was depriving black men of a sense of manhood and that a reassertion of masculinity was essential to black liberation. In the entire three-hour program of the 1963 March on Washington, there was not a single female speaker. Similarly, while women participated in SDS from the beginning, the organization's leadership was almost entirely male-dominated: in 1964, women comprised only 6 percent of the executive committee.[40]

Echoing the words of Abby Kelley a century earlier, young SNCC activists Casey Hayden and Mary King concluded in a 1965 memorandum that "there seem to be many parallels that can be drawn between the treatment of Negroes and the treatment of women in our society as a whole." But what really galled Hayden and King was the status of women within the movement. The same complaints soon arose in SDS, where, as countercultural ideas of free love began to circulate, many male activists defined freedom for women almost exclusively in sexual terms. Young women embraced the sexual revolution, especially its assault on the traditional double standard. But many complained that it reinforced prevailing images of women as objects of sexual pleasure for men. "The Movement is supposed to be for human liberation," wrote the young novelist Marge Piercy. "How come the condition of women inside it is no better than outside?" By 1967, women throughout the country were establishing small "consciousness-raising" groups to discuss the sources of their discontent. The time, many concluded, had come to establish a movement of their own, one demanding not simply the equal rights championed by NOW but women's "liberation."[41]

A new, radical feminism, spearheaded by the young, burst into national consciousness at the Miss America beauty pageant of September 1968, when protesters filled a "freedom trash can" with objects of "oppression": girdles, brassieres, high-heeled shoes, copies of *Playboy* and *Ladies Home Journal.* (Contrary to legend, they did not set the contents on fire, but the media quickly invented a new epithet for radical women, "bra-burners.") Inside the hall, protesters unfurled banners carrying the slogans, "Women's Liberation" and "Freedom for Women." Four months later, a group of women burned their voter registration cards during the inauguration of President Nixon, an action that not only offered a female analogue to men burning their draft cards, but also indicated that the sources of women's inequality remained unaffected by the winning of the vote.[42]

When the sixties began, the Port Huron Statement had struggled to link conventional politics with the "private troubles" of Americans. The counterculture had insisted that politics involved far more than electoral activity or mass demonstrations. But more than any other group, the women's liberation movement tried to think through the full meaning of the slogan, "The personal is political." Introducing the terms "sexism" and "sexual politics" into the political language, they insisted that unequal power and lack of freedom could be found in private affairs as well as public. Sexual relations, conditions of marriage, standards of beauty, the nature of family life—these were as much "political" questions as the war and civil rights. "There is no private domain of a person's life," wrote the feminist Charlotte Bunch, "that is not political and there is no political issue that is not ultimately personal. The old barriers have fallen." Radical feminists' first major public campaign demanded the repeal of laws that either banned abortions or left the decision to terminate a pregnancy in the hands of physicians, underscoring women's lack of genuine self-determination. "Without the full capacity to limit her own reproduction," wrote one activist, "woman's other 'freedoms' are tantalizing mockeries that cannot be exercised." Here was the nineteenth-century demand that a woman enjoy control over her own body, charged with the sixties' emphasis on the right to sexual pleasure, within marriage or outside.[43]

But the demands of women's liberation went far beyond sexuality. "People seem to believe," complained Dana Densmore, an early radical feminist leader, "that sexual freedom is freedom." In fact, *Sisterhood Is Powerful*, an influential collection of essays, polemics, and personal experiences published in 1970, touched on a remarkable array of issues, from violence against women to inequalities in the law, churches, and workplaces. At the center, however, stood the family. "Winning our freedom," declared the New York feminist group Redstockings in 1969, required recognizing that unequal relationships between men and women were no less fundamental than the class oppression that had traditionally inspired radical protest. At its most radical, the movement identified the family itself as the essential locus of women's lack of freedom—a stunning repudiation of the family-oriented public culture of the 1950s. If devising coherent alternatives to the family proved maddeningly difficult, radical feminists succeeded in introducing into public debate the idea that family life is not off-limits to considerations of power, justice, and freedom.[44]

The Rights Revolution

It is hardly surprising that the civil rights revolution, soon followed by the rise of the New Left and the second wave of feminism, inspired many other Amer-

LIBERTY'S CROWN

Karl Hubenthal's 8 December 1976 cartoon from the *Los Angeles Herald-Examiner* celebrates the rights revolution. (Karl Hubenthal Cartoon: L. A. Herald–Examiner)

icans to articulate their grievances and claim their own rights. By the late sixties, movements for Chicano rights, homosexual rights, Native American rights, consumer rights, and others dotted the political landscape. Many borrowed the confrontational tactics of the black movement and the New Left, adopting their language of "power" and "liberation" and their derisive stance toward traditional organizations and legal approaches.

It is one of the era's more striking ironies that if the "rights revolution" began in the streets, it achieved constitutional legitimacy through the Supreme Court, historically the most conservative branch of government. Under the guidance of Earl Warren, who served as Chief Justice from 1953 to 1969, the Court vastly expanded the rights enjoyed by all American citizens, and placed them beyond the reach of legislative and local majorities. Fulfilling, at long last, the promise of Reconstruction, the Court became a powerful ally of the revolution in race relations, infusing political and social substance into the constitutional guarantee of equal protection of the laws. It also redefined how political democracy must operate and revitalized the Bill of Rights as a broad protection of citizens' liberties.[45]

The Court's emergence as a vigorous protector of civil liberties had been foreshadowed in 1937, when the justices abandoned freedom of contract while arguing that the First Amendment right of free expression deserved enhanced protection. McCarthyism, however, shattered progress toward a broader conception of civil liberties. It was the civil rights movement that forced the Court to reassess the status of freedom of expression and of political association.

If freedom of speech had gained strength in the 1930s at least partly because of its association with the rights of labor, in the 1950s and 1960s it became intertwined with civil rights. Beginning with *NAACP* v. *Alabama* in 1958, the Court struck down southern laws that sought to destroy civil rights organizations by forcing them to make public their membership lists and requiring schoolteachers to disclose the names of groups to which they belonged. It also shielded the movement from legislative investigations of its activities. Similar measures and investigations had been upheld when directed at the Communist Party, and at first the Court insisted that government harassment of civil rights groups was "wholly different" from similar action against Communists. As late as 1961, the Court upheld the conviction under the Smith Act of the chairman of the North Carolina Communist Party. But the justices soon moved from defending the NAACP to a far broader protection of free speech and freedom of association as the lifeblood of a democracy.

By the end of Warren's tenure, the Court had reaffirmed the right of even the most unpopular viewpoints to First Amendment protection, dismantled the Cold War loyalty security system, and ruled that even advocacy of violence could not be prohibited unless the danger of inciting lawless acts was imminent. In addition, in the landmark freedom of the press ruling in *New York Times* v. *Sullivan* (1964), the Court overturned libel judgments by an Alabama jury against the nation's leading newspaper for carrying an advertisement critical of how local officials treated civil rights demonstrators. The "central meaning of the First Amendment," the ruling declared, lay in the right of citizens to criticize their government; for good measure, it declared the Sedition Act of John Adams's administration unconstitutional over a century and a half after it had expired. Before the 1960s, few Supreme Court cases had dealt with newspaper publishing. It was *Sullivan*, one scholar concludes, that began "the modern constitutional law of freedom of the press."[46]

Simultaneously, the Court pushed forward the process of "incorporating" the Bill of Rights. The states were now required to abide by protections against self-incrimination, illegal search and seizure, the rights to a speedy trial and to confront hostile witnesses, the prohibition against cruel and unusual punishment, and the right of indigent defendants to publicly supplied attorneys. It also proved increasingly sensitive to local efforts to breach the "wall of separation" between church and state. In 1961, the justices unanimously invalidated an oxymoronic clause in the Maryland constitution declaring that there could be no test oath for public office except "a declaration of belief in the existence of God." Soon afterward, it decreed that non-sectarian prayers and Bible readings in public schools also violated the First Amendment, in effect disestablishing Protestantism as the nation's unofficial religion. The Court also assumed the power to oversee the fairness of democratic procedures at the state and local levels, insisting, in a series of "one-man, one-vote" decisions, that legislative districts must contain equal populations, and in 1966 invalidating the poll tax.[47]

The Warren Court not only vastly expanded the substantive protection of the civil rights and civil liberties of all Americans (especially those likely to suffer discrimination at the hands of local majorities), but discovered entirely new rights in response to the rapidly changing contours of American society. Most dramatic was the assertion of a constitutional right to privacy in the 1965 decision in *Griswold* v. *Connecticut*, which overturned a state law prohibiting the use of contraceptive devices. When first introduced into legal discourse by Louis D. Brandeis and Samuel D. Warren in 1890, "privacy" referred to protection against brazen journalistic intrusion into people's lives and the unauthorized use of an individual's likeness by advertisers. By the 1960s, it had come to mean the ability to conduct private life without fear of governmental intrusion. In striking down the Connecticut statute, Justice William O. Douglas— who had once written that "the right to be let alone is the beginning of all freedom"—faced a difficulty: apart from decisions of the 1920s that affirmed the right to marry and raise and educate children without government interference, there was little by way of privacy jurisprudence to build on. The Constitution, moreover, nowhere makes explicit reference to privacy. Douglas solved the problem by concluding that a constitutional right to privacy could be inferred from the "penumbras" and "emanations" of the Bill of Rights, which created a "zone of privacy" legislatures could not invade. In his concurring opinion, Justice Arthur Goldberg wrote that "the concept of liberty protects those personal rights that are fundamental," including the right to privacy "in the marital relation and the marital home."

If *Griswold* linked privacy to the sanctity of marriage and the family, the principle was soon transformed into an individual right with unimpeded access to birth control extended to unmarried adults and ultimately to minors—an admission by the Court that law could not reverse the sexual revolution. These decisions led directly to perhaps the most controversial ruling of the "Warren Court" (even though it occurred in 1973, four years after Warren left the bench), *Roe* v. *Wade,* which created a constitutional right to terminate a pregnancy. Access to abortion, the Court declared, was a fundamental individual freedom protected by the Constitution, a striking vindication of radical feminism's earliest demand. *Roe* proved far more controversial than *Griswold* and has continued so to this day. When *Griswold* was decided, only two states banned contraception; *Roe* invalidated the laws of no fewer than forty-six.[48]

"A constitutionally protected right to privacy," the political philosopher Jean Cohen has written, "is indispensable to any modern conception of freedom." As late as 1970, the Ohio Supreme Court held that a wife was "at most a superior servant to her husband," without "legally recognized feelings or rights." But *Griswold* and *Roe* unleashed a flood of rulings and legislation that finally seemed to accept the feminist view of the family as a collection of individuals, rather than a single unit with a single head. Thus, the legal rights of women within the domestic sphere expanded dramatically. "No-fault" divorce laws replaced statutes that made adultery, cruelty, or desertion the only grounds for terminating marriages, and law enforcement authorities came to accept the idea of prosecuting marital rape and assault. In the law, the old debate between egalitarian and "difference" feminism was resolved in favor of the former, a result that offered millions of women legal recourse against previously unprosecuted crimes, yet also brought unforeseen hardships. No-fault divorce, for example, virtually eliminated the old entitlement to alimony; but in an economy in which most women still found themselves with far less earning power than men, the termination of a marriage became a major cause of female poverty. It is indeed ironic that the notion of "privacy"—once condemned by many feminists as an obfuscation of the ways that public power and social relations shape family life—became the first line of legal defense in women's continuing struggle for equality. But "privacy" now rested on a vision of society composed not of families within a "private sphere" but of sovereign individuals, male and female.[49]

The "rights revolution" completed the transformation of American freedom from a finite body of entitlements enjoyed mainly by white men into an open-ended claim to equality, recognition, and self-determination. By the end of the sixties, and well thereafter, the government and legal system were inundated by rights claims from all sorts of aggrieved groups—blacks, women, gays, welfare recipients, ethnic groups, the elderly, the handicapped. Claims were also advanced for the rights of the voiceless—the "unborn" (as foes of abortion termed the fetus), the environment, endangered plant and animal species. Congress and the Supreme Court would spend much of the rest of the century defining the rights of various groups of Americans and the role of government in advancing or restricting their enjoyment.[50]

As the social movements spawned by the sixties adopted first "power" and then "rights" as their favored idiom, they ceded the vocabulary of "freedom" to a resurgent conservatism, its mass constituency itself a product of that tumultuous decade. The very fact that "rights" were being protected and invented by the most undemocratic branch of government opened the door for the rise of a populist reaction, which fed on the argument that bureaucrats in Washington were riding roughshod over local traditions and preferences. By the end of the sixties, conservative political leaders would seize upon the sense that change had gone "too far" to call for a renewed commitment to "law and order" and social stability. The election of Republican Richard Nixon in 1968 ushered in a period of growing conservative dominance in American politics, interrupted for a time by revulsion against the Watergate scandal that led to Nixon's resignation from office in 1974. With the conservative ascendancy would come yet another turn in the story of American freedom.[51]

Like the "long nineteenth century," which began in 1789 with the French Revolution and ended in 1914 with the outbreak of World War I, the sixties overspilled its chronological boundaries. The Great Society reached an unlikely culmination during the Nixon administration, when affirmative action programs for blacks, only in their infancy under Johnson, were fully institutionalized, spending on Medicare and Medicaid burgeoned, and, for a time, the president even spoke of government recognition of a "right" to a guaranteed annual income. The high water mark of the student movement came in 1970, when in the wake of the American invasion of Cambodia and the killing of four antiwar protesters at Kent State University by troops of the National Guard, more than five hundred colleges and universities experienced strikes that canceled classes and brought the National Guard to twenty-one campuses. Although SDS had already disintegrated, the antiwar movement persisted until the Paris Peace Agreement of 1973. It was in the early 1970s that movements born in the late sixties reached their peak of militancy, such as gay liberation and the American Indian Movement, which seized the Bureau of Indian Affairs Building in Washington and took part in the Sioux takeover of Wounded Knee, site of a notorious massacre over eight decades earlier.[52]

Of all the achievements of the sixties, none was so enduring as its success in transforming popular attitudes regarding women's roles and rights, sexuality, and the family. The 1970s was the decade when the sexual revolution passed from the counterculture into the social mainstream, producing a rapid rise in the divorce rate, a great increase in the number of women in paid work (over half of all married women by 1980), and a drastic fall in the number of Americans who told public opinion pollsters that premarital sex was wrong. As pre–World War I bohemians saw many of their values absorbed into the mass culture of the 1920s, so sixties values and styles, often in depoliticized form, became part of seventies America. When asked in a Gallup Poll to rate the importance of a series of values, respondents gave the highest ranking to "freedom to choose," placing it above "following God's will," "high income," or "a sense of accomplishment." The same telescoping of the personal and political that widened the experience of individual freedom for so many Americans also contributed to a growing estrangement from formal politics, and, indeed, from any notion of a common civil life. In some ways, despite the New Left's critique of consumerism, the growing demand for liberation and personal fulfillment reflected the language and aspirations of postwar consumer culture. There was more continuity than might at first appear between the protesters' demand that individuals be empowered to "choose" their own lifestyle in the quest for personal realization, and the self-absorbed "me decade" that followed.[53]

Just as the Civil War established the framework for several generations of American politics, and political campaigns revolved around the New Deal for many years after Roosevelt's death, so, it seemed, Americans were condemned to refight the battles of the sixties long after the decade had ended. Race relations, feminism, the role of the government in attacking social ills, and the nation's proper role in world affairs—these questions hardly originated in the 1960s, but the events of those years made them more salient and more divisive. As the country turned more conservative, the sixties came to be blamed for every ill, real and imagined, of American society, from crime, drug abuse, and teenage pregnancy to a decline of respect for authority (as if through Vietnam, Watergate, and decades of complicity in racism, authority had not effectively discredited itself). Yet because of the sixties, the United States became a more open, more tolerant—in a word, a freer country.

A 1967 rally by members of Young Americans for Freedom,
a conservative group that flourished in the 1960s.
(UPI/Corbis-Bettman)

13

Conservative
Freedom

B*EGINNING WITH* the dramatic 1960 contest between John F. Kennedy and Richard M. Nixon, the journalist Theodore White published four highly popular accounts of the quadrennial race for the presidency. Traversing the country in 1964, White attended countless civil rights demonstrations as well as numerous rallies for Barry Goldwater, the conservative Republican nominee. White noticed something that struck him as odd:

> The dominant word of these two groups, which loathe each other, is "freedom." Both demand either Freedom Now or Freedom for All. The word has such emotive power behind it that . . . a reporter is instantly denounced for questioning what they mean by the word "freedom." . . .

To White, the conclusion was inescapable: the United States sorely needed "a commonly agreed-on concept of freedom."[1]

White had witnessed firsthand both the struggle over possession of "freedom" set in motion by the 1960s and the revival of conservatism in the midst of a decade fabled for its radicalism. And although few realized it at the time, despite Lyndon Johnson's landslide reelection victory, the Goldwater campaign marked a milestone in the resurgence of American conservatism as a political movement, and the growing popularity of its ideological creed, including its understanding of freedom.

The Rebirth of Conservatism

From the vantage point of the late twentieth century, it is difficult to recall conservatism's beleaguered condition at the end of World War II. Associated in many minds with the crimes of European fascism and the economic policies that had produced the Great Depression, and identified with conspiracy theories, anti-Semitism, and an elitist belief in social hierarchy, conservatism appeared to lack the intellectual resources to deal effectively with the problems of the postwar world. "In the United States at this time," wrote the literary critic Lionel Trilling in *The Liberal Imagination*, published in 1950, "liberalism is not only the dominant but even the sole intellectual tradition. For it is the plain fact that nowadays there are no conservative or reactionary ideas in general circulation." Clearly, Trilling exaggerated; as McCarthyism would soon demonstrate, conservative ideas had hardly been expelled from American life. Yet for Trilling and his generation of liberal intellectuals, conservatism, like radicalism, was a relic of the past, since ideologies of all kinds had been superseded by a broad consensus in support of the New Deal welfare state. When conservative ideas did begin to circulate, liberals explained them as a transitory reaction of the alienated, psychologically disturbed, or status-deprived against "modernity" itself.[2]

"I am still puzzled," Friedrich A. Hayek wrote in 1956, that conservatives in the United States had allowed "the left" to control the definition of liberty, "this almost indispensable term." During the 1950s, a group of conservative thinkers began the task of reclaiming the idea of freedom. Although largely ignored outside their own immediate circle, they articulated the major strands that would dominate conservative thought to the turn of the century. One was antistatism, an outlook, rooted in classical liberalism, which had been given new political life in conservatives' bitter reaction against the New Deal and new intellectual legitimacy in Hayek's own writings. Freedom, in this view, meant decentralized political power, limited government, and a free market economy—an argument promoted in the journal *The Freeman*, which began publication in 1950, and in the writings of neoclassical economists like Milton Friedman. In some ways, this critique echoed common laments of the 1950s about the decline of individual autonomy in a mass society. At a 1956 conference on "The Problem of Man's Freedom," John Dos Passos, the radical Depression-era novelist turned conservative ideologue, called for a "reapplication of the vocabulary of freedom" to criticize assembly-line production and social conformism, as well as intrusive government.[3]

What set these "libertarian" conservatives apart from other social critics, however, was their equation of individual freedom with unregulated capitalism. At the 1956 conference, Friedman insisted that conservatives must stop apologizing for capitalism and emphasize instead that a free market is the necessary foundation for individual freedom. In 1962, the year that witnessed the appearance of Michael Harrington's *The Other America* and the Port Huron Statement, Friedman published *Capitalism and Freedom,* no less uncompromising a critique of mainstream liberalism. Echoing Hayek, Friedman insisted that an unregulated marketplace was the truest "expression of freedom," since competition "gives people what they want," rather than what government planners or regulators think they ought to have. But carrying his argument far beyond his mentor and other critics of economic planning, Friedman called for the privatization of virtually all government functions, down to national parks, and the abrogation of minimum wage laws, the graduated income tax, and the Social Security system.[4]

Conservative libertarianism extended the idea of market choice into virtually every realm of life, in some respects anticipating the language of lifestyle pluralism soon to be adopted by the New Left and the women's movement. It was not the role of the state, Friedman wrote, "to say . . . what an individual does with his freedom." Government could not legislate morality; "the ethical problem," he insisted, was one for each individual to resolve for himself. Indirectly, Friedman was criticizing the "new conservatism," a second strand of thought that became increasingly prominent in the 1950s. Convinced that the free world needed to arm itself morally and intellectually, not just militarily, for the battle against communism, writers like Russell Kirk and Richard Weaver rejected the "relativism" that had supposedly corroded Western self-confidence and called for the reassertion of absolute values grounded in religion and timeless notions of good and evil. Weaver's *Ideas Have Consequences* (1948) a rambling philosophical treatise that surprisingly became the most influential expression of this new traditionalism, lamented the moral "dissolution of the West," and called for a return to a civilization based on the primacy of "transcendental," primarily Christian, values. Toleration of difference—the cardinal virtue of modern liberalism—was no substitute for the search for absolute truth.

The new conservatives shared the libertarians' hostility toward the modern liberal state. But they had little interest in economics and often expressed distaste for crass materialism. To Hayek and Friedman, the market embodied individual freedom. To Weaver, the commercial ethos exemplified the degradation of modern society, which exalted "material interests over spiritual." Freedom, he insisted, was a moral state, not simply the absence of coercion, and it could not be reconciled with the single-minded pursuit of either consumer goods or personal fulfillment. Americans, wrote the conservative historian Clinton Rossiter, echoing John Winthrop and other devotees of the Christian idea of freedom, were "obsessed with liberty" when they ought to be concerned with duty, responsibility, and moral order.[5]

Here lay the origins of a division in conservative ranks that would persist to the close of the twentieth century. Was the purpose of conservatism to liberate individuals from intrusive government or to encourage them to lead moral lives? Was its aim, as Rossiter put it, to create the "free man" or the "good man"? And if men and women declined to act in a moral manner, could the state, having been expelled from the economy, be trusted to regulate personal behavior? Some conservative writers, like M. Stanton Evans, tried to have it both ways, simultaneously condemning the government for being too "permissive" in matters of ethics and too "statist" in public policy. But the differences among conservatives were indeed profound. They were illustrated by the fact that Friedman condemned McCarthy-era blacklists as an illegitimate interference with the individual's right to pursue a livelihood, while Evans endorsed loyalty oaths on the grounds that patriotism was one of those transcendent values the government had a right to encourage, even coercively. Ultimately, the philosophical contradiction rested on an inescapable fact of modern life: one cannot with logical consistency defend both an unregulated market and timeless values, since capitalism is profoundly antitraditional. Its expansion has remolded in its image families, communities, schools, and churches, subordinating all relationships to the calculus of the bottom line. The capitalist market, as Karl Marx pointed out over a century ago, "left no other nexus between man and man than naked self-interest," hardly the foundation of a moral community.[6]

Virtue and unrestrained individual choice are radically different starting points from which to discuss freedom. One sees society as an organic entity united by moral bonds, the other as a collection of autonomous individuals. One blames the problems of modern society on an excess of individualism, the other on an excess of impediments to individual freedom. Nonetheless, many conservatives searched for a way of reconciling these strands of thought, an effort that has continued to this day.

No one played a more prominent part in this quest than William F. Buckley, editor of the *National Review*, which since its founding in 1955 has offered a weekly forum for the various expressions of conservative thought. Buckley soon emerged as the most important single influence on conservatism's intellectual revival. He carefully sought to dissociate the movement from fringe groups like the Liberty Lobby, an anti-Semitic organization that denied the reality of the Holocaust, and the John Birch Society, which portrayed President Dwight Eisenhower as a conscious agent of international communism. He also tried, without complete success, to reconcile the two dominant wings of conservatism. In a series of writings in the early 1960s, his *National Review* associate Frank S. Meyer sought to demonstrate the compatibility of libertarian freedom and "moral authority." A "free economy" might not be equivalent to the "virtuous life," but without it, Meyer argued, "the preservation of freedom" was impossible. In the end, however, Meyer's "fusionism" came down on the side of the antistatist libertarians. Men could be free, he insisted, even if they did not "choose the Good." Meyer pleaded with the two groups to be more civil to one another (Evans had called traditionalists "authoritarians" and Kirk had dubbed libertarians "libertines" who rejected all moral authority) and to recognize that the movement had no need for a "monolithic party line."[7]

Fortunately for conservatives, intellectual coherence often contributes less to the growth of a political movement than a common foe, and these they had in abundance. To begin with, two powerful antagonists offered themselves as focal points for conservative unity—the USSR abroad and the liberal state at home. To be sure, some conservatives, including Herbert Hoover himself, initially expressed reservations about the Truman Doctrine and the increase in governmental power certain to result if the United States became the world's policeman. By the mid-1950s, however, nearly all conservatives had concluded that, as Buckley put it, they would have to "accept Big Government for the duration," since only a powerful state could wage an aggressive political and military crusade against the Soviets. Indeed, unlike Friedman, most conservatives were strong supporters of McCarthyism, evidently believing that individual liberty did not extend to Communists or their alleged sympathizers. As for foreign policy, conservatives came to believe that the problem with Truman and Eisenhower was not that they were doing too much to combat communism, but too little. Anticommunism, however, did not clearly distinguish conservatives from liberals, who by and large avidly supported the Cold War. What made the movement distinct was its antagonism to "big government" at home. The "crystallization of an American conservative movement," Meyer wrote, was a "delayed reaction to the *revolutionary* transformation of America" that began with Roosevelt's election in 1932. Then, in the 1960s, another set of foes emerged against whom conservatives could define themselves.[8]

The sixties, the decade when ideologically charged young people altered the landscape of American society in the name of freedom, had conservative as well as radical dimensions. Conservatives had their own Freedom School, established in Colorado by newspaper editor Robert LeFevre to teach laissez-faire economics and unfettered individualism, and a Freedom Center, developed by Walter Knott on his California berry farm to promote free enterprise and condemn the welfare state as a communist conspiracy that would reduce "a free nation" to "slavery." With the founding in 1960 of Young Americans for Freedom (YAF), conservative students emerged as a significant force in politics. Indeed, there are striking parallels between the ninety-odd young conservatives who gathered at Buckley's home in Sharon, Connecticut, to establish YAF and their counterparts who created SDS that same year, and between the Sharon Statement of 1960 and the Port Huron Statement two years later. In contrast to Port Huron's lengthy analysis of social ills, to be sure, the YAF manifesto consisted of a single page of general principles. Both, however, portrayed the United States as confronting a crisis and youth as the cutting edge of a new radicalism, and both claimed to offer a route to greater freedom. The Sharon Statement summarized maxims that had circulated among conservatives during the past decade: the free market was the underpinning of "personal freedom"; government must be limited to preserving order, administering justice, and conducting foreign affairs; and "international communism" was the gravest threat to liberty and must be destroyed.[9]

Much of YAF's activity was aimed at wresting control of the Republican Party away from leaders prepared to make their peace with the New Deal and "appease" communism. YAF members soon became the shock troops for Barry Goldwater's campaign for the 1964 Republican nomination. Having established himself as the nation's most prominent conservative public official by winning election to the Senate from Arizona in 1958, Goldwater two years later published The Conscience of a Conservative, which sold over 3 million copies and was especially popular on college campuses. Like the Sharon Statement, the book combined an antistatist vision with a demand for more aggressive conduct of the Cold War (he even suggested that nuclear war might be "the price of freedom"). But most of Goldwater's critique was directed against "internal" dangers to freedom, especially the welfare state, which destroyed individual autonomy by encouraging reliance on the government, thus serving as the entering wedge for socialism. "No people dependent upon the subsidies of central government," Goldwater insisted, "can claim to be free." While admitting that his plans might appear "callous and contemptuous of the plight of less fortunate citizens," Goldwater called for the substitution of private charity for public welfare programs and Social Security and the abolition of the graduated income tax. But unlike the YAF manifesto, Goldwater spoke the language of traditionalism as well. The principles of conservatism, he insisted, were fundamentally "spiritual," derived from "the nature of man, and from the truths that God has revealed." It was liberalism, Goldwater charged, that promoted materialism by viewing society in purely economic terms.[10]

Goldwater's nomination in 1964 was a remarkable triumph for a movement widely viewed as composed of fanatics out to "repeal the twentieth century." He devoted his campaign to reclaiming "the words of freedom" from Johnson and the New Deal state. His acceptance speech, long remembered for the explosive sentence, "extremism in the defense of liberty is no vice," also contained a remarkably academic discussion of the relationship between freedom and order partly written by the libertarian political scientist Harry Jaffa. Drawing on deeply rooted American ideas, Goldwater insisted that God had intended "this mighty republic to be . . . the land of the free," and invoked the vision of a world united, under American leadership, in "a mighty system" of freedom, prosperity, and interdependence.[11]

Stigmatized by the Democrats as an extremist who would repeal Social Security and risk nuclear war, Goldwater went down to a devastating defeat, winning only 40 percent of the vote. Nonetheless, the campaign energized conservatives. The 1964 election helped to crystallize ideas that would remain the bedrock of conservative appeals for years to come. To anticommunism (a position that did not distinguish Republicans from Democrats) Goldwater added a critique of the welfare state for destroying "the dignity of the individual," and demanded a reduction in taxes and governmental regulations, themes Republicans would reiterate for the next thirty years. Goldwater showed that with liberals in control in Washington, conservatives could appropriate the tradition of antigovernment populism, thus broadening their electoral base and dispelling their traditional image as elitists. At one campaign rally, he even declared, "I fear Washington and centralized government more than I do Moscow." (Following this logic, a few Goldwater supporters, including the speechwriter Karl Hess, would within a few years repudiate the Cold War for spawning a leviathan state.) Goldwater also appealed directly to a growing desire for social stability, calling for "law and order" in the face of civil rights and student demonstrations, ghetto riots, and rising urban crime rates.[12]

Goldwater brought new constituencies to the conservative cause. His support in the rapidly expanding suburbs of Southern California and the Southwest, and the funds that poured into his campaign from the Sun Belt's nouveau riche oilmen and aerospace entrepreneurs, presaged a new popular and financial base for conservatism. And the fact that he carried five states of the Deep South—the first Republican in the century to do so —indicated that the civil rights revolution was already redrawing the nation's political map, opening the door to a "Southern strategy" that four years later would reclaim the White House for Republicans.

Well before the rise of Black Power, indeed, a backlash against black civil rights offered conservatives new opportunities and threatened the stability of the Democratic coalition. There was no intrinsic reason why conservatives should be attracted to racism—why, as the literary critic Edmund Wilson quipped, those repelled by "Soviet knavery" should favor "restoring slavery." But in the United States, hostility to federal authority has historically been linked to the defense of slavery and segregation, while blacks, since the Civil War, have been among the most consistent supporters of an active and powerful national state. During the 1950s, many conservatives responded favorably to southern whites' condemnation of the *Brown* v. *Board of Education* desegregation decision as an invasion of local autonomy and freedom of association. Sometimes, their writings revealed a crude racism, as when Frank Meyer spoke of the "pre-civilized cultures" of Africa, or the *National Review* referred to southern whites as "the advanced race" and defended black disenfranchisement on the grounds that "the claims of civilization supersede those of universal suffrage."[13]

If moral conservatives were prone to view the white South as a last bastion of traditional Christian civilization, libertarians proved amazingly indifferent to the denial of blacks' economic and educational opportunities. Friedman, for example, insisted against all historical evidence that fair employment laws were unnecessary since the free market would penalize firms that discriminated on the basis of race. He favored replacing public schools with state-funded private acadmies even though he acknowledged that many such institutions had sprung up solely to avoid "compulsory integration." Goldwater himself condemned legal segregation but voted against the 1964 Civil Rights Act and insisted that racial equality must come voluntarily, not through federal dictation. His aim, he said, was not an "integrated society" but a "free society," in which individuals enjoyed "the freedom *not* to associate" with those they disliked. As for YAF, the organization always viewed civil rights through the lens of limited government, while never offering an alternative to federal intervention as a means of achieving racial justice in the face of local resistance. Indeed, the entire conservative emphasis on self-governing local communities rarely discussed relations of power within such communities, and left unspecified how the rights of dissenters and despised minorities were to be protected. In 1962, YAF bestowed a "Freedom Award" on South Carolina senator Strom Thurmond, one of the country's most prominent opponents of civil rights.[14]

By the early 1960s, Buckley was backing away from his earlier support for segregation, and fewer and fewer conservatives spoke explicitly of racial superiority and inferiority, with some forthrightly rejecting such language. But there could be no denying that the conservative litany of law and order, local autonomy, "freedom of association," the evils of welfare, and the sanctity of property often had strong racial overtones. The surprisingly strong showing in the 1964 Democratic primaries of George Wallace, who as governor of Alabama had won national notoriety with his cry, "Segregation now, segregation tomorrow, segregation forever," indicated that politicians could strike electoral gold by appealing to white uneasiness with civil rights gains, an uneasiness by no means confined to the South.[15]

An even stronger premonition of the future was offered in California that year, with the passage by popular referendum of Proposition 14, which repealed a 1963 law banning racial discrimination in the sale of real estate. Homeownership had by now become a central component of the idea of freedom. No less important, as far as whites were concerned, was the right to dispose of their property without outside interference. Backed by the state's realtors and developers, California conservatives made freedom the rallying cry of the 1964 campaign against the fair housing law. The cover of the Real Estate Association's monthly magazine superimposed the Statue of Liberty on a drawing of suburban houses, with a caption equating the defeat of open housing with "the preservation of freedom." Although Lyndon Johnson swept to victory in California, Proposition 14 received a considerable majority, winning three of every four votes among whites. When the state Supreme Court reinstated the open housing law two years later, it reinforced the impression that racial reform was being promoted against the will of the democratic majority. The issue contributed to the 1966 gubernatorial victory of former film star Ronald Reagan, who explicitly defended the right of homeowners in a "free society" to "discriminate against Negroes" if they chose.

The California housing battle presaged subsequent conflicts—over court-ordered busing to achieve school integration in Boston, for example—in which racism, concern for neighborhood stability, and fear of crime fused to create a fertile ground for conservative attacks on the activist liberal state among previously Democratic ethnic working-class voters. The often crude epithets hurled against blacks by opponents of busing and open housing in South Boston, New York's Canarsie, and other such neighborhoods helped to consolidate the image of the blue-collar ethnic as a retrograde racist. But affluent suburbanites who had learned to discard such language were no less determined to keep their neighborhoods lily-white, as the California referendum showed.[16]

The "backlash" among formerly Democratic voters helped propel Richard Nixon into the White House in 1968 and again in 1972. But conservatives were no more satisfied with Nixon than his predecessors. Nixon could echo conservative language, especially in his condemnation of antiwar protesters and calls for law and order, but he proved in office to be a mainstream Republican, expanding the welfare state and pursuing detente, not confrontation, with the Soviets. During the 1970s, however, national and international events further reshaped American politics and created the preconditions for the conservative triumph of 1980. Foremost among them was the end, in 1973, of the long period of postwar economic expansion and consumer prosperity and the onset of a period of slow growth and high inflation. The result was a breakdown of the postwar social compact, with corporations—faced with declining profits and rising overseas competition—demanding contract concessions and productivity gains, and accelerating the shift, already underway, of well-paid manufacturing jobs to low-wage areas of the United States and overseas. Always a junior partner in the Democratic coalition, the labor movement was forced onto the defensive by this mobilization of corporate conservatism. It has remained there ever since. This was one among many causes of a long-term stagnation in Americans' real wages, which essentially did not rise for two decades beginning in 1973. The economic crisis and the widespread sense of anxiety it produced enhanced the attraction of conservative calls for lower taxes, reduced government regulation, and cuts in social spending to spur business investment and restore productivity. Such demands appealed to both moralistic and libertarian conservatives, making it possible for them to continue to work together despite their divergent definitions of freedom.[17]

Economic dislocation contributed to a growing sense of national unease. One small indication was the fate of the American Freedom Train, launched in December 1974 as part of the celebration of the bicentennial of American independence. To be sure, the train, funded by General Motors and four other corporations, differed in significant respects from its renowned predecessor of 1947. The historic documents on board were replicas, not originals, and the addition of artifacts like comedian Jack Benny's violin, basketball player Bob Lanier's size twenty sneakers, Judy Garland's dress from *The Wizard of Oz*, and a hula hoop seemed to identify freedom with modern-day consumer culture and popular entertainment rather than the nation's political and intellectual heritage. But in a country still reeling from defeat in Vietnam and the resignation of President Nixon in the Watergate scandal, the train's low attendance seemed to bespeak a crisis of national self-esteem. Soon, the seizure of several score

Americans as hostages in Iran would reinforce the sense that the era in which the United States was the predominant world power had come to a close. In 1979, President Jimmy Carter himself warned that the nation faced a "crisis of confidence." He blamed it, in part, on Americans' "mistaken idea of freedom," which privileged "self-indulgence and consumption" at the expense of devotion to a common national purpose.[18]

All these developments brought new constituents to the conservative cause. One set of recruits was the self-styled neoconservatives, a group of formerly liberal intellectuals who charged that the 1960s had produced a decline in moral standards and respect for authority. Adopting this strand of conservative thought soon led them to embrace others, including the idea that even well-intentioned government social programs did more harm than good. They also repudiated Carter's attempt to reorient foreign policy away from the Cold War (the United States, said the president, suffered from "an inordinate fear of communism") and toward the promotion of human rights, even within countries of the "free world". Resurrecting the doctrine of totalitarianism, largely abandoned during the 1960s, neoconservatives insisted that the "survival of freedom" was endangered by Carter's alleged blindness to the Soviet threat.[19]

More significant as a mass movement was another phenomenon of the 1970s—the rise of religious conservatives as a major force in politics. The catalyst was yet another political "backlash," this one inspired not so much by the civil rights movement as by Warren Court decisions banning prayer in public schools, protecting pornography as free speech, and legalizing abortion. More generally, the religious Right was repelled by the sexual revolution and the rise of second-wave feminism, which it perceived as undermining the stability of the family and women's role within it. There was, of course, nothing new about either evangelical Christianity, which in America dated back to the colonial era, or its involvement in politics. In the nineteenth century, religious revivals had helped to inspire abolitionism and a host of other reform movements. In the twentieth, however, evangelical Christians became more and more estranged from a culture that seemed to trivialize religion and exalt immorality. When religious evangelicals stepped onto the stage of party politics in the 1970s, they were primarily aligned with the right.[20]

Christian conservatives (many of whose leaders proved highly adept at using the mass media to raise funds and disseminate their ideas) fully embraced the free market economics of libertarian conservatives. The reverend Jerry Falwell, founder of the self-styled Moral Majority, proclaimed that "the Word of God in both the Old and New Testaments" offered a justification for "capitalism and free enterprise." But the Christian Right's definition of freedom owed far more to the idea that genuine freedom meant living a moral life—voluntarily if possible, but if necessary as a result of coercion.[21]

If Christian conservatives gave religious sanction to the pursuit of self-interest in the marketplace, they repudiated the sixties' goal of emancipation in private life, especially when it came to the sexual revolution and the role of women. That many women were themselves unhappy with the new definition of their sex as autonomous rights-bearing individuals was revealed in the battle over the proposed Equal Rights Amendment (ERA) to the Constitution. Originally proposed during the 1920s by Alice Paul and the Women's Party, the ERA was revived by second-wave feminists. In the wake of the rights revolution, the amendment's affirmation that "equality of rights under the law" could not be abridged "on account of sex" seemed uncontroversial. In 1972, with little opposition, it was approved by Congress and sent to the states. Designed to eliminate obstacles to the full participation of women in public life, the proposal soon aroused unexpected protest from those who claimed it would undermine the family, discredit the role of wife and homemaker, and, in an echo of 1920s debates, abrogate gender-specific laws beneficial to women such as maternity leaves and the presumption favoring awarding the mother custody of children in the event of divorce.

The ERA debate reflected a division among women as much as a battle of the sexes. To its proponents, the amendment offered a guarantee of women's freedom. To its foes, freedom for women still resided in the divinely appointed roles of wife and mother. By treating its members as fully autonomous individuals, the amendment, opponents claimed, would destroy the organic unity of the family and let men "off the hook" by denying their responsibility to provide for their wives and children. Feminism, wrote Phyllis Schlafly, leader of the anti-ERA forces, exalted "the freedom of self, at the expense of marital union and social compromise." Polls consistently showed that a majority of Americans, male and female, favored the ERA. But like the Prohibition movement before it, the campaign against the amendment, launched in the name of protecting marriage and the family, brought thousands of women into the public arena. The amendment's failure to achieve ratification by the required thirty-eight states was a major victory for this grassroots mobilization of conservative women. It revealed that many women still adhered to traditional gender categories condemned by feminists as obstacles to American freedom.[22]

Even more divisive was the battle over abortion rights, another example, in conservative eyes, of how the liberal state promoted sexual immorality and

selfish individualism at the expense of moral values. To feminists, the right to
a safe, legal abortion was indispensable to a woman's ability to control her own
body. To conservatives, especially those rooted in evangelical Protestant denominations and the Catholic Church, abortion was nothing less than murder.
Between these positions, compromise was all but impossible. Thanks to the
Supreme Court's *Roe* v. *Wade* decision of 1973, women would continue to the end
of the century to enjoy the right to terminate a pregnancy. But the abortion
issue drew a bitter, sometimes violent line through American politics, and set
religiously devout women against more secular ones and homemakers against
those who worked outside the home. As in the case of the ERA, the abortion
conflict reflected, in part, a debate over women's freedom. Defenders of abortion rights exalted "the right to choose" as the essence of freedom, a definition
endorsed by a majority of the Supreme Court in a 1992 decision reaffirming *Roe*
v. *Wade*. "At the heart of liberty," said the Court, "is the right to define one's
own concept of existence," and to make "the most intimate and personal
choices" without outside interference. Those who opposed abortion tended to
understand freedom as something enjoyed within the family unit, and to dis-
approve of homosexuality, premarital sex, looser divorce laws, and contraception. In essence, they repudiated the entire sexual revolution. Ironically, however,
while condemning second-wave feminism for promoting an excessive emphasis on self-determination as opposed to collective responsibility, opponents of
abortion adopted the now-ubiquitous language of the rights revolution, calling themselves the "right to life" movement and claiming to represent the
"rights" of the "unborn child."

In one sense, opponents of ERA and abortion rights were fighting a rear-
guard action against an irreversible revolution in gender roles. Indeed, even as
conservatives reasserted the primacy of what Jane Addams had called the "family claim," the number of women in the workforce (including mothers of young
children) continued its relentless upward climb. Two very different kinds of
women were responsible: those seeking careers in professions and skilled jobs
previously open only to men; and women who flooded into the traditional
low-wage, "pink-collar" sector, spurred by the need to augment family income
as men's wages stagnated. Nonetheless, the campaigns against ERA and abortion rights added another element to the expanding conservative coalition. In
1980, riding a wave of dissatisfaction with economic dislocation, declining
world power, and a perceived weakening of traditional social roles and values,
Ronald Reagan swept into the White House. The Reagan Revolution would
complete the transformation of freedom from the rallying cry of the left to a
possession of the right.[23]

The Reagan Revolution and After

Ronald Reagan followed a most unusual path to the presidency. Originally a New Deal Democrat and head of the Screen Actors Guild (the only union leader ever to reach the White House), he emerged in the fifties as a publicist for the General Electric Corporation, whose lectures preached the virtues of unregulated capitalism. Reagan's nominating speech for Goldwater at the 1964 Republican convention brought him to national attention, and his election two years later as governor of California established him as conservatives' best hope of capturing the presidency. His victory in 1980 brought to power a polyglot coalition of old and new conservatism—Sun Belt suburbanites and working-class ethnic Catholics; antigovernment crusaders and advocates of a more aggressive foreign policy; libertarian ideologues and those seeking to restore "traditional moral values" to American life.

Like Roosevelt, Reagan was a master of the media, who possessed an uncanny ability to appropriate the vocabulary of his political opponents and give it new meaning. To the annoyance of his adversaries, for example, he delighted in quoting liberalism's heroes, from Thomas Paine to Franklin D. Roosevelt and John F. Kennedy. He could invoke feminist language for conservative purposes, hailing his administration's repeal of a New Deal ban on industrial home work as a victory for women's right to seek employment. He promised to free government from the control of "special interests," but these were not lobbyists or businessmen seeking governmental favors—the traditional targets of liberals—but blacks, trade unionists, and others hoping to use Washington's power to redress social inequalities. In Reagan's Justice Department, John Marshall Harlan's maxim that the Constitution must be "color-blind"—a remark hurled at the Supreme Court's majority a century earlier to challenge a system of unequal freedom mandated by law—was invoked to justify gutting civil rights enforcement.[24]

An expert at symbolic leadership, Reagan associated himself with emblems of nationality, especially the flag, and repeatedly invoked the time-honored rhetoric of America's divinely appointed mission as a "beacon of liberty and freedom." Republicans, wrote the journalist Daniel Schorr, had "laid siege to 'free.' " Many of Reagan's specific policies, from tax cuts and reduced government regulation to large increases in military spending, had been pioneered by Carter. It was Reagan, however, who championed them in the language of freedom. "Freedom," indeed, became the watchword of the Reagan Revolution, and in his public appearances and state papers, Reagan used the word more often than any president before or since. Reagan's years in office completed the process by which freedom, having been progressively abandoned by liberals and the left, became fully identified with conservative goals and values.[25]

In foreign policy, Reagan breathed new life into the rhetorical division of the world into a free West and slave East that made the United States and its allies, by definition, part of a "crusade for freedom." He boldly gave the term "freedom fighters"—previously applied to Hungarians rebelling against their Communist government in 1956, and appropriated by the New Left to describe anticolonial movements in the Third World—a new definition. Carter had already applied the phrase to Afghans battling a Soviet-backed regime. Reagan expanded the category to include armed groups struggling to overthrow recently established Third World governments friendly to the Soviet Union. The ranks of "freedom fighters" now included former supporters of the Nicaraguan dictator Anastasio Somoza and of Cambodia's Pol Pot, whose regime had killed millions of his countrymen, as well as disgruntled losers of national elections in Angola, and Islamic fundamentalists bent on eliminating public rights for women in Afghanistan. All these, Reagan insisted, were motivated by "freedom . . . the same ideals that inspired our forefathers." He never applied the term to South Africans struggling to overturn apartheid, or to opponents of pro-American dictatorships no matter how brutal. The inhabitants of the free world already "ha[d] their freedom." To underscore his vision of the world, Reagan even proclaimed that the word "freedom" did not exist in the Russian language. If true, this exercise in linguistic diplomacy would have revealed a deep difference between Soviet and American cultures. As it happens, however, Russian has a perfectly good word for freedom, *svoboda*.[26]

In his 1964 nominating speech for Goldwater, Reagan had declared freedom the central value of American life and identified two threats to its survival: communism abroad and big government at home. As president, he conducted a rhetorical Cold War against both. The "free market" took its place alongside the free world as the essence of freedom. Reagan's administration marked the end of the New Deal as a politically dominant set of public policies, ideas, and political alliances. Like Roosevelt and Johnson before him, Reagan spoke of "economic freedom" and proposed an "economic Bill of Rights." But in contrast to his predecessors—who used these phrases to support creating jobs, combatting poverty, and enhancing social security—economic freedom for Reagan meant dismantling economic regulations and reducing the power of unions, all to ensure the individual's right to "contract freely for goods and services." The key to "economic freedom," however, was a radical reduction in taxes. High taxes, said Reagan, produced "servitude" to government, while "the right to earn your own keep and keep what you earn" was "what it means to be free." The cuts not only reduced the level of taxation, they all but eliminated the principle of progressivity, one of the ways twentieth-century capitalist societies have tried to redress the unequal distribution of incomes produced by a market system. The result was a massive shift of wealth from poorer to wealthier Americans. By the mid-1990s, the richest 1 percent of Americans owned 40 percent of the nation's wealth, twice their share twenty years earlier.[27]

The year 1986, midway into Reagan's second term, resounded with conservative uses of "freedom." Jerry Falwell changed the name of his Moral Majority to the Liberty Federation, complete with Liberty University, located outside Lynchburg, Virginia. Pat Robertson, a prominent evangelical minister, established the Freedom Council, with a budget of $5.5 million, to prepare for a possible run for the presidency. But by far the year's most significant event, so far as the language of freedom was concerned, was Liberty Weekend, marking the centennial of the Statue of Liberty. With its parade of tall ships and impressive fireworks display, the event, designed by Hollywood producer David Wolper, was an extravagant pageant dedicated to freedom. It was also an orgy of commercialism, replete with corporate sponsorships and the sale of broadcast rights to a single television network. This celebration of the "American spirit of freedom" left "no cliché unturned," as *Time* magazine noted. *Time* itself, however, was hardly innocent; its special issue on the commemoration abounded in hackneyed, sometimes incomprehensible prose. "Freedom is a powerful animal that fights the barriers," its editors declared. But inadvertently, the magazine offered a graphic example of how Reagan had transformed public discourse. The special issue rewrote history to erase non-conservative meanings of freedom, insisting that from the beginning, Americans had been concerned only with "freedom *from*, specifically from the evils of repressive government," and never with "freedom *to*."[28]

Reagan himself used the centennial to declare freedom from "government interference" the key to American greatness. In so doing, he offered a narrative of American history as the saga of the white ethnics—descendants of upwardly striving individuals who had emigrated from Europe in search of "freedom and opportunity," especially the ability to "support themselves and their families by their own labor." Reagan's version of the past appeared to eliminate from the "imagined community" African-Americans, whose ancestors came in slave ships and whose labor for centuries supported families other than their own. Indeed, among many black Americans, a certain skepticism prevailed on Liberty Weekend. "For us, the Statue of Liberty is a bitter joke," wrote James Baldwin. Some black leaders, like John Jacob, head of the Urban League, urged

Americans in 1986 were inundated by efforts to capitalize commercially on the Statue of Liberty's centennial. S. D. Warren was a division of Scott Paper Company. (Courtesy, Creative Services, Inc., Design, Atlanta)

blacks to take part in the ceremonies. "We must refuse to cede the symbols of liberty, freedom, and equality," Jacob wrote, "to ideologues of the right." His plea, however, may well have come too late.[29]

Reagan's presidency revealed the contradictions at the heart of modern conservative thought. Rhetorically, he sought to address the concerns of the religious Right, strongly opposing abortion and advocating a "return to spiritual values" as a way to strengthen traditional families and local communities. Freedom, he insisted, carried with it responsibility: "We're not set free so that we can become slaves to sin." Like most conservatives, however, he exempted the economy from his abhorrence of self-interested behavior and his demand for moral action, making the unremitting pursuit of profit the sole arbiter of right and wrong. In the end, the Reagan Revolution undermined the very values and social institutions conservatives professed to hold dear. Intended to discourage reliance on government handouts by rewarding honest work and entrepreneurial initiative, Reagan's policies inspired a speculative frenzy that enriched architects of corporate takeovers, plungers in the stock market, and sellers of "junk bonds." In their wake were left plant closings, job losses, and devastated communities. Nothing was more threatening to local traditions or family stability than deindustrialization, pervasive insecurity about employment, and the relentless downward pressure on wages spurred by the Reagan Revolution. Nothing did more to prevent a revitalized sense of common national purpose more than the widening gap between rich and poor.[30]

In terms of public policy, the Reagan Revolution disappointed many conservatives. Despite his radical income tax reduction, federal spending, spurred by increased funds for the military, continued to rise, thus producing the largest budget deficits in American history. And while Great Society antipoverty programs were gutted, core elements of the welfare state such as Social Security, Medicare, and Medicaid remained intact. In his second term, Reagan even softened his anticommunist rhetoric, establishing good relations with Soviet premier Mikhail Gorbachev. Nor did conservative control of the presidency under Reagan and his successor George Bush, or of Congress after 1994, do much to create a more virtuous society or persuade women to abandon public aspirations and "go about the business of marrying and raising children," as Republican congressional leader Richard Armey indelicately put it. By the mid-1990s, traditionalists wondered whether conservatives ought to rethink the notion that freedom is the paramount social value. Jurist Robert Bork urged Americans to repudiate "our modern, virtually unqualified, enthusiasm for liberty." Some conservatives even gazed wistfully at Singapore, where a rapidly growing market economy coexisted with an authoritarian polity and culture, as a model for the United States—quite a departure from the idea that market liberty and personal and political freedom were inextricably connected.[31]

Nonetheless, few figures have changed the language of politics as successfully as Ronald Reagan. By the 1990s, virtually no politician would admit to being a liberal. Conservative assumptions about the sanctity of the free market and the evils of "big government" dominated the mass media and political debates, and were embraced as fully by President Bill Clinton, a Democrat, as by many Republicans. Instead of acting as a vehicle for social or racial progress, the 1990s saw government at all levels seeking to grow smaller and repudiating the tradition of combatting social inequality.[32]

In other ways as well, the 1990s were a decade of conservative triumph, which began with the collapse of communism as an ideological force and of the Soviet Union as a nation-state. In 1994, spearheaded by the party's conservative wing, Republicans gained control of Congress for the first time since the 1950s. They proclaimed their triumph the "Freedom Revolution," although the words sometimes seemed little more than a form of salesmanship. "No matter what cause you advocate," Richard Armey, now House majority leader, noted, "you must sell it in the language of freedom." Among other things, the victors insisted, the end of the Cold War had eliminated the only justification for a powerful central government actively involved in the affairs of the American people. Now that one of their historic bêtes noires had disappeared, conservatives turned their full fury against the other, the federal government—especially remaining New Deal and Great Society programs and agencies (although they somewhat incongruously promoted large increases in military spending). In 1996, with the approval of Democratic president Clinton, Congress abolished entirely the New Deal program of Aid to Dependent Children, commonly known as "welfare," replacing it with grants to the states and the hope that the needy would make do with what Armey called "the natural safety-net—family, friends, churches, and charities."[33]

Perhaps the most striking thing about American discussions of freedom during the nineties was how frequently old ideas and debates seemed to resurface. Freedom of expression, a central component of freedom in modern America, provides one example. In 1942, David Riesman had warned that Americans were "ill-prepared for crisis" when confronting threats to free speech, given their tendency to fall back on "inherited slogans." This remained true half a century later, when writings by civil libertarians continued to focus almost exclusively on the danger of governmental action to restrict expression. The most vigorous defenders of free speech were "netizens"—"citizens" of the Internet, who insisted on the right to absolute free expression in the face of the Communications Decency Act of 1996, which made indecent "speech" in cyberspace a federal crime. But the traditional view that government posed the major threat to free speech seemed ill-equipped to deal with the effects of concentrated wealth on the dissemination of ideas and on the democratic process itself. In the nineties, the typical free speech claimant before the courts was no longer a persecuted heretic but a powerful corporation fighting public regulation of campaign financing and restrictions on concentrated ownership of the media. The Supreme Court, supported by the American Civil Liberties Union, endorsed the corporate view that spending money was a form of speech deserving First Amendment protection. It remained for future generations to ponder the implications for freedom of the ever-closer connection between power in the economic marketplace and power in the marketplace of ideas.[34]

So, too, shifting debates over social citizenship reflected the renewed hold of ideas once thought discredited. In 1944, in his classic study *Social Darwinism in American Life*, Richard Hofstadter concluded that this intellectual system, "once pervasive and powerful," had "crumbled and been forgotten." He could hardly have foreseen the resurrection, half a century later, of the Social Dar-winist mentality, if not the name itself: the belief that government should not intervene to affect the "natural" working of the economy; that the distribution of wealth reflects individual merit rather than historical circumstances; that the plight of the less fortunate, whether conceived as individuals, classes, or races, arises from their own failings. As in the late nineteenth century, indifference to the plight of the poor came to be seen as a sign of realism, not callousness.

On the age-old question of how social and economic conditions shape the exercise of freedom, leaders of both parties had little to say other than to let the market take its course. During the 1890s, Henry Demarest Lloyd had noted with a sense of foreboding that "the financial, commercial, possessory powers of modern industrial life are organized internationally." This was all the more true a century later. Yet the implications of economic internationalization for inherited ideas of freedom had yet to receive full consideration. In conserva-tive treatises of the 1990s, concentrated economic power was never mentioned, nor were the implications for democracy when basic economic decisions were made by business leaders, investors, and currency traders without even the sem-blance of accountability to any constituency but themselves. Threats to freedom continued to arise wholly from intrusive political power.[35]

Despite the triumph of market fundamentalism, older ideas concerning economic security did not entirely disappear, although they were no longer ar-ticulated in terms of freedom. Polls continued to show that a large majority of Americans supported government action to create jobs, and Congress's whole-sale assault on federal "entitlement" programs alienated many voters, con-tributing significantly to Clinton's reelection in 1996. It was an irony of late twentieth-century life that Americans enjoyed more autonomy than ever before in their private lives, but less and less of what earlier generations called "in-dustrial freedom." The sustained recovery from the recession of the early nineties did not entirely relieve a widespread sense of economic insecurity—a product of stagnant wages, the widening gap between rich and poor, and grow-ing part-time employment. The continued internationalization of economic en-terprise, which treated workers as factors of production capable of being uprooted or dismissed without warning, seemed to render individual (and even national) sovereignty all but meaningless.[36]

Even as American consumer culture triumphed throughout the world, doubts about the future proliferated. In 1996, BusinessWeek reported that two-thirds of all Americans believed that "equal opportunity, personal freedom, and social mobility" had become increasingly elusive. Conservative writers insisted that the market economy was not the source of economic discontent. The cul-

Statue of Liberty Barbie® Doll
The first Barbie in the new American Beauties Collection™ has arrived on our shores! Our doll of freedom captures the drama and beauty of the original Lady Liberty... giving new meaning to America the beautiful! Girls ages 3 to 11 receive an average of three Barbie dolls per year, made for Mattel by dedicated men and women in Malaysia, Indonesia and China. You, our shareholders, are also part of the team, as are our board members and customers.

"Barbie's Liberty," a satirical work by the artist Hans Haacke, recasts the ubiquitous Barbie doll in the image of the Statue of Liberty to comment on the loss of manufacturing jobs to low-wage areas overseas. (© 1998 Artists Rights Society [ARS], New York/VG Bild-Kunst, Bonn)

prit was a set of unrealistic expectations and an exaggerated sense of entitlement spawned by the post–World War II economic boom and reinforced when the promise of abundance became a weapon in the Cold War. The American standard of living—so central to the twentieth-century vocabulary of freedom—was a luxury society could no longer afford.[37]

In some ways, the increasingly strident conservative rhetoric picturing the federal government as an alien and menacing presence rather than an embodiment of the popular will reflected a powerful strain of American political culture that dated back to the eighteenth century. But its renewed popular appeal pointed to a broad disengagement from politics. In 1985, at the height of the

Reagan Revolution, *Habits of the Heart*, a best-selling exploration of American values by a team of sociologists headed by Robert Bellah, lamented the "cancerous" growth of individualism and the concomitant decline of social solidarity in the United States. The book placed the blame squarely on Americans' understanding of freedom. This "most resonant, deeply held American value," the authors claimed, now meant little more than "being left alone by others" and not being coerced into adhering to "other people's values, ideas, or style of life." Such a definition of freedom made it almost impossible to think in terms of a shared vision of the good life, or what social or political structures were essential to a good society. In the 1990s, the exalting of private over public concerns and the decline of a common civic culture continued unabated. Somehow, the end of the Cold War produced not euphoria but a broad crisis of confidence in democratic institutions. Public cynicism about political institutions and leaders abounded. Voter turnout remained far below that in other leading democracies. As governments at all levels competed to "privatize" their activities, and millions of Americans took up residence in socially homogeneous gated communities, the very idea of a shared public culture seemed to dissolve.[38]

At the radical fringe of conservatism, the belief that freedom needed to be defended against the federal government spawned a host of groups—self-proclaimed patriots, militias, and freedom fighters—who armed themselves to fend off oppressive authority. For millions of Americans, owning a gun became a prime symbol of liberty. "We're here because we love freedom," declared a participant in a 1995 Washington rally against proposed legislation banning semi-automatic assault weapons. The right to bear arms, proclaimed the National Rifle Association, was the "first freedom," on which all others depended. Many militia groups employed the symbolism and language of the American Revolution, sprinkling their appeals with images of the Minutemen, slogans like "Don't Tread on Me," and warnings about the dangers of despotic central authority culled from the writings of Thomas Jefferson, Patrick Henry, and other leaders of the War for Independence. Although such organizations had been growing for years, they burst into the national spotlight in 1995 when one disgruntled patriot, in the name of freedom, placed a bomb at a federal office building in Oklahoma City, killing 168 persons.[39]

In 1996, a group calling themselves the Freemen fought a pitched battle with federal agents in Montana and called on Americans to "free" themselves by not paying taxes and destroying their Social Security cards. Like many other self-proclaimed patriots, such as the Aryan Nation, they also sought to reinvigorate a racialized definition of Americanism. Citizens, the Freemen proclaimed, came in two categories: "We the People," or whites, enfranchised by the original

Constitution and "God's law"; and other racial groups, enfranchised only by "man's law" (the Fourteenth Amendment) and not really Americans at all. "Free" white men, the Freemen warned, had lost control of the government and were now ruled by "foreigners and aliens."

Bizarre as they appeared, the existence of groups like the Freemen underscored the persistent tension between civic and cultural definitions of Americanism—a tension, seemingly resolved by World War II, the Cold War, and the civil rights movement, that resurfaced in the nineties. Around the world, the end of the Cold War and the growth of a global economy spawned not a new sense of cosmopolitanism but what the Argentine political philosopher Ernesto Laclau called a "rebellion of particularisms"—renewed assertions of racial and ethnic identity, and insistent demands for group recognition and power. Perhaps the reaffirmation of regional and tribal loyalties reflected the declining power of nation-states in a world united as never before by capital flows, consumer culture, and instantaneous communication. In the United States, with the rapid growth of the Asian and Hispanic populations, racial diversity was more visible than ever. But this inspired not so much celebration of the triumph of pluralism as alarm over perceived cultural fragmentation. Public discussion of immigration policy spilled over into increasingly rancorous debates on bilingual education, "multicultural" school curricula, proposals to make English the nation's "official language," and ways of restricting applications for political asylum. The Republican National Convention of 1996 even proposed to rescind the principle of birthright citizenship embedded in the Fourteenth Amendment. These debates heralded yet another redrawing of the boundaries of nationality.[40]

In the aftermath of the civil rights movement, the celebration of difference and demands for group recognition emanated from aggrieved minorities—racial, cultural, and sexual. In the 1990s, conservatives—and many liberals as well—decried "identity politics" and "multiculturalism" for undermining a common sense of American identity and assuming that one's race or "culture" determines one's destiny. Yet, simultaneously, one wing of conservatism developed an "identity politics" of its own, based on the old presumption that the world is divided into permanent racial groups who inhabit distinct places on a spectrum from superior to inferior. Conservative foundations funded and conservative journals praised The Bell Curve, a 1994 bestseller by Charles Murray and Richard Herrnstein that sought to demonstrate scientifically the innate intellectual inferiority of non-whites. Peter Brimelow, a naturalized citizen born in England, argued in Alien Nation (1995) that non-white immigration posed a threat to the country's historical cultural identity. Rejecting the civic definition of American nationality, Brimelow insisted that a nation is "an ethno-cultural community," and that any successful culture must possess a "link by blood." These books probably inspired a feeling of déjà vu among readers with a knowledge of history. Murray and Herrnstein recalled World War I–era eugenicists in their elevation of IQ scores to measures of inborn group intelligence. And Brimelow echoed turn-of-the-century theorists who invoked differential birth rates to "prove" that real Americans—that is, whites—were in danger of being overwhelmed by lesser races. Brimelow even blamed recent immigrants for the fact that Southern California "is being paved over," although red-blooded white citizens had long since accomplished this themselves.[41]

Brimelow's screed split conservative ranks, with some repudiating his crude racism and insisting that immigrants contributed to economic growth and the preservation of "family values." The difference reflected a wider disagreement over whether freedom itself could still be deemed a universal value. In the euphoria at the close of the Cold War, Francis Fukuyama had proclaimed "the end of history" and the worldwide triumph of liberal democracy among all nations, cultures, and peoples—the long-anticipated universalization of American values. By the mid-1990s, many conservatives seemed both more pessimistic and more parochial. Samuel P. Huntington's *The Clash of Civilizations* (1996) depicted a post–Cold War world in which civilizations grounded in divergent cultural and racial identities battled for supremacy. For Huntington, freedom was the product of specific historical, cultural, and racial circumstances, not a universal entitlement—a view which, although he did not make the point explicitly, recalled the heritage of "British liberty" of the eighteenth century and the racialized Anglo-Saxonism of the nineteenth. He rejected the "relevance of Western culture" for the rest of the world, a remarkable departure from the universalist view of freedom dating back to the American Revolution, which had been so powerfully reinforced by World War II and the Cold War.[42]

As the century drew to a close, freedom remained both a source of contention and a crucial point of self-definition for individuals and society at large. Asked in a public opinion survey, "What are you proudest of about America?" 69 percent answered, "freedom."[43] In the late 1990s, a search of the Internet for sites associated with freedom yielded striking evidence of how fully the word had come to be associated with the free market and hostility to government. Apart from companies using freedom to market their wares (the Freedom software company, for example), the largest number of sites were those of antigovernment libertarians, groups promoting the sanctity of private property and the ideology of free trade, and armed patriot and militia organi-

 ### The Militia of Montana

This Information is Presented as a Service to the Patriots of the Republic of The United States and The State of Montana ...

"...... to defend the <u>Constitution of The United States of America</u> and the <u>Constitution of The State of Montana</u> against All Enemies, Both Foreign and Domestic."

JOIN THE ARMY AND SERVE THE UN or

JOIN THE MILITIA AND SERVE AMERICA

IT'S YOUR CHOICE === FREEDOM OR SLAVERY

JOIN OR FORM YOUR LOCAL MILITIA TODAY!!

BE MILITANT IN YOUR SEARCH FOR TRUTH AND IN THE DEFENSE OF LIBERTY!!

In the late 1990s, browsers on the Internet could encounter militia groups, right-wing libertarians, and other self-proclaimed patriots claiming for themselves the language of freedom. (United States Freedom Fighters; Militia of Montana; Netscape is a Registered Trademark of Netscape Communications Corporation; Software System 7.6.1 © 1983–1996 Apple Computer, Inc. Used with permission. Apple ® and the Apple logo are Registered Trademarks of Apple Computer, Inc. All Rights Reserved.)

zations. Civil liberties, too, were well represented, at sites offering information on the First Amendment, religious freedom, and the Communications Decency Act.[44] It remained to be seen whether an understanding of freedom grounded in access to the consumer marketplace and a series of negations—of government, of social citizenship, of restraints on individual self-definition, of a common public culture—could provide an adequate language for comprehending the world of the twenty-first century.

Americans have sometimes believed they enjoy the greatest freedom of all—freedom from history. No people can escape being bound, to some extent, by their past. But if history teaches anything, it is that the definitions of freedom and of the community entitled to enjoy it are never fixed or final. We may not have it in our power, as Thomas Paine proclaimed in 1776, "to begin the world over again."[45] But we can decide for ourselves what freedom is. No one can predict the ultimate fate of current understandings of freedom, or whether alternative traditions now in eclipse—freedom as economic security, freedom as active participation in democratic governance, freedom as social justice for those long disadvantaged—will be rediscovered and reconfigured to meet the challenges of the new century. All one can hope is that in the future, the better angels of our nature (to borrow Lincoln's words) will reclaim their place in the forever unfinished story of American freedom.

Notes

INTRODUCTION

1. Gunnar Myrdal, *An American Dilemma* (New York, 1944), 4. For discussions of whether "freedom" and "liberty" are identical, see Hanna P. Pitkin, "Are Freedom and Liberty Twins?", *Political Theory*, 16 (November 1988), 523–52; Quentin Skinner, "The Idea of Negative Liberty: Philosophical and Historical Perspectives," in *Philosophy in History*, ed. Richard Rorty, et al. (New York, 1984), 194n.; and David T. Konig, ed., *Devising Liberty: Preserving and Creating Liberty in the New American Republic* (Stanford, 1995).
2. James Bryce, *The American Commonwealth* (2 vols. London, 1889), II, 635; Herbert McCloskey and John Zaller, *The American Ethos: Public Attitudes Toward Capitalism and Democracy* (Cambridge, MA, 1984), 18; Seymour M. Lipset, *American Exceptionalism: A Double-Edged Sword* (New York, 1996), 101, 145; Pamela J. Conover, et al., "The Nature of Citizenship in the United States and Great Britain: Empirical Comments on Theoretical Themes," *Journal of Politics*, 53 (August 1991), 819.
3. Homer C. Hockett and Arthur M. Schlesinger, *Land of the Free: A Short History of the American People* (New York, 1944); Oscar and Lillian Handlin, *Liberty in America, 1600 to the Present* (4 vols. New York, 1986–94); R. W. Davis, "The Center for the History of Freedom," *The Historian*, 55 (Summer 1993), 629–34; Donald W. Treadgold, *Freedom: A History* (New York, 1990); M. Stanton Evans, *The Theme Is Freedom: Religion, Politics, and the American Tradition* (Washington, DC, 1994); Bloom in Todd Gitlin, *The Twilight of Common Dreams* (New York, 1995), 40; Higginson in Willie L. Rose, *Rehearsal for Reconstruction: The Port Royal Experiment* (Indianapolis, 1964), 408.
4. Carl Becker, *New Liberties for Old* (New Haven, 1941), 3; W. B. Gallie, "Essentially Contested Concepts," *Proceedings of the Aristotelian Society*, n.s., 56 (1955–56), 167–98.

5. Marc Bloch, *The Historian's Craft* (New York, 1953), 173.

6. Cynthia S. Jordan, " 'Old Words' in 'New Circumstances': Language and Leadership in Post-Revolutionary America," *American Quarterly*, 40 (December 1988), 491; Henry Demarest Lloyd, *Wealth Against Commonwealth* (New York, 1899), 498.

7. Joseph Raz, *The Morality of Freedom* (New York, 1986), 17–19; Theodor Adorno, "Messages in a Bottle," *New Left Review*, 200 (July–August 1993), 7.

8. Martin Oswald, "Freedom and the Greeks," in *The Origins of Modern Freedom in the West*, ed. R. W. Davis (Stanford, 1995), 35; Joan W. Scott, *Gender and the Politics of History* (New York, 1989), 5–7.

9. Robert B. Westbrook, *John Dewey and American Democracy* (Ithaca, 1991), 165.

10. William E. Connolly, *The Terms of Political Discourse* (Lexington, 1974), 166; J. R. Pole, *The Pursuit of Equality in American History* (rev. ed. Berkeley, 1993), 6.

11. Myrdal, *American Dilemma*, 2–5; Lipset, *American Exceptionalism*, 19; Arthur M. Schlesinger, Jr., *The Disuniting of America: Reflections on a Multicultural Society* (New York, 1992), 27, 118; Ross E. Paulson, *Liberty, Equality, and Justice: Civil Rights, Women's Rights, and the Regulation of Business, 1865–1932* (Durham, NC, 1997), 2; Louis D. Brandeis, "True Americanism," in *Immigration and Americanization*, ed. Philip Davis (Boston, 1920), 639.

12. Benedict Anderson, *Imagined Communities: Reflections on the Origin and Spread of Nationalism* (rev. ed. London, 1991).

13. Kenneth L. Karst, *Belonging to America: Equal Citizenship and the Constitution* (New Haven, 1989); Rogers L. Smith, *Civic Ideals: Conflicting Visions of Citizenship in U.S. History* (New Haven, 1997)

14. Clayborne Carson, ed., *The Papers of Martin Luther King, Jr.* (Berkeley, 1991–), III, 204.

15. Lynne V. Cheney, *Telling the Truth: A Report on the State of the Humanities in Higher Education* (Washington, DC, 1992), 40–44; *New York Times*, January 19, 1995; Eric Hobsbawm, *The Age of Extremes: A History of the World, 1914–1991* (New York, 1994), 3.

CHAPTER 1

1. Seneca, *Letters from a Stoic*, ed. and trans. Robin Campbell (London, 1969), 95; Orlando Patterson, *Freedom* (New York, 1991), xvi; David B. Davis, *The Problem of Slavery in Western Culture* (Ithaca, 1966), 85–90; II Corinthians 3:17; Romans 6:20–22.

2. Perry Miller and Thomas H. Johnson, eds., *The Puritans* (2 vols. New York, 1938), I, 205–07; Edmund S. Morgan, *The Puritan Family: Religion and Domestic Relations in Seventeenth-Century New England* (rev. ed. New York, 1966), 26; David H. Fischer, *Albion's Seed: Four British Folkways in America* (New York, 1989), 202–03; Harry S. Stout, *The New England Soul: Preaching and Religious Culture in Colonial New England* (New York, 1986), 15; Hooker in Allen Carden, "The Communal Ideal in Puritan New England, 1630–1700," *Fides et Historia* (Fall–Winter 1984), 25–38.

3. Helena M. Wall, *Fierce Communion: Family and Community in Early America* (Cambridge, MA, 1990); Richard L. Bushman, *From Puritan to Yankee: Character and the Social Order in Connecticut, 1690–1765* (Cambridge, MA, 1967); Jack P. Greene, *Pursuits of Happiness*

(Chapel Hill, 1988), 35–76; Barry A. Shain, *The Myth of American Individualism: The Protestant Origins of American Political Thought* (Princeton, 1994), 193–240; Jonathan Boucher, *A View of the Causes and Consequences of the American Revolution: In Thirteen Discourses . . . 1763–1775* (London, 1797), 511.

4. John P. Reid, *The Concept of Liberty in the Age of the American Revolution* (Chicago, 1988), 32; *Aristotle's Politics*, trans. Benjamin Jowett (Oxford, 1908), 261; Charles S. Hyneman and Donald S. Lutz, eds., *American Political Writing During the Founding Era 1760–1805* (2 vols. Indianapolis, 1983), I, 23; John Locke, *Two Treatises of Government*, ed. Peter Laslett (Cambridge, 1988), 284, 306.

5. Eric Hobsbawm and Terence Ranger, eds., *The Invention of Tradition* (New York, 1983); Linda Colley, *Britons: Forging the Nation, 1707–1837* (New Haven, 1992), 35, 53–55; E. P. Thompson, *The Making of the English Working Class* (New York, 1963), 77–101; John P. Reid, "Liberty and the Original Understanding," in *Essays in the History of Liberty: Seaver Lectures at the Huntington Library* (San Marino, CA, 1988), 3–6; Forrest McDonald, *Novus Ordo Seclorum: The Intellectual Origins of the Constitution* (Lawrence, 1985), 36–40; Reid, *Concept of Liberty*, 48–50.

6. James Kinsley, ed., *The Poems of John Dryden* (4 vols. Oxford, 1958), I, 450; Colley, *Britons*, 351–52; David Eltis, "Europeans and the Rise and Fall of African Slavery in the Americas: An Interpretation," *American Historical Review*, 98 (December 1993), 1415–23.

7. Gordon S. Wood, *The Radicalism of the American Revolution* (New York, 1992), 57; W. A. Speck, *Stability and Strife: England, 1714–1760* (London, 1977), 16; Joseph Priestley, *An Essay on the First Principles of Government, and on the Nature of Political, Civil, and Religious Liberty* (London, 1768), 12–14; Jonathan A. Bush, " 'Take This Job and Shove It': The Rise of Free Labor," *Michigan Law Review*, 91 (May 1993), 1396; J. H. Baker, "Personal Liberty Under the Common Law of England, 1200–1600," in *The Origins of Modern Freedom in the West*, ed. R. W. Davis (Stanford, 1995), 178; Fischer, *Albion's Seed*, 201; Graham R. Hodges, *New York Craftsmen, 1667–1850* (New York, 1986), 3–5.

8. Wood, *Radicalism of the American Revolution*, 13–14; Michael Kammen, *Sovereignty and Liberty: Constitutional Discourse in American Culture* (Madison, 1988), 55–56, 74–75; Reid, "Liberty," 2.

9. Liah Greenfeld, *Nationalism: Five Roads to Modernity* (Cambridge, MA, 1992), 71–74; Bernard Bailyn, *The Ideological Origins of the American Revolution* (Cambridge, MA, 1967), 56–70; Bush, " 'Take This Job,' " 1397; Bushman, *Puritan to Yankee*, 271; Allan Kulikoff, "The American Revolution, Capitalism, and the Formation of the Yeoman Classes," in *Beyond the American Revolution*, ed. Alfred F. Young (DeKalb, 1993), 92. Here, as throughout the book, italics are in the original sources.

10. Philip Pettit, *Republicanism: A Theory of Freedom and Government* (Oxford, 1997); Albert H. Smythe, ed., *The Writings of Benjamin Franklin* (10 vols. New York, 1906), X, 80; Morton J. Horwitz, "Republicanism and Liberalism in American Constitutional Thought," *William and Mary Law Review*, 29 (Fall 1987), 66–67.

11. Quentin Skinner, *Liberty Before Liberalism* (Cambridge, UK, 1998); Locke, *Two Treatises*, II, 22; M. M. Goldsmith, "Liberty, Virtue, and the Rule of Law, 1689–1770," in *Republicanism, Liberty, and Commercial Society, 1649–1776*, ed. David Wootton (Stanford, 1994),

197–98; James P. Young, *Reconsidering American Liberalism: The Troubled Odyssey of the Liberal Idea* (Boulder, 1996), 25–36.

12. Pierre Manent, *An Intellectual History of Liberalism*, trans. Rebecca Balinski (Princeton, 1994), x; *The Correspondence of Edmund Burke* (10 vols. Cambridge, UK, 1958–78), VI, 42; Isaac Kramnick, *Republicanism and Bourgeois Radicalism: Political Ideology in Late Eighteenth-Century England and America* (Ithaca, 1990), 4–11.

13. Richard Price, *Observations on the Nature of Civil Liberty ...* (London, 1776), 2–3. Recent discussions of the interconnections between eighteenth-century liberalism and republicanism include Nathan Tarcov, "A 'Non-Lockean' Locke and the Character of Liberalism," in *Liberalism Reconsidered*, ed. Douglas MacLean and Claudia Mills (Totowa, 1983), 130–40; Lance Banning, "Jeffersonian Ideology Revisited: Liberal and Classical Ideas in the New American Republic," *William and Mary Quarterly*, 3 ser. 43 (January 1986), 3–19; James T. Kloppenberg, "The Virtues of Liberalism: Christianity, Republicanism, and Ethics in Early American Political Discourse," *Journal of American History*, 74 (June 1987), 9–29; and Joyce Appleby, "Introduction," *American Quarterly*, 37 (Fall 1985), 469–70.

14. Zenger in Michael Kammen, *Spheres of Liberty: Changing Perceptions of Liberty in American Culture* (Madison, 1986), 24–26; Samuel Johnson, *A Dictionary of the English Language* (2 vols. London, 1755); Thomas Jefferson, *Notes on the State of Virginia* (New York, 1964), 157; William Blackstone, *Commentaries on the Laws of England* (Portland, 1807), Bk 1, 171; Reid, *Concept of Liberty*, 73–92; Christopher Hill, *Change and Continuity in Seventeenth-Century England* (London, 1974), 219–38.

15. Philip J. Barbour, ed., *The Complete Works of Captain John Smith (1530–1631)* (3 vols. Chapel Hill, 1986), I, 332; Jack P. Greene, *The Intellectual Construction of America: Exceptionalism and Identity from 1492 to 1800* (Chapel Hill, 1993), 75, 104; Greene, *Pursuits of Happiness*, 193.

16. Eric Foner, *Tom Paine and Revolutionary America* (New York, 1976), 27; Linda G. DePauw, "Land of the Unfree: Legal Limitations on Liberty in Pre-revolutionary America," *Maryland Historical Magazine*, 68 (Winter 1973), 355–68; Elaine F. Crane, "Dependence in the Era of Independence: The Role of Women in a Republican Society," in *The American Revolution: Its Character and Limits*, ed. Jack P. Greene (New York, 1987), 259–61.

17. Robert J. Steinfeld, *The Invention of Free Labor: The Employment Relation in English and American Law and Culture, 1350–1870* (Chapel Hill, 1991), 3–5, 46, 101–02; Jean B. Lee, *The Price of Nationhood: The American Revolution in Charles County* (New York, 1994), 44; Bernard Bailyn, *Voyagers to the West: A Passage in the Peopling of America on the Eve of the Revolution* (New York, 1986), 166; Wood, *Radicalism*, 51–55; Isabel M. Calder, ed., *Colonial Captivities, Marches and Journeys* (New York, 1935), 151–52.

18. Shane White, *Somewhat More Independent: The End of Slavery in New York City, 1770–1810* (Athens, GA, 1991), 6–12; Gary B. Nash and Jean R. Sonderland, *Freedom by Degrees: Emancipation in Pennsylvania and Its Aftermath* (New York, 1991), 20–21; John M. Faragher, "History from the Inside-Out: Writing the History of Women in Rural America," *American Quarterly*, 33 (Winter 1981), 540–48; Linda K. Kerber, " 'I Have Don ... much to Carrey on the Warr': Women and the Shaping of Republican Ideology After the American Revolution," *Journal of Women's History*, 1 (Winter 1990), 236–39; Robert G. McCloskey, ed., *The Works of James Wilson* (2 vols. Cambridge, MA, 1967), II, 725.

19. Lee, *Price of Nationhood*, 17; Allan Kulikoff, *The Agrarian Origins of American Capitalism* (Charlottesville, 1992), 7, 21–22; John L. Brooke, *The Heart of the Commonwealth: Society and Political Culture in Worcester County, Massachusetts, 1713–1861* (New York, 1989), 42–44; Greene, *Pursuits of Happiness*, 72, 188; Joyce Appleby, *Liberalism and Republicanism in the Historical Imagination* (Cambridge, MA, 1992), 155.

20. J. Hector St. John Crèvecoeur, *Letters from an American Farmer*, ed. Alfred E. Stone (New York, 1981), 67; Ronald Schultz, "The Small-Producer Tradition and Artisan Radicalism in Philadelphia, 1720–1810," *Past and Present*, 127 (May 1990), 85–86.

21. McDonald, *Novus Ordo Seclorum*, 4–13; Kammen, *Sovereignty and Liberty*, 56–57; Alan Heimert, *Religion and the American Mind: From the Great Awakening to the Revolution* (Cambridge, MA, 1966), 400–01; Ann F. Withington, *Toward a More Perfect Union: Virtue and the Formation of the American Republic* (New York, 1991), 145–47; James MacGregor Burns, *The Vineyard of Liberty* (New York, 1982), 23; Lee, *Price of Nationhood*, 118.

22. Theodore Draper, *A Struggle for Power: The American Revolution* (New York, 1996), 33, 219; John M. Murrin, "A Roof Without Walls: The Dilemma of American National Identity," in Richard Beeman, et al., ed., *Beyond Confederation: Origins of the Constitution and American National Identity* (Chapel Hill, 1987), 340; Hyneman and Lutz, *American Political Writing*, I, 45–46; Julian Boyd, ed., *The Papers of Thomas Jefferson* (Princeton, 1950–), I, 141; Greenfeld, *Nationalism*, 410–16.

23. Pauline Maier, *From Resistance to Revolution: Colonial Radicals and the Development of American Opposition to Britain, 1765–1776* (New York, 1972), 161; Bailyn, *Ideological Origins*, 119; Nathan O. Hatch, *The Sacred Cause of Liberty: Republican Thought and the Millennium in Revolutionary New England* (New Haven, 1977), 50–54.

24. Edmund Burke, *The Works of the Right Honourable Edmund Burke* (16 vols. London, 1803), III, 49–50; Hatch, *Sacred Cause of Liberty*, 3–14; Ruth H. Bloch, *Visionary Republic: Millennial Themes in American Thought, 1756–1800* (New York, 1985); Foner, *Paine*, 78.

25. Foner, *Paine*, 75; Greenfeld, *Nationalism*, 423.

26. Adrienne Koch, *Power, Morals, and the Founding Fathers* (Ithaca, 1961), 105; Boyd, *Jefferson Papers*, I, 199; Foner, *Paine*, 78; Hans L. Kohn, *American Nationalism: An Interpretive Essay* (New York, 1957).

27. Philip S. Foner, ed., *The Complete Writings of Thomas Paine* (2 vols. New York, 1945), II, 243, 286–87; Wood, *Radicalism*, 6–7, 24–27, 232–40; Lee, *Price of Nationhood*, 42.

28. Charles F. Adams, ed., *Familiar Letters of John Adams and His Wife Abigail Adams During the Revolution* (Boston, 1875), 149–50, 155.

29. Draper, *Struggle for Power*, 468; Gary B. Nash, "Artisans and Politics in Eighteenth-Century Philadelphia," in *The Origins of Anglo-American Radicalism*, ed. Margaret and James Jacob (London, 1984), 174–77; Ruth Bogin, "Petitioning and the New Moral Economy of Post-Revolutionary America," *William and Mary Quarterly*, 3 ser., 45 (July 1988), 391–94; Kammen, *Sovereignty and Liberty*, 78; James A. Henretta, "The Nineteenth-Century Revolution in Civil Liberties: From 'Rights in Property' to 'Property in Rights,' " *This Constitution*, 19 (Fall 1991), 19.

30. *Maryland Gazette* (Annapolis), August 15, 1776; Marc Kruman, *Between Authority and Liberty: State Constitution Making in Revolutionary America* (Chapel Hill, 1997), 87–96.

31. Robert J. Taylor, ed., *Papers of John Adams* (10 vols. Cambridge, MA, 1977), IV, 210–11; Foner, *Paine*, 143–44; Kruman, *Between Authority and Liberty*, 91–95.

32. Robert J. Dinkin, *Voting in Revolutionary America: A Study of Elections in the Original Thirteen States, 1776–1789* (Westport, 1982), 27–39; Kulikoff, "The American Revolution," 98.

33. Steinfeld, *Invention of Free Labor*, 102–03, 122–28; Sharon V. Salinger, *"To Serve Well and Faithfully": Labor and Indentured Servants in Pennsylvania, 1682–1800* (New York, 1987), 142–53; Bernard Elbaum, "Why Apprenticeship Persisted in Britain But Not in the United States," *Journal of Economic History*, 49 (June 1989), 346; Bailyn, *Ideological Origins*, 234; New York *Independent Journal*, January 24, 1784; Albert Matthews, "Hired Man and Help," *Publications of the Colonial Society of Massachusetts*, 5 (March 1898), 225–56.

34. Rowland Berthoff, "Independence and Attachment, Virtue and Interest: From Republican Citizen to Free Enterpriser, 1787–1837," in *Uprooted Americans*, ed. Richard L. Bushman, et al. (Boston, 1979), 105–07; *The Debate on the Constitution* (2 vols. New York, 1993), I, 155–58; James L. Hutson, "The American Revolutionaries, the Political Economy of Aristocracy, and the American Concept of the Distribution of Wealth, 1765–1900," *American Historical Review*, 98 (October 1993), 1079–84; Charles Francis Adams, ed., *The Works of John Adams* (10 vols. Boston, 1850–56), IX, 376–77.

35. Merrill D. Peterson, *Thomas Jefferson and the New Nation: A Biography* (New York, 1970), 289, 304; Foner, *Paine*, 90–97; Appleby, *Liberalism and Republicanism*, 261–73. The phrase "the pursuit of happiness" was not uncommon in the eighteenth century. Jefferson probably encountered it in his voluminous reading and it "lingered in his memory"— Pauline Maier, *American Scripture: Making the Declaration of Independence* (New York, 1997), 134.

36. Alan Taylor, "Land and Liberty on the Post-Revolutionary Frontier," in *Devising Liberty*, ed. Konig, 81–88; Christopher L. Tomlins, *Law, Labor, and Ideology in the Early American Republic* (New York, 1993), 81–82; J. R. Pole, *The Pursuit of Equality in American History* (rev. ed. Berkeley, 1993), 134–35; Gordon S. Wood, *The Creation of the American Republic, 1776–1787* (Chapel Hill, 1969), 403–05.

37. Garrett W. Sheldon, *The Political Philosophy of Thomas Jefferson* (Baltimore, 1991), 72–77; Boyd, ed., *Jefferson Papers*, II, 308; Peterson, *Jefferson*, 106.

38. Gaillard Hunt, ed., *The Writings of James Madison* (9 vols. 1900–10), VI, 86, 96–99; Max Farrand, ed., *The Records of the Federal Convention of 1787* (4 vols. New Haven, 1911–37), II, 203–04; Jennifer Nedelsky, *Private Property and the Limits of American Constitutionalism* (Chicago, 1990), 2–7; Lance Banning, "Political Economy and the Creation of the Federal Republic," in *Devising Liberty*, ed. Konig, 41–42.

39. Foner, *Paine*, 91; Kammen, *Sovereignty and Liberty*, 56–57.

40. Herbert J. Storing, ed., *The Complete Anti-Federalist* (7 vols. Chicago, 1981), IV, 144; Gordon S. Wood, "Freedom and the Constitution," in *Freedom in America: A 200-Year Perspective*, ed. Norman A. Graebner (University Park, 1977), 47; Jacob E. Cooke, ed., *The Federalist* (Middletown, CT, 1961), 428; David P. Szatmary, *Shays' Rebellion: The Making of an Agrarian Insurrection* (Amherst, 1980), 60–69.

41. Jonathan Elliott, *Debates in the Several State Conventions on the Adoption of the Federal Constitution* (5 vols. Washington, DC, 1830–36), III, 536–37; Harold C. Syrett, ed., *The Papers of*

Alexander Hamilton (27 vols. New York, 1961–87), II, 649–51; Jack N. Rakove, *Original Meanings: Politics and Ideas in the Making of the Constitution* (New York, 1996), 289–97.

42. L. H. Butterfield, ed., *Letters of Benjamin Rush* (2 vols. Philadelphia, 1951), I, 418–19; Elliott, *Debates*, III, 53, 607.

43. *The Address and Reasons of Dissent of the Minority Convention of the State of Pennsylvania to Their Constituents* (Philadelphia, 1787), 52; Rakove, *Original Meanings*, 316, 332–35; Jack N. Rakove, "Parchment Barriers and the Politics of Rights," in *A Culture of Rights: The Bill of Rights in Philosophy, Politics, and Law 1791 and 1991*, ed. Michael J. Lacey and Knud Haakonssen (New York, 1991), 136–38.

44. Kenneth R. Bowling, " 'A Tub to the Whale': The Founding Fathers and Adoption of the Federal Bill of Rights," *Journal of the Early Republic*, 8 (Fall 1988), 223–26; Celeste M. Condit and John L. Lucaites, *Crafting Equality: America's Anglo-African Word* (Chicago, 1993), 48; Martha Minow, "Interpreting Rights: An Essay for Robert Cover," *Yale Law Journal*, 96 (July 1987), 1860–1915. Joseph Raz, *The Morality of Freedom* (New York, 1986), 249–53.

45. Leonard W. Levy, *Emergence of a Free Press* (New York, 1985), 3–19, 37, 129; Bernard Bailyn, "Jefferson and the Ambiguities of Freedom," *Proceedings of the American Philosophical Society*, 137 (December 1993), 509.

46. John P. Roche, "American Liberty: An Examination of the 'Tradition' of Freedom," in *Aspects of Liberty*, ed. Milton R. Konvitz and Clinton Rossiter (Ithaca, 1958), 131; Leonard W. Levy, *The Establishment Clause: Religion and the First Amendment* (Chapel Hill, 1994), 1–17; Robert T. Handy, "The Contribution of Pennsylvania to the Rise of Religious Liberty in America," in *Quest for Faith, Quest for Freedom: Aspects of Pennsylvania's Religious Experience*, ed. Otto Reimherr (Cranbury, 1987), 21–25; William G. McLoughlin, ed., *The Diary of Isaac Backus* (3 vols. Providence, 1977), II, 774.

47. William L. Miller, *The First Liberty: Religion and the American Republic* (New York, 1986), 56–63; Levy, *Establishment Clause*, 27–29, 56; Bill J. Leonard, "Varieties of Freedom in the Baptist Experience," *Baptist History and Heritage*, 5 (January 1990), 3–5; Stephen Botein, "Religious Dimensions of the Early American State," in *Beyond Confederation*, ed. Beeman, 317–20; Isaac Kramnick and R. Laurence Moore, *The Godless Constitution: The Case Against Religious Correctness* (New York, 1996), 32.

48. Robert A. Rutland, ed., *The Papers of James Madison* (17 vols. Chicago, 1962–91), XIV, 266–68; Hunt, ed., *Writings of Madison*, XI, 188; Lance Banning, *The Sacred Fire of Liberty: James Madison and the Founding of the Federal Republic* (Ithaca, 1995), 128–31; Kramnick and Moore, *Godless Constitution*, 17.

49. Nathan O. Hatch, "The Second Great Awakening and the Market Revolution," in *Devising Liberty*, ed. Konig, 253–56; Elizabeth Sommer, "A Different Kind of Freedom? Order and Discipline Among the Moravian Brethren in Germany and Salem, North Carolina 1771–1801," *Church History*, 63 (June 1994), 221–34; Marvin E. Frankel, *Faith and Freedom: Religious Liberty in America* (New York, 1994), 84.

50. Heimert, *Religion and the American Mind*, 391.

CHAPTER 2

1. David B. Davis, *Slavery and Human Progress* (New York, 1984), 19; Roger Bruns, ed., *Am I Not a Man and a Brother: The Antislavery Crusade in Revolutionary America* (New York, 1977), 136, 341; John P. Reid, *The Concept of Liberty in the Age of the American Revolution* (Chicago, 1988), 38–45; F. Nwabueze Okoye, "Chattel Slavery as the Nightmare of the American Revolutionaries," *William and Mary Quarterly*, 3 ser., 37 (January 1980), 3–28.

2. Bernard Bailyn, ed., *Pamphlets of the American Revolution* (Cambridge, MA, 1965–), I, 420–22, 446–47.

3. John Dickinson, *Letters from a Farmer in Pennsylvania to the Inhabitants of the British Colonies* (Philadelphia, 1768), 3; Philip S. Foner, ed., *The Complete Writings of Thomas Paine* (2 vols. New York, 1945), I, 390; Henry S. Commager and Richard B. Morris, eds., *The Spirit of Seventy-Six* (2 vols. Indianapolis, 1958), I, 297–98; Gordon S. Wood, *The Creation of the American Republic* (Chapel Hill, 1969), 32; *Pennsylvania Packet* (Philadelphia), April 8, 1776; Peter Force, ed., *American Archives*, 4 ser. (6 vols. Washington, DC, 1837), I, 512.

4. *The Works of the Right Honourable Edmund Burke* (16 vols. London, 1803), III, 54; Charles S. Hyneman and Donald S. Lutz, eds., *American Political Writing During the Founding Era 1760–1805* (2 vols. Indianapolis, 1983), II, 723.

5. Moses I. Finley, *Economy and Society in Ancient Greece* (New York, 1983), 12; Bill J. Leonard, "Varieties of Freedom in the Baptist Experience," *Baptist History and Heritage*, 25 (January 1990), 10; Dr. Johnson in David B. Davis, *The Problem of Slavery in the Age of Revolution 1770–1823* (New York, 1975), 275; Thomas Hutchinson, *Strictures Upon the Declaration of the Congress at Philadelphia* (London, 1776), 9–10; Julian Boyd, ed., *The Papers of Thomas Jefferson* (Princeton, 1950–), VIII, 259.

6. Marquis de Chastellux, *Travels in North-America, in the Years 1780, 1781, and 1782* (2 vols. London, 1787), II, 56–57; John C. Miller, *The Wolf by the Ears: Thomas Jefferson and Slavery* (New York, 1977).

7. Edmund S. Morgan, *American Slavery, American Freedom: The Ordeal of Colonial Virginia* (New York, 1975), 380–85; Adam Smith, *Lectures on Jurisprudence*, ed. R. L. Meek, et al. (Oxford, 1976), 181; John P. Diggins, *The Lost Soul of American Politics: Virtue, Self-Interest, and the Foundations of Liberalism* (New York, 1984), 12, 141–42; James W. Ely, Jr., "Property Rights and Liberty: Allies or Enemies?" *Presidential Studies Quarterly*, 22 (Fall 1992), 703; Sylvia R. Frey, "Liberty, Equality, and Slavery: The Paradox of the American Revolution," in *The American Revolution: Its Character and Limits*, ed. Jack P. Greene (New York, 1987), 241–42.

8. Joyce Appleby, *Liberalism and Republicanism in the Historical Imagination* (Cambridge, MA, 1992), 158; Henry P. Johnston, ed., *The Correspondence and Public Papers of John Jay* (4 vols. New York, 1890–93), III, 342; Robin Blackburn, *The Overthrow of Colonial Slavery 1776–1848* (London, 1988), 51–52; Bernard Bailyn, *The Ideological Origins of the American Revolution* (Cambridge, MA, 1967), 237; Bruns, *Am I Not a Man*, 325; Boyd, ed., *Jefferson Papers*, X, 63.

9. Thomas J. Davis, "Emancipation Rhetoric, Natural Rights, and Revolutionary New England: A Note on Four Black Petitions in Massachusetts, 1773–1777," *New England*

Quarterly, 62 (June 1989), 255; Sylvia R. Frey, *Water from the Rock: Black Resistance in a Revolutionary Age* (Princeton, 1991), 49–57, 174–94; John C. Fitzpatrick, ed., *The Writings of George Washington, 1745–1799* (39 vols. Washington, DC, 1931–44), XXII, 14n.

10. Ruth Bogin, " 'Liberty Further Extended': A 1776 Antislavery Manuscript by Lemuel Haynes," *William and Mary Quarterly*, 3 ser., 40 (January 1983), 85–105; Davis, "Emancipation Rhetoric," 250–52, 261–62.

11. Ira Berlin, *Slavery: The First Two Centuries of African American Captivity in Mainland North America* (Cambridge, MA, 1998), ch. 5; *Poems of Phyllis Wheatley: A Native African and a Slave* (Bedford, MA, 1995), 47–48; Orlando Patterson, *Freedom* (New York, 1991), 24.

12. Bailyn, *Ideological Origins*, 237; Davis, *Problem of Slavery*, 87–88.

13. Max Farrand, ed., *The Records of the Federal Convention of 1787* (4 vols. New Haven, 1911–37), I, 135; Merrill Jensen, ed., *The Documentary History of the Ratification of the Constitution* (Madison, 1976–), XIV, 707–08; L. H. Butterfield, ed., *Letters of Benjamin Rush* (2 vols. Philadelphia, 1951), I, 442; Herbert J. Storing, ed., *The Complete Anti-Federalist* (7 vols. Chicago, 1981), II, 60.

14. Edward Countryman, *Americans: A Collision of Histories* (New York, 1996), 67; Richard B. Morris, et al., eds., *John Jay* (New York, 1975–), II, 155–56; Davis, *Problem of Slavery*, 472–73; James W. Ely, Jr., " 'The Good Old Cause': The Ratification of the Constitution and Bill of Rights in South Carolina," in *The South's Role in the Creation of the Bill of Rights*, ed. Robert J. Haws (Jackson, 1991), 116.

15. Ira Berlin, "The Revolution in Black Life," in *The American Revolution*, ed. Alfred F. Young (DeKalb, 1976), 363–82.

16. Edgar F. Smith, *Priestley in America 1794–1804* (Philadelphia, 1920), 35–37; U.S. Department of Commerce, Bureau of the Census, *Historical Statistics of the United States* (2 vols. Washington, DC, 1975), I, 14.

17. Blackburn, *Overthrow of Colonial Slavery*, 224–26, 248, 333–75; Austin Dobson, ed., *The Complete Poetical Works of Oliver Goldsmith* (London, 1906), 18.

18. Edmund S. Morgan, *Inventing the People: The Rise of Popular Sovereignty in England and America* (New York, 1988); John M. Murrin, "A Roof Without Walls: The Dilemma of American National Identity," in *Beyond Confederation: Origins of the Constitution and American National Identity*, ed. Richard Beeman, et al. (Chapel Hill, 1987), 333–39.

19. Rogers Brubaker, *Citizenship and Nationhood in France and Germany* (Cambridge, MA, 1992); Hans Kohn, *American Nationalism: An Interpretive Essay* (New York, 1957).

20. Jon Gjerde, "Tensions Amidst Complementary Identities: Citizenship and Ethnicity in the Nineteenth Century United States," Unpublished paper, Organization of American Historians annual meeting, 1996; Rogers M. Smith, *Civic Ideals: Conflicting Visions of Citizenship in U.S. History* (New Haven, 1997); Judith Shklar, *American Citizenship: The Quest for Inclusion* (Cambridge, MA, 1991), 1–2.

21. Liah Greenfeld, *Nationalism: Five Roads to Modernity* (Cambridge, MA, 1992), 437; J. Hector St. John de Crèvecoeur, *Letters from an American Farmer*, ed. Alfred E. Stone (New York, 1981), 69; Duncan J. MacLeod, *Slavery, Race and the American Revolution* (New York, 1974), 62; Edmund Randolph, *History of Virginia*, ed. Arthur H. Shaffer (Charlottesville, 1970), 253.

22. James H. Kettner, *The Development of American Citizenship, 1608–1870* (Chapel Hill, 1978), 235–46; E. P. Hutchinson, *Legislative History of American Immigration Policy 1798–1965* (Philadelphia, 1981), 405–33. Robert A. Divine, *American Immigration Policy, 1924–1952* (New Haven, 1957), 1, refers to pre-1880 immigration policy as "open."

23. Thomas Jefferson, *Notes on the State of Virginia* (New York, 1964), 132–37, 155; Winthrop D. Jordan, *White Over Black: American Attitudes Toward the Negro, 1550–1812* (Chapel Hill, 1968), 288–89, 455; Merrill D. Peterson, *Thomas Jefferson and the New Nation: A Biography* (New York, 1970), 55; Drew R. McCoy, *The Last of the Founders: James Madison and the Republican Legacy* (New York, 1989), 262–77; David F. Ericson, *The Shaping of American Liberalism: The Debates Over Ratification and Slavery* (Chicago, 1993), 12–20.

24. Uday S. Mehta, "Liberal Strategies of Exclusion," *Politics and Society*, 18 (December 1990), 427–30; David B. Davis, "Reconsidering the Colonization Movement: Leonard Bacon and the Problem of Evil," *Intellectual History Newsletter*, 14 (1992), 4; John Locke, *Two Treatises of Government*, ed. Peter Laslett (Cambridge, UK, 1988), 309; Audrey Smedley, *Race in North America: Origin and Evolution of a Worldview* (Boulder, 1993), 185–205.

25. Jan Lewis, " 'of every age sex and condition': The Representation of Women in the Constitution," *Journal of the Early Republic*, 15 (Fall 1995), 359–60; Joan Hoff, *Law, Gender, and Injustice* (New York, 1991), 81–101; Linda K. Kerber, *Women of the Republic: Intellect and Ideology in Revolutionary America* (Chapel Hill, 1980), 10–12, 204–28; Carole Pateman, *The Sexual Contract* (Cambridge, UK, 1988); Adams in Michael Grossberg, *Governing the Hearth: Law and the Family in Nineteenth-Century America* (Chapel Hill, 1985), 3.

26. Rogers M. Smith, " 'One United People': Second-Class Female Citizenship and the American Quest for Community," *Yale Journal of Law and the Humanities*, I (1989) 241; Davis, "Emancipation Rhetoric," 258; Genevieve Lloyd, *The Man of Reason: "Male" and "Female" in Western Philosophy* (Minneapolis, 1984); Kerber, *Women of the Republic*, 31–35; Edwin G. Burrows and Michael Wallace, *Gotham: A History of New York City* (2 vols. New York, 1998–), I, ch. 25; Countryman, *Americans*, 71.

27. James Richardson, ed., *A Compilation of the Messages and Papers of the Presidents* (10 vols. Washington, DC, 1896–99), I, 48, 58; Thomas P. Slaughter, *The Whiskey Rebellion: Frontier Epilogue to the American Revolution* (New York, 1986), 127, 138; King in David H. Fischer, *The Revolution of American Conservatism: The Federalist Party in the Era of Jeffersonian Democracy* (New York, 1965), 303, 358.

28. Fischer, *Revolution of American Conservatism*, 236; Robert E. Shalhope, "Republicanism, Liberalism, and Democracy: Political Culture in the Early Republic," *Proceedings of the American Antiquarian Society*, 102, pt. 1 (1992), 132–39; Michael H. Hunt, *Ideology and U.S. Foreign Policy* (New Haven, 1987), 23–25.

29. Joyce Appleby, *Capitalism and a New Social Order: The Republican Vision of the 1790s* (New York, 1984), 77; Philip S. Foner, ed., *The Democratic-Republican Societies, 1790–1800* (Westport, 1976), 99, 264; Minutes, Democratic Society of Pennsylvania, January 9, 1794, Historical Society of Pennsylvania; Lucas A. Powe, Jr., *The Fourth Estate and the Constitution: Freedom of the Press in America* (Berkeley, 1991), 58–60.

30. John C. Miller, *Crisis in Freedom: The Alien and Sedition Acts* (Boston, 1952), 106–08, 124–25; Leonard W. Levy, *Emergence of a Free Press* (New York, 1985), 297–310; Lester J. Cappon,

ed., *The Adams-Jefferson Letters* (Chapel Hill, 1959), 279; Peterson, *Jefferson*, 613, 640, 716–17; Richardson, ed., *Messages and Papers*, I, 369.

31. Donald R. Hickey, "America's Response to the Slave Revolt in Haiti, 1791–1806," *Journal of the Early Republic*, 2 (Winter 1982), 361–80; Tim Mattheson, "Jefferson and Haiti," *Journal of Southern History*, 61 (May 1995), 209–48; Michael Zuckerman, "The Color of Counterrevolution: Thomas Jefferson and the Rebellion in San Domingo," in *The Languages of Revolution*, ed. Loretta V. Mannucci (Milan, 1988), 83–109.

32. Douglas R. Egerton, *Gabriel's Rebellion: The Virginia Slave Conspiracies of 1800 and 1802* (Chapel Hill, 1993), 26–27, 40; Frey, *Water from the Rock*, 320.

33. MacLeod, *Slavery, Race and Revolution*, 154–55; Ira Berlin, *Slaves Without Masters: The Free Negro in the Antebellum South* (New York, 1974), 95–101; *Virginia Argus* (Richmond), January 17, 1806.

34. Jack P. Greene, *Pursuits of Happiness* (Chapel Hill, 1988), 208.

CHAPTER 3

1. Fred Somkin, *Unquiet Eagle: Memory and Desire in the Idea of American Freedom, 1815–1860* (Ithaca, 1967), 170–72; Walt Whitman, *Leaves of Grass*, ed. Malcolm Cowley (New York, 1959), 6.

2. John Higham, "Indian Princess and Roman Goddess: The First Female Symbols of America," *Proceedings of the American Antiquarian Society*, 100, pt. 1 (1990), 59–66; Nancy Jo Fox, *Liberties with Liberty* (New York, 1985), 8–13; Rush Welter, *The Mind of America 1820–1860* (New York, 1975), 47; James T. Schleifer, "Tocqueville and Some American Views of Liberty," in *Liberty/Liberté: The American and French Experiences*, ed. Joseph Klaits and Michael H. Haltzel (Washington, DC, 1991), 51; Hans Kohn, *American Nationalism* (New York, 1957), 141; James Richardson, ed., *A Compilation of the Messages and Papers of the Presidents* (10 vols. Washington, DC, 1896–99), II, 1526.

3. Judith N. Shklar, *American Citizenship: The Quest for Inclusion* (Cambridge, MA, 1991), 1–3, 22.

4. Anders Stephanson, *Manifest Destiny: American Expansion and the Empire of Right* (New York, 1995); Robert W. Tucker and David C. Hendrickson, *Empire of Liberty: The Statecraft of Thomas Jefferson* (New York, 1990), 14–20; Thomas R. Hietala, *Manifest Design: Anxious Aggrandizement in Late Jacksonian America* (Ithaca, 1985), 214–15; Wallace Stegner, *Angle of Repose* (New York, 1971), 133.

5. Michel Chevalier, *Society, Manners and Politics in the United States* (Boston, 1839), 330; Drew R. McCoy, *The Elusive Republic: Political Economy in Jeffersonian America* (Chapel Hill, 1980), 203–07; Major L. Wilson, *Space, Time, and Freedom: The Quest for Nationality and the Irrepressible Conflict 1815–1861* (Westport, 1974), 107–12.

6. Gregory Nobles, *American Frontiers: Cultural Encounter and Continental Conquest* (New York, 1997), 126–30, 209–10; Alan Taylor, "Land and Liberty on the Post-Revolutionary Frontier," in *Devising Liberty: Preserving and Creating Liberty in the New American Republic*, ed. David T. Konig (Stanford, 1995), 82; Thomas P. Slaughter, *The Whiskey Rebellion: Frontier Epilogue to the American Revolution* (New York, 1986), 142.

7. Christopher Collier, "The American People as Christian White Men of Property: Suffrage and Elections in Colonial and Early National America," and Sean Wilentz, "Property and Power: Suffrage Reform in the United States, 1787–1860," both in *Voting and the Spirit of American Democracy*, ed. Donald W. Rogers (Hartford, 1990), 19–41; Merrill D. Peterson, ed., *Democracy, Liberty, and Property: The State Constitutional Conventions of the 1820's* (Indianapolis, 1966); Drew R. McCoy, *The Last of the Founders; James Madison and the Republican Legacy* (New York, 1989), 192–98.

8. Robert J. Steinfeld, "Property and Suffrage in the Early American Republic," *Stanford Law Review*, 41 (January 1989), 335–76; Judith Wellman, "Women's Rights, Republicanism, and Revolutionary Rhetoric in Antebellum New York State," *New York History*, 69 (July 1988), 366; Francis Lieber, *On Civil Liberty and Self-Government* (Philadelphia, 1859), 176–77.

9. Robert H. Wiebe, *Self-Rule: A Cultural History of American Democracy* (Chicago, 1995), 71–73; William J. Novak, *The People's Welfare: Law and Regulation in Nineteenth-Century America* (Chapel Hill, 1996), 10; Alexis de Tocqueville, *Democracy in America* (New York, 1946), 59.

10. Wiebe, *Self-Rule*, 83; Jean H. Baker, *Affairs of Party: The Political Culture of Northern Democrats in the Mid-Nineteenth Century* (Ithaca, 1983), 266–71; Noah Webster, *A Dictionary of the English Language* (2 vols. London, 1852); William B. Scott, *In Pursuit of Happiness: American Conceptions of Property from the Seventeenth to the Twentieth Century* (Bloomington, 1977), 76–78.

11. Duncan J. MacLeod, *Slavery, Race and the American Revolution* (New York, 1974), 119.

12. Novak, *People's Welfare*, 35 and *passim*; Adrienne Koch and William Peden, eds., *Selected Writings of John and John Quincy Adams* (New York, 1946), 342; Daniel W. Howe, *The Political Culture of the American Whigs* (Chicago, 1979), 33–36; Michael J. Sandel, *Democracy's Discontent: American in Search of Public Philosophy* (Cambridge, MA, 1996), 165; J. William Frost, *A Perfect Freedom: Religious Liberty in Pennsylvania* (New York, 1990), 5–8.

13. Carl Bode and Malcolm Cowley, eds., *The Portable Emerson* (New York, 1981), 594–95; "Introduction," *United States Magazine and Democratic Review*, I (October 1837), 1–15; Michael A. Morrison, "Martin Van Buren, the Democracy, and the Partisan Politics of Texas Annexation," *Journal of Southern History*, 61 (November 1995), 712–13; W. J. Rorabaugh, *The Alcoholic Republic: An American Tradition* (New York, 1979), 200–01; Roy Rosenzweig, *Eight Hours for What We Will: Workers and Leisure in an Industrial City, 1870–1920* (New York, 1983), 177; L. Ray Gunn, *The Decline of Authority: Public Economic Policy and Political Development in New York: 1800–1860* (Ithaca, 1988), 1–9, 155.

14. Welter, *Mind of America*, 127; Novak, *People's Welfare*, 184–85; Francis Lieber, *Manual of Political Ethics* (Boston, 1838), 167; Lawrence F. Kohl, *The Politics of Individualism: Parties and the American Character in the Jacksonian Era* (New York, 1989), 104–09.

15. Charles Sellers, *The Market Revolution: Jacksonian America 1815–1846* (New York, 1991); Christopher Clark, *The Roots of Rural Capitalism: Western Massachusetts, 1780–1860* (Ithaca, 1990), 4.

16. Joyce Appleby, et al., *Telling the Truth About History* (New York, 1994), 121; Steven Watts, *The Republic Reborn: War and the Making of Liberal America, 1790–1820* (Baltimore, 1987), 68–72; Henry C. Carey, *Principles of Social Science* (3 vols. Philadelphia, 1858–59), III, 234;

"The Story of the Great Seal of the State of New Jersey," Unpublished paper, New Jersey Historical Commission, 1983; J. Franklin Reigart, *The United States Album* (Lancaster, 1844).

17. George M. Marsden, *Fundamentalism and American Culture: The Shaping of Twentieth-Century Evangelicism 1870–1925* (New York, 1980), 16, 28–30, 99–100; Watts, *Republic Reborn*, 10–14, 119–39; Nathan O. Hatch, *The Democratization of American Christianity* (New Haven, 1989), 3–4, 43–44.

18. Bode and Cowley, eds., *Portable Emerson*, 594–95; Yehoshua Arieli, *Individualism and Nationalism in American Ideology* (Cambridge, MA, 1964), 276–84.

19. Thomas L. Haskell, "Capitalism and the Origins of the Humanitarian Sensibility," *American Historical Review*, 90 (April–June 1985), 339–61, 547–66; Wilfred McClay, *The Masterless: Self and Society in Modern America* (Chapel Hill, 1994), 40–73.

20. Rorabaugh, *Alcoholic Republic*, 200–01, 214–15; Heman Humphrey, *Parallel Between Intemperance and the Slave Trade: An Address Delivered at Amherst College, July 4, 1828* (Amherst, 1828); Scott A. Sandage, "Deadbeats, Drunkards, and Dreamers: A Cultural History of Failure in America, 1819–1893," Ph.D. dissertation, Rutgers University, 1995; Tyler Anbinder, *Nativism and Slavery: The Northern Know-Nothings and the Politics of the 1850s* (New York, 1992), 104–05; Amy Bridges, *A City in the Republic: Antebellum New York and the Origins of Machine Politics* (New York, 1984), 31.

21. Lacy K. Ford, *Origins of Southern Radicalism: The South Carolina Upcountry 1800–1860* (New York, 1988); Jonathan Prude, "Town-Country Conflicts in Antebellum Rural Massachusetts," and John M. Faragher, "Open-Country Community," both in *The Countryside in the Age of Capitalist Transformation: Essays in the Social History of Rural America*, ed. Steven Hahn and Jonathan Prude (Chapel Hill, 1985), 75–76, 245–47; Randolph A. Roth, *The Democratic Dilemma: Religion, Reform, and the Social Order in the Connecticut River Valley of Vermont, 1791–1850* (New York, 1987), 297; Wiebe, *Self-Rule*, 24–26.

22. Richard Stott, "Artisans and Capitalist Development," *Journal of the Early Republic*, 16 (Summer 1996), 267–69; Sean Wilentz, "The Rise of the American Working Class, 1776–1877," in *Perspectives on American Labor History*, ed. J. Carroll Moody and Alice Kessler-Harris (DeKalb, 1989), 83–151; Peter Knights, *The Plain People of Boston, 1830–1860* (New York, 1971), 120; Bridges, *A City in the Republic*, 46–58; U.S. Department of Commerce, Bureau of the Census, *Historical Statistics of the United States* (2 vols. Washington, DC, 1975), I, 139; Stanley Lebergott, "The Pattern of Employment Since 1800," in *American Economic History*, ed. Seymour E. Harris (New York, 1961), 290–91; Christopher L. Tomlins, *Labor, Law, and Ideology in the Early American Republic* (New York, 1993); Robert J. Steinfeld, *The Invention of Free Labor: The Employment Relation in English and American Law and Culture, 1350–1870* (Chapel Hill, 1991), 144–60.

23. Haskell, "Capitalism and the Origins of the Humanitarian Sensibility," 339–61, 547–66; Sean Wilentz, *Chants Democratic: New York City and the Rise of the American Working Class, 1788–1850* (New York, 1984), 63–103; Ronald Schultz, *The Republic of Labor: Philadelphia Artisans and the Politics of Class, 1720–1830* (New York, 1993), 206–29.

24. David Turley, *The Culture of English Antislavery, 1780–1860* (London, 1991), 182–84; Marcus Cunliffe, *Chattel Slavery and Wage Slavery: The Anglo-American Context 1830–1860* (Athens,

GA, 1979), 9–14; Noah Webster, *An American Dictionary of the English Language* (2 vols. New York, 1828); Wilentz, *Chants Democratic*, 271–84; Christopher Lasch, *The True and Only Heaven: Progress and Its Critics* (New York, 1991), 203.

25. Barry Goldberg, "Slavery, Race and the Languages of Class: 'Wage Slaves' and White 'Niggers,' " *New Politics*, n.s., 3 (Summer 1991), 64–70; John R. Commons, et al., *History of Labor in the United States* (4 vols. New York, 1918–35), I, 141–42; Tomlins, *Law, Labor, Ideology*, 128–30, 163n.; David A. Zonderman, *Aspirations and Anxieties: New England Workers and the Mechanized Factory System 1815–1850* (New York, 1992), 113–16, 161–62.

26. Bronson essay in Joseph L. Blau, ed., *Social Theories of Jacksonian Democracy* (Indianapolis, 1954), 306–10; Lasch, *The True and Only Heaven*, 191n; "The Tartarus of Maids," *Selected Writings of Herman Melville* (New York, 1952), 195–96; Wilentz, *Chants Democratic*, 332; Zonderman, *Aspirations and Anxieties*, 116, 293.

27. Bruce Levine, "The Migration of Ideology and the Contested Meaning of Freedom: German Americans in the Mid-Nineteenth Century," *Occasional Paper No. 7, German Historical Institute* (Washington, DC, 1992), 11–12; Wilentz, "Rise of the Working Class," 88; Arieli, *Individualism and Nationalism*, 241; Blau, ed., *Social Theories*, 310.

28. Blau, ed., *Social Theories*, 141; J. F. C. Harrison, *Quest for the New Moral World: Robert Owen and the Owenites in Britain and America* (New York, 1969), 52–58; Christopher Clark, *The Communitarian Moment: The Radical Challenge of the Northampton Association* (Ithaca, 1995), 99–108.

29. Thomas Skidmore, *The Rights of Man to Property* (New York, 1829); Wilentz, *Chants Democratic*, 193–95; Jackson in Scott, *In Pursuit of Happiness*, 59–66; Arieli, *Individualism and Nationalism*, 313; Bernard Mandel, *Labor Free and Slave* (New York, 1955), 85.

30. Cunliffe, *Chattel Slavery*, 4–7; Eugene D. Genovese, *The Slaveholders' Dilemma: Freedom and Progress in Southern Conservative Thought, 1820–1860* (Columbia, SC, 1992), 33–34, 48; James Oakes, *Slavery and Freedom: An Interpretation of the Old South* (New York, 1990), 80; *Congressional Globe*, 35th Congress, 2d sess., 1339; *Charleston Mercury*, March 7, 1860.

31. Oakes, *Slavery and Freedom*, 72–77; Chilton Williamson, *American Suffrage: From Property to Democracy 1760–1860* (Princeton, 1960), 156; J. Mills Thornton III, *Politics and Power in a Slave Society: Alabama, 1800–1860* (Baton Rouge, 1978), 216; Bradley G. Bond, *Political Culture in the Nineteenth-Century South: Mississippi 1830–1900* (Baton Rouge, 1995), 96; Richard K. Crallé, ed., *The Works of John C. Calhoun* (6 vols. New York, 1851–56), I, 55; "Diversity of the Races; Its Bearing upon Negro Slavery," *Southern Quarterly Review*, n.s., 3 (April 1851), 406; William M. Wiecek, *The Sources of Antislavery Constitutionalism in America, 1760–1848* (Ithaca, 1977), 180–81.

32. Drew G. Faust, ed., *The Ideology of Slavery: Proslavery Thought in the Antebellum South, 1830–1860* (Baton Rouge, 1981), 176, 285, 293; Mitchell Snay, *Gospel of Disunion: Religion and Separatism in the Antebellum South* (Chapel Hill, 1997), 68–71; George Fitzhugh, "Revolutions of '76 and '61 Contrasted," *De Bow's Review*, n.s., 4 (July–August 1867), 36–47; George Fitzhugh, *Sociology for the South* (Richmond, 1854), 238–39.

33. *The Speeches of the Right Honourable Edmund Burke, in the House of Commons, and in Westminster-Hall* (4 vols. London, 1816), I, 235; William W. Freehling, *The Reintegration of American History: Slavery and the Civil War* (New York, 1994), 100; Oakes, *Slavery and Freedom*, 80.

34. Istvan Hont and Michael Ignatieff, "Needs and Justice in the *Wealth of Nations*: An In-

troductory Essay," in *Wealth and Virtue: The Shaping of Political Economy of the Scottish Enlight-enment*, ed. Istvan Hont and Michael Ignatieff (Cambridge, UK, 1983), 13–15; Scott, *In Pursuit of Happiness*, 87–93.

35. Wilentz, *Chants Democratic*, 271–86, 303–04; Sean Wilentz, "Many Democracies: On Toc-queville and Jacksonian America," in *Reconsidering Tocqueville's "Democracy in America"*, ed. Abraham S. Eisenstadt (New Brunswick, 1988), 218–19; John Ashworth, *"Agrarians" and "Aristocrats": Party Political Ideology in the United States, 1837–1846* (London, 1983), 68; Calvin Colton, *The Rights of Labor*, 3d ed. (New York, 1847), 9.

36. Eric Foner, *Politics and Ideology in the Age of the Civil War* (New York, 1980), 65; Jonathan A. Glickstein, " 'Poverty Is Not Slavery': American Abolitionists and the Competitive Labor Market," in *New Perspectives on the Abolitionists*, ed. Lewis Perry and Michael Fell-man (Baton Rouge, 1979), 207–11; Phillips in John R. Commons, et al., eds., *A Docu-mentary History of American Industrial Society* (10 vols. Cleveland, 1910–14), VII, 220–21; Phillips in *Liberator*, February 10, 1845, October 1, 1847.

37. *Narrative of the Life of Frederick Douglass, an American Slave* (Boston, 1845), 113; *Liberator*, March 26, 1847.

38. Robert J. Steinfeld, "Property and Suffrage in the Early American Republic," *Stanford Law Review*, 41 (January 1989), 335–76; Rowland Berthoff, "Independence and Attach-ment, Virtue and Interest: From Republican Citizen to Free Enterpriser, 1787–1837," in *Uprooted Americans*, ed. Richard L. Bushman, et al. (Boston, 1979), 115–16.

39. Gordon S. Wood, *The Radicalism of the American Revolution* (New York, 1992), 33, 136–39, 171, 277; *New York Tribune*, November 11, 1857; Shklar, *American Citizenship*, 64–67.

40. Zonderman, *Aspirations and Anxieties*, 288; Charles Stephenson, " 'There's Plenty Waitin' at the Gates': Mobility, Opportunity, and the American Worker," in *Life and Labor: Di-mensions of Working-Class History*, ed. Charles Stephenson and Robert Asher (Albany, 1986), 72–91; Jonathan Prude, *The Coming of Industrial Order: Town and Factory Life in Rural Massachusetts, 1810–1860* (New York, 1983), 114–15; Clark, *Roots of Rural Capitalism*, 305–13; Walter D. Kamphoefner, et al., eds., *News from the Land of Freedom: German Immigrants Write Home* (Ithaca, 1991), 393.

41. Eric Foner, *Free Soil, Free Labor, Free Men: The Ideology of the Republican Party Before the Civil War* (New York, 1970), 11–39; James A. Stevenson, "Lincoln vs. Douglas Over the Repub-lican Ideal," *American Studies*, 35 (Spring 1994), 66–67; Roy F. Basler, et al., eds., *The Col-lected Works of Abraham Lincoln* (9 vols. New Brunswick, 1953–55), II, 364, 405, III, 462, 477–79.

42. Foner, *Free Soil*, 9, 43, 83; George E. Baker, ed., *The Works of William H. Seward* (5 vols. Boston, 1853–84), I, 74.

CHAPTER 4

1. Daniel T. Rodgers and Sean Wilentz, "Languages of Power in the United States," in *Language, History and Class*, ed. Penelope J. Corfield (Oxford, 1991), 254; Robert H. Wiebe, *Self-Rule: A Cultural History of American Democracy* (Chicago, 1995), 110.

2. John Stuart and Harriet Taylor Mill, *Essays on Sex Equality*, ed. Alice S. Rossi (Chicago, 1970), 137; Richard Bellamy, *Liberalism and Modern Society: A Historical Argument* (University Park, 1992), 25–28; *New York Herald* in Elizabeth Cady Stanton, Susan B. Anthony, and Matilda J. Gage, eds., *History of Woman Suffrage* (6 vols. Rochester, 1881–1922), I, 854.

3. Joan R. Gunderson, "Independence, Citizenship, and the American Revolution," *Signs*, 13 (Autumn 1987), 65–66; Merrill D. Peterson, ed., *Democracy, Liberty, and Property: The State Constitutional Conventions of the 1820's* (Indianapolis, 1966), 293–94.

4. Christopher Lasch, *Women and the Common Life: Love, Marriage, and Feminism* (New York, 1997), xxiii; Joan C. Williams, "Domesticity as the Dangerous Supplement of Liberalism," *Journal of Women's History*, 2 (Winter 1991), 69–88; Paula Baker, "The Domestication of Politics: Women and American Political Society, 1780–1920," *American Historical Review*, 89 (June 1984), 628–31.

5. Julian Boyd, ed., *Papers of Thomas Jefferson* (Princeton, 1950–), I, 503–05; Carole Pateman, *The Sexual Contract* (Cambridge, 1988), 3–4; Jeanne Boydston, *Home and Work: Housework, Wages, and the Ideology of Labor in the Early Republic* (New York, 1990), 44; Anne Phillips, *Engendering Democracy* (University Park, 1991), 25; Edward W. Emerson and Wallace E. Forbes, eds., *Journals of Ralph Waldo Emerson* (10 vols. Boston, 1909–14), VI, 72. *New York Herald*, April 4, 1858.

6. Stephanie McCurry, "The Politics of Yeoman Households in South Carolina," in *Divided Houses: Gender and the Civil War*, ed. Catherine Clinton and Nina Silber (New York, 1992), 31; Alice Kessler-Harris, *A Woman's Wage: Historical Meanings and Social Consequences* (Lexington, 1990), 8–10, 36; Norma Basch, *In the Eyes of the Law: Women, Marriage, and Property in Nineteenth-Century New York* (Ithaca, 1982), 17–26; Marylynn Salmon, *Women and the Law of Property in Early America* (Chapel Hill, 1986), 41–44.

7. Amy D. Stanley, "Home Life and the Morality of the Market," in *The Market Revolution in America: Social, Political, and Religious Expressions, 1800–1800*, ed. Melvyn Stokes and Stephen Conway (Charlottesville, 1996), 76–79; Elizabeth Blackmar, *Manhattan for Rent, 1785–1850* (Ithaca, 1989), 112–21; Carolyn L. Karcher, *The First Woman in the Republic: A Cultural Biography of Lydia Maria Child* (Durham, NC, 1994), 127–28; Reva B. Siegel, "Home as Work: The First Woman's Rights Claims Concerning Wives' Household Labor, 1850–1880," *Yale Law Journal*, 103 (March 1994), 1089–90; Faye E. Dudden, *Serving Women: Household Service in Nineteenth-Century America* (Middletown, CT, 1983), 1–8, 59.

8. Amy Bridges, *A City in the Republic: Antebellum New York and the Origins of Machine Politics* (New York, 1984), 56–58; Thomas Dublin, "Women and Outwork in a Nineteenth-Century New England Town," in *The Countryside in the Age of Capitalist Transformation: Essays in the Social History of Rural America*, ed. Steven Hahn and Jonathan Prude (Chapel Hill, 1985), 51–66; Mary H. Blewett, *Men, Women, and Work: Class, Gender, and Protest in the New England Shoe Industry, 1780–1910* (Urbana, 1988), 45–61; Boydston, *Home and Work*, 40, 59, 76–93; McCurry, "Politics," 28, 37.

9. Boydston, *Home and Work*, 47–55; Kessler-Harris, *A Woman's Wage*, 3–10, 36–39; Basch, *In the Eyes of the Law*, 125; Martha May, "Bread Before Roses: American Workingmen, Labor Unions and the Family Wage," in *Women, Work and Protest: A Century of U.S. Women's Labor History*, ed. Ruth Milkman (Boston, 1985), 3–7.

10. Rowland Berthoff, "Conventional Mentality: Free Blacks, Women, and Business Corporations as Unequal Persons, 1820–1870," *Journal of American History*, 76 (December 1989), 760–73; Robert J. Dinkin, *Voting in Revolutionary America: A Study of Elections in the Original Thirteen States, 1776–1789* (Westport, 1982), 41–42; Ira Berlin, *Slaves Without Masters: The Free Negro in the Antebellum South* (New York, 1974), 7, 91; Leon F. Litwack, *North of Slavery: The Negro in the Free States 1790–1860* (Chicago, 1961), 74–93.

11. Gary Nash, *Forging Freedom: The Formation of Philadelphia's Black Community 1720–1840* (New York, 1988), 172–73; Litwack, *North of Slavery*, 77; Berthoff, "Conventional Mentality," 780–83; Kenneth L. Karst, *Belonging to America: Equal Citizenship and the Constitution* (New Haven, 1989), 44–45; Priscilla Wald, "Terms of Assimilation," in *Cultures of United States Imperialism*, ed. Amy Kaplan and Donald E. Pease (Durham, NC, 1993), 64.

12. Roy F. Basler, et al., eds., *The Collected Works of Abraham Lincoln* (9 vols. New Brunswick, 1953–55), II, 405, III, 479.

13. Gary B. Nash and Jean R. Sonderlund, *Freedom by Degrees: Emancipation in Pennsylvania and Its Aftermath* (New York, 1991), 173–77.

14. Howard Lamar, "From Bondage to Contract: Ethnic Labor in the American West," in *The Countryside*, ed. Hahn and Prude, 293–326; Alexander Saxton, *The Indispensable Enemy: Labor and the Anti-Chinese Movement in California* (Berkeley, 1971), 3–8; Tomás Almaguer, *Racial Fault Lines: The Historical Origins of White Supremacy in California* (Berkeley, 1994), 131–41.

15. Nash and Sonderlund, *Freedom by Degrees*, 173–77; Gary B. Nash, *Forging Freedom: The Formation of Philadelphia's Black Community 1720–1840* (Cambridge, MA, 1988), 146; Graham R. Hodges, *New York City Cartmen, 1667–1850* (New York, 1986), 158–59; Leonard P. Curry, *The Free Black in Urban America 1800–1850* (Chicago, 1981), 260; Eric Foner, *Free Soil, Free Labor, Free Men: The Ideology of the Republican Party Before the Civil War* (New York, 1970), 261.

16. *Democratic Review*, 18 (June 1846), 434; Reginald Horsman, *Race and Manifest Destiny: The Origins of American Racial Anglo-Saxonism* (Cambridge, MA, 1981), 1–4, 146–53; Anita H. Goldman, *From Emerson to King: Democracy, Race, and the Politics of Protest* (New York, 1997), 131–32.

17. Joyce Appleby, et al., *Telling the Truth About History* (New York, 1994), 104–12; Dorothy Ross, "Grand Narrative in American Historical Writing: From Romance to Uncertainty," *American Historical Review*, 100 (June 1995), 652; Thomas Hietala, *Manifest Design: Anxious Aggrandizement in Late Jacksonian America* (Ithaca, 1985), 164–65; Major L. Wilson, *Space, Time, and Freedom: The Quest for Nationality and the Irrepressible Conflict 1815–1861* (Westport, 1974), 32.

18. Daniel W. Howe, *The Political Culture of the American Whigs* (Chicago, 1979), 38–42; Horsman, *Race and Manifest Destiny*, 190; Priscilla Wald, *Constituting Americans: Cultural Anxiety and Narrative Form* (Durham, NC, 1995), 24–39.

19. Berlin, *Slaves Without Masters*, 117–20; Ronald Takaki, *A Different Mirror: A History of Multicultural America* (Boston, 1993), 177–80; Almaguer, *Racial Fault Lines*, 4–9; Robert W. Larson, *New Mexico's Quest for Statehood 1846–1912* (Albuquerque, 1968), 124–28; Roger Daniels, *Coming to America: A History of Immigration and Ethnicity in American Life* (New York, 1990), 308.

20. U.S. Department of Commerce, Bureau of the Census, *Historical Statistics of the United States* (2 vols. Washington, DC, 1975), I, 106; Almaguer, *Racial Fault Lines*, 11; Judith N. Shklar, *American Citizenship: The Quest for Inclusion* (Cambridge, MA, 1991), 3–4; Foner, *Free Soil*, 250–53.

21. Mary H. Blewett, *Men, Women, and Work: Class, Gender, and Protest in the New England Shoe Industry, 1780–1910* (Urbana, 1988), 36–39, 123–40.

22. Kessler-Harris, *A Woman's Wage*, 27–28; Harriet H. Robinson, *Loom and Spindle; or Life Among the Early Mill Girls* (New York, 1898), 69; Ellen C. DuBois, "Outgrowing the Compact of the Fathers: Equal Rights, Woman Suffrage, and the United States Constitution, 1820–1878," *Journal of American History*, 74 (December 1987), 847; Davis in Jean Matthews, "Race, Sex, and the Dimensions of Liberty in Antebellum America," *Journal of the Early Republic*, 6 (Fall 1986), 282.

23. *Course of Popular Lectures as Delivered by Frances Wright* (New York, 1829), 52–53; Anne C. Rose, *Transcendentalism as a Social Movement, 1830–1850* (New Haven, 1981), 59–60; Stanton, *History of Woman Suffrage*, 189–90; Lydia Maria Child to Charles Sumner, July 9, 1872, Charles Sumner Papers, Houghton Library, Harvard University; *Proceedings of the Woman's Rights Convention, Held at the Broadway Tabernacle, in the City of New York* (New York, 1853), 29; Ellen C. DuBois, ed., *Elizabeth Cady Stanton Susan B. Anthony: Correspondence, Writings, Speeches* (New York, 1981), 31.

24. Stanton, *History of Woman Suffrage*, I, 842–43; DuBois, *Stanton Anthony*, 34; Joan Hoff, *Law, Gender, and Injustice* (New York, 1991), 18, 36; Nancy J. Hirschmann, "Toward a Feminist Theory of Freedom," *Political Theory*, 24, (February 1996), 46–48, 61–63; *Report of the Woman's Rights Meeting, at Mercantile Hall* (Boston, 1859), 8.

25. John L. Brooke, *The Heart of the Commonwealth: Society and Political Culture in Worcester County, Massachusetts, 1713–1861* (New York, 1989), 360; Blanche G. Hersh, *The Slavery of Sex: Feminist-Abolitionists in America* (Urbana, 1978), 9, 34, 89–90, 190; George Eliot, *Felix Holt, The Radical*, ed. Fred C. Thomson (Oxford, 1980), 45; Frances E. Olsen, "The Family and the Market: A Study of Ideology and Legal Reform," *Harvard Law Review*, 96 (May 1983), 1511.

26. Clare Midgley, *Women Against Slavery: The British Campaigns 1780–1870* (London, 1992), 27; Basch, *In the Eyes of the Law*, 120, 162; Stephanie McCurry, "The Two Faces of Republicanism: Gender and Proslavery Politics in Antebellum South Carolina," *Journal of American History*, 78 (March 1992), 1251–55.

27. Basch, *In the Eyes of the Law*, 162; Amy D. Stanley, "Conjugal Bonds and Wage Labor: Rights of Contract in the Age of Emancipation," *Journal of American History*, 75 (September 1988), 477–82; Elizabeth B. Clark, "Matrimonial Bonds: Slavery and Divorce in Nineteenth-Century America," *Law and History Review*, 8 (Spring 1990), 34–35, 48–49; Mill and Mill, *Essays*, 174; Carol A. Kolmerten, *Women in Utopia: The Ideology of Gender in American Owenite Communities* (Bloomington, 1990), 8–11, 79–94; Raymond L. Muncy, *Sex and Marriage in Utopian Communities* (Bloomington, 1973), 204; Jeanette C. and Robert H. Lauer, "Sex Roles in Nineteenth-Century American Utopian Societies," *Communal Societies*, 3 (Fall 1983), 17–25.

28. Goldman, *From Emerson to King*, 128; William H. and Jane H. Pease, eds., *The Antislavery*

Argument (Indianapolis, 1965), 68; Linda K. Kerber, "A Constitutional Right to Be Treated Like American Ladies: Women and the Obligations of Citizenship," in *U.S. History as Women's History: New Feminist Essays*, ed. Linda K. Kerber, et al. (Chapel Hill, 1995), 22; Reva B. Siegel, " 'The Rule of Love,': Wife Beating as Prerogative and Privacy," *Yale Law Journal*, 105 (June 1996), 2118–20; Henry C. Wright, *The Unwelcome Child; or, The Crime of an Undesigned and Undesired Maternity* (Boston, 1858), 86; U.S. Department of Commerce, *Historical Statistics*, I, 49.

29. Myra C. Glenn, *Campaigns Against Corporal Punishment: Prisoners, Sailors, Women, and Children in Antebellum America* (Albany, 1984), 70–71; Remond in Clare Midgley, "Anti-Slavery and Feminism in Nineteenth-Century Britain," *Gender and History*, 5 (Autumn 1993), 352; Remond in C. Peter Ripley, et al., eds., *The Black Abolitionist Papers* (5 vols. Chapel Hill, 1985–93), I, 23, 445; Kristin Hoganson, "Garrisonian Abolitionists and the Rhetoric of Gender, 1850–1860," *American Quarterly*, 45 (December 1993), 558–70.

30. Elizabeth B. Clark, "Religion, Rights, and Difference in the Early Women's Rights Movement," *Wisconsin Women's Law Journal*, 3 (1987), 29–58; Debra G. Hansen, *Strained Sisterhood: Gender and Class in the Boston Female Anti-Slavery Society* (Amherst, 1993), 143–53; Jean V. Matthews, "Consciousness of Self and Consciousness of Sex in Antebellum Feminism," *Journal of Women's History*, 5 (Spring 1993), 62–67; Basch, *In the Eyes of the Law*, 180.

31. "Social freedom" in Hersh, *Slavery of Sex*, 66; Luisa Cetti, "The Radicals and the Wrongs of Marriage: The Rutland Free Convention of 1858," in *Making, Unmaking and Remaking America: Popular Ideology Before the Civil War*, ed. Loretta V. Mannucci (Milan, 1986), 94.

32. Jonathan A. Glickstein, " 'Poverty Is Not Slavery': American Abolitionists and the Competitive Labor Market," in *Antislavery Reconsidered: New Perspectives on the Abolitionists*, ed. Lewis Perry and Michael Fellman (Baton Rouge, 1979), 207–11; Lewis Perry, "The Panorama and the Mills: A Review of 'The Letters of John Greenleaf Whittier,' " *Civil War History*, 22 (September 1976), 247; Lewis Perry, *Radical Abolitionism: Anarchy and the Government of God in Antislavery Thought* (Ithaca, 1973), 24, 51–59; *The Emancipator*, March 26, 1840.

33. Russell B. Nye, *Fettered Freedom: Civil Liberties and the Slavery Controversy 1830–1860* (East Lansing, 1949), 36–65, 98–104; Seyla Benhabib, "Models of Public Space: Hannah Arendt, the Liberal Tradition, and Jurgen Habermas," in *Habermas and the Public Sphere*, ed. Craig Calhoun (Cambridge, MA, 1992), 79; Karcher, *The First Woman*, 267; Walter M. Merrill, ed., *The Letters of William Lloyd Garrison* (6 vols. Cambridge, MA, 1971–81), IV, 160; William E. Nelson, *The Roots of American Bureaucracy, 1830–1900* (Cambridge, MA, 1982), 42–50.

34. Gilbert H. Barnes and Dwight L. Dumond, eds., *Letters of Theodore Dwight Weld, Angelina Grimké, and Sarah Grimké, 1822–1844* (2 vols. New York, 1934), I, 98; Nelson, *Roots*, 42–56.

35. Stanley N. Katz, "The Strange Birth and Unlikely History of Constitutional Equality," *Journal of American History*, 75 (December 1988), 753; Lydia Maria Child, *An Appeal in Favor of That Class of Americans Called Africans* (Boston, 1833); Celeste M. Condit and John L. Lucaites, *Crafting Equality: America's Anglo-African Word* (Chicago, 1993), 6, 61, 84–97.

36. Larry Ceplair, ed., *The Public Years of Sarah and Angelina Grimké: Selected Writings 1835–1839*

(New York, 1989), 194–95; Nelson, *Roots*, 51–52; William M. Wiecek, *The Sources of Antislavery Constitutionalism in America, 1760–1848* (Ithaca, 1977), 248–60; Harold M. Hyman and William M. Wiecek, *Equal Justice Under Law: Constitutional Development, 1835–1875* (New York, 1982), 490.

37. Philip S. Foner, ed., *The Life and Writings of Frederick Douglass* (4 vols. New York, 1950–55), I, 191, 281, III, 191; Ripley, et al., eds., *Black Abolitionist Papers*, I, 45, 54; IV, 74, 256–57; Geneviève Fabre, "African American Commemorative Celebrations in the Nineteenth Century," in *History and Memory in African-American Culture*, ed. Geneviève Fabre and Robert O'Meally (New York, 1994), 72–87; John R. McKivigan and Jason H. Silverman, "Monarchial Liberty and Republican Slavery: West Indian Emancipation Celebrations in Upstate New York and Canada," *Afro-Americans in New York Life and History*, 10 (January 1986), 10–12; Len Travers, *Celebrating the Fourth: Independence Day and the Rites of Nationalism in the Early Republic* (Amherst, 1997), 143–44; James Forten, et al., *To the Honourable the Senate and House of Representatives of the Commonwealth of Pennsylvania* (Philadelphia, 1832), 1; Paul E. Teed, "Racial Nationalism and Its Challengers: Theodore Parker, John Rock, and the Antislavery Movement," *Civil War History*, 41 (June 1995), 152–54.

38. Foner, ed., *Douglass*, IV, 167–68; J. Morgan Kousser, " 'The Supremacy of Equal Rights': The Struggle Against Racial Discrimination in Antebellum Massachusetts and the Foundations of the Fourteenth Amendment," *Northwestern University Law Review*, 82 (Summer 1988), 941–1010; Ripley, et al., eds., *Black Abolitionist Papers*, III, 6, 365–66; Jane H. and William H. Pease, *They Who Would Be Free: Blacks' Search for Freedom, 1830–1861* (New York, 1974), 3–9; Julia Griffiths, ed., *Autographs for Freedom*, ser. 2 (Auburn, 1854), 11.

39. Barbara J. Fields, *Slavery and Freedom on the Middle Ground: Maryland During the Nineteenth Century* (New Haven, 1985), 30–35; Ripley, et al., eds., *Black Abolitionist Papers*, II, 246; John H. Bracey, Jr., et al., eds., *Black Nationalism in America* (Indianapolis, 1970), 87–90; Berlin, *Slaves Without Masters*, 168, 269–71.

40. Foner, ed., *Douglass*, I, 210–11, II, 189–92; Philip S. Foner and George Walker, eds., *Proceedings of the Black State Conventions, 1840–1865* (2 vols. Philadelphia, 1979), I, 310; Eric J. Sundquist, *To Wake the Nations: Race in the Making of American Literature* (Cambridge, MA, 1993), 85; Wald, *Constituting Americans*, 92.

41. Pauline Maier, *American Scripture: Making the Declaration of Independence* (New York, 1997), 190; David Kimball, *Venerable Relic: The Story of the Liberty Bell* (Philadelphia, 1989), 38, 44, 55–60; James B. Stewart, "Boston, Abolition, and the Atlantic World, 1820–1861," in *Courage and Conscience: Black and White Abolitionists in Boston*, ed. Donald M. Jacobs (Bloomington, 1993), 102–05.

42. Yehoshua Arieli, *Individualism and Nationalism in American Ideology* (Cambridge, MA, 1964), 308–09; Basler, et al., eds., *Lincoln Works*, II, 250, 255, 405, 532, III, 95, 375–76; David F. Ericson, *The Shaping of American Liberalism: The Debates Over Ratification and Slavery* (Chicago, 1993), 70–71, 133; *Congressional Globe*, 31st Congress, 1st sess., 73.

43. Wald, *Constituting Americans*, 60; Basler, et al., eds., *Lincoln Works*, II, 255, 406, III, 374–75; Foner, *Free Soil*, 27–29.

44. Paul M. Angle, ed., *Created Equal?: The Complete Lincoln-Douglas Debates* (Chicago, 1958), 111–12; Basler, et al., eds., *Lincoln Works*, II, 405, 499–500, III, 95.

45. Vivien G. Fyrd, *Art and Empire: The Politics of Ethnicity in the United States Capitol, 1815–1860* (New Haven, 1992), 177–93; Lynda L. Crist and Mary S. Dix, eds., *The Papers of Jefferson Davis* (6 vols. Baton Rouge, 1971–89), VI, 6–7; James Epstein, "Understanding the Cap of Liberty: Symbolic Practice and Social Conflict in Early Nineteenth-Century England," *Past and Present,* 122 (February 1989), 76–88.

CHAPTER 5

1. Frank Moore, ed., *The Rebellion Record* (12 vols. New York, 1861–68), I, 44–49; James M. McPherson, *What They Fought For 1861–1865* (Baton Rouge, 1994), 9–11, 48; James M. McPherson, *For Cause and Comrades: Why Men Fought the Civil War* (New York, 1997), 19–21, 105–06.

2. Earl J. Hess, *Liberty, Virtue, and Progress: Northerners and Their War for the Union* (New York, 1988), 29; McPherson, *What They Fought For,* 30, 57–67; McPherson, *For Cause and Comrades,* 90–112, 128; Roy F. Basler, et al., eds., *The Collected Works of Abraham Lincoln* (9 vols. New Brunswick, 1953–55), V, 537.

3. Basler, et al., eds., *Lincoln Works,* VI, 301–02.

4. *National Anti-Slavery Standard,* June 3, 1865; George A. Levesque, "Boston's Black Brahmin: Dr. John S. Rock," *Civil War History,* 26 (December 1980), 336; Francis Lieber to Edward Bates, November 25, 1862, Francis Lieber Papers, Huntington Library; Herman Belz, *A New Birth of Freedom: The Republican Party and Freedmen's Rights 1861–1866* (Westport, 1976), 24; Basler, et al., eds., *Lincoln Works,* VII, 243; Charles E. Norton, ed., *Orations and Addresses of George William Curtis* (3 vols. New York, 1894), I, 172.

5. Melinda Lawson, "Patriot Fires: Loyalty and National Identity in the Civil War North," Ph.D. dissertation, Columbia University, 1998; David Potter, *The South and the Sectional Conflict* (Baton Rouge, 1968), 56; *Congressional Record,* 43d Congress, 1st sess., 4116; Frank Friedel, *Francis Lieber: Nineteenth-Century Liberal* (Baton Rouge, 1947), 302; Edward E. Hale, *The Man Without a Country and Other Stories* (Boston, 1898).

6. Mark E. Neely, *The Fate of Liberty: Abraham Lincoln and Civil Liberties* (New York, 1991), 52–67, 116–30, 176–77, 206; *New York Times,* May 28, 1863; David H. Donald, *Lincoln* (New York, 1995), 303–04; Eric Foner, *Reconstruction: America's Unfinished Revolution 1863–1877* (New York, 1988), 15–17.

7. George M. Fredrickson, *The Inner Civil War: Northern Intellectuals and the Crisis of the Union* (New York, 1965); William J. Novak, *The People's Welfare: Law and Regulation in Nineteenth-Century America* (Chapel Hill, 1996), 241.

8. Hess, *Liberty, Virtue, Progress,* 26; Philip S. Foner, ed., *The Life and Writings of Frederick Douglass* (4 vols. New York, 1950–55), III, 214; *Congressional Globe,* 38th Congress, 1st sess., 523.

9. Wilfred M. McClay, *The Masterless: Self and Society in Modern America* (Chapel Hill, 1994), 19; George S. Phillips, *American Republic and Human Liberty Foreshadowed in Scripture* (Cincinnati, 1864); Basler, et al., eds., *Lincoln Works,* VIII, 333; Paul C. Nagel, *This Sacred Trust: American Nationality 1798–1898* (New York, 1971), 166–67; Eric Foner and Olivia Mahoney, *America's Reconstruction: People and Politics After the Civil War* (New York, 1996), 33.

10. V. Jacque Voegeli, *Free But Not Equal: The Midwest and the Negro During the Civil War* (Chicago, 1967), 162–63; Carl Schurz, *For the Great Empire of Liberty, Forward!* (New York, 1864).

11. Burke A. Hinsdale, ed., *The Works of James Abram Garfield* (2 vols. Boston, 1882–83), I, 86.

12. Foner, *Reconstruction*, 77–78; John W. Blassingame, ed., *Slave Testimony: Two Centuries of Letters, Speeches, Interviews, and Autobiographies* (Baton Rouge, 1977), 135; James Richardson, ed., *A Compilation of the Messages and Papers of the Presidents* (10 vols. Washington, DC, 1896–99), V, 3157–58.

13. Richard H. King, *Civil Rights and the Idea of Freedom* (New York, 1992), 16, 29–31; Derek Q. Reeves, "Beyond the River Jordan: An Essay on the Continuity of the Black Prophetic Tradition," *Journal of Religious Thought*, 47 (Winter–Spring 1990–91), 42–54.

14. Reginald F. Hildebrand, *The Times Were Strange and Stirring: Methodist Preachers and the Crisis of Emancipation* (Durham, NC, 1995), 32–39, 53–65; Vincent G. Harding, "Wrestling Toward the Dawn: The Afro-American Freedom Movement and the Changing Constitution," *Journal of American History*, 74 (December 1987), 723; Foner, *Reconstruction*, 3–4.

15. Foner, ed., *Douglass*, IV, 159, 167; Foner, *Reconstruction*, 110–12, 291; Earl S. Miers, ed., *When the World Ended: The Diary of Emma LeConte* (New York, 1957), 113–15; Elsa Barkley Brown, "Negotiating and Transforming the Public Sphere: African American Political Life in the Transition from Slavery to Freedom," *Public Culture*, 7 (Fall 1994), 115.

16. "Colloquy with Colored Ministers," *Journal of Negro History*, 16 (January 1931), 88–94; Merrimon Howard to Adelbert Ames, November 28, 1873, Ames Family Papers, Sophia Smith Collection, Smith College.

17. James O. Robertson, *American Myth, American Reality* (New York, 1980), 98–99; Gyora Binder, "Did the Slaves Author the Thirteenth Amendment? An Essay in Redemptive History," *Yale Journal of Law and the Humanities*, 5 (Summer 1993), 471–505.

18. J. William Harris, *Plain Folk and Gentry in a Slave Society: White Liberty and Black Slavery in Augusta's Hinterlands* (Middletown, CT, 1985), 184; Sidney Andrews, "Three Months Among the Reconstructionists," *Atlantic Monthly*, 16 (February 1866), 243–44; Foner, *Reconstruction*, 129, 134, 198–201; Brown, "Public Sphere," 117.

19. H. S. Beals to Samuel Hunt, December 30, 1865, American Missionary Association Archives, Amistad Research Center, Tulane University; Lea S. Vander Velde, "The Labor Vision of the Thirteenth Amendment," *University of Pennsylvania Law Review*, 138 (December 1989), 437–504; *Congressional Globe*, 38th Congress, 1st sess., 1962, 2d sess., 193, 215.

20. *Congressional Globe*, 38th Congress, 1st sess., 343; 39th Congress, 1st sess., 42, 111, 343, 474; Celeste M. Condit and John L. Lucaites, *Crafting Equality: America's Anglo-African Word* (Chicago, 1993), 8; Foner, *Reconstruction*, 243–45.

21. *Congressional Globe*, 39th Congress, 1st sess., 1833; William S. Burns to Henry M. Haight, October 28, 1867, Henry M. Haight Papers, Huntington Library; Foner, *Reconstruction*, 256–59, 446.

22. Foner, *Reconstruction*, 24; Frederic Bancroft, ed., *Speeches, Correspondence and Political Papers of Carl Schurz* (6 vols. New York, 1913), I, 487–88; Akhil R. Amar, *The Bill of Rights: Creation and Reconstruction* (New Haven, 1998); Robert J. Kaczorowski, "To Begin the Nation Anew: Congress, Citizenship, and Civil Rights After the Civil War," *American*

Historical Review, 92 (February 1987), 47–49; Donald G. Nieman, "The Language of Liberation: African Americans and Equalitarian Constitutionalism, 1830–1950," in *The Constitution, Law, and American Life: Critical Aspects of the Nineteenth-Century Experience*, ed. Donald G. Nieman (Athens, GA, 1992), 67–90.

23. John Rawls, *Political Liberalism* (New York, 1993), 238–39; Foner, *Reconstruction*, 250, 278–79.

24. Douglass in Philip S. Foner and Daniel Rosenberg, eds., *Racism, Dissent, and Asian Americans from 1850 to the Present* (Westport, 1993), 223–24; Luella Gettys, *The Law of Citizenship in the United States* (Chicago, 1934), 62–69.

25. Ellen C. DuBois, ed., *Elizabeth Cady Stanton Susan B. Anthony: Correspondence, Writings, Speeches* (New York, 1981), 132; Ellen C. DuBois, "Outgrowing the Compact of the Fathers: Equal Rights, Woman Suffrage, and the United States Constitution, 1820–1878," *Journal of American History*, 74 (December 1987), 846; Jane C. Croly, *For Better or Worse* (Boston, 1875), 191; Virginia Penny, *Think and Act: A Series of Articles Pertaining to Men and Women, Work and Wages* (Philadelphia, 1869), 183.

26. DuBois, ed., *Stanton Anthony*, 98, 141; David Montgomery, *The Fall of the House of Labor: The Workplace, the State, and American Labor Activism, 1865–1925* (New York, 1987), 136–37; Steven M. Buechler, *The Transformation of the Woman Suffrage Movement: The Case of Illinois, 1850–1920* (New Brunswick, 1986), 72–78; Ruth B. Moynihan, *Rebel for Rights: Abigail Scott Duniway* (New Haven, 1983), 88; Reva B. Siegel, "Home as Work: The First Woman's Rights Claims Concerning Wives' Household Labor, 1850–1880," *Yale Law Journal*, 103 (March 1994), 1156–57.

27. DuBois, ed., *Stanton Anthony*, x–xi, 100, 132, 148, 207, Amy D. Stanley, "Conjugal Bonds and Wage Labor: Rights of Contract in the Age of Emancipation," *Journal of American History*, 75 (September 1988), 478–81; Siegel, "Home as Work," 1112.

28. Victoria Woodhull, *"And the Truth Shall Make You Free"* (New York, 1871).

29. Luisa Cetti, "The Radicals and the Wrongs of Marriage: The Rutland Free Convention of 1858," in *Making, Unmaking and Remaking America: Popular Ideology Before the Civil War*, ed. Loretta V. Mannucci (Milan, 1986), 77–94; Foner, *Reconstruction*, 520–21.

30. Foner, *Reconstruction*, 82–88; Andrew M. Kerr, *Lucy Stone: Speaking Out for Equality* (New Brunswick, 1992), 156; Elizabeth Pleck, "Feminist Responses to 'Crimes Against Women,' 1868–1896," *Signs*, 8 (Spring 1983), 456–60.

31. Barbara Epstein, *The Politics of Domesticity: Women, Evangelicism, and Temperance in Nineteenth-Century America* (Middletown, CT, 1981), 125–27; Ross E. Paulson, *Liberty, Equality, and Justice: Civil Rights, Women's Rights, and the Regulation of Business, 1865–1932* (Durham, NC, 1997), 88; Samuel Gompers, *Seventy Years of Life and Labor* (2 vols. New York, 1925), I, 54–56; Mari Jo Buhle, *Women and American Socialism, 1870–1920* (Urbana, 1981), xiv–xv; Linda K. Kerber, "A Constitutional Right to Be Treated Like American Ladies: Women and the Obligations of Citizenship," in *U.S. History as Women's History: New Feminist Essays*, ed. Linda K. Kerber, et al. (Chapel Hill, 1995), 26.

32. Martin H. Blatt, *Free Love and Anarchism: The Biography of Ezra Heywood* (Urbana, 1989), 100–18; John D'Emilio and Estelle B. Freedman, *Intimate Matters: A History of Sexuality in America* (New York, 1988), 159.

33. David W. Blight, *Frederick Douglass' Civil War: Keeping Faith in Jubilee* (Baton Rouge, 1989), 192; *Congressional Globe*, 38th Congress, 2d sess., 193, 528; Foner, *Reconstruction*, 255; Gage in Stanley, "Conjugal Bonds," 471.

34. Norma Basch, "The Emerging Legal History of Women in the United States: Property, Divorce, and the Constitution," *Signs*, 12 (Autumn 1986), 111; Ellen C. DuBois, "Taking the Law into Our Own Hands: *Bradwell, Minor,* and Suffrage Militance in the 1870s," in *Visible Women: New Essays on American Activism,* ed. Nancy A. Hewitt and Suzanne Lebsock (Urbana, 1993), 19–26; Norma Basch, "Reconstructing Female Citizenship: *Minor v. Happersett,*" in *The Constitution, Law, and American Life,* ed. Nieman, 60–61; Rogers M. Smith, *Civic Ideals: Conflicting Visions of Citizenship in U.S. History* (New Haven, 1997), 341.

35. DuBois, "Outgrowing the Compact," 848–51; Buechler, *Transformation,* 110–17; Ellen C. DuBois, *Feminism and Suffrage: The Emergence of an Independent Women's Movement in America, 1848–1869* (Ithaca, 1978), 162–202.

36. *Report of the Committee of the Senate Upon the Relations Between Labor and Capital, and Testimony Taken by the Committee* (5 vols. Washington, DC, 1885), IV, 450–51; Foner, *Reconstruction,* 346–459, 564–601, 610.

37. Foner, *Reconstruction,* 160, 245–46; George P. Rawick, ed., *The American Slave: A Composite Autobiography* (39 vols. Westport, 1972–79), Supp., ser. 2, III, 877.

CHAPTER 6

1. *New York Times,* October 29, 1886; Neil G. Kitler, "The Statue of Liberty as Idea, Symbol, and Historical Presence," and Christian Blanchet, "The Universal Appeal of the Statue of Liberty," both in *The Statue of Liberty Revisited,* ed. Wilton S. Dillon and Neil G. Kotler (Washington, DC, 1994), 1–7, 34–35; Roger A. Fischer, *Them Damned Pictures: Explorations in American Political Cartoons* (North Haven, CT, 1996), 150–62; Nancy Jo Fox, *Liberties with Liberty* (New York, 1985), 14–16.

2. Jo Ann Boydston, ed., *John Dewey: The Middle Works, 1899–1924* (15 vols. Carbondale, 1976–83), I, 6; Eric Foner, *Reconstruction: America's Unfinished Revolution, 1863–1877* (New York, 1988), 461–62; David Montgomery, *The Fall of the House of Labor: The Workplace, the State, and American Labor Activism, 1865–1925* (New York, 1987), 44–57, 112–70; John A. Garraty, *The New Commonwealth 1877–1890* (New York, 1968), 78–127.

3. Montgomery, *Fall of the House of Labor,* 46–48, 138–40; Garraty, *New Commonwealth,* 128–40; Alan Trachtenberg, *The Incorporation of America: Culture and Society in the Gilded Age* (New York, 1982), 99; Henry Demarest Lloyd, *Wealth Against Commonwealth* (New York, 1899), 517–19.

4. David Montgomery, "Workers Control of Machine Production in the 19th Century," *Labor History,* 17 (Fall 1976), 485–509; Carter Goodrich, *The Miner's Freedom* (Boston, 1925), 15–18, 39–42; Frances G. Couvares, *The Remaking of Pittsburgh: Class and Culture in an Industrializing City, 1877–1919* (Albany, 1984), 9–30; Edward Atkinson to Charles Eliot Norton, March 7, 1864, Charles Eliot Norton Papers, Houghton Library, Harvard University; *The Nation,* June 27, 1867.

5. Nancy Cohen, "The Problem of Democracy in the Age of Capital: Reconstructing American Liberalism, 1865–1890," Ph.D. dissertation, Columbia University, 1996; James L. Hutson, *To Secure the Fruits of Labor: The American Concept of the Distribution of Wealth, 1765–1900* (Baton Rouge, 1998), ch. 10; Sarah L. Watts, *Order Against Chaos: Business Culture and Labor Ideology in America, 1880–1915* (New York, 1991), 4; Allan Nevins, ed., *Selected Writings of Abram Hewitt* (New York, 1937), 277.

6. John G. Sproat, *"The Best Men": Liberal Reformers in the Gilded Age* (New York, 1968); Foner, *Reconstruction*, 488–93; Michael E. McGerr, *The Decline of Popular Politics: The American North, 1865–1928* (New York, 1986), 43–54.

7. Jonathan B. Harrison, "Limited Sovereignty in the United States," *Atlantic Monthly*, 43 (February 1879), 186; Dorman B. Eaton, "Municipal Government," *Journal of Social Science*, 5 (1873), 7; Michael Les Benedict, "Laissez-Faire and Liberty: A Re-Evaluation of the Meaning and Origins of Laissez-Faire Constitutionalism," *Law and History Review*, 3 (Fall 1985), 293–331.

8. George W. Welch to Benjamin F. Butler, May 19, 1874, Benjamin F. Butler Papers, Library of Congress; Henry S. Maine, *Ancient Law*, 10th ed. (London, 1881), 165.

9. Wells in Daniel T. Rodgers, *The Work Ethic in Industrial America 1850–1920* (Chicago, 1978), 35; White in Cohen, "Problem of Democracy," 86; *The Nation*, June 22, 1871; Foner, *Reconstruction*, 482, 490.

10. Richard Hofstadter, *Social Darwinism in American Thought* (Philadelphia, 1944), 33–59.

11. Olivier Zunz, *The Changing Face of Inequality: Urbanization, Industrial Development, and Immigrants in Detroit, 1880–1920* (Chicago, 1982), 261–62; Michael Les Benedict, "Victorian Moralism and Civil Liberty in the Nineteenth-Century United States," in *The Constitution, Law, and American Life: Critical Aspects of the Nineteenth-Century Experience*, ed. Donald G. Nieman (Athens, GA, 1992), 93–95; Stefan Collini, "The Idea of 'Character' in Victorian Political Thought," *Transactions of the Royal Historical Society*, 5 ser., 35 (1985), 39–43; Eileen Boris, " 'A Man's Dwelling House Is His Castle': Tenement House Cigarmaking and the Judicial Imperative," in *Work Engendered: Toward a New History of American Labor*, ed. Ava Baron (Ithaca, 1991), 134–35.

12. Jeffrey P. Sklansky, "The Fall of Political Economy and the Rise of Social Psychology in the United States, 1830–1930," Ph.D. dissertation, Columbia University, 1996, ch. 4; Hostadter, *Social Darwinism*, 51, 63; Robert G. McCloskey, *American Conservatism in the Age of Enterprise 1865–1910* (Cambridge, MA, 1951), 64–67; William Graham Sumner, *What Social Classes Owe to Each Other* (New York, 1883), 24; Mark A. Graber, *Transforming Free Speech: The Ambiguous Legacy of Civil Libertarianism* (Berkeley, 1991), 53.

13. William E. Forbath, "The Ambiguities of Free Labor: Labor and the Law in the Gilded Age," *Wisconsin Law Review*, 1985, 768; Charles W. McCurdy, "Justice Field and the Jurisprudence of Government-Business Relations: Some Parameters of Laissez-Faire Constitutionalism, 1863–1897," *Journal of American History*, 61 (March 1975), 970–81; Rogers M. Smith, *Civic Ideals: Conflicting Visions of Citizenship in U.S. History* (New Haven, 1997), 333.

14. Eileen Boris, *Home to Work: Motherhood and the Politics of Industrial Homework in the United States* (New York, 1994), 42–43; Forbath, "Ambiguities," 795–98; Kathryn K. Sklar, *Florence*

Kelley and the Nation's Work: The Rise of Women's Public Culture, 1830–1900 (New Haven, 1995), 234–83; Leon Fink, "Labor, Liberty, and the Law: Trade Unionism and the Problem of the American Constitutional Order," *Journal of American History*, 74 (December 1987), 909–11.

15. Melvyn Urofsky, "State Courts and Protective Legislation During the Progressive Era: A Reevaluation," *Journal of American History*, 72 (June 1985), 63–66; Philippa Strum, *Louis D. Brandeis: Justice for the People* (Cambridge, MA, 1984), 116–17; Rudolph J. R. Peritz, *Competition Policy in America 1888–1992* (New York, 1996), 45–46; John Mitchell, "The Workingman's Conception of Industrial Liberty," *American Federationist*, 17 (May 1910), 406–07.

16. Carlos A. Schwantes, "Protest in a Promised Land: Unemployment, Disinheritance, and the Origin of Labor Militancy in the Pacific Northwest, 1885–1886," *Western Historical Quarterly*, 13 (October 1982), 373–75; Leon Fink, "The New Labor History and the Powers of Historical Pessimism: Consensus, Hegemony, and the Case of the Knights of Labor," *Journal of American History*, 75 (June 1988), 115.

17. Ira Steward, *Poverty* (Boston, 1873), 4; Barry Goldberg, "Slavery, Race and the Languages of Class: 'Wage Slaves' and White 'Niggers,' " *New Politics*, n.s., 3 (Summer 1991), 71–77; Florence Kelley Wischnewetsy, *The Labour Question, Is Slavery yet Abolished? A Social Democratic Address in Memory of Thomas Paine* (London, n.d.), 5; Boston *Daily Evening Voice*, December 13, 1865; William E. Forbath, *Law and the Shaping of the American Labor Movement* (Cambridge, MA, 1991), 136–39; Fink, "Labor, Liberty, and the Law," 912; George E. McNeill, *The Labor Movement: The Problem of Today* (Boston, 1887), 161, 456, 462.

18. Leon Fink, *Workingmen's Democracy: The Knights of Labor and American Politics* (Urbana, 1983), 6; *Report of the Committee of the Senate Upon the Relations of Capital and Labor, and Testimony Taken by the Committee* (5 vols. Washington, DC, 1885), I, 49, 91, 217; Barry Goldberg, "Beyond Free Labor: Labor, Socialism, and the Idea of Wage Slavery, 1890–1920," Ph.D. dissertation, Columbia University, 1979, ch. 1; *Chicago Times*, July 31, August 10, 11, 12, 1888; John K. Ingram, *A History of Slavery and Serfdom* (London, 1895), 261.

19. Marx in Ian Shapiro, *The Evolution of Rights in Liberal Theory* (New York, 1986), 141n.; Christopher L. Tomlins, *The State and the Unions: Labor Relations, Law, and the Organized Labor Movement in America, 1880–1960* (New York, 1985), 49–51; *Haverhill Laborer*, May 15, 1886; Edward T. O'Donnell, "Henry George and the 'New Political Forces': Ethnic Nationalism, Labor Radicalism, and Politics in Gilded Age New York City," Ph.D. dissertation, Columbia University, 1995, 183; Montgomery, *Fall of the House of Labor*, 4.

20. Philip S. Foner, ed., *We, the Other People* (Urbana, 1976), 131; Nick Salvatore, *Eugene V. Debs: Citizen and Socialist* (Urbana, 1982), 153–54.

21. Lawrence Goodwyn, *Democratic Promise: The Populist Moment in America* (New York, 1976), 138; Robert W. Larson, *Populism in the Mountain West* (Albuquerque, 1986).

22. Gene Clanton, *Populism: The Humane Preference in America, 1890–1900* (Boston, 1991), 46–47; George McKenna, ed., *American Populism* (New York, 1974), 89–93.

23. McKenna, ed., *American Populism*, 89–91; Norman Pollack, ed., *The Populist Mind* (Indianapolis, 1967), 18–20, 51; Steven Hahn, *The Roots of Southern Populism: Yeoman Farmers and the Transformation of the Georgia Upcountry, 1850–1890* (New York, 1983), 285.

24. Henry George to Terence V. Powderly, April 19, 1883, Terence V. Powderly Papers,

Catholic University; John L. Thomas, *Alternative America: Henry George, Edward Bellamy, Henry Demarest Lloyd and the Adversary Tradition* (Cambridge, MA, 1983), 118–22; Charles Barker, *Henry George* (New York, 1955), 509, 519; O'Donnell, "George," 46, 324; Sklansky, "Fall of Political Economy," ch. 4; Henry George, *Progress and Poverty* (New York, 1884), 489–93.

25. John A. Kasson, *Civilizing the Machine* (New York, 1976), 196–99; Mari Jo Buhle, *Women and American Socialism, 1870–1920* (Urbana, 1981), 76–77, Edward Bellamy, *Looking Backward, 2000–1887* (New York, 1986), 188.

26. George M. Marsden, *Fundamentalism and American Culture: The Shaping of Twentieth-Century Evangelicism 1870–1925* (New York, 1980), 13–14, 36–37; Susan Curtis, *A Consuming Faith: The Social Gospel and Modern American Culture* (Baltimore, 1991), 2–9; James T. Kloppenberg, *Uncertain Victory: Social Democracy and Progressivism in European and American Thought, 1870–1920* (New York, 1986), 284.

27. David Green, *Shaping Political Consciousness: The Language of Politics in America from McKinley to Reagan* (Ithaca, 1987), 30–31; Carl Resek, ed., *The Progressives* (Indianapolis, 1967), 21; Henry S. Commager, ed., *Lester Ward and the Welfare State* (Indianapolis, 1967), xxi–xxxiv, 159–60.

28. Thomas G. Dyer, *Theodore Roosevelt and the Idea of Race* (Baton Rouge, 1980), 23–28; Collini, "Idea of 'Character,' " 31–35; John Higham, *Strangers in the Land: Patterns of American Nativism, 1860–1925* (New Brunswick, 1955), 131–47; Linda R. Monk, ed., *Ordinary Americans: U.S. History Through the Eyes of Everyday People* (Alexandria, 1994), 137.

29. Rayford Logan, *The Betrayal of the Negro: From Rutherford Hayes to Woodrow Wilson* (New York, 1965); John W. Burgess, *Reconstruction and the Constitution 1866–1876* (New York, 1902), 44–45, 133, 244–46; Woodrow Wilson, "The Reconstruction of the Southern States," *Atlantic Monthly*, 87 (January 1901), 6.

30. Philip S. Foner, ed., *The Life and Writings of Frederick Douglass* (4 vols. New York, 1950–55), IV, 430; David Howard-Pitney, *The Afro-American Jeremiad: Appeals for Justice in America* (Philadelphia, 1990), 73–83; W. E. B. Du Bois, *The Souls of Black Folk* (New York, 1903), 219; Lofgren, *The Plessy Case* (New York, 1987), 28, 193.

31. T. Alexander Aleinikoff, "Re-Reading Justice Harlan's Dissent in *Plessy* v. *Ferguson*: Freedom, Antiracism, and Citizenship," *University of Illinois Law Review* (1992, 4), 961–78; Donald G. Nieman, *Promises to Keep: African Americans and the Constitutional Order, 1776 to the Present* (New York, 1991), 359–61; George M. Fredrickson, *The Black Image in the White Mind: The Debate on Afro-American Character and Destiny, 1817–1914* (New York, 1971), 255.

32. Harold H. Koh, "Bitter Fruit of the Asian Immigration Cases," *Constitution*, 6 (Fall 1994), 69–77; Charles J. McClain, *In Search of Equality: The Chinese Struggle Against Discrimination in Nineteenth-Century America* (Berkeley, 1994), 1–4; Rudolph J. Vecoli, "The Lady and the Huddled Masses: The Statue of Liberty as a Symbol of Immigration," in *Statue of Liberty*, ed. Dillon and Kotler, 45; E. P. Hutchinson, *Legislative History of American Immigration Policy 1798–1965* (Philadelphia, 1981), 405–15; Pollack, ed., *Populist Mind*, 153.

33. Simon Patten, "The Theory of Social Forces," *Annals of the American Association of Social and Political Science*, 7, Supp. (January 1896), 143.

34. Stuart McConnell, "Reading the Flag: A Reconsideration of the Patriotic Cults of the

1890s," in *Bonds of Affection: Americans Define Their Patriotism*, ed. John Bodnar (Princeton, 1996), 102–11; Nina Silber, *The Romance of Reunion: Northerners and the South, 1865–1900* (Chapel Hill, 1993), 161; Cecelia E. O'Leary, "To Die For: The Cultural Politics of American Patriotism, 1865–1918," Ph.D. dissertation, University of California, Berkeley, 1996.

35. Silber, *Romance of Reunion*, 137–41, 178–81; Higham, *Strangers in the Land*, 76–77; E. Berkeley Tompkins, *Anti-Imperialism in the United States: The Great Debate, 1890–1920* (Philadelphia, 1970), 129, 141–44.

36. Michael H. Hunt, *Ideology and U.S. Foreign Policy* (New Haven, 1987), 17–18, 39–40; James Richardson, ed., *A Compilation of the Messages and Papers of the Presidents* (10 vols. Washington, DC, 1896–99), IX, 6398, 6467; Tony Smith, *America's Mission: The United States and the Worldwide Struggle for Democracy in the Twentieth Century* (Princeton, 1994), 43–45, 51–55.

37. Hunt, *Ideology*, 80–81; Tomás Almaguer, *Racial Fault Lines: The Historical Origins of White Supremacy in California* (Berkeley, 1994), 100–02; Christopher Lasch, *The Agony of the American Left* (New York, 1969), 19–22; Howard-Pitney, *Afro-American Jeremiad*, 54–64; Leslie H. Fishel, Jr., "The 'Negro Question' at Mohonk: Microcosm, Mirage, and Message," *New York History*, 74 (July 1993), 227–314; Robert H. Wiebe, *Self-Rule: A Cultural History of American Democracy* (Chicago, 1995), 150–54.

38. Lasch, *Agony*, 17–19; Andrew Neather, "Labor Republicanism, Race, and Popular Patriotism in the Era of Empire, 1890–1914," in *Bonds of Affection*, ed. Bodnar, 88–89; Forbath, *Law and the Shaping*, 130; Eric Arnesen, " 'Like Banquo's Ghost, It Will Not Down': The Race Question and the American Railroad Brotherhoods, 1880–1920," *American Historical Review*, 99 (December 1994), 1612, 1632–33; Michael Kazin, *The Populist Persuasion* (New York, 1995), 59–60.

39. Suzanne M. Marilley, *Woman Suffrage and the Origins of Liberal Feminism in the United States 1820–1920* (Cambridge, MA, 1996), 6–14, 159–64; Nancy F. Cott, *The Grounding of Modern Feminism* (New Haven, 1987), 19–20; Catt in Aileen S. Kraditor, *The Ideas of the Woman Suffrage Movement, 1890–1920* (New York, 1965), 125–42, 197.

40. Kraditor, *Ideas*, 52–55, 163–203; Marilley, *Woman Suffrage*, 168–73; *The Pacific Empire* (Portland), December 9, 1897; Ruth B. Moynihan, *Rebel for Rights: Abigail Scott Duniway* (New Haven, 1983), 111–13, 149, 151–52, 159–60.

41. George R. Taylor, ed., *The Turner Thesis* (Boston, 1956), 18; William Dean Howells, "The Nature of Liberty," *Forum*, 20 (December 1895), 408.

CHAPTER 7

1. *The Independent*, 54 (May 1, 1902), 1027, 1036–44, 1055, 1072.

2. Otis Pease, ed., *The Progressive Years: The Spirit and Achievement of American Reform* (New York, 1962), 3–5; H. G. Wells, *The Future in America* (New York, 1906), 82–83; Steven J. Diner, *A Very Different Age: Americans of the Progressive Era* (New York, 1998), 30–49; Eldon J. Eisenach, *The Lost Promise of Progressivism* (Lawrence, 1994), 14–15; Benjamin P. DeWitt, *The Progressive Movement* (New York, 1915), 14.

3. Edward A. Stettner, *Shaping Modern Liberalism: Herbert Croly and Progressive Thought* (Lawrence, 1993), 48–52; Gunther Roth and Wolfgang Schluchter, *Max Weber's Vision of History* (Berkeley, 1979), 201–02; Herbert Croly, *Progressive Democracy* (New York, 1914), 384.

4. Robert Westbrook, *John Dewey and American Democracy* (Ithaca, 1991), 183; Walter E. Weyl, *The New Democracy* (New York, 1912), 3, 164.

5. Milton Derber, *The American Idea of Industrial Democracy 1865–1965* (Urbana, 1970), 6–11; Nelson Lichtenstein and Howell J. Harris, eds., *Industrial Democracy in America: The Ambiguous Promise* (New York, 1993), 2–5, 28; Manly in Pease, ed., *Progressive Years*, 157–60.

6. Diner, *A Very Different Age*, 61–68; Croly, *Progressive Democracy*, 384; Walter Lippmann, *Drift and Mastery* (Madison, 1985), 59; Louis D. Brandeis, *Business—A Profession* (Boston, 1914), 18–19; Philippa Strum, *Brandeis: Beyond Progressivism* (Lawrence, 1993), 144–45; Melvin I. Urofsky and David W. Levy, eds., *Letters of Louis D. Brandeis* (5 vols. Albany, 1971–78), V, 45–46; Philippa Strum, *Louis D. Brandeis: Justice for the People* (Cambridge, MA, 1984), 151, 184–95.

7. Rogert Fagge, " 'Citizens of This Great Republic': Politics and the West Virginia Miners, 1900–1922," *International Review of Social History*, 40 (April 1995), 46–47; Philip S. Foner, ed., *Mother Jones Speaks: Collected Writings and Speeches* (New York, 1983), 87–89, 165.

8. Diner, *A Different Age*, 155–75; Cindy S. Aron, *Ladies and Gentlemen of the Civil Service* (New York, 1987), 38; Daniel T. Rodgers, *The Work Ethic in Industrial America 1850–1920* (Chicago, 1978), 55–56, 166–67; David Montgomery, "The 'New Unionism' and the Transformation of Workers' Consciousness in America, 1909–22," *Journal of Social History*, 7 (Summer 1974), 515; Samuel Gompers, "Fundamental Universal Service," *American Federationist* (November 1916), 1037–41.

9. Andrzej Walicki, *Marxism and the Leap to the Kingdom of Freedom: The Rise and Fall of the Communist Utopia* (Stanford, 1995), 1–6, 14–15; James Weinstein, *The Decline of Socialism in America 1912–1925* (New York, 1967), 16–27; Irving Howe, *World of Our Fathers* (New York, 1976), 311–24; Nick Salvatore, *Eugene V. Debs: Citizen and Socialist* (Urbana, 1982), 191; Jean Y. Tussey, ed., *Eugene V. Debs Speaks* (New York, 1972), 99, 122; Albert Fried, ed., *Socialism in America* (New York, 1970), 404; John Laslett, *Labor and the Left* (New York, 1970), 253.

10. *The Carpenter*, September 11, 1919; David G. Phillips, "Economic Independence the Basis of Freedom," *Arena*, 41 (March–June 1909), 17–19; Lawrence B. Glickman, *A Living Wage: Workers and the Making of American Consumer Society* (Ithaca, 1997); John A. Ryan, *A Living Wage*, 2nd ed. (New York, 1912), 44, 68–69; Francis L. Broderick, *Right Reverend New Dealer: John A. Ryan* (New York, 1963), 2–24.

11. James B. Atleson, *Values and Assumptions in American Labor Law* (Amherst, 1983), 12; Glickman, *A Living Wage*; Philip Davis, ed., *Immigration and Americanization* (Boston, 1920), 17; Nancy F. Cott, *The Grounding of Modern Feminism* (New Haven, 1987), 146; Mark T. Connelly, *The Response to Prostitution in the Progressive Era* (Chapel Hill, 1980), 114–18.

12. Martha May, "The Historical Problem of the Family Wage: The Ford Motor Company and the Five Dollar Day," *Feminist Studies*, 8 (Summer 1982), 404–07; Martha May, "Bread Before Roses: American Workingmen, Labor Unions and the Family

Wage," in *Women, Work and Protest: A Century of U.S. Women's Labor History*, ed. Ruth Milkman (Boston, 1985), 9–10; John Mitchell, "The Workingman's Conception of Industrial Liberty," *American Federationist*, 17 (May 1910), 405–06; Ryan, *Living Wage*, 108; Alice Kessler-Harris, *A Woman's Wage: Historical Meanings and Social Consequences* (Lexington, 1990), 11.

13. Alice Kessler-Harris, *Out to Work: A History of Wage-Earning Women in the United States* (New York, 1982), 109–26, 237; Ellen C. DuBois, *Harriot Stanton Blatch and the Winning of Woman Suffrage* (New Haven, 1997), 93–94; Charlotte Perkins Gilman, *Women and Economics* (Boston, 1898), 10–20, 152.

14. Polly W. Allen, *Building Domestic Liberty: Charlotte Perkins Gilman's Architectural Feminism* (Amherst, 1988), 5–6, 20–24, 63–75; Gilman, *Women and Economics*, 241, 270; DuBois, *Blatch*, 94–95; June Sochen, *The New Woman: Feminism in Greenwich Village, 1910–1920* (New York, 1972), 47–59.

15. Emma Goldman, *Anarchism and Other Essays* (New York, 1917), 216–17; Louise Odencranz, *Italian Women in Industry: A Study of Conditions in New York City* (New York, 1919), 176; Abraham Bisno, *Union Pioneer* (Madison, 1967), 212; Kathy Peiss, *Cheap Amusements: Working Women and Leisure in Turn-of-the-Century New York* (Philadelphia, 1986), 34–47, 62.

16. Donna Gabaccia, *From the Other Side: Women, Gender, and Immigrant Life in the U.S., 1820–1990* (Bloomington, 1994), 68–69; Howe, *World of Our Fathers*, 128, 183, 253; George J. Sánchez, *Becoming Mexican American: Ethnicity, Culture, and Identity in Chicano Los Angeles, 1900–1945* (New York, 1993), 3–5, 137–47; Gary Cross and Peter Shergold, " 'We Think We are of the Oppressed': Gender, White Collar Work, and Grievances of Late Nineteenth-Century Women," *Labor History*, 28 (Winter 1987), 38–42; Robert S. and Helen M. Lynd, *Middletown in Transition: A Study in Cultural Conflicts* (New York, 1937), 181.

17. Daniel Horowitz, *The Morality of Spending: Attitudes Toward the Consumer Society in America, 1875–1940* (Baltimore, 1985), xxiv–xxv, 30–41; Richard L. Bushman, *The Refinement of America: Persons, Houses, Cities* (New York, 1992); William Leach, *Land of Desire: Merchants, Power, and the Rise of a New American Culture* (New York, 1993), 11, 30–35, 147–48; Diner, *A Very Different Age*, 3–4; Richard W. Fox and T. Jackson Lears, eds., *The Culture of Consumption: Critical Essays in American History, 1880–1980* (New York, 1983), xi–xii.

18. Roland Marchand, *Advertising the American Dream: Making Way for Modernity, 1920–1940* (Berkeley, 1985), 160, 294–95; Stuart Ewen, *Captains of Consciousness: Advertising and the Social Roots of Consumer Culture* (New York, 1976), 28–30; Dana Frank, *Purchasing Power: Consumer Organizing, Gender, and the Seattle Labor Movement, 1919–1929* (New York, 1994), 3; *Saturday Evening Post*, September 8, 1928.

19. Warren I. Susman, *Culture as History: The Transformation of American Society in the Twentieth Century* (New York, 1984), xx; T. Jackson Lears, "From Salvation to Self-Realization," in *Culture of Consumption*, ed. Fox and Lears, 3–9; Susan Levine, "Workers' Wives: Gender, Class and Consumerism in the 1920s United States," *Gender and History*, 3 (Spring 1991), 53–54; Lippmann, *Drift and Mastery*, 53–55.

20. Helen Campbell, *Prisoners of Poverty* (Boston, 1889), 31; Kathryn K. Sklar, *Florence Kelley*

and the Nation's Work: The Rise of Women's Public Culture, 1830–1900 (New Haven, 1995), 142–51.

21. Tugwell in Horowitz, *Morality of Spending*, 30–34, Simon W. Patten, *The New Basis of Civilization* (New York, 1907), 10–15, 90–91, 220; Christopher Lasch, *The True and Only Heaven: Progress and Its Critics* (New York, 1991), 69–70.

22. Siegfried and Straus in Leach, *Land of Desire*, 266; Robert S. and Helen M. Lynd, *Middletown: A Study in American Culture* (New York, 1929), 88, 416–20; Robert H. Wiebe, *Self-Rule: A Cultural History of American Democracy* (Chicago, 1995), 134–37.

23. Ryan, *Living Wage*, 297–98; Harold E. Stearns, ed., *Civilization in the United States* (New York, 1922), 283.

24. Stephen Skowronek, *Building a New American State* (New York, 1982), 42–43; Leach, *Land of Desire*, 177; Horace Kallen, "Why Freedom Is a Problem," in *Freedom in the Modern World*, ed. Horace Kallen (New York, 1928), 13–15; Herbert Croly, *The Promise of American Life* (New York, 1914), 44–45.

25. James T. Kloppenberg, *Uncertain Victory: Social Democracy and Progressivism in European and American Thought, 1870–1920* (New York, 1986), 182; John Dewey and James Tufts, *Ethics* (New York, 1908), 439; Daniel F. Rice, *Reinhold Niebuhr and John Dewey: An American Odyssey* (Albany, 1993), 243–44; Westbrook, *John Dewey*, 37–49, 165–66; Randolph Bourne, *The Radical Will: Selected Writings 1911–1918*, ed. Olaf Hansen (New York, 1977), 252.

26. Croly, *Promise*, 23; R. Jeffrey Lustig, *Corporate Liberalism: The Origins of Modern American Political Theory, 1890–1920* (Berkeley, 1982), 129–30; John Dewey, "Philosophies of Freedom," in *Freedom in the Modern World*, ed. Kallen, 245–54; Alan Ryan, *John Dewey and the High Tide of American Liberalism* (New York, 1995), 234; John L. Recchiuti, "The Origins of American Progressivism: New York's Social Science Community 1880–1917," Ph.D. dissertation, Columbia University, 1991, 100.

27. Sarah Henry, "Progressivism and Democracy: Electoral Reform in the United States, 1888–1919," Ph.D. dissertation, Columbia University, 1995; James A. Henretta, "The Rise and Decline of 'Democratic-Republicanism': Political Rights in New York and the Several States, 1800–1915," in *Toward a Usable Past: Liberty Under State Constitutions*, ed. Paul Finkelman and Stephen E. Gottlieb (Athens, GA, 1991), 51.

28. Wiebe, *Self-Rule*, 162–64; Westbrook, *John Dewey*, xiv–xvi, 179–89; Eisenach, *Lost Promise*, 7; Lustig, *Corporate Liberalism*, 172–89.

29. Stettner, *Shaping Modern Liberalism*, 63; Lippmann, *Drift and Mastery*, 6, 45–52; Lustig, *Corporate Liberalism*, 152–54.

30. Aileen S. Kraditor, *The Ideas of the Woman Suffrage Movement, 1890–1920* (New York, 1965), 66–71; Suzanne M. Marilley, *Woman Suffrage and the Origins of Liberal Feminism in the United States 1820–1920* (Cambridge, MA, 1996), 188–92; Diner, *A Very Different Age*, 209–12.

31. Rosalind Rosenberg, *Divided Lives: American Women in the Twentieth Century* (New York, 1992), 58; Molly Ladd-Taylor, *Mother-Work: Women, Child Welfare, and the State, 1890–1930* (Urbana, 1994), 3, 43–75.

32. Ladd-Taylor, *Mother-Work*, 135–49; Gwendolyn Mink, *The Wages of Motherhood: Inequality in*

the Welfare State, 1917–1942 (Ithaca, 1995), 31–51; Linda Gordon, *Pitied But Not Entitled: Single Mothers and the History of Welfare* (New York, 1994), 58.

33. Nancy S. Erickson, "Muller v. Oregon Reconsidered: The Origin of a Sex-Based Doctrine of Liberty of Contract," *Labor History*, 30 (Spring 1989), 228–50; Strum, *Louis D. Brandeis*, 114; Susan Lehrer, *Origins of Protective Legislation for Women 1905–1925* (Albany, 1987), 1–3.

34. Gordon, *Pitied But Not Entitled*, 147–81; Mark A. Graber, *Transforming Free Speech: The Ambiguous Legacy of Civil Libertarianism* (Berkeley, 1991), 120; Broderick, *Right Reverend New Dealer*, 57–60.

35. Kathryn K. Sklar, "Two Political Cultures in the Progressive Era: The National Consumers' League and the American Association for Labor Legislation," in *U.S. History as Women's History: New Feminist Essays*, ed. Linda K. Kerber, et al. (Chapel Hill, 1995), 36–62.

36. James Gilbert, *Designing the Industrial State: The Intellectual Pursuit of Collectivism in America, 1880–1940* (Chicago, 1972), 48–49; Thomas J. Knock, *To End All Wars: Woodrow Wilson and the Quest for a New World Order* (New York, 1992), 15; Fried, *Socialism*, 391–94.

37. John W. Davidson, ed., *A Crossroads of Freedom: The 1912 Campaign Speeches of Woodrow Wilson* (New Haven, 1956), ix–x, 3–9; Woodrow Wilson, *The New Freedom* (New York, 1913), 284; Arthur S. Link, ed., *The Papers of Woodrow Wilson* (Princeton, 1966–), XX, 443, XXV, 99, 124, 228; Urofsky and Levy, eds., *Brandeis Letters*, II, 635n.

38. Davidson, ed., *Crossroads of Freedom*, 72–79, 130; Lippmann, *Drift* and Mastery, 81–84; *The Works of Theodore Roosevelt, Memorial Edition* (24 vols. New York, 1923–26), XIX, 170–76, 419–29, 519.

39. *Works of Roosevelt*, XIX, 372–76; Recchiuti, "Origins of American Progressivism," 278–95; Knock, *To End All Wars*, 23.

40. Stettner, *Shaping Modern Liberalism*, 1–3; Ronald D. Rotunda, *The Politics of Language: Liberalism as Word and Symbol* (Iowa City, 1986), 31–40.

CHAPTER 8

1. Geoffrey R. Stone, "Reflections on the First Amendment: The Evolution of the American Jurisprudence of Free Expression," *Proceedings of the American Philosophical Society*, 131 (September 1987), 251–52; Samuel Walker, *In Defense of American Liberties: A History of the ACLU* (New York, 1990), 22–29; Paul L. Murphy, *World War I and the Origin of Civil Liberties in the United States* (New York, 1979), 17, 32–36; David M. Rabban, *Free Speech in Its Forgotten Years 1870–1920* (New York, 1997); Linda C. Reilly, "The Meaning of Freedom of Speech and the Press in the Progressive Era: Historical Roots of Modern First Amendment Theory," Ph.D. dissertation, University of Utah, 1986, 268–83, 344–45; Zechariah Chaffee, *Freedom of Speech* (New York, 1920).

2. John W. Wertheimer, "Free-Speech Fights: The Roots of Modern Free-Expression Litigation in the United States," Ph.D. dissertation, Princeton University, 1992, 3–13, 112.

3. James G. Pope, "Labor's Constitution of Freedom," *Yale Law Journal*, 106 (January

1997), 942–44, 967; Rudolph J. R. Peritz, *Competition Policy in America 1888–1992* (New York, 1996), 101; Jerold S. Auerbach, *Labor and Liberty: The La Follette Committee and the New Deal* (Indianapolis, 1966), 14–15.

4. Philip S. Foner, ed., *Fellow Workers and Friends: I.W.W. Free-Speech Fights as Told by Participants* (Westport, 1981), 12–14, 20, 53 (Flynn), 134, 198; Reilly, "Meaning of Freedom of Speech," 167–82; Melvyn Dubofsky, *We Shall Be All: A History of the Industrial Workers of the World* (New York, 1969).

5. Edward Abrahams, *The Lyrical Left: Randolph Bourne, Alfred Stieglitz and the Origins of Cultural Radicalism in America* (Charlottesville, 1986), ix–xii, 2–8; Ann Daly, *Done into Dance: Isadora Duncan in America* (Bloomington, 1995); Ronald Steel, *Walter Lippmann and the American Century* (Boston, 1980), 51; Casey Blake, *Beloved Community: The Cultural Criticism of Randolph Bourne, Van Wyck Brooks, Waldo Frank, and Lewis Mumford* (Chapel Hill, 1990), 2–5, 51–52, 87; Christine Stansell, *American Moderns: Sex, Art and Radicalism, 1890–1919* (New York, 1999).

6. Leslie Fishbein, *Rebels in Bohemia: The Radicals of "The Masses"* (Chapel Hill, 1982), 74–81; Nancy F. Cott, *The Grounding of Modern Feminism* (New Haven, 1987), 3–8, 35–49, 186–93; Blanche W. Cook, ed., *Crystal Eastman on Women and Revolution* (New York, 1978), 53.

7. George Chauncey, "Long-Haired Men and Short-Haired Women: Building a Gay World in the Heart of Bohemia," in *Greenwich Village: Culture and Counterculture*, ed. Rick Beard and Leslie C. Berlowitz (New Brunswick, 1993), 151–58; Caroline F. Ware, *Greenwich Village 1920–1930* (Boston, 1935), 235–40; Linda Gordon, *Woman's Body, Woman's Right* (New York, 1976), 203; John D'Emilio and Estelle B. Freedman, *Intimate Matters: A History of Sexuality in America* (New York, 1988), 194–97, 226–29.

8. D'Emilio and Freedman, *Intimate Matters*, 231; Cook, ed., *Crystal Eastman*, 47, 56; Gordon, *Woman's Body*, 95–106; Richard Drinnon, *Rebel in Paradise: A Biography of Emma Goldman* (Boston, 1961), 121–40; Alice Wexler, *Emma Goldman: An Intimate Life* (New York, 1984) 209–15; Mark A. Graber, *Transforming Free Speech: The Ambiguous Legacy of Civil Libertarianism* (Berkeley, 1991), 53–54.

9. Ellen Chesler, *Woman of Valor: Margaret Sanger and the Birth Control Movement in America* (New York, 1992), 56–58, 97–150; Gordon, *Woman's Body*, 207–11, 229–30; Linda R. Monk, ed., *Ordinary Americans: U.S. History Through the Eyes of Everyday People* (Alexandria, 1994), 76–77.

10. Randolph Bourne, *The Radical Will: Selected Writings 1911–1918*, ed. Olaf Hansen (New York, 1977), 359; Thomas J. Knock, *To End All Wars: Woodrow Wilson and the Quest for a New World Order* (New York, 1992), viii–x; Steel, *Walter Lippmann*, 114–15; Eldon J. Eisenach, *The Lost Promise of Progressivism* (Lawrence, 1994), 249–52; Blake, *Beloved Community*, 159; Robert Westbrook, *John Dewey and American Democracy* (Ithaca, 1991), 236–37; David M. Kennedy, *Over Here: The First World War and American Society* (New York, 1980), 50.

11. Kennedy, *Over Here*, 126–38, 267–74; Alan Dawley, *Struggles for Justice: Social Responsibility and the Liberal State* (Cambridge, MA, 1991), 194–207; Steven J. Diner, *A Very Different Age: Americans of the Progressive Era* (New York, 1998), 234–46.

12. Alfred Fried, ed., *Socialism in America* (Garden City, NY, 1970), 521–27; *Complete Report of the Chairman of the Committee on Public Information* (Washington, DC, 1920), 2; James R.

Mock and Cedric Larson, *Words That Won the War: The Story of the Committee on Public Information 1917–1919* (Princeton, 1939), 5–7, 113–25, 158–66, 183; George T. Blakey, *Historians on the Homefront: American Propagandists for the Great War* (Lexington, 1970), 3–4, 16–35; Bernays in Michael Kazin, *The Populist Persuasion* (New York, 1995), 69–70.

13. Mock and Larson, *Words That Won the War*, 6–7, 190–98, 211; Stephen Vaughan, *Holding Fast the Inner Lines: Democracy, Nationalism, and the Committee on Public Information* (Chapel Hill, 1980), 5–6, 24–35, 56; Peter Novick, *That Noble Dream: The "Objectivity Question" and the American Historical Profession* (New York, 1988), 129; David Montgomery, *The Fall of the House of Labor: The Workplace, the State, and American Labor Activism, 1865–1925* (New York, 1987), 417–18; Steven Fraser, *Labor Will Rule: Sidney Hillman and the Rise of American Labor* (New York, 1991), 123–28.

14. David Green, *Shaping Political Consciousness: The Language of Politics in America from McKinley to Reagan* (Ithaca, 1987), 79–91; Vaughan, *Holding Fast*, 186; Rudolph J. Vecoli, "The Lady and the Huddled Masses: The Statue of Liberty as a Symbol of Immigration," in *The Statue of Liberty Revisited: Making a Universal Symbol*, ed. Wilton S. Dillon and Neil G. Kotler (Washington, DC, 1994), 53; Shawn Aubitz and Gail E. Stern, "Americans All! Ethnic Images in World War I Posters," *Prologue*, 19 (Spring 1987), 41–45; Murphy, *World War I*, 15.

15. Robert B. Fowler, *Carrie Catt: Feminist Politician* (Boston, 1986), 139–49; Christine Lunardini, *From Equal Suffrage to Equal Rights; Alice Paul and the National Woman's Party, 1910–1928* (New York, 1986), 1–17, 132–45; Cott, *Feminism*, 59–69; Robert H. Wiebe, *Self-Rule: A Cultural History of American Democracy* (Chicago, 1995), 168.

16. Ralph E. Luker, *The Social Gospel in Black and White: American Racial Reform, 1885–1912* (Chapel Hill, 1991), 1.

17. W. E. B. Du Bois, "This Freedom," manuscript speech, March 1950, W. E. B. Du Bois Papers, University of Massachusetts, Amherst; David L. Lewis, ed., *W. E. B. Du Bois: A Reader* (New York, 1995), 367.

18. William Jordan, " 'The Damnable Dilemma': African-American Accommodation and Protest during World War I," *Journal of American History*, 81 (March 1995), 1562–83; *The Crisis*, September 1917; Steven A. Reich, "Soldiers of Democracy: Black Texans and the Fight for Citizenship, 1917–1921," *Journal of American History*, 82 (March 1996), 1478–80.

19. Gilbert Osofsky, *Harlem: The Making of a Ghetto* (New York, 1965), 22–23; Peter Gottlieb, "Rethinking the Great Migration: A Perspective from Pittsburgh," in *The Great Migration in Historical Perspective: New Dimensions of Race, Class, and Gender*, ed. Joe M. Trotter, Jr. (Bloomington 1991), 70–72; James R. Grossman, *Land of Hope: Chicago, Black Southerners, and the Great Migration* (Chicago, 1989), 13; Milton C. Sernett, *Bound for the Promised Land: African American Religion and the Great Migration* (Durham, NC, 1997), 3, 57–60; Neil McMillen, *Dark Journey: Black Mississippians in the Age of Jim Crow* (Urbana, 1989), 263–65.

20. Alain Locke, *The New Negro: An Interpretation* (New York, 1925), 6; Grossman, *Land of Hope*, 259–60; Neil Betten and Raymond Mohl, "The Evolution of Racism in an Industrial City, 1906–1940: A Case Study of Gary, Indiana," *Journal of Negro History*, 59 (January 1974), 60; John Bodnar, et al., *Lives of Their Own: Blacks, Italians, and Poles in Pittsburgh,*

1900–1960 (Urbana, 1982), 242–48; Kevin K. Gaines, *Uplifting the Race: Black Leadership, Politics, and Culture in the Twentieth Century* (Chapel Hill, 1996), 235; Reich, "Soldiers of Democracy," 1502; N. Gordon Levin, Jr., *Woodrow Wilson and World Politics: America's Response to War and Revolution* (New York, 1968), 242–47.

21. *The Crisis*, February 1920; Amy Jacques-Garvey, ed., *Philosophy and Opinions of Marcus Garvey* (2 vols. New York, 1923–25), I, 94–96; Adele Oltman, "Sacred Mission, Worldly Ambition: A Social History of Black Baptists in Savannah, Georgia, 1918–1939," Ph.D. dissertation, Columbia University, 1998, ch. 1.

22. Samuel Gompers, *Seventy Years of Life and Labor* (2 vols. New York, 1925), II, 385; Joseph A. McCartin, " 'An American Feeling': Workers, Managers, and the Struggle Over Industrial Democracy in the World War I Era," in *Industrial Democracy in America: The Ambiguous Promise*, ed. Nelson Lichtenstein and Howell J. Harris (New York, 1993), 69–73; Montgomery, *Fall of the House of Labor*, 332; Fraser, *Labor Will Rule*, 144.

23. Carl H. Chrislock, *Watchdog of Loyalty: The Minnesota Commission of Public Safety During World War I* (St. Paul, 1991), 62; Fernando Fasce, "Freedom in the Workplace? Immigrants at the Scovill Manufacturing Company, 1915–1921," in *In the Shadow of the Statue of Liberty: Immigrants, Workers, and Citizens in the American Republic, 1880–1920*, ed. Marianne Debouzy (Urbana, 1992), 104–05; Jacqueline D. Hall, et al., *Like a Family: The Making of a Southern Cotton Mill World* (Chapel Hill, 1987), 186–94; David A. Corbin, *Life, Work, and Rebellion in the Coal Fields: The Southern West Virginia Miners 1880–1922* (Urbana, 1981), 176–90, 241–47; Pope, "Labor's Constitution," 945.

24. David Brody, *Steelworkers in America: The Nonunion Era* (Cambridge, MA, 1960), 180–242; Ewa Morawska, "From Myth to Reality: America in the Eyes of East European Peasant Migrant Laborers," in *Distant Magnets: Expectations and Realities in the Immigrant Experience, 1840–1930*, ed. Dirk Hoerder and Horst Rössler (New York, 1993), 245–46; Irving Howe, *World of Our Fathers* (New York, 1976), 35; Camille Guerin-Gonzales, *Mexican Workers and American Dreams: Immigration, Repatriation, and California Farm Labor, 1900–1939* (New Brunswick, 1994), 2–4; John A. Fitch, *The Steel Workers* (New York, 1911), 11–12; John A. Fitch, "The Closed Shop," *Survey*, 43, November 8, 1919, 91.

25. Bourne, *Radical Will*, 307–08, 338–45; John P. Diggins, *The Promise of Pragmatism: Modernism and the Crisis of Knowledge and Authority* (Chicago, 1994), 252–54.

26. Murphy, *World War I*, 25–30, 72–83, 99–118; Graber, *Transforming Free Speech*, 75; Jean Y. Tussey, ed., *Eugene V. Debs Speaks* (New York, 1972), 251–62, 281–88; Lucas A. Powe, Jr., *The Fourth Estate and the Constitution: Freedom of the Press in America* (Berkeley, 1991), 73–76.

27. Walker, *Defense of American Liberties*, 25; William Preston, Jr., *Aliens and Dissenters: Federal Suppression of Radicals, 1903–1933* (Cambridge, MA, 1963), 118–50; Rudolph J. Vecoli, " 'Free Country': The American Republic Viewed by the Italian Left, 1880–1920," in *Statue of Liberty*, ed. Debouzy, 37–38.

28. Walker, *Defense of American Liberties*, 43; Murphy, *World War I*, 128–30; Chrislock, *Watchdog of Loyalty*, 57–60, 89–90, 114–17, 270; Kennedy, *Over Here*, 54.

29. Walter Lippmann, "The Basic Problem of Democracy," *Atlantic Monthly*, 124 (November 1919), 616; Arthur S. Link, ed., *The Papers of Woodrow Wilson* (Princeton, 1966–),

XLIV, 272, 393–94; Murphy, *World War I*, 138–50; R. Jeffrey Lustig, *Corporate Liberalism: The Origins of Modern American Political Theory, 1890–1920* (Berkeley, 1982), 148; Powe, *Fourth Estate*, 69.

30. Richard W. Fox, *Reinhold Niebuhr: A Biography* (New York, 1985), 57–59; *The Nation*, July 4, 1923; Walker, *Defense of American Liberties*, 71; D. H. Lawrence, *Studies in Classic American Literature* (New York, 1923), 4.

31. McCartin, " 'An American Feeling,' " 79–80; Lizabeth Cohen, *Making a New Deal: Industrial Workers in Chicago, 1919–1939* (New York, 1990), 163–209; Lyman P. Powell, ed., *The Social Unrest: Capital, Labor, and the Public in Turmoil* (2 vols. New York, 1919), I, 133–35; Dana Frank, *Purchasing Power: Consumer Organizing, Gender, and the Seattle Labor Movement, 1919–1929* (New York, 1994), 96–110.

32. Lois Quam and Peter J. Rachleff, "Keeping Minneapolis an Open-Shop Town: The Citizens' Alliance in the 1930s," *Minnesota History*, 50 (Fall 1986), 105–06; Frank, *Purchasing Power*, 1–2, 139–46; Hall, *Like a Family*, 200–13; Bryant Simon, "Prelude to the New Deal: The Political Response of South Carolina Textile Workers to the Great Depression, 1929–1933," in *Race, Class, and Community in Southern Labor History*, ed. Gary N. Fink and Merl E. Reed (Tuscaloosa, 1994), 41–45.

33. Susan Lehrer, *Origins of Protective Legislation for Women 1905–1925* (Albany, 1987), 70–73; Molly Ladd-Taylor, *Mother-Work: Women, Child Welfare, and the State, 1890–1930* (Urbana, 1994), 93–95; Joan G. Zimmerman, "The Jurisprudence of Equality: The Women's Minimum Wage, the First Equal Rights Amendment, and *Adkins v. Children's Hospital*, 1905–1923," *Journal of American History*, 78 (June 1991), 190, 221–22 (Kelley).

34. Lehrer, *Origins*, 107–12, 174; Cott, *Feminism*, 70; Ellen C. DuBois, *Harriot Stanton Blatch and the Winning of Woman Suffrage* (New Haven, 1997), 224–29; Zimmerman, "Jurisprudence of Equality," 207–17; Florence Kelley, *Twenty Questions About the Federal Amendment Proposed by the National Woman's Party* (New York, 1922), 4–6; Linda Gordon, *Pitied But Not Entitled: Single Mothers and the History of Welfare* (New York, 1994), 94.

35. Fishbein, *Rebels in Bohemia*, 158–59; Alice Kessler-Harris, *Out to Work: A History of Wage-Earning Women in the United States* (New York, 1982), 224–26; Stuart Ewen, *Captains of Consciousness: Advertising and the Social Roots of Consumer Culture* (New York, 1976), 160–61; Roland Marchand, *Advertising the American Dream: Making Way for Modernity, 1920–1940* (Berkeley, 1985), 172–74; Ruth S. Cowan, "Two Washes in the Morning and a Bridge Party at Night: The American Housewife Between the Wars," in *Decades of Discontent: The Women's Movement, 1920–1940* (Westport, 1983), 177–82; *Give Me Liberty* (Cleveland, 1969), 56.

36. Horace Kallen, *Culture and Democracy in the United States* (New York, 1924), 10; Westbrook, *John Dewey*, 278–86; Andrew Feffer, *The Chicago Pragmatists and American Progressivism* (Ithaca, 1993), 1–2; Wiebe, *Self-Rule*, 173–77; Marchand, *Advertising*, 66–68.

37. Christopher Lasch, *The True and Only Heaven: Progress and Its Critics* (New York, 1991), 363–64; Steel, *Walter Lippmann*, 180–83; Westbrook, *John Dewey*, 294–99; Jo Ann Boydston, ed., *John Dewey: The Later Works, 1925–1953* (17 vols. Carbondale, 1981–90), II, 308.

38. Edward A. Stettner, *Shaping Modern Liberalism: Herbert Croly and Progressive Thought* (Lawrence, 1993), 111–15; Murphy, *World War I* passim.

39. Murphy, *World War I*, 9, 153–68, 175; Walker, *Defense of American Liberties*, 3–4, 11, 21; Alan Ryan, *John Dewey and the High Tide of American Liberalism* (New York, 1995), 169.

40. Walker, *Defense of American Liberties*, 26–27; Graber, *Transforming Free Speech*, 36, 106–08; David Riesman, "Civil Liberties in a Period of Transition," in *Public Policy*, ed. C. J. Freidrich and Edward S. Mason (Cambridge, MA, 1942), 36–37; Philippa Strum, *Louis D. Brandeis: Justice for the People* (Cambridge, MA, 1984), 314–20.

41. Henry J. Abraham, *Freedom and the Court: Civil Rights and Liberties in the United States*, 5th ed. (New York, 1988), 67–69; Rochelle Gurstein, *The Repeal of Reticence* (New York, 1996), 109–10, 209.

42. Strum, *Louis D. Brandeis*, 327–28; Vincent Blasi, "The First Amendment and the Ideal of Civic Courage: The Brandeis Opinion in *Whitney v. California*," *William & Mary Law Review*, 29 (Summer 1988), 655, 664–65, 696–97; Walker, *Defense of American Liberties*, 90.

43. Sarah Henry, "Progressivism and Democracy: Electoral Reform in the United States, 1888–1919," Ph.D. dissertation, Columbia University, 1995, 311–12; Eileen Boris, *Home to Work: Motherhood and the Politics of Industrial Homework in the United States* (New York, 1994), 119; Walter E. Weyl, *The New Democracy* (New York, 1912), 345–46; David L. Lewis, *W. E. B. Du Bois: Biography of a Race, 1868–1919* (New York, 1993), 395.

44. Tomas G. Dyer, *Theodore Roosevelt and the Idea of Race* (Baton Rouge, 1980), 16–19, 70–80, 100–09; Lewis, *W. E. B. Du Bois*, 422–23; Link, ed., *Wilson Papers*, XXIII, 551–52, XXIV, 112; Desmond King, *Separate and Unequal: Black Americans and the U.S. Federal Government* (Oxford, 1995), 11–14, 28–31, 107–08; Gaines, *Uplifting the Race*, 215.

45. U.S. Immigration Commission, *Dictionary of Races or Peoples* (Washington, DC, 1911), 81–85; Madison Grant, *The Passing of the Great Race* (New York, 1916); Judith Stein, "Defining the Race, 1890–1930," in *The Invention of Ethnicity*, ed. Werner Sollors (New York, 1989), 78–80.

46. Rivka S. Lissak, *Pluralism and Progressives: Hull House and the New Immigrants, 1890–1919* (Chicago, 1989), 25–34; Olivier Zunz, *The Changing Face of Inequality: Urbanization, Industrial Development, and Immigrants in Detroit, 1880–1920* (Chicago, 1982), 311–13; Gary Gerstle, *Working-Class Americanism: The Politics of Labor in a Textile City, 1914–1960* (New York, 1989), 43–44.

47. William Griffith, ed., *The Roosevelt Policy* (3 vols. New York, 1919), III, 887–89; John Higham, *Strangers in the Land* (New Brunswick, 1955), 242–55; James R. Barrett, "Americanization from the Bottom Up: Immigration and the Remaking of the Working Class in the United States, 1880–1930," *Journal of American History*, 79 (December 1992), 1018; William G. Ross, *Forging New Freedoms: Nativism, Education, and the Constitution, 1917–1927* (Lincoln, 1994), 61–68, 148; Ronald Edsforth, *Class Conflict and Cultural Consensus: The Making of a Mass Consumer Society in Flint, Michigan* (New Brunswick, 1987), 102–04; John F. McClymer, "Gender and the 'American Way of Life': Women in the Americanization Movement," *Journal of American Ethnic History*, 10 (Spring 1991), 3.

48. Paul McBride, *Culture Class: Immigrants and Reformers, 1880–1920* (San Francisco, 1975), 27; Powell, *The Social Unrest*, II, 663–71; Gwendolyn Mink, *The Wages of Motherhood: Inequality in the Welfare State, 1917–1942* (Ithaca, 1995), 23–26.

49. Leonard J. Moore, *Citizen Klansmen: The Ku Klux Klan in Indiana, 1921–1928* (Chapel Hill,

1991); Nancy MacLean, *Behind the Mask of Chivalry: The Making of the Second Ku Klux Klan* (New York, 1994).

50. Higham, *Strangers in the Land*, 311–13; Thomas F. Gossett, *Race: The History of an Idea in America* (Dallas, 1963), 405–07.

51. Virginia Sapiro, "Women, Citizenship, and Nationality: Immigration and Naturalization Policies in the United States," *Politics and Society*, 13 (March 1984), 1–14; Mae M. Ngai, "Illegal Aliens and Alien Citizens: U.S. Immigration Policy and Racial Formation, 1924–1965," Ph.D. dissertation, Columbia University, 1998, ch. 1.

52. Kallen in Philip Gleason, *Speaking of Diversity: Language and Ethnicity in Twentieth-Century America* (Baltimore, 1992), 19–20, 147–54; *Brandeis on Zionism* (New York, 1942), 3–11; Bourne, *Radical Will*, 248–56; David A. Hollinger, *In the American Province: Studies in the History and Historiography of Ideas* (Bloomington, 1985), 56–65; Elazar Barkan, *The Retreat of Scientific Racism: Changing Concepts of Race in Britain and the United States Between the World Wars* (New York, 1992), 76–95.

53. Gleason, *Speaking of Diversity*, 57; Lynn Dumenil, *The Modern Temper: America in the Twenties* (New York, 1995), 250–83; John J. Bukowczyk, *And My Children Did Not Know Me: A History of the Polish Americans* (Bloomington, 1987), 70; McClymer, "Gender and Americanization," 7.

54. Cohen, *Making a New Deal*, 55–64, 100–17; Barrett, "Americanization from the Bottom Up," 1004–06; Maddalena Tirabassi, "Not to Be Afraid, Rosa's Travel," *Quaderni dei Nuovi Annali*, 31 (1993), 603–13; Elizabeth Ewen, *Immigrant Women in the Land of Dollars: Life and Culture on the Lower East Side, 1890–1925* (New York, 1985), 15–16; Bruce Stave and John F. Sutherland, eds., *From the Old Country: An Oral History of European Migration to America* (New York, 1994), 158.

55. Ross, *Forging New Freedoms*, 3–6, 115–30, 148–89; Martha Minow, "We, the Family: Constitutional Rights and American Families," *Journal of American History*, 74 (December 1987), 963–64.

56. Horace M. Kallen, ed., *Freedom in the Modern World* (New York, 1928), viii–xi, 1, 17, 23–24, 29–33, 159–61, 250.

57. *The Public Papers of the Presidents: Herbert Hoover 1929* (Washington, DC, 1974), 1.

CHAPTER 9

1. Anthony Badger, *The New Deal: The Depression Years, 1933–1940* (New York, 1989), 11–65; William E. Leuchtenberg, *Franklin D. Roosevelt and the New Deal* (New York, 1963), 102; Robert S. McElvaine, ed., *Down and Out in the Great Depression: Letters from the "Forgotten Man"* (Chapel Hill, 1983), 17–19.

2. Alan Dawley, *Struggles for Justice: Social Responsibility and the Liberal State* (Cambridge, MA, 1991), 342; Samuel I. Rosenman, ed., *The Public Papers and Addresses of Franklin Delano Roosevelt* (13 vols. New York, 1938–50), V, 233; Robert S. Lynd and Helen M. Lynd, *Middletown in Transition: A Study in Cultural Conflicts* (New York, 1937), 413; Leuchtenberg, *Roosevelt and the New Deal*, 18–22; Irwin Edman, *Fountainheads of Freedom* (New York, 1941), 7, 186.

3. Francis L. Broderick, *Right Reverend New Dealer: John A. Ryan* (New York, 1963), 195.

4. Lizabeth Cohen, *Making a New Deal: Industrial Workers in Chicago, 1919–1939* (New York, 1990), 261–71; Leuchtenberg, *Roosevelt and the New Deal*, 24.

5. Gerald Markowitz and David Rosner, eds., *"Slaves of the Depression": Workers' Letters About Life on the Job* (Ithaca, 1987), 1, 19, 103–04, 178; McElvaine, *Down and Out*, 195, 208.

6. Terry A. Cooney, *Balancing Acts: American Thought and Culture in the 1930s* (New York, 1995), 10, 44; David J. O'Brien, *American Catholics and Social Reform: The New Deal Years* (New York, 1968), 46–51, Aaron I. Abell, ed., *American Catholic Thought on Social Questions* (Indianapolis, 1968), 378–80; Herbert Agar, *Land of the Free* (Boston, 1935); Archibald MacLeish, *Land of the Free* (New York, 1938), 7–8, 84–86; Frederick Heimberger, "Our Outworn Civil Liberties," *Christian Century*, April 22, 1936; McElvaine, *Down and Out*, 11–12; John Dewey, *Liberalism and Social Action* (New York, 1935), 48.

7. Robert H. Zieger, *The CIO 1935–1955* (Chapel Hill, 1995), 1–2; *Steel Labor*, August 1, 1936; Kenneth Casebeer, "Alaquippa: The Company Town and Contested Power in the Construction of Law," *Buffalo Law Review*, 43 (Winter 1995), 645, 665–66; Steven Fraser, *Labor Will Rule: Sidney Hillman and the Rise of American Labor* (New York, 1991), 260–64; Ronald Edsforth, *Class Conflict and Cultural Consensus: The Making of a Mass Consumer Society in Flint, Michigan* (New Brunswick, 1987), 175; Patrick Renshaw, *American Labour and Consensus Capitalism, 1935–1990* (London, 1991), 14–21.

8. Steve Fraser, "The 'Labor Question,' " in *The Rise and Fall of the New Deal Order, 1930–1980*, ed. Steve Fraser and Gary Gerstle (Princeton, 1989), 78; John Dewey, *Individualism Old and New* (New York, 1930), 54; Zieger, *CIO*, 13–15, 118; John L. Lewis, "The Battle for Industrial Democracy," *Vital Speeches of the Day*, July 15, 1936, 678; Ronald W. Schatz, *The Electrical Workers: A History of Labor at General Electric and Westinghouse 1923–60* (Urbana, 1983), 114–21; Joshua B. Freeman, *In Transit: The Transport Workers Union in New York City, 1933–1966* (New York, 1989), 127; Gary Gerstle, *Working-Class Americanism: The Politics of Labor in a Textile City, 1914–1960* (New York, 1989), 182–83, 207–12; David Brody, "Workplace Contractualism in Comparative Perspective," in *Industrial Democracy in America: The Ambiguous Promise*, ed. Nelson Lichtenstein and Howell J. Harris (New York, 1993), 179.

9. Cohen, *Making a New Deal*, 2–3; Michael Kazin, *The Populist Persuasion* (New York, 1995), 112–32, 138–39; T. Harry Williams, *Huey Long* (New York, 1969), 692–701; Alan Brinkley, *Voices of Protest: Huey Long, Father Coughlin, and the Great Depression* (New York, 1982); Linda Gordon, *Pitied But Not Entitled: Single Mothers and the History of Welfare* (New York, 1994), 215–30.

10. Richard Hofstadter, *The American Political Tradition* (New York, 1948), 315–52; Rosenman, ed., *Public Papers*, I, 742–56; Alonzo L. Hamby, *Liberalism and Its Challengers: FDR to Reagan* (New York, 1985), 23–28; Leuchtenberg, *Roosevelt and the New Deal*, 167–97.

11. Colin Gordon, *New Deals: Business, Labor, and Politics in America, 1920–1935* (New York, 1994), 299; J. Joseph Huthmacher, *Senator Robert F. Wagner and the Rise of Urban Liberalism* (New York, 1968), 131–33; Ronald Steel, *Walter Lippmann and the American Century* (Boston, 1980), 308.

12. James P. Young, *Reconsidering American Liberalism: The Troubled Odyssey of the Liberal Idea* (Boul-

der, 1996), 170–71; David Green, *Shaping Political Consciousness: The Language of Politics in America from McKinley to Reagan* (Ithaca, 1987), 119; Dorothy Thompson, "Women and Freedom," *Vital Speeches of the Day*, December 16, 1935, 155; James MacGregor Burns, *Roosevelt: The Lion and the Fox* (New York, 1956), 264–88; Rosenman, ed., *Public Papers*, III, 422; VI, 122–23; VII, 232–34, 246–47; Howard Zinn, ed., *New Deal Thought* (Indianapolis, 1966), 121–22.

13. Richard Oestereicher, "Urban Working-Class Political Behavior and Theories of American Electoral Politics, 1870–1940," *Journal of American History*, 74 (March 1988), 1264, 1283; George Soule, *The Future of Liberty* (New York, 1936), 53–54, 118–20, 149–50; Ronald D. Rotunda, *The Politics of Language: Liberalism as Word and Symbol* (Iowa City, 1986), 15–17, 55–64; Russell Kirk and James McClellan, *The Political Principles of Robert A. Taft* (New York, 1967), 34–36; W. J. Cameron, "Industrial Freedom," *Vital Speeches of the Day*, December 1, 1938, 122; Milton Derber, *The American Idea of Industrial Democracy, 1865–1965* (Urbana, 1970), 357.

14. Herbert Hoover, "Holy Crusade for Liberty," *Vital Speeches of the Day*, June 15, 1936, 570–73; Herbert Hoover, *Further Addresses Upon the American Road* (New York, 1940), 7; Green, *Shaping Political Consciousness*, 121.

15. William E. Leuchtenberg, *The Supreme Court Reborn: The Constitutional Revolution in the Age of Roosevelt* (New York, 1995), 216–23; Rudolph J. R. Peritz, *Competition Policy in America 1888–1992* (New York, 1996), 163.

16. Frances Perkins, *The Roosevelt I Knew* (New York, 1946), 282–83; Gordon, *Pitied But Not Entitled*, 3–11, 253–55; Alice Kessler-Harris, "Designing Women and Old Fools: The Construction of the Social Security Amendments of 1939," in *U.S. History as Women's History: New Feminist Essays*, ed. Linda K. Kerber, et al. (Chapel Hill, 1995), 88–106; Frank Freidel, *Franklin D. Roosevelt: A Rendezvous with Destiny* (Boston, 1990), 150; Gwendolyn Mink, *The Wages of Motherhood: Inequality in the Welfare State, 1917–1942* (Ithaca, 1995), 135–37.

17. Alice Kessler-Harris, *Out to Work: A History of Wage-Earning Women in the United States* (New York, 1982), 250–72; Nancy F. Gabin, *Feminism in the Labor Movement: Women and the United Auto Workers, 1935–1975* (Ithaca, 1990), 36–37; Mink, *Wages of Motherhood*, 126–33; Markowitz and Rosner, *Slaves of the Depression*, 65.

18. Gordon, *Pitied But Not Entitled*, 236–38, 266–76; Dona C. Hamilton and Charles V. Hamilton, "The Dual Agenda of African American Organizations since the New Deal: Social Welfare Policies and Civil Rights," *Political Science Quarterly*, 107 (Fall 1992), 436–42; Robert C. Lieberman, *Shifting the Color Line: Race and the American Welfare State* (New York, 1998); Kessler-Harris, "Designing Women," 103.

19. Alan Brinkley, "The New Deal and Southern Politics," in *The New Deal and the South*, ed. James C. Cobb and Michael V. Namorato (Jackson, 1984), 99–112; Ira Katznelson, "Limiting Liberalism: The Southern Veto in Congress, 1933–1950," *Political Science Quarterly*, 108 (Summer 1993), 284–86; National Resources Planning Board, *Security, Work, and Relief Policies* (Washington, DC, 1942), 224–25.

20. Walter A. Jackson, *Gunnar Myrdal and America's Conscience* (Chapel Hill, 1990), 5–6;

Cooney, *Balancing Acts*, 120; David Howard-Pitney, *The Afro-American Jeremiad: Appeals for Justice in America* (Philadelphia, 1990), 111.

21. McElvaine, *Down and Out*, 83–84; Kevin Starr, *Endangered Dreams: The Great Depression in California* (New York, 1996), 299; James C. Cobb, *The Most Southern Place on Earth: The Mississippi Delta and the Roots of Regional Identity* (New York, 1992), 188–89; Richard Polenberg, *War and Society: The United States 1941–1945* (Philadelphia, 1972), 98; James T. Patterson, *Congressional Conservatism and the New Deal: The Growth of the Conservative Coalition in Congress, 1933–1939* (Lexington, 1967), 43.

22. Kenneth T. Jackson, *Crabgrass Frontier: The Suburbanization of the United States* (New York, 1985), 50, 118; Olivier Zunz, *The Changing Face of Inequality: Urbanization, Industrial Development, and Immigrants in Detroit, 1880–1920* (Chicago, 1982), 153–53; John Bodnar, et al., *Lives of Their Own: Blacks, Italians, and Poles in Pittsburgh, 1900–1960* (Urbana, 1982), 148–62; Becky M. Nicolaides, "In Search of the Good Life: Community and Politics in Working-Class Los Angeles, 1920–1955," Ph.D. dissertation, Columbia University, 1993, 30–31.

23. Gail Radford, *Modern Housing for America: Policy Struggles in the New Deal Era* (Chicago, 1996), 75–76, 86–87; Constance Perin, *Everything in Its Place: Social Order and Land Use in America* (Princeton, 1977), 72; Hoover in John M. Gries and James Ford, eds., *Housing Objectives and Programs* (Washington, DC, 1932), 1–2; John M. Gries and James Ford, eds., *Slums, Large-Scale Housing and Decentralization* (Washington, DC, 1932), x–xii.

24. Radford, *Modern Housing*, 51–57, 91–104; Rosenman, ed., *Public Papers*, III, 292; Ronald Tobey, et al., "Moving Out and Settling In: Residential Mobility, Home Owning, and the Public Enframing of Citizenship, 1921–1950," *American Historical Review*, 95 (December 1990), 1395, 1416–18.

25. Jackson, *Crabgrass Frontier*, 195–226; Carlos A. Schwantes, "Wage Earners and Wealth Makers," in *The Oxford History of the American West*, ed. Clyde A. Milner II, et al. (New York, 1994), 441; Radford, *Modern Housing*, 104–05.

26. Thomas Gobel, "Becoming American: Ethnic Workers and the Rise of the CIO," *Labor History*, 29 (Spring 1988), 173–98; Russell A. Kazal, "Revisiting Assimilation: The Rise, Fall, and Reappraisal of a Concept in American Ethnic History," *American Historical Review*, 100 (April 1995), 438; George J. Sánchez, *Becoming Mexican American: Ethnicity, Culture, and Identity in Chicano Los Angeles, 1900–1945* (New York, 1993), 249–50; Kazin, *Populist Persuasion*, 143–45; Markowitz and Rosner, *Slaves of the Depression*, 97.

27. Michael Denning, *The Cultural Front: The Laboring of American Culture in the Twentieth Century* (New York, 1996); Fraser M. Ottanelli, *The Communist Party of the United States: From the Depression to World War II* (New Brunswick, 1991); Dewey, *Liberalism*, 88–92; Louis Adamic, *My America* (New York, 1938), 329–30.

28. Mark Naison, "Remaking America: Communists and Liberals in the Popular Front," in *New Studies in the Politics and Culture of U.S. Communism*, ed. Michael E. Brown, et al. (New York, 1993), 45–73; Ottanelli, *Communist Party*, 107–28; Judy Kutulas, *The Long War: The Intellectual People's Front and Anti-Stalinism, 1930–1940* (Durham, NC, 1995), 104–07, 144–53, 167–69.

29. Robert Cantell, *When We Were Good: The Folk Revival* (Cambridge, MA, 1996), 92–100; William Stott, *Documentary Expression and Thirties America* (New York, 1973); Warren I. Susman, *Culture as History: The Transformation of American Society in the Twentieth Century* (New York, 1984), 153–57, 205; Roosevelt in Bruce I. Bustard, *A New Deal for the Arts* (Washington, DC, 1997), 21, 49.

30. Adamic, *My America*, 218; Naison, "Remaking America," 45–48; Denning, *Cultural Front*, 9; Cohen, *Making a New Deal*, 333–41.

31. Denning, *Cultural Front*, 116–17; Paul Buhle, "Themes in American Jewish Radicalism," in *The Immigrant Left in the United States*, ed. Paul Buhle and Dan Georgakis (Albany, 1996), 99; Ottanelli, *Communist Party*, 121–24; Elizabeth Fones-Wolf, "Industrial Unionism and Labor Movement Culture in Depression-Era Philadelphia," *Pennsylvania Magazine of History and Biography*, 109 (January 1985), 8–16; Peter Novick, *That Noble Dream: The "Objectivity Question" and the American Historical Profession* (New York, 1988), 225–26; Ellen Graff, *Stepping Left: Dance and Politics in New York City, 1928–1942* (Durham, NC, 1997), 127; Cantell, *When We Were Good*, 106.

32. Naison, "Remaking America," 60–62; Stuart Svonkin, *Jews Against Prejudice: American Jews and the Fight for Civil Liberties* (New York, 1997), 11–16; Patricia Sullivan, *Days of Hope: Race and Democracy in the New Deal Era* (Chapel Hill, 1996), 85, 97–108; Sánchez, *Becoming Mexican American*, 229–43; Charles H. Martin, "The Rise and Fall of Popular Front Liberalism in the South: The Southern Conference for Human Welfare, 1938–1948," *Perspectives on the American South*, 3 (1985), 119–22; Dan T. Carter, *Scottsboro: A Tragedy of the American South* (Baton Rouge, 1969).

33. Kazin, *Populist Persuasion*, 147–48; Beth Bates, " 'The Unfinished Task of Emancipation': Protest Politics Comes of Age in Black Chicago, 1925–1943," Ph.D. dissertation, Columbia University, 1997; Michael K. Honey, *Southern Labor and Black Civil Rights: Organizing Memphis Workers* (Urbana, 1993), 117–38.

34. Denning, *Cultural Front*, 13; Michael J. Klarman, "Rethinking the Civil Rights and Civil Liberties Revolutions," *Virginia Law Review*, 82 (February 1996), 39–42; Jerold S. Auerbach, *Labor and Liberty: The La Follette Committee and the New Deal* (Indianapolis, 1966), 1–11, 24–27, 75, 103–07; Starr, *Endangered Dreams*, 268–69.

35. Auerbach, *Labor and Liberty*, 210–13; David Riesman, "Civil Liberties in a Period of Transition," in *Public Policy*, ed. C. J. Freidrich and Edward S. Mason (Cambridge, MA, 1942), 78–81; Henry J. Abraham, *Freedom and the Court: Civil Rights and Liberties in the United States*, 5th ed. (New York, 1988), 7–25; Peritz, *Competition Policy*, 161–64; Mark A. Graber, *Transforming Free Speech: The Ambiguous Legacy of Civil Libertarianism* (Berkeley, 1991), 156.

36. Auerbach, *Labor and Liberty*, 205–08; Samuel Walker, *In Defense of American Liberties: A History of the ACLU* (New York, 1990), 125–34; Michael Kammen, *A Machine That Would Go of Itself: The Constitution in American Culture* (New York, 1987), 336–39; Alan Brinkley, *The End of Reform: New Deal Liberalism in Recession and War* (New York, 1995), 140–41.

37. Patterson, *Congressional Conservatism*, 212–13, 236–37, 323–30; Fraser, " 'Labor Question,' " 75; John W. Jeffries, *Wartime America: The World War II Home Front* (Chicago, 1996), 159.

CHAPTER 10

1. John W. Jeffries, *Wartime America: The World War II Home Front* (Chicago, 1996), 4–5; Marilynn S. Johnson, *The Second Gold Rush: Oakland and the East Bay in World War II* (Berkeley, 1993), 2–9; Alan Brinkley, "World War II and American Liberalism," in *The War in American Culture: Society and Consciousness During World War II*, ed. Lewis A. Erenberg and Susan B. Hirsch (Chicago, 1996), 317.

2. Roland Marchand, *Advertising the American Dream: Making Way for Modernity, 1920–1940* (Berkeley, 1985), 20; Daniel T. Rodgers, *Contested Truths: Keywords in American Politics Since Indepedence* (New York, 1987), 214.

3. Mark L. Chadwin, *The Hawks of World War II* (Chapel Hill, 1968), v. 69–70, 161–68, 223–28, 275; *The Nation*, September 27, 1941; *Freedom House, 1941–1991* (New York, 1991), 5–9, 21.

4. Samuel I. Rosenman, *Working with Roosevelt* (New York, 1952), 258–64; James MacGregor Burns, *Roosevelt: The Soldier of Freedom* (New York, 1970), 33–34; Samuel I Rosenman, ed., *The Public Papers and Addresses of Franklin Delano Roosevelt* (13 vols. New York, 1938–50), IX, 672.

5. Rosenman, ed., *Public Papers*, X, 192, 335, xi, 287–88; Burns, *Roosevelt*, 387–88.

6. Frederick F. Siegel, *Troubled Journey: From Pearl Harbor to Ronald Reagan* (New York, 1984), 8; Alan Brinkley, *The End of Reform: New Deal Liberalism in Recession and War* (New York, 1995), 164; Samuel Walker, *In Defense of American Liberties: A History of the ACLU* (New York, 1990), 109–12; Michael J. Klarman, "Rethinking the Civil Rights and Civil Liberties Revolutions," *Virginia Law Review*, 82 (February 1996), 43–44.

7. "Freedom from Want," *Fortune*, 26 (October 1942), 126–28; Gerald Markowitz and David Rosner, eds., *"Slaves of the Depression": Workers' Letters About Life on the Job* (Ithaca, 1987), 32; Harold F. Gosnell, "Symbols of National Solidarity," *Annals of the American Academy of Political and Social Science*, 223 (September 1942), 160; Warren I. Susman, *Culture as History: The Transformation of American Society in the Twentieth Century* (New York, 1984), 194; Rosenman, ed., *Public Papers*, X, 184; Burns, *Roosevelt*, 387.

8. Lawrence R. Samuel, *Pledging Allegiance: American Identity and the Bond Drive of World War II* (Washington, DC, 1997), 67–68; *Life*, November 10, 1941, 103–13; unidentified newspaper clipping, October 16, 1942, Norman Rockwell Museum; *New York Times*, September 29, 1943.

9. *Life*, October 12, 1942, 63; Robert B. Westbrook, "Fighting for the American Family: Private Interests and Political Obligation in World War II," in *The Power of Culture: Critical Essays in American History*, ed. Richard W. Fox and T. Jackson Lears (Chicago, 1993), 202–04, 218–21; Lester C. Olson, "Portraits in Praise of a People: A Rhetorical Analysis of Norman Rockwell's Icons in Franklin Roosevelt's 'Four Freedoms' Campaign," *Quarterly Journal of Speech*, 69 (February 1983), 15–24; Stuart Murray and James McCabe, eds., *Norman Rockwell's Four Freedoms: Images that Inspire a Nation* (Stockbridge, MA, 1993), 62–91; *Saturday Evening Post*, February 20, 27; March 6, 13, 1943.

10. Richard Polenberg, *One Nation Divisible: Class, Race, and Ethnicity in the United States Since 1938*

(New York, 1980), 47; Siegel, *Troubled Journey*, 3–4; Allan M. Winkler, *The Politics of Propaganda: The Office of War Information 1942–1945* (New Haven, 1978), 1–6; Jeffries, *Wartime America*, 176; Charles D. Lloyd, "American Society and Values in World War II from the Publications of the Office of War Information," Ph.D. dissertation, Georgetown University, 1975, 46–48; Murray and McCabe, eds., *Norman Rockwell's Four Freedoms*, 111.

11. Murray and McCabe, eds., *Norman Rockwell's Four Freedoms*, 67; Leila J. Rupp, *Mobilizing Women for War: German and American Propaganda, 1939–1945* (Princeton, 1978), 91–94; Winkler, *Politics of Propaganda*, 18–19, 27–31; Sydney Weinberg, "What to Tell America: The Writers' Quarrel in the Office of War Information," *Journal of American History*, 55 (June 1968), 73–89.

12. John M. Blum, *V Was for Victory: Politics and American Culture During World War II* (New York, 1976), 118–24; Samuel, Pledging Allegiance, 23; Jeffries, *Wartime America*, 5, 44.

13. Joshua Freeman, "Delivering the Goods: Industrial Unionism During World War II," *Labor History*, 19 (Fall 1978), 590; Brinkley, *End of Reform*, 201–25; Nelson Lichtenstein, "The Making of the Postwar Working Class: Cultural Pluralism and Social Structure in World War II," *The Historian*, 51 (November 1988), 44–50; Jeffries, *Wartime America*, 23, 55–57.

14. Frank W. Fox, *Madison Avenue Goes to War: The Strange Military Career of American Advertising* (Provo, UT, 1975), 56, 25–37, 68–73; Francis X. Sutton, et al., *The American Business Creed* (Cambridge, MA, 1956), 296; Edith Nourse Rogers to Norman Rockwell, ca. January 1944, Norman Rockwell Museum; Robert Gaylord, "Free Enterprise in the Postwar Period," *Vital Speeches of the Day*, May 15, 1944, 457; *Saturday Evening Post*, May 13, 1944; Elizabeth A. Fones-Wolf, *Selling Free Enterprise: The Business Assault on Labor and Liberalism 1945–1960* (Urbana, 1994), 27.

15. Fox, *Madison Avenue*, 96; Westbrook, "Fighting for the Family," 198–201; Rupp, *Mobilizing Women*, 138–53; Maria Diedrich and Dorothea Fischer-Nornung, eds., *Women and War: The Changing Status of American Women from the 1930s to the 1950s* (New York, 1990), 4–7.

16. Nancy F. Gabin, *Feminism in the Labor Movement: Women and the United Auto Workers, 1935–1975* (Ithaca, 1990), 47, 51–71, 83–87, 95–99; Karen Anderson, *Wartime Women: Sex Roles, Family Relations, and the Status of Women During World War II* (Westport, 1981), 59; Studs Terkel, *"The Good War": An Oral History of World War Two* (New York, 1984), 122; Westbrook, "Fighting for the American Family," 213; Elaine T. May, *Homeward Bound: American Families in the Cold War Era* (New York, 1988), 60.

17. Murray and McCabe, eds., *Norman Rockwell's Four Freedoms*, 51; Henry R. Luce, *The American Century* (New York, 1941), 22–37.

18. Luce, *American Century*, 33; Henry A. Wallace, *The Century of the Common Man*, ed. Russell Lord (New York, 1943), 11–19; Henry A. Wallace, *The Price of Freedom* (Washington, DC, 1940), xiii–xiv; Norman D. Markowitz, *The Rise and Fall of the People's Century: Henry A. Wallace and American Liberalism, 1941–1948* (New York, 1973), 47–52.

19. John M. Blum, ed., *The Price of Vision: The Diary of Henry A. Wallace 1942–1946* (Boston, 1973), 25–29, 76n.; Dwight Macdonald, "The (American) People's Century," *Partisan Review*, 9 (July–August 1942), 294–301.

20. National Resources Planning Board, *Security, Work, and Relief Policies* (Washington, DC,

1942), 1–3, 545–49; National Resources Planning Board, *Report for 1943* (3 vols. Washington, DC, 1943), I, 3–4; Keith W. Olsen, "The American Beveridge Plan," *Mid-America*, 65 (April–July 1983), 87–100; Brinkley, *End of Reform*, 254.

21. Alan Brinkley, "The New Deal and the Idea of the State," in *The Rise and Fall of the New Deal Order, 1930–1980*, ed. Steve Fraser and Gary Gerstle (Princeton, 1989), 87–112; Brinkley, *End of Reform*, 7–8, 138–39, 171; *The New Republic*, March 22, 1943.

22. Rosenman, ed., *Public Papers*, XI, 52–53, XII, 122–23, XIII, 32–43, 370–77; Margaret Weir, *Politics and Jobs: The Boundaries of Employment Policy in the United States* (Princeton, 1992), 52; Olsen, "Beveridge Plan," 90–92; Blum, *V Was for Victory*, 247–50.

23. Markowitz, *Rise and Fall*, 85; Steven Fraser, *Labor Will Rule: Sidney Hillman and the Rise of American Labor* (New York, 1991), 506–09, 539; *Steel Labor*, May 28, 1943.

24. Henry A. Wallace, *Democracy Reborn*, ed. Russell Lord (New York, 1944), 29; J. Joseph Huthmacher, *Senator Robert F. Wagner and the Rise of Urban Liberalism* (New York, 1968), 291–318; Brinkley, *End of Reform*, 228–33; *The New Republic*, September 24, 1945.

25. Robert Griffith, "Forging America's Postwar Order: Domestic Politics and Political Economy in the Age of Truman," in *The Truman Presidency*, ed. Michael J. Lacey (New York, 1989), 68–70; Alonzo L. Hamby, *Beyond the New Deal: Harry S. Truman and American Liberalism* (New York, 1973), 60–69; Brinkley, *End of Reform*, 261–62; Jeffries, *Wartime America*, 158.

26. F. A. Hayek, *The Road to Serfdom* (Chicago, 1994), 16–31, 132, 173; Hughes in George W. Nash, *The Conservative Intellectual Movement in America Since 1945* (New York, 1976), 35; Eric A. Johnson, "America Unlimited," *Vital Speeches of the Day*, June 15, 1943, 521–25; Abbott Gleason, *Totalitarianism: The Inner History of the Cold War* (New York, 1995), 64; John Gray, *Hayek on Liberty* (Oxford, 1984); Theodore Rosenof, "Freedom, Planning, and Totalitarianism: The Reception of F. A. Hayek's *Road to Serfdom*," *Canadian Review of American Studies*, 5 (Fall 1974), 149.

27. Hayek, *Road to Serfdom*, 21, 41–51, 133–34; Frank S. Meyer, ed., *What Is Conservatism?* (New York, 1964), 91–97; *The Nation*, April 28, 1945; Jerome L. Himmelstein, *To the Right: The Transformation of American Conservatism* (Berkeley, 1990), 6.

28. Lichtenstein, "Postwar Working Class," 42–43; Philip Gleason, *Speaking of Diversity: Language and Ethnicity in Twentieth-Century America* (Baltimore, 1992), xi–xii.

29. Nelson Lichtenstein uses the phrase "patriotic assimilation" in a forthcoming history of the United States from 1941 to 2000; Erenberg and Hirsch, *War in American Culture*, 6; John J. Bukowczyk, *And My Children Did Not Know Me: A History of the Polish Americans* (Bloomington, 1987), 96; Lloyd, "American Society and Values," 263.

30. Ronald Takaki, *A Different Mirror: A History of Multicultural America* (Boston, 1993), 374; Lloyd, "American Society and Values," 56, 226; Gleason, *Speaking of Diversity*, 58; Samuel, *Pledging Allegiance*, xiv–xv.

31. Polenberg, *One Nation Divisible*, 52–54; Serge Guibault, *How New York Stole the Idea of Modern Art: Abstract Expressionism, Freedom, and the Cold War*, trans. Arthur Goldhammer (Chicago, 1983), 88–89; "Dance Libretto: American Document, by Martha Graham," *Theater Arts*, 26 (September 1942), 565–74.

32. Murray and McCabe, eds., *Norman Rockwell's Four Freedoms*, 38–39; Polenberg, *One Nation*

Divisible, 70; David H. Bennett, *The Party of Fear: From Nativist Movements to the New Right in American History* (Chapel Hill, 1988), 284–85; Gleason, *Speaking of Diversity*, 86; Barkan, *Retreat*, 279–81.

33. Blum, *V Was for Victory*, 63; Lary May, "Making the American Consensus: The Narrative of Conversion and Subversion in World War II Films," in *The War in American Culture*, ed. Erenberg and Hirsch, 76; Lary May, "Movie Star Politics: The Screen Actors' Guild, Cultural Conversion, and the Hollywood Red Scare," in *Recasting America: Culture and Politics in the Age of the Cold War*, ed. Lary May (Chicago, 1989), 136–37.

34. T. C. Upham to Norman Rockwell, February 25, 1943, Norman Rockwell Museum; Gary Gerstle, *Working-Class Americanism: The Politics of Labor in a Textile City, 1914–1960* (New York, 1989), 264, 278–93; Lichtenstein, "Postwar Working Class," 53–56; Gary Gerstle, "The Working Class Goes to War," in *The War and American Culture*, ed. Erenberg and Hirsch, 118.

35. Alan Dawley and Joe W. Trotter, Jr., "Race and Class," *Labor History*, 35 (Fall 1994), 487; Abraham Hoffman, *Unwanted Mexican Americans in the Great Depression: Repatriation Pressures, 1929–1939* (Tucson, 1974), 95; Camille Guerin-Gonzales, *Mexican Workers and American Dreams: Immigration, Repatriation, and California Farm Labor, 1900–1939* (New Brunswick, 1994), 77–79.

36. Guerin-Gonzales, *Mexican Workers*, 134–35; Ronald Takaki, *A Different Mirror*, 387.

37. John W. Dower, "Race, Language, and War in Two Cultures: World War II in Asia," in *The War and American Culture*, ed. Erenberg and Hirsch, 169–73; John W. Dower, *War Without Mercy: Race and Power in the Pacific War* (New York, 1986), 9–13, 81; Mary L. Dudziak, "Cold War Civil Rights: The Relationship Between Civil Rights and Foreign Affairs in the Truman Administration," Ph.D. diss, Yale University, 1992, 23.

38. Roger Daniels, *Prisoners Without Trial: Japanese Americans in World War II* (New York, 1993), 3, 29–46; Polenberg, *One Nation Divisible*, 59–60.

39. Ronald Steel, *Walter Lippmann and the American Century* (Boston, 1980), 395; Cheryl Greenberg, "Black and Jewish Responses to Japanese Internment," *Journal of American Ethnic History*, 14 (Winter 1995), 4; Daniels, *Prisoners*, 47, 59–62; Terkel, *"Good War,"* 30.

40. Rosenman, ed., *Public Papers*, X, 69; Dower, *War Without Mercy*, 5; Office of War Information, Bureau of Intelligence, Intelligence Report 35, August 7, 1942, Library of Congress (copy at Norman Rockwell Museum).

41. David Riesman, "Civil Liberties in a Period of Transition," in *Public Policy*, ed. C. J. Freidrich and Edward S. Mason (Cambridge, MA, 1942), 85–86; Jeffries, *Wartime America*, 107–10; August Meier, et al., eds., *Black Protest Thought in the Twentieth Century* (Indianapolis, 1971), 221–22.

42. Terkel, *"Good War,"* 337–38, 340; Beth Bates, " 'The Unfinished Task of Emancipation': Protest Politics Comes of Age in Black Chicago, 1925–1943," Ph.D. dissertation, Columbia University, 1997, 381–83; Martha Biondi, "The Struggle for Black Equality in New York City, 1945–1955," Ph.D. dissertation, Columbia University, 1997, 22–29; Shema B. Gluck, *Rosie the Riveter Revisited: Women, the War and Social Change* (Boston, 1987), 23–24.

43. Sullivan, *Days of Hope*, 119; Lloyd, "American Society and Values," 206–07; Gretchen Lemke-Santangelo, *Abiding Courage: African American Migrant Women and the East Bay Community* (Chapel Hill, 1996), 6, 64; Johnson, *Second Gold Rush*, 83–96; Nelson Lichtenstein, *Labor's War at Home: The CIO in World War II* (New York, 1982), 125–26; Takaki, *A Different Mirror*, 394; Steven F. Lawson, *Running for Freedom: Civil Rights and Black Politics in America Since 1941* (Philadelphia, 1991), 2–15.

44. Philip S. Foner and Ronald L. Lewis, eds., *The Black Worker: A Documentary History from Colonial Times to the Present* (7 vols. Philadelphia, 1978–83), VII, 385; Adam Fairclough, *Race and Democracy: The Civil Rights Struggle in Louisiana, 1915–1972* (Athens, GA, 1995), 74–82; C. Alvin Hughes, "Let Us Do Our Part: The New York City Based Negro Labor Victory Committee, 1941–1945," *Afro-Americans in New York Life and History*, 10 (January 1986), 19–30; Blum, *V Was for Victory*, 180–85; Gosnell, "Symbols of National Solidarity," 157–60; Jeffries, *Wartime America*, 111.

45. Cheryl Greenberg, "Pluralism and Its Discontents: The Case of Blacks and Jews," in David Biale, et al., eds., *Insider/Outsider: American Jews and Multiculturalism* (Berkeley, 1997), 10; Paul Milkman, *PM: A New Deal in Journalism, 1940–1948* (New Brunswick, 1997), 146–49; Aaron Levensein, *Freedom's Advocate: A Twenty-Five Year Chronicle* (New York, 1965), 45–50.

46. Robert Korstad and Nelson Lichtenstein, "Opportunities Found and Lost: Labor, Radicals, and the Early Civil Rights Movement," *Journal of American History*, 75 (December 1988), 786–88; August Meier and Elliott Rudwick, *Black Detroit and the Rise of the UAW* (New York, 1979), 175–206.

47. Rayford Logan, ed., *What the Negro Wants* (Chapel Hill, 1944), 7, 110–11, 137; Penny M. Von Eschen, *Race Against Empire: Black Americans and Anticolonialism 1937–1957* (Ithaca, 1997), 22–43.

48. Chadwin, *The Hawks*, 159; Walter A. Jackson, *Gunnar Myrdal and America's Conscience* (Chapel Hill, 1990), 251; Kenneth R. Janken, *Rayford Logan and the Dilemma of the African-American Intellectual* (Amherst, 1993), 154–61; John T. Kneebone, *Southern Liberal Journalists and the Issue of Race, 1920–1944* (Chapel Hill, 1985), xiii–xx, 180–96; Morton Sosna, *In Search of the Silent South: Southern Liberals and the Race Issue* (New York, 1977), 109.

49. John M. Jordan, "A Small World of Little Americans: The $1 Diplomacy of Wendell Willkie's *One World*," *Indiana Magazine of History*, 88 (September 1992), 173–204; Philip Beindler, "Remembering Wendell Willkie's *One World*," *Canadian Review of American Studies*, 24 (Spring 1994), 87–104.

50. Gunnar Myrdal, *An American Dilemma* (New York, 1944), 3–5, 997; Jackson, *Gunnar Myrdal*, 186–97.

51. Jackson, *Gunnar Myrdal*, xi; Brinkley, *End of Reform*, 168–70; Myrdal, *American Dilemma*, 209–14; Jack Goodman, ed., *While You Were Gone: A Report on Wartime Life in the United States* (New York, 1946), 107–10.

52. Biondi, "Struggle for Black Equality," 99–159; Sullivan, *Days of Hope*, 167–80; Brinkley, *End of Reform*, 10, 170; Logan, *What the Negro Wants*, 185.

53. *The Public Papers of the Presidents: Harry S. Truman 1945* (Washington, DC, 1961), 223, 256.

CHAPTER 11

1. Frank Monaghan, *Heritage of Freedom: The History and Significance of the Basic Documents of American Liberty* (Princeton, 1948); Michael Kammen, *Mystic Chords of Memory: The Transformation of Tradition in American Culture* (New York, 1991), 576–79; Stuart J. Little, "The Freedom Train: Citizenship and Postwar Political Culture 1946–1949," *American Studies*, 34 (Spring 1993), 35–67; James G. Bradsher, "Taking America's Heritage to the People: The Freedom Train Story," *Prologue*, 17 (Winter 1985), 229–34; *The New Republic*, September 20, 1948.

2. Little, "Freedom Train," 53–61; *The New Republic*, September 15, 1947; Bradsher, "America's Heritage," 234–41; *Library Journal*, February 1, 1948.

3. Kammen, *Mystic Chords of Memory*, 573–76; Bradsher, "America's Heritage," 237–38; Robert Griffith, "The Selling of America: The Advertising Council and American Politics, 1942–1960," *Business History Review*, 57 (Autumn 1983), 397–98.

4. Melvyn P. Leffler, *A Preponderance of Power: National Security, the Truman Administration, and the Cold War* (Stanford, 1992), 99–109; Lynn B. Hinds and Theodore O. Windt, Jr., *The Cold War as Rhetoric: The Beginnings, 1945–1950* (New York, 1991), 89–94.

5. Dean Acheson, *Present at the Creation: My Years in the State Department* (New York, 1969), 220–21; Joseph M. Jones, *The Fifteen Weeks* (New York, 1955), 138–43; Thomas J. McCormack, *America's Half-Century: United States Foreign Policy in the Cold War* (Baltimore, 1989), 77–78; Leffler, *Preponderance of Power*, 146–51; *The Public Papers of the Presidents: Harry S. Truman 1947* (Washington, DC, 1963), 178.

6. J. William Fulbright, *The Crippled Giant* (New York, 1972), 6–24; *Life*, August 7, 1950; Ernest R. May, ed., *American Cold War Strategy: Interpreting NSC 68* (Boston, 1993), 1–27; Leffler, *Preponderance of Power*, 313–56, 495.

7. George F. Kennan, *Memoirs* (2 vols. Boston, 1967–72), I, 312–22; Walter Lippmann, *The Cold War: A Study in U.S. Foreign Policy* (New York, 1947), 13–26, 44–46; Barton J. Bernstein, "Walter Lippmann and the Early Cold War," and Ronald Radosh and Leonard P. Liggio, "Henry Wallace and the Open Door," in *Cold War Critics: Alternatives to American Foreign Policy in the Truman Years*, ed. Thomas G. Patterson (Chicago, 1971), 19–40, 76–107; Steven M. Gillon, *Politics and Vision: The ADA and American Liberalism, 1947–1985* (New York, 1987), 25–31, 55–58.

8. Leffler, *Preponderance of Power*, 14–16; Melvyn P. Leffler, *The Specter of Communism: The United States and the Origins of the Cold War, 1917–1953* (New York, 1994), 126; Tony Smith, *America's Mission: The United States and the Worldwide Struggle for Democracy in the Twentieth Century* (Princeton, 1994), 197–98; Allen Dulles, "Progress of Freedom Abroad," *Vital Speeches of the Day*, December 1, 1954, 869.

9. Hinds and Windt, *Cold War as Rhetoric*, 129, 139; Michael H. Hunt, *Ideology and U.S. Foreign Policy* (New Haven, 1987), 165–67; *The Public Papers of the Presidents: Dwight D. Eisenhower 1954* (Washington, DC, 1960), 399; *Dwight D. Eisenhower 1959* (Washington, DC, 1960), 871; Glenn E. Hoover, "Freedom vs. Power," *Vital Speeches of the Day*, October 15, 1959, 22.

10. Samuel Walker, *In Defense of American Liberties: A History of the ACLU* (New York, 1990),

174–88; Albert Fried, ed., *McCarthyism: The Great American Red Scare* (New York, 1997), 7, 24–34; Ellen W. Schrecker, *No Ivory Tower: McCarthyism and the Universities* (New York, 1986), 9, 117, 309–39; Peter Novick, *That Noble Dream: The "Objectivity Question" and the American Historical Profession* (New York, 1988), 328.

11. Howard K. Beale to Merle Curti, April 8, 1950, Merle Curti Papers, State Historical Society of Wisconsin; *Life,* July 5, 1954.

12. Frederick F. Siegel, *Troubled Journey: From Pearl Harbor to Ronald Reagan* (New York, 1984), 48, 78; M. J. Heale, "The Triumph of Liberalism? Red Scare Politics in Michigan, 1938–1954," *Proceedings of the American Philosophical Society,* 139 (March 1995), 44; Leffler, *Specter of Communism,* 121; Charles H. Martin, "The Rise and Fall of Popular Front Liberalism in the South: The Southern Conference for Human Welfare, 1938–1948," *Perspectives on the American South,* 3 (1985), 124–30; John D'Emilio and Estelle B. Freedman, *Intimate Matters: A History of Sexuality in America* (New York, 1988), 292–93.

13. Frank in Michael J. Klarman, "Rethinking the Civil Rights and Civil Liberties Revolutions," *Virginia Law Review,* 82 (February 1996), 34; Walker, *Defense of American Liberties,* 175, 187; Richard H. Pells, *The Liberal Mind in a Conservative Age: American Intellectuals in the 1940s and 1950s* (New York, 1985), 264; Fried, ed., *McCarthyism,* 64; Michael Wrezsin, *A Rebel in Defense of Tradition: The Life and "Politics" of Dwight Macdonald* (New York, 1994), 273.

14. May, *NSC 68,* 154; David Plotke, *Building a Democratic Political Order: Reshaping American Liberalism in the 1930s and 1940s* (New York, 1996), 311–12; Ira Katznelson, "Was the Great Society a Lost Opportunity?" in *The Rise and Fall of the New Deal Order, 1930–1980* (Princeton, 1989), ed. Steve Fraser and Gary Gerstle, 187–94.

15. Alonzo L. Hamby, *Liberalism and Its Challengers: FDR to Reagan* (New York, 1985), 63–70; Robert Griffith, "Forging America's Postwar Order: Domestic Politics and Political Economy in the Age of Truman," and Nelson Lichtenstein, "Labor in the Truman Era: Origins of the 'Private Welfare State,' " both in *The Truman Presidency,* ed. Michael J. Lacey (New York, 1989), 83–84, 148–55; Marilynn S. Johnson, *The Second Gold Rush: Oakland and the East Bay in World War II* (Berkeley, 1993), 218–20.

16. Steve Rosswurm, ed., *The CIO's Left-Led Unions* (New Brunswick, 1992); Robert H. Zieger, *The CIO 1935–1955* (Chapel Hill, 1995), 253, 291–93.

17. Walter A. Jackson, *Gunnar Myrdal and America's Conscience* (Chapel Hill, 1990), 274–79; Robert Korstad and Nelson Lichtenstein, "Opportunities Found and Lost: Labor, Radicals, and the Early Civil Rights Movement," *Journal of American History,* 75 (December 1988), 799–800; President's Committee on Civil Rights, *To Secure These Rights* (Washington, DC, 1947); David S. Horton, ed., *Freedom and Equality; Addresses by Harry S. Truman* (Columbia, MO, 1960), 16; Harvard Sitkoff, "Harry Truman and the Election of 1948: The Coming of Age of Civil Rights in American Politics," *Journal of Southern History,* 37 (November 1971), 597–613.

18. Martha Biondi, "The Struggle for Black Equality in New York City, 1945–1955," Ph.D. dissertation, Columbia University, 1997, 386–461; *The Autobiography of W. E. B. Du Bois* (New York, 1968), 380–95; C. Alvin Hughes, "We Demand Our Rights: The Southern Negro Youth Congress, 1937–1949," *Phylon,* 48 (March 1987), 38–50; Adam Fair-

clough, *Race and Democracy: The Civil Rights Struggle in Louisiana, 1915–1972* (Athens, GA, 1995), 146–47.

19. Penny M. Von Eschen, *Race Against Empire: Black Americans and Anticolonialism 1937–1957* (Ithaca, 1997), 2–17, 194, 216–20, 291; Mary L. Dudziak, "Cold War Civil Rights: The Relationship Between Civil Rights and Foreign Affairs in the Truman Administration," Ph.D. dissertation, Yale University, 1992, iii, 170–71.

20. Acheson, *Present at the Creation*, 227–29; Nan E. Woodruff, "Mississippi Delta Planters and Debates Over Mechanization, Labor, and Civil Rights in the 1940s," *Journal of Southern History*, 60 (May 1994), 264–84; David M. Oshinsky, *"Worse Than Slavery": Parchman Farm and the Ordeal of Jim Crow Justice* (New York, 1996), 55; Neil McMillen, *Dark Journey: Black Mississippians in the Age of Jim Crow* (Urbana, 1989), 124–25.

21. Biondi, "Struggle for Black Equality," 163–69, 459, 538–41; Plotke, *Democratic Political Order*, 282–84; Gillon, *Politics and Vision*, 87–101; Richard Hofstadter, *The Age of Reform* (New York, 1955), 13–14.

22. Robert B. Fowler, *Believing Skeptics: American Political Intellectuals, 1945–1964* (Westport, 1978), 229; Herbert McCloskey, "Consensus and Ideology in American Politics," *American Political Science Review*, 58 (June 1964), 365; John F. Kennedy, "Freedom's Cause," *Vital Speeches of the Day*, June 15, 1961, 514–18; Thomas Bender, *New York Intellect* (New York, 1987), 338–39; Miller in Kammen, *Mystic Chords of Memory*, 573.

23. Mortimer J. Adler, *Philosopher at Large: An Intellectual Autobiography* (New York, 1977), 225–79; Mortimer J. Adler, *The Idea of Freedom: A Dialectical Examination of the Conceptions of Freedom* (2 vols. New York, 1958–61).

24. Michael D. Torre, ed., *Freedom in the Modern World: Jacques Martain, Yves R. Simon, Mortimer J. Adler* (Notre Dame, 1989), 69; Isaiah Berlin, *Four Essays on Liberty* (New York, 1969), xliii–xlix, 118–72; John N. Gray, "On Negative and Positive Liberty," *Political Studies*, 28 (December 1980), 518; Nancy J. Hirschmann, "Toward a Feminist Theory of Freedom," *Political Theory*, 24 (February 1996), 50; Perry Anderson, *A Zone of Engagement* (London, 1992), 239–40.

25. Abbott Gleason, *Totalitarianism: The Inner History of the Cold War* (New York, 1995), 3, 10–28, 61, 87–88; Les K. Adler and Thomas G. Patterson, "Red Fascism: The Merger of Nazi Germany and Soviet Russia in the American Image of Totalitarianism, 1930's–1950's," *American Historical Review*, 75 (April 1970), 1046–48; Arthur M. Schlesinger, Jr., *The Vital Center: The Politics of Freedom* (New York, 1988), x–xiv; Hannah Arendt, *Between Past and Future: Eight Essays in Political Thought* (New York, 1968), 149–58.

26. MacLeish in Studs Terkel, *"The Good War": An Oral History of World War Two* (New York, 1984), 13; John D'Emilio, *Sexual Politics, Sexual Communities: The Making of a Homosexual Minority in the United States* (Chicago, 1983), 43–44.

27. Raymond D. Gastil, ed., *Freedom in the World: Political Rights and Civil Liberties 1978* (Boston, 1978), 4–5; Louis Hartz, *The Liberal Tradition in America* (New York, 1955), 306.

28. Robert Skidelsky, *The Road from Serfdom: The Economic and Political Consequences of the End of Communism* (New York, 1995), 5–8; *Public Papers of the Presidents: Truman 1947*, 169.

29. Elizabeth A. Fones-Wolf, *Selling Free Enterprise: The Business Assault on Labor and Liberalism 1945–1960* (Urbana, 1994), 1–3, 44–51; Robert H. Haddow, *Pavilions of Plenty: Exhibit-*

ing American Culture Abroad in the 1950s (Washington, DC, 1997), 46–52; Griffith, "Selling of America," 388–412; Francis X. Sutton, et al., *The American Business Creed* (Cambridge, MA, 1956), vii–2, 22–26, 253; Marver H. Bernstein, "Political Ideas of Selected American Business Journals," *Public Opinion Quarterly*, 17 (Summer 1953), 258–67; Howell J. Harris, *The Right to Manage: Industrial Relations Policies of American Business in the 1940s* (Madison, 1982), 8–9, 189–92; Herbert McCloskey and John Zaller, *The American Ethos: Public Attitudes Toward Capitalism and Democracy* (Cambridge, MA, 1984), 133.

30. Norbert Elias, *Reflections on a Life*, trans. Edmund Jephcott (Cambridge, UK, 1994), 138–39; Sutton, *American Business Creed*, 253; Eric Hobsbawm, *The Age of Extremes: A History of the World, 1914–1991* (New York, 1994), 8; David E. Lilienthal, *Big Business: A New Era* (New York, 1952), ix–9, 40, 137–40; Stuart Ewen, *Captains of Consciousness: Advertising and the Social Roots of Consumer Culture* (New York, 1976), 211.

31. Ronald Edsforth, "Affluence, Anti-Communism, and the Transformation of Industrial Unionism Among Automobile Workers, 1933–1973," in *Popular Culture and Political Change in Modern America*, ed. Ronald Edsforth and Larry Bennett (Albany, 1991), 106–10; Elaine T. May, *Homeward Bound: American Families in the Cold War Era* (New York, 1988), 162–70; David Halle, *America's Working Man: Work, Home, and Politics among Blue-Collar Property Owners* (Chicago, 1984), 11–14; Matthew Edel, et al., *Shaky Palaces: Homeownership and Social Mobility in Boston's Suburbanization* (New York, 1984), 3–13; Barbara M. Kelly, *Expanding the American Dream: Building and Rebuilding Levittown* (Albany, 1993), 11–16.

32. Thomas Hine, *Populuxe* (New York, 1986), 4; Ewen, *Captains of Consciousness*, 200; Clark Kerr, et al., *Industrialism and Industrial Man* (Cambridge, MA, 1960), 33–41, 295; Howell, *Right to Manage*, 99–105.

33. Hine, *Populuxe*, 3–17; Richard W. Fox, "Epitaph for Middletown," in *The Culture of Consumption: Critical Essays in American History, 1880–1980*, ed. Richard W. Fox and T. Jackson Lears (New York, 1983), 103; *Life*, August 14, 1950; Potter in David Farber, *The Age of Great Dreams: America in the 1960s* (New York, 1994), 15–16.

34. Everett Case, "The Idea of Freedom: 1959," *Saturday Review*, July 4, 1959, 8; Karal Ann Marling, *As Seen on TV: The Visual Culture of Everyday Life in the 1950s* (Cambridge, MA, 1994), 133–34; Kenneth T. Jackson, *Crabgrass Frontier: The Suburbanization of the United States* (New York, 1985), 187; May, *Homeward Bound*, 162; James O. Robertson, *American Myth, American Reality* (New York, 1980), 128; Roland Marchand, *Advertising the American Dream: Making Way for Modernity, 1920–1940* (Berkeley, 1985), 360–61.

35. Leila J. Rupp, *Mobilizing Women for War: German and American Propaganda, 1939–1945* (Princeton, 1978), 179; Maureen Honey, *Creating Rosie the Riveter: Class, Gender, and Propaganda During World War II* (Amherst, 1984), 23–24; *Look*, October 16, 1956; May, *Homeward Bound*, 137; Christopher Lasch, *Women and the Common Life: Love, Marriage, and Feminism* (New York, 1997), 94–104; Judith Sealander, "Moving Painfully and Uncertainly: Policy Formation and 'Women's Issues,' 1940–1980," in *Federal Social Policy: The Historical Dimension*, ed. Donald T. Critchlow and Ellis W. Hawley (University Park, 1988), 85.

36. May, *Homeward Bound*, 4–9, 22; Stephanie Coontz, *The Way We Never Were: American Families and the Nostalgia Trap* (New York, 1992), 24–27; Hine, *Populuxe*, 24–29.

37. Becky M. Nicolaides, "In Search of the Good Life: Community and Politics in

Working-Class Los Angeles, 1920–1955," Ph.D. dissertation, Columbia University, 1993, 3–13, 45–54; George Lipsitz, "The Possessive Investment in Whiteness: Racialized Social Democracy and the 'White' Problem in American Studies," *American Studies*, 47 (September 1995), 373–74.

38. President's Committee, *To Secure These Rights*, 67–70; Gail Radford, *Modern Housing for America: Policy Struggles in the New Deal Era* (Chicago, 1996), 199–204; Richard Polenberg, *One Nation Divisible: Class, Race, and Ethnicity in the United States Since 1938* (New York, 1980), 163; Arnold Hirsch, *Making the Second Ghetto: Race and Housing in Chicago, 1940–1960* (New York, 1983), 3–9, 125–73, 269.

39. Thomas J. Sugrue, *The Origins of the Urban Crisis: Race and Inequality in Postwar Detroit* (Princeton, 1996), 76–88, 127–28, 194, 209–27; Thomas J. Sugrue, "Crabgrass-Roots Politics: Race, Rights, and the Reaction Against Liberalism in the Urban North, 1940–1964," and Arnold R. Hirsch, "Massive Resistance in the Urban North: Trumbull Park, Chicago, 1953–1966," *Journal of American History*, 82 (September 1995), 522–78; Nicolaides, "In Search of the Good Life," 1–3, 368–73.

40. Hobsbawm, *Age of Extremes*, 264–73; Pells, *Liberal Mind*, 130–39; Fowler, *Believing Skeptics*, 4–18; *Fortune*, 39 (July 1955), 87; Rudolph J. R. Peritz, *Competition Policy in America 1888–1992* (New York, 1996), 181–88; David Riesman, *The Lonely Crowd: A Study of the Changing American Character* (New Haven, 1961), xxxvi.

41. Mark Silk, "Notes on the Judeo-Christian Tradition in America," *American Quarterly*, 36 (Spring 1984), 65–85; Philip Gleason, *Speaking of Diversity: Language and Ethnicity in Twentieth-Century America* (Baltimore, 1992), 177, 212, 246; David Campbell, *Writing Security: United States Foreign Policy and the Politics of Identity* (Minneapolis, 1992), 168; Marvin E. Frankel, *Faith and Freedom: Religious Liberty in America* (New York, 1994), 34–42, 59; Will Herberg, *Protestant—Catholic—Jew: An Essay in American Religious Sociology* (New York, 1955), 46–49, 88–93.

42. Hans J. Morgenthau, "The Dilemmas of Freedom," in *The Essentials of Freedom: The Idea and Practice of Ordered Liberty in the Twentieth Century*, ed. Raymond English (Gambier, 1960), 137–38; C. Wright Mills, *The Power Elite* (New York, 1957); C. Wright Mills, *The Sociological Imagination* (New York, 1959), 174.

43. Schlesinger, *Vital Center*, 1, 52–53, 65; Erich Fromm, *Escape from Freedom* (New York, 1941); Riesman, *Lonely Crowd*, xiv, xxxii–xxxiii; Pells, *Liberal Mind*, viii–ix, 185, 232; Wilfred M. McClay, *The Masterless: Self and Society in Modern America* (Chapel Hill, 1994), 197–211, 236–63; Paul Lazarsfeld and Robert K. Merton, "Mass Communication, Popular Taste and Organized Social Action," in Lyman Bryson, ed., *The Communication of Ideas* (New York, 1948), 96–99; Joseph T. Klapper, "Mass Media and the Engineering of Consent," *American Scholar*, 17 (Autumn 1948), 419–29.

44. Dorothy Ross, "Grand Narrative in American Historical Writing: From Romance to Uncertainty," *American Historical Review*, 100 (June 1995), 659–60; McClay, *The Masterless*, 222–24, 234; John K. Galbraith, *The Affluent Society* (Boston, 1958); Robert M. Collins, "Growth Liberalism in the Sixties," in *The Sixties: From Memory to History*, ed. David Farber (Chapel Hill, 1994), 26; Joanne Meyerowitz, ed., *Not June Cleaver: Women and Gender in Postwar America, 1945–1960* (Philadelphia, 1994), 8.

45. James J. Farrell, *The Spirit of the Sixties: The Making of Postwar Radicalism* (New York, 1997), 149; Edward Shils, "Daydreams and Nightmares: Reflections on the Critique of Mass Culture," *Sewanee Review* 65 (Fall 1957), 587–608; Rochelle Gurstein, *The Repeal of Reticence* (New York, 1996), 263–67; M. C. Patterson, "Word and Deed in a Changing America," *Vital Speeches of the Day*, October 1, 1960, 758–59; Haddow, *Pavilions of Plenty*, 44.

46. *New York Times*, July 25, 1959; *Newsweek*, August 3, 1959; Richard M. Nixon, "What Freedom Means to Us," *Vital Speeches of the Day*, September 1, 1959, 677–78; May, *Homeward Bound*, 16–18, 162; Hine, *Populuxe*, 129–69; Haddow, *Pavilions of Plenty*, 2, 213–29; Marling, *As Seen on TV*, 244–52.

CHAPTER 12

1. Martin Luther King, Jr., *Stride Toward Freedom* (New York, 1958); David Riesman, *The Lonely Crowd: A Study of the Changing American Character* (New Haven, 1961), xxxv.

2. Richard H. King, *Civil Rights and the Idea of Freedom* (New York, 1992), 141; David Farber, *The Age of Great Dreams: America in the 1960s* (New York, 1994), 67; James Baldwin, *Nobody Knows My Name* (New York, 1961), 66; Sally Belfrage, *Freedom Summer* (Charlottesville, 1990), xx.

3. Juan Williams, *Eyes on the Prize: America's Civil Rights Years, 1954–1965* (New York, 1987), 72.

4. King, *Civil Rights*, 13, 56–57, 148; Daniel P. Hinman-Smith, " 'Does the Word Freedom Have a Meaning?' The Mississippi Freedom Schools, the Berkeley Free Speech Movement, and the Search for Freedom Through Education," Ph.D. dissertation, University of North Carolina at Chapel Hill, 1993), 2, 98–101, 184; Daniel Perlstein, "Teaching Freedom: SNCC and the Creation of the Mississippi Freedom Schools," *History of Education Quarterly*, 30 (Fall 1990), 297–303.

5. Hinman-Smith, "Does the Word Freedom," 98; King, *Civil Rights*, 4–7; John Ditmer, "The Politics of the Mississippi Movement, 1954–1964," in *The Civil Rights Movement in America*, ed. Charles W. Eagles (Jackson, 1986), 65–66; Theodore Rosengarten, *All God's Dangers: The Life of Nate Shaw* (New York, 1974), 7.

6. Merrill Proudfoot, *Diary of a Sit-In* (Chapel Hill, 1962), 52; Martha Solomon, "Covenanted Rights: The Metaphoric Matrix of 'I Have a Dream,' " in *Martin Luther King, Jr., and the Sermonic Power of Public Discourse*, ed. Carolyn Calloway-Thomas and John L. Lucaites (Tuscaloosa, 1993), 77; Charlene Mires, "We the People: Defining Citizenship in the Shadow of Independence Hall," Unpublished paper, Organization of American Historians annual meeting, 1997; Howell Raines, *My Soul Is Rested: Movement Days in the Deep South Remembered* (New York, 1977), 76.

7. Mary King, *Freedom Song: A Personal Story of the 1960s Civil Rights Movement* (New York, 1987), 440, 456; Charles M. Payne, *I've Got the Light of Freedom: The Organizing Tradition and the Mississippi Freedom Struggle* (Berkeley, 1995), 331; Sara Evans, *Personal Politics* (New York, 1979), 94; Clayborne Carson, *In Struggle: SNCC and the Black Awakening of the 1960s* (Cambridge, MA, 1981), 170, 303; King, *Civil Rights*, 143–44.

8. David Howard-Pitney, *The Afro-American Jeremiad: Appeals for Justice in America* (Philadelphia, 1990), 142–45; Clayborne Carson, et al., eds., *The Eyes on the Prize Civil Rights Reader* (New York, 1991), 48–52; Diana Wells, ed., *We Have a Dream: African-American Visions of Freedom* (New York, 1993), 168–72.

9. James J. Farrell, *The Spirit of the Sixties: The Making of Postwar Radicalism* (New York, 1997), 82–93; Clayborne Carson, ed., *The Papers of Martin Luther King, Jr.* (Berkeley, 1991–), III, 428; King, *Civil Rights*, 29–31; Keith D. Miller, "Alabama as Egypt: Martin Luther King, Jr., and the Religion of Slaves," in *Martin Luther King, Jr.*, ed. Calloway-Thomas and Lucaites, 28–31; Taylor Branch, *Parting the Waters: America in the King Years 1954–63* (New York, 1988), 743; Carson, *Eyes on the Prize Reader*, 48–51.

10. King, *Stride Toward Freedom*, 131–32; Dennis C. Dickerson, *Out of the Crucible: Black Steelworkers in Western Pennsylvania, 1875–1980* (Albany, 1986), 1–5; Patricia Sullivan, *Days of Hope: Race and Democracy in the New Deal Era* (Chapel Hill, 1996), 274; Harvard Sitkoff, *The Struggle for Black Equality* (New York, 1993), 23.

11. *The Public Papers of the Presidents: John F. Kennedy 1961* (Washington, DC, 1962), 1; Branch, *Parting the Waters*, 824–25; David J. Garrow, *Bearing the Cross: Martin Luther King, Jr., and the Southern Christian Leadership Conference* (New York, 1986), 408–09.

12. Rogers Smith, *Civic Ideals: Conflicting Visions of Citizenship in American Public Law* (New Haven, 1997), 473; Herbert McCloskey and John Zaller, *The American Ethos: Public Attitudes Toward Capitalism and Democracy* (Cambridge, MA, 1984), 23.

13. Garrow, *Bearing the Cross*, 284; Carson, *Eyes on the Prize Reader*, 163; Penny M. Von Eschen, *Race Against Empire: Black Americans and Anticolonialism 1937–1957* (Ithaca, 1997), 377; Martin Luther King, Jr., *Why We Can't Wait* (New York, 1964), 23–4, 133–39; Alonzo L. Hamby, *Liberalism and Its Challengers: FDR to Reagan* (New York, 1985), 168–77; Jervis Anderson, *Bayard Rustin: Troubles I've Seen* (New York, 1997), 284–89.

14. James R. Ralph, Jr., *Northern Protest: Martin Luther King, Jr., Chicago, and the Civil Rights Movement* (Cambridge, MA, 1993), 1–14; 30–33, 70–71, 102–23, 220; Martin Luther King, Jr., *Where Do We Go from Here: Chaos or Community?* (New York, 1968), 6–13, 190–93; Garrow, *Bearing the Cross*, 420, 539–40.

15. Alexander Bloom and Wini Breines, eds., *"Takin' It to the Streets": A Sixties Reader* (New York, 1995), 141.

16. King, *Where Do We Go?*, 34–51; John T. McCartney, *Black Power Ideologies: An Essay in African-American Political Thought* (Philadelphia, 1992), 120–22; *New York Times*, August 5, 1966; Bloom and Breines, eds., *Takin' It to the Streets*, 159; August Meier, et al., eds., *Black Protest Thought in the Twentieth Century* (Indianapolis, 1971), 484; Philip Gleason, *Speaking of Diversity: Language and Ethnicity in Twentieth-Century America* (Baltimore, 1992), 75–76.

17. Kevin Boyle, *The UAW and the Heyday of American Liberalism 1945–1968* (Ithaca, 1995), 7; Frederick F. Siegel, *Troubled Journey: From Pearl Harbor to Ronald Reagan* (New York, 1984), 156, 250; Jill Quadrango, *The Color of Welfare: How Racism Undermined the War on Poverty* (New York, 1994), 9–12, 89.

18. Barbara Ehrenreich, *Fear of Falling: The Inner Life of the Middle Class* (New York, 1989), 42–47; Gareth Davies, "War on Dependency: Liberal Individualism and the Economic Opportunity Act of 1964," *Journal of American Studies*, 26 (August 1992), 205–30;

Quadrango, *Color of Welfare*, 67–75; Herbert McCloskey, "Consensus and Ideology in American Politics," *American Political Science Review*, 58 (June 1964), 369, Farber, *Age of Great Dreams*, 106–08.

19. *The Public Papers of the Presidents: Lyndon B. Johnson 1963–64* (Washington, DC, 1965), 130, 1012; *Public Papers: Johnson 1965* (Washington, DC, 1966), 636; *Public Papers: Johnson 1966* (Washington, DC, 1967), 210; Michael J. Sandel, *Democracy's Discontent: America in Search of a Public Philosophy* (Cambridge, MA, 1996), 281–83.

20. Hamby, *Liberalism*, 258–62; Farber, *Age of Great Dreams*, 108–09; Jennifer L. Hochschild, *Facing Up to the American Dream: Race, Class, and the Soul of the Nation* (Princeton, 1995), 40–49; John Dittmer, *Local People: The Struggle for Civil Rights in Mississippi* (Urbana, 1994), 426–34.

21. Meier, et al., eds., *Black Protest Thought*, 447–50; Robert M. Collins, "Growth Liberalism in the Sixties," in *The Sixties: From Memory to History*, ed. David Farber (Chapel Hill, 1994), 11–31.

22. John P. Diggins, *The American Left in the Twentieth Century* (New York, 1973), 156; Terry H. Anderson, *The Movement and the Sixties: Protest in America from Greensboro to Wounded Knee* (New York, 1995), 19; Mungo in Massimo Teodori, ed., *The New Left: A Documentary History* (Indianapolis, 1969), 349; Kirkpatrick Sale, *SDS* (New York, 1973), 318.

23. Sale, *SDS*; Teodori, ed., *New Left*, 73.

24. Wilfred M. McClay, *The Masterless: Self and Society in Modern America* (Chapel Hill, 1994), 270; Farrell, *Spirit of the Sixties*, 2–7, 16–19; Michael Kazin, *The Populist Persuasion* (New York, 1995), 199–200.

25. James Miller, *"Democracy Is in the Streets": From Port Huron to the Siege of Chicago* (New York, 1987), 79–101, 143, 275; Sale, *SDS*, 50–53; Richard J. Ellis, *American Political Cultures* (New York, 1993), 56, 71–72; Teodori, ed., *New Left*, 49–51, 195; Paul Berman, *A Tale of Two Utopias: The Political Journey of the Generation of 1968* (New York, 1996), 52–53.

26. Teodori, ed., *New Left*, 30; Sale, *SDS*, 163–67; Hinman-Smith, "Does the Word Freedom," 3, 302–13; Bloom and Breines, eds., *Takin' It to the Streets*, 120.

27. Michael H. Hunt, *Lyndon Johnson's War* (New York, 1996), 3–18; Siegel, *Troubled Journey*, 140; *Public Papers: Johnson 1964*, 842, 1048.

28. Anderson, *Rustin*, 294; Teodori, ed., *New Left*, 54; Bloom and Breines, eds., *Takin' It to the Streets*, 228–29.

29. Sale, *SDS*, 54–58, 177–79; Miller, *"Democracy,"* 116; Abbott Gleason, *Totalitarianism: The Inner History of the Cold War* (New York, 1995), 130; Bloom and Breines, eds., *Takin' It to the Streets*, 215–16.

30. Berman, *Tale of Two Utopias*, 59; Teodori, ed., *New Left*, 182; Sale, *SDS*, 242–45.

31. Herbert Marcuse, *One-Dimensional Man* (Boston, 1964); Peter Clecak, *Radical Paradoxes: Dilemmas of the American Left: 1945–1970* (New York, 1973), 186–203; Robert B. Fowler, *Believing Skeptics: American Political Intellectuals, 1945–1964* (Westport, 1978), 218–24; Bloom and Breines, eds., *Takin' It to the Streets*, 126–27.

32. Anderson, *The Movement and the Sixties*, 241–87; Clecak, *Radical Paradoxes*, 252; Jay Stevens, *Storming Heaven: LSD and the American Dream* (New York, 1987), 171, 203; Farrell, *Spirit of the Sixties*, 203–04.

33. Jonah Raskin, *For the Hell of It: The Life and Times of Abbie Hoffman* (Berkeley, 1996).

34. Herbert Marcuse, *Eros and Civilization* (Boston, 1955); Ruth Rosen, "The Female Generation Gap: Daughters of the Fifties and the Origins of Contemporary American Feminism," in *U.S. History as Women's History: New Feminist Essays*, ed. Linda K. Kerber, et al. (Chapel Hill, 1995), 325–30; Anderson, *Movement and the Sixties*, 357; Sally Banes, *Greenwich Village 1963: Avant-Garde Performance and the Effervescent Body* (Durham, NC, 1993), 2–9, 212–17.

35. Michael Wrezsin, *A Rebel in Defense of Tradition: The Life and "Politics" of Dwight Macdonald* (New York, 1994), 194–95; Stanley Aronowitz, "When the New Left was New," in *The 60s Without Apology*, ed. Sohnya Sayres, et al. (Minneapolis, 1984), 24.

36. Betty Friedan, *The Feminine Mystique* (New York, 1983), 15–24, 43, 77, 282, 306–20; Daniel Horowitz, "Rethinking Betty Friedan and *The Feminine Mystique:* Labor Union Radicalism and Feminism in Cold War America," *American Quarterly*, 48 (March 1996), 1–17, 22–29; Glenna Matthews, *"Just a Housewife": The Rise and Fall of Domesticity in America* (New York, 1987), 199–218.

37. Letters to Betty Friedan [correspondents' names omitted], May 14, 1963, Brookline; June 23, 1963, Atlanta; March 9, 1964, South Carolina; March 12, 1964, Sioux City; June 22, 1964, Pomona; Nella Yount to Friedan, April 22, 1964; Betty Friedan Papers, Schlesinger Library, Radcliffe College.

38. Letters to *McCall's* by Mildred Wells, February 19, 1963; Dorothy Knapp, February 22, 1963; Shirley A. Gadd, February 26, 1963; Friedan Papers.

39. Joan Hoff, *Law, Gender, and Injustice* (New York, 1991), 233; Donald G. Mathews and Jane S. De Hart, *Sex, Gender, and the Politics of ERA* (New York, 1990), 31–33; Nancy F. Gabin, *Feminism in the Labor Movement: Women and the United Auto Workers, 1935–1975* (Ithaca, 1990), 189–93.

40. Letter to Betty Friedan, March 13, 1963, Ridgewood, Friedan Papers; Alice Echols, *Daring to Be Bad: Radical Feminism in America 1967–1975* (Minneapolis, 1989), 26–31; Bloom and Breines, eds., *Takin' It to the Streets*, 45; Branch, *Parting the Waters*, 880; Elsa Barkley Brown, "Negotiating and Transforming the Public Sphere: African American Political Life in the Transition from Slavery to Freedom," *Public Culture*, 7 (Fall 1994), 144–45; Evans, *Personal Politics*, 112.

41. Bloom and Breines, eds., *Takin' It to the Streets*, 48; Evans, *Personal Politics*, 83–101, 152–54; Piercy in Robin Morgan, ed., *Sisterhood Is Powerful* (New York, 1970), 421; Ellen Willis, *Beginning to See the Light: Sex, Hope, and Rock-and-Roll* (Hanover, 1992), 62; Echols, *Daring to Be Bad*, 42–44; Teodori, ed., *New Left*, 355.

42. Alice Echols, "Nothing Distant About It: Women's Liberation and Sixties Radicalism," in *The Sixties*, ed. Farber, 149–51; Echols, *Daring to Be Bad*, 3–12; Evans, *Personal Politics*, 206–07.

43. Echols, "Nothing Distant," 163; Dick Cluster, ed., *They Should Have Served that Cup of Coffee* (Boston, 1979), 194; Echols, *Daring to Be Bad*, vii–ix, 13–17; Bunch in Evans, *Personal Politics*, 212; Morgan, *Sisterhood Is Powerful*, 246.

44. John D'Emilio and Estelle B. Freedman, *Intimate Matters: A History of Sexuality in America* (New York, 1988), 312; Morgan, ed., *Sisterhood Is Powerful*; Bloom and Breines, eds., *Takin' It to the Streets*, 486; Willis, *Beginning to See the Light*, xiii.

45. Morton J. Horwitz, *The Warren Court and the Pursuit of Justice* (New York, 1998); Stanley N. Katz, "The Strange Birth and Unlikely History of Constitutional Equality," *Journal of American History*, 75 (December 1988), 757–59.

46. Michael J. Klarman, "Rethinking the Civil Rights and Civil Liberties Revolutions," *Virginia Law Review*, 82 (February 1996), 42; Samuel Walker, *In Defense of American Liberties: A History of the ACLU* (New York, 1990), 217, 240–41; Adam Fairclough, *Race and Democracy: The Civil Rights Struggle in Louisiana, 1915–1972* (Athens, GA, 1995), 324–25; Geoffrey R. Stone, "Reflections on the First Amendment: The Evolution of the American Jurisprudence of Free Expression," *Proceedings of the American Philosophical Society*, 131 (September 1987), 253–55; Lucas A. Powe, Jr., *The Fourth Estate and the Constitution: Freedom of the Press in America* (Berkeley, 1991), ix, 92–96.

47. Walker, *In Defense of Liberties*, 219–24; Marvin E. Frankel, *Faith and Freedom: Religious Liberty in America* (New York, 1994), 66; Henry J. Abraham, *Freedom and the Court: Civil Rights and Liberties in the United States*, 5th ed. (New York, 1988), 73–115.

48. David J. Garrow, *Liberty and Sexuality: The Right to Privacy and the Making of "Roe" v. "Wade"* (New York, 1994), 213–60, 376–77; William W. Fisher III, "The Development of Modern American Legal Theory and the Judicial Interpretation of the Bill of Rights," in *A Culture of Rights: The Bill of Rights in Philosophy, Politics, and Law 1791 and 1991*, ed. Michael J. Lacey and Knud Haakonssen (New York, 1991), 348–49; Martha Minow, "We, the Family: Constitutional Rights and American Families," *Journal of American History*, 74 (December 1987), 960–61; Osmond K. Frankel, ed., *The Curse of Bigness: Miscellaneous Papers of Louis D. Brandeis* (New York, 1934), 289–315; Michael Kammen, *Sovereignty and Liberty: Constitutional Discourse in American Culture* (Madison, 1988), 90–91.

49. Jean L. Cohen, "Redescribing Privacy: Identity, Difference, and the Abortion Controversy," *Columbia Journal of Gender and Law*, 3 (1992), 44; Hoff, *Law, Gender, and Injustice*, 277–81; Sandel, *Democracy's Discontent*, 108–11; Reva B. Siegel, " 'The Rule of Love': Wife Beating as Prerogative and Privacy," *Yale Law Journal*, 105 (June 1996), 2171–96; Mary Poovey, "The Abortion Question and the Death of Man," in *Feminists Theorize the Political*, ed. Judith Butler and Joan W. Scott (New York, 1992), 240–41.

50. Lacey and Haakonssen, *A Culture of Rights*, 1; Robert H. Wiebe, *Self-Rule: A Cultural History of American Democracy* (Chicago, 1995), 223–26; Daniel T. Rodgers, *Contested Truths: Keywords in American Politics Since Independence* (New York, 1987), 217–20.

51. Kazin, *Populist Persuasion*, 222–55.

52. Hamby, *Liberalism*, 318–21; Anderson, *Movement and the Sixties*, 250–51; D'Emilio and Freedman, *Intimate Matters*, 318; Paul C. Smith and Robert A. Warrior, *Like a Hurricane: The Indian Movement from Alcatraz to Wounded Knee* (New York, 1997), 201–65.

53. E. J. Dionne, Jr., *Why Americans Hate Politics* (New York, 1991), 53–54, 98; Elaine T. May, *Homeward Bound: American Families in the Cold War Era* (New York, 1988), 217–23; William G. Mayer, *The Changing American Mind* (Ann Arbor, 1993), 36, 225; Robert Wuthnow, *The Restructuring of American Religion: Society and Faith Since World War II* (Princeton, 1988), 260; Peter Clecak, *America's Quest for the Ideal Self: Dissent and Fulfillment in the 60s and 70s* (New York, 1983), 4.

CHAPTER 13

1. Theodore White, *The Making of the President, 1964* (New York, 1965), 332n.

2. Lionel Trilling, *The Liberal Imagination* (New York, 1950), ix; John A. Andrew III, *The Other Side of the Sixties: Young Americans for Freedom and the Rise of Conservative Politics* (New Brunswick, 1997), 12; Jerome L. Himmelstein, *To the Right: The Transformation of American Conservatism* (Berkeley, 1990), 1–3, 137–38.

3. F. A. Hayek, *The Road to Serfdom* (Chicago, 1994), xxxv–vi; George W. Nash, *The Conservative Intellectual Movement in America Since 1945* (New York, 1976), 22–27; Felix Morley, ed., *Essays on Individuality* (Philadelphia, 1958), 4–5, 15–33.

4. Himmelstein, *To the Right,* 46; Morley, ed., *Essays on Individuality,* 168–74; Milton Friedman, *Capitalism and Freedom* (Chicago, 1962), 1–4, 12–15, 31–36.

5. Friedman, *Capitalism and Freedom,* 12–14; Nash, *Conservative Intellectual Movement,* xiii, 38–69, 82; Himmelstein, *To the Right,* 49; Richard M. Weaver, *Ideas Have Consequences* (Chicago, 1948), 1–3, 29–40; Clinton Rossiter, *Conservatism in America* (New York, 1955), 72.

6. Rossiter, *Conservatism,* 72; M. Stanton Evans, *Revolt on the Campus* (Chicago, 1961), 13–22, 75–87, 179–82; Friedman, *Capitalism and Freedom,* 20; Christopher Lasch, *The Revolt of the Elites and the Betrayal of Democracy* (New York, 1994), 98; Robert C. Tucker, ed., *The Marx-Engels Reader,* 2d ed. (New York, 1978), 475.

7. E. J. Dionne, Jr., *Why Americans Hate Politics* (New York, 1991), 154–61, 266–81; Andrew, *Other Side of the Sixties,* 8–16, 102; David H. Bennett, *The Party of Fear: From Nativist Movements to the New Right in American History* (Chapel Hill, 1988), 356; John B. Judis, *William F. Buckley, Jr.: Patron Saint of the Conservatives* (New York, 1988), 147–69; Frank S. Meyer, *In Defense of Freedom: A Conservative Credo* (Chicago, 1962), 1–9, 20–23, 38–59, 68–70, 150–51; Nash, *Conservative Intellectual Movement,* 172–77; Frank S. Meyer, ed., *What Is Conservatism?* (New York, 1964), 8–19, 68–74.

8. Hodgson, *World Turned Right Side Up,* 89–90; Himmelstein, *To the Right,* 15–17, 32–45; Ronald Lora, "Conservative Intellectuals, the Cold War, and McCarthyism," in *The Specter: Original Essays on the Cold War and the Origins of McCarthyism,* ed. Robert Griffith and Athan Theoharis (New York, 1974), 54–60; Nash, *Conservative Intellectual Movement,* 148–61; Meyer, ed., *What is Conservatism?,* 15.

9. Evans, *Revolt,* 109–11, 167; Lisa McGirr, "Suburban Warriors: Grassroots Conservatism in the 1960s," Ph.D. dissertation, Columbia University, 1995, 117–18; Andrew, *Other Side of the Sixties,* 8, 55–58; *National Review,* September 24, 1960.

10. Mary C. Brennan, *Turning Right: The Conservative Capture of the GOP* (Chapel Hill, 1995); Andrew, *Other Side of the Sixties,* 5–6, 17; Barry Goldwater, *The Conscience of a Conservative* (Shepherdsville, 1960), 3–5, 10–22, 70–74, 89–91, 118–22; Barry Goldwater, "We Cannot Have Economic Freedom and Political Dictation," *Vital Speeches of the Day,* March 15, 1960, 337–39.

11. *Commonweal,* April 14, 1961; *Vital Speeches of the Day,* April 15, 1964, 642–44; Dionne, *Why Americans Hate Politics,* 176–79.

12. Andrew, *Other Side of the Sixties,* 211–14; Michael Kazin, *The Populist Persuasion* (New York,

1995), 4; Jonathan M. Kolkey, *The New Right, 1960–68, with Epilogue, 1969–1980* (Washington, DC, 1983), 183–84; Murray N. Rothbard, *For a New Liberty* (New York, 1973), 3–11, 184–229; Michael W. Flamm, " 'Law and Order': Street Crime, Civil Disorder, and the Crisis of Liberalism," Ph.D. dissertation, Columbia University, 1997, 60–114.

13. McGirr, "Suburban Warriors"; Frederick F. Siegel, *Troubled Journey: From Pearl Harbor to Ronald Reagan* (New York, 1984), 157–59; John P. Diggins, *Up from Communism: Conservative Odysseys in American Intellectual History* (New York, 1975), 8–9; Hodgson, *World Turned Right Side Up*, 65–81; Nash, *Conservative Intellectual Movement*, 199–200; Meyer, *In Defense of Freedom*, 8; Judis, *Buckley*, 138.

14. Friedman, *Capitalism and Freedom*, 110–18; Goldwater, *Conscience of a Conservative*, 31–37; White, *Making of the President*, 332; Diggins, *Up from Communism*, 8.

15. Judis, *Buckley*, 191–207; Kazin, *Populist Persuasion*, 224–36, 246–51; Kenneth Durr, "When Southern Politics Came North: The Roots of White Working-Class Conservatism in Baltimore, 1940–1964," *Labor History*, 37 (Summer 1996), 309–31.

16. Thomas Casstevens, *Politics, Housing, and Race Relations: The Defeat of Berkeley's Fair Housing Ordinance* (Berkeley, 1965), 9–11, 72–73, 99–108; *California Real Estate Magazine*, 44 (September 1964), cover; McGirr, "Suburban Warriors," 227–28, 246–47; Jill Quadrango, *The Color of Welfare: How Racism Undermined the War on Poverty* (New York, 1994), 96–98; Ronald P. Formisano, *Boston Against Busing: Race, Class, and Ethnicity in the 1960s and 1970s* (Chapel Hill, 1991); Jonathan Rieder, *Canarsie: The Jews and Italians of Brooklyn Against Liberalism* (Cambridge, MA, 1985); Arnold Hirsch, *Making the Second Ghetto: Race and Housing in Chicago 1940–1960* (New York, 1983), 171, 198.

17. Judith Stein, *Running Steel, Running America* (Chapel Hill, 1998), chs. 9–10; Hodgson, *World Turned Right Side Up*, 189–91; Dionne, *Why Americans Hate Politics*, 247–57; Himmelstein, *To the Right*, 132–45.

18. *Time*, July 28, 1975; *New Yorker*, April 21, 1975; Wilfred M. McClay, *The Masterless: Self and Society in Modern America* (Chapel Hill, 1994), 279.

19. John Ehrman, *The Rise of Neoconservatism: Intellectuals and Foreign Affairs 1945–1994* (New Haven, 1995), 28–31, 108–22; Alonzo L. Hamby, *Liberalism and Its Challengers: FDR to Reagan* (New York, 1985), 300–01; Abbott Gleason, *Totalitarianism: The Inner History of the Cold War* (New York, 1995), 11, 192–203.

20. Hodgson, *World Turned Right Side Up*, 176; George M. Marsden, *Fundamentalism and American Culture: The Shaping of Twentieth-Century Evangelicism 1870–1925* (New York, 1980), 3–7, 86–92, 141–70; Dionne, *Why Americans Hate Politics*, 110–12, 219–43.

21. Kazin, *Populist Persuasion*, 247–56; Robert Wuthnow, *The Restructuring of American Religion: Society and Faith Since World War II* (Princeton, 1988), 248–49.

22. Donald G. Mathews and Jane S. De Hart, *Sex, Gender, and the Politics of ERA* (New York, 1990), x–xii, 67–79, 152–56, 169–71; Kazin, *Populist Persuasion*, 259; Rebecca E. Klatch, *Women of the New Right* (Philadelphia, 1987), 7, 122–28; Jane S. De Hart, "Rights and Representation: Women, Politics, and Power in the Contemporary United States," in *U.S. History as Women's History: New Feminist Essays*, ed. Linda K. Kerber, et al. (Chapel Hill, 1995), 219.

23. Kristin Luker, *Abortion and the Politics of Motherhood* (Berkeley, 1984); Klatch, *Women of the New Right*, 26–30, 45; Michael J. Sandel, *Democracy's Discontent: America in Search of a Public Philosophy* (Cambridge, MA, 1996), 99; Christopher Shannon, *Conspicuous Criticism: Tradition, the Individual, and Culture in American Social Thought, from Veblen to Mills* (Baltimore, 1996), 186–87; Dionne, *Why Americans Hate Politics*, 105.

24. Hodgson, *World Turned Right Side Up*, 11–12, 18; Alfred A. Balitzer and Gerald M. Bonetto, eds., *A Time for Choosing: The Speeches of Ronald Reagan 1961–1982* (Chicago, 1983), 41–57, 232; Eileen Boris, *Home to Work: Motherhood and the Politics of Industrial Homework in the United States* (New York, 1994), 16–17, 358; Kazin, *Populist Persuasion*, 261; T. Alexander Aleinikoff, "Re-Reading Justice Harlan's Dissent in Plessy v. Ferguson: Freedom, Antiracism, and Citizenship," *University of Illinois Law Review*, 92, (1992, 4), 973.

25. Daniel T. Rodgers, *Contested Truths: Keywords in American Politics Since Independence* (New York, 1987), 213–16; Schorr in Ronald D. Rotunda, *The Politics of Language: Liberalism as Word and Symbol* (Iowa City, 1986), xi; *The Public Papers of the Presidents: Ronald Reagan 1981* (Washington, DC, 1982), 1; *Public Papers: Reagan 1985*, 70, 118 (Washington, DC, 1988); *Public Papers: Reagan 1986* (Washington, DC, 1988), 1505.

26. Mark P. Lagon, *The Reagan Doctrine: Sources of American Conduct in the Cold War's Last Chapter* (Westport, 1994), xii–3, 81–89, 113; *Public Papers: Reagan 1985*, 770, 1310; *Public Papers: Reagan 1986*, 444–45, 739.

27. Balitzer and Bonetto, *A Time for Choosing*, 41–57; Tony Smith, *America's Mission: The United States and the Worldwide Struggle for Democracy in the Twentieth Century* (Princeton, 1994), 291; Steve Fraser and Gary Gerstle, eds., *The Rise and Fall of the New Deal Order, 1930–1980* (Princeton, 1989), ix; *The Public Papers of the Presidents: Ronald Reagan 1984* (Washington, DC, 1986), 1282, 1627; *Public Papers: Reagan 1985*, 1186; *Public Papers: Reagan 1986*, 1624; *Public Papers: Reagan 1987* (Washington, DC, 1989), 741–44; *The Nation*, August 26, 1996.

28. Bennett, *Party of Fear*, 402; Kathy Evertiz, "The 1986 Statue of Liberty Centennial: 'Commercialization' and Reaganism," *Journal of Popular Culture*, 29 (Winter 1995), 214–19; David E. Procter, *Enacting Political Culture: Rhetorical Transformations of Liberty Weekend 1986* (New York, 1991), 14–32, 77–91; *Time*, June 16, July 14, 1986.

29. *The Public Papers of the Presidents: Ronald Reagan 1986*, 896, 916; Mike Wallace, *Mickey Mouse History* (Philadelphia, 1996), 57; Baldwin and Jacob in Procter, *Enacting Political Culture*, 38–45, 61–65.

30. *The Public Papers of the Presidents: Ronald Reagan 1983* (Washington, DC, 1984), 1450; John Gray, *Enlightenment's Wake: Politics and Culture at the Close of the Modern Age* (New York, 1996); Rudolph J. R. Peritz, *Competition Policy in America 1888–1992* (New York, 1996), 265; Eugene D. Genovese, *The Southern Tradition: The Achievement and Limitations of an American Conservatism* (Cambridge, MA, 1994), 82–83.

31. Siegel, *Troubled Journey*, 251; Dick Armey, *The Freedom Revolution* (Washington, DC, 1995), 306; Robert H. Bork, *Slouching Towards Gomorrah* (New York, 1996), 65; *The New Republic*, April 18, 1994, December 9, 1996.

32. Hodgson, *World Turned Right Side Up*, 18, 248; Christopher Lasch, "Liberalism in Retreat," in *Liberalism Reconsidered*, ed. Douglas MacLean and Claudia Mills (Totowa, 1983),

105–06; Margaret Weir, *Politics and Jobs: The Boundaries of Employment Policy in the United States* (Princeton, 1992), 3–4.

33. Armey, *Freedom Revolution*, 49, 67, 229; Newt Gingrich, *To Renew America* (New York, 1995), 102; *Wall Street Journal*, April 7, 1995.

34. David Riesman, "Civil Liberties in a Period of Transition," in *Public Policy*, ed. C. J. Freidrich and Edward S. Mason (Cambridge, MA, 1942), 33, 73–76; Jon Katz, "The Netizen: Birth of a Digital Nation," *Wired* (April 1997), 49–50, 184–91; Peritz, *Competition Policy*, 249–50, 292; Mark A. Graber, *Transforming Free Speech: The Ambiguous Legacy of Civil Libertarianism* (Berkeley, 1991), 13, 168, 207–22.

35. Richard Hofstadter, *Social Darwinism in American Thought* (Philadelphia, 1944), 68–71; George McKenna, ed., *America Populism* (New York, 1974), 128–29; Richard J. Barnet and John Cavanaugh, *Global Dreams: Imperial Corporations and the New World Order* (New York, 1994); Gingrich, *To Renew America;* Lamar Alexander and Chester E. Finn, eds., *The New Promise of American Life* (Indianapolis, 1995).

36. Seymour M. Lipset, *American Exceptionalism: A Double-Edged Sword* (New York, 1996), 75; Sandel, *Democracy's Discontent*, 118; James L. Hutson, *To Secure the Fruits of Labor: The American Concept of the Distribution of Wealth, 1765–1900* (Baton Rouge, 1998), ch. 12.

37. *BusinessWeek*, March 11, 1996; Robert J. Samuelson, *The Good Life and Its Discontents: The American Dream in the Age of Entitlement 1945–1995* (New York, 1995).

38. Robert H. Wiebe, *Self-Rule: A Cultural History of American Democracy* (Chicago, 1995), 3–5, 243; Robert N. Bellah, et al., *Habits of the Heart: Individualism and Commitment in American Life* (Berkeley, 1985), vi–vii, 23–25; Sandel, *Democracy's Discontent*, 203.

39. Christine Stock, *Rural Radicals: Righteous Rage in the American Grain* (Ithaca, 1996), 148; Chip Berlet, *Eyes Right!* (Boston, 1995); James R. Kennedy and Walter D. Kennedy, *Why Not Freedom! America's Revolt Against Big Government* (Gretna, 1995); *Philadelphia Inquirer*, June 5, 1995; *New York Times*, April 20, 23, May 15, 1995, September 11, 1997.

40. *New York Times*, April 12, August 13, 1996; Ernesto Laclau, *Emancipation(s)* (New York, 1996), vii; Eric Hobsbawm, *The Age of Extremes: A History of the World, 1914–1991* (New York, 1994), 428; Arthur M. Schlesinger, Jr., *The Disuniting of America* (New York, 1992).

41. Charles Murray and Richard Hernnstein, *The Bell Curve* (New York 1994); Peter Brimelow, *Alien Nation: Common Sense About America's Immigration Disaster* (New York, 1995), xvii, 10–15, 46, 188, 203–22.

42. Francis Fukuyama, *The End of History and the Last Man* (New York, 1992); Samuel P. Huntington, *The Clash of Civilizations and the Remaking of World Order* (New York, 1996), 20–31, 310.

43. Wunthrow, *Restructuring of American Religion*, 260.

44. These results were obtained by searching the Internet for "freedom" in September 1997, using the programs Excite and AltaVista.

45. Eric Foner, *Tom Paine and Revolutionary America* (New York, 1976), 78.

Acknowledgments

ALL WORKS OF HISTORY are in a sense collaborative endeavors, for no matter how original, they necessarily build on previous scholarship. This is even more true for books, like *The Story of American Freedom*, based largely on secondary literature. My greatest debt is to the legions of American historians on whose work I have relied. My Notes are intended not only to direct attention to sources of insights and information and the location of quotations, but to pay tribute to the vast scholarly literature that in the past generation has so greatly enriched our understanding of the American past.

I am deeply indebted to Joyce Appleby, Thomas Bender, Alan Brinkley, Joshua Freeman, and Arthur Wang, who read the manuscript and offered invaluable comments and suggestions. For reading portions of the book, I also wish to thank the members of the Yale Legal Theory Workshop, the Seminar on Twentieth Century Politics at Columbia University, and Professor Anders Stephanson's first-year graduate colloquium. Over the last few years I have benefited enormously from discussions about the theme of this book with Fred Siegel. Other friends and colleagues who passed along ideas, information, and salutary warnings, and to whom I extend my thanks, are Neil Besen, Ira Berlin, Betsy Blackmar, Nancy Cott, Ellen C. DuBois, Willie Forbath, Ira Katznelson, Wilbur Miller, Leslie S. Rowland, James P. Shenton, and Amy Stanley. My father, Jack D. Foner, offered his usual sage advice. Joshua Brown and Olivia Mahoney generously gave assistance on the book's illustrations.

While researching and writing this book, I had the good fortune to work with a group of brilliant graduate students at Columbia University. Some of their dissertations and books are cited in the Notes; others shared ideas and material culled from their own research. All contributed greatly to the evolution of my thinking on freedom and I am happy to be able to thank them individually: Beth Bates, Sven Beckert, Martha Biondi, Nancy Cohen, Peter Field, Margaret Garb (who also did invaluable work as my research assistant), Michael Green, Sarah Henry, Mark Higbee, Anne Kornhauser (who also read and commented on the manuscript), Melinda Lawson, Lisa McGirr, Rebecca McLennan, Premilla Nadesen, Mae Ngai, Becky Nicolaides, Adele Oltman, John Recchuiti, Manisha Sinha, David Stebenne, Michael Sugrue, Midori Takagi, Lara Vapnek, Cyrus Veeser, Penny Von Eschen, Wang Xi, and Michael Zakim. Two other Columbia graduate students, Charles Forcey and Ellen Stroud, deserve thanks for introducing me to the wonders and pitfalls of research on the Internet.

I am indebted to the many librarians who assisted my research, beginning with the staff of the Columbia University libraries, especially the reference, rare books, and interlibrary loans divisions, and the electronic text service. In 1993–94, while teaching as Harmsworth Professor of American History at the University of Oxford, I enjoyed the generous assistance of the librarians at Rhodes House. Thanks, too, to those archivists who assisted me in locating illustrations for the book, especially Georgia B. Barnhill of the American Antiquarian Society and Maja Keech of the Library of Congress.

My editor at W. W. Norton, Steve Forman, offered encouragement and insightful comments at every stage of this project. Ann Adelman did a superlative job of copyediting. Thanks, as well, to Sandra Dijkstra, a most talented literary agent. I am also grateful to the National Endowment for the Humanities for a Fellowship for Senior Scholars, which covered the year during which most of this book was written. The Tenured Faculty Research Program of Columbia University helped to defray research expenses.

To my wife, Lynn Garafola, I once again extend my heartfelt thanks for a rare comradeship and for her own example as an intellectual, writer, and editor extraordinaire. The book is dedicated to my daughter, Daria, for whom this project must have been quite a trial, but who never let it diminish her affection, generosity of spirit, and enthusiasm for life.

Index

Page numbers in *italics* refer to illustrations.